Legal Practice in the Digital Age

Paul Caddy | David Jackson | Tony Randle

Authors
Paul Caddy, David Jackson and Tony Randle

Managing director
Sian O'Neill

Legal Practice in the Digital Age
is published by

Globe Law and Business Ltd
3 Mylor Close
Horsell
Woking
Surrey GU21 4DD
United Kingdom
Tel: +44 20 3745 4770
www.globelawandbusiness.com

Printed and bound in Great Britain by Ashford Colour Press Ltd

Legal Practice in the Digital Age

ISBN 9781787429314
EPUB ISBN 9781787429321
Adobe PDF ISBN 9781787429338

DISCLAIMER
This publication is intended as a general guide only. The information and opinions which it contains are not intended to be a comprehensive study, or to provide legal or financial advice, and should not be treated as a substitute for legal advice concerning particular situations. Legal advice should always be sought before taking any action based on the information provided. The publishers bear no responsibility for any errors or omissions contained herein.

Table of contents

David Jackson
For Lizzie, Izzie & Noah. My crazy ones.

Tony Randle
For Maria; for her tolerance of the hours I have spent in my study, for her humour when I have needed it, and for her (frequent and unsolicited) reminders whenever she thinks I am getting 'big-headed'.

Paul Caddy
For my parents and family, to whom I owe everything.

The authors would also like to thank their valued colleagues at Shoosmiths and everyone else who helped in the creation of this book.

All royalties from the sale of this book will be paid to Shoosmiths LLP for application to charitable causes through the Shoosmiths Foundation (a Charities Aid Foundation fund, registered charity number 268369).

Preface

At the turn of the century, the late author Douglas Adams came up with a short set of rules to determine our approach to tech. The rules went roughly like this:

- rule 1: everything around us when we're born is normal;
- rule 2: new inventions between then and the age of 30 are amazing. Careers are founded on them. Life is fabulous and exciting;
- rule 3: everything changes. After the age of 30 new inventions are, as Adams noted, "against the natural order of things". Civilisation itself is threatened until the invention has been on the scene for a decade or so "when it gradually turns out to be alright really".[1]

At that time, the 'information superhighway' was a thing of wonder. If you were lucky, after a series of metallic bleeps and hisses, you might get a connection. It was exciting, exasperating (when the connection dropped for the umpteenth time) but extraordinary nonetheless. As Adams noted, news presenters would feel the need to go out of their way to mention 'the internet' if some misdemeanour was planned using it, although they didn't bother mentioning when criminals, say, used the telephone or the M4 motorway.

And there's the rub.

As Adams explains, everything is new once. New technology and ways of doing things can be deeply unsettling.

As late as the 1930s, many people thought phones were dangerous. Some fretted that the electric wiring might give them a shock. If they came across the technology, they'd often try to move away from it or, failing that, they'd pick up the receiver in a suspicious and guarded manner. Motorways would flood our green and pleasant land with ne'er-do-wells from the nearby cities.

Most of us now use or enjoy these things routinely and instinctively. We don't give them a second thought: few lawyers physically distance themselves from their phones nowadays, as much as they might like to. Motorways criss-cross the country. The internet is now so ubiquitous we don't notice it, until it's not there – a reversal from 20 years ago when we'd be dizzy with excitement when we turned the net on and 'surfed' it.

These societal changes and technologies have merged into the landscape of our everyday lives. Newscasters have tired of them. They just 'are'. Following Adams' rough rule of thumb, these things have gone from ☺ to ☺ crashed down to ☹ and then, after a period of adjustment, ended up back at ☺.

We chart this in Figure 1.

Figure 1. Douglas Adams' three rules for approaching technology

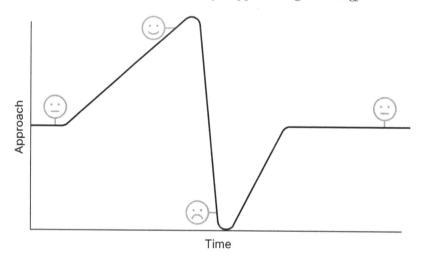

This book, *Legal Practice in the Digital Age*, looks at the anticipated 'just-ares' of legal practice in the future and the evolving landscape of our working lives as we enter a time of great change.

It explores questions, such as:

- What's in store and what things will we take for granted in the years to come?
- What do we need to do to prepare ourselves for the change ahead of us?

Of course, everyone has a different tolerance to technology and change, so wherever you sit on Adams' scale – or, indeed, whether you agree with it at all – this book will serve as a useful guide, whatever your level of knowledge and practising experience.

It features plenty of technology, but it isn't a homage to tech for tech's sake. Instead, it focuses on the people who use technology (eg, lawyers). It also looks at the trends which are likely to impact our working lives and the practice of law in the future.

What's more, it takes an insider's perspective, based on the authors' collective experience of over three-quarters of a century of working in firms and in-house. The goal of this book is to take a client-focused approach as, ultimately, the things we set out in this book are for our clients, not us.

Each one of us has a part to play in the future of legal practice in the digital age.

This book is your companion for the inevitable change that lies ahead.

We know that making predictions is hard, particularly when, as the saying goes, it's all about the future.

And there's a lot about our collective future in this book.

The temptation is strong to fall back on a few shop-soiled clichés. It wouldn't be tricky to conclude here, for example, that there'll be many twists and turns and bumps in the road ahead, but the authors can't help feeling these hackneyed expressions are a lazy disclaimer. While they're no doubt true, it also misses a vital point.

Bumps, twists and turns are exciting.

Ask any child – or grown-up child – that has ever pleaded to go the long way round to a destination because the roads are windy. Ask any adventure tourist who wants to ride Route 66 or go overland through the Andes of Patagonia.

Twists, turns and bumps are a vital part of what it's all about.

In a world where being optimistic is *déclassé* and corrosive pessimism is *de rigueur*, there's something seductive about giving up. But this would be like stopping your car in the middle of the road before a bump, getting out and walking away.

The future won't be dystopian, nor will it be utopian. There'll be good bits and bad bits. But it's where we are heading and, frankly, we have no choice in the matter, so it's time for us to be optimistic and use this book as a possible road map for our future; a future where we get to determine the outcome. We get to narrate our story. It's a book of hope.

So, buckle up and enjoy the journey!

Paul Caddy, David Jackson and Tony Randle
February 2022

Notes

1   Douglas Adams, "How to stop worrying and learn to love the Internet" (*The Sunday Times*, 29 August 1999).

Introduction

And now the shipping forecast issued by the Met Office on behalf of the Maritime and Coastguard Agency at double O one five. There are warnings of gales in Viking, North Utsire, South Utsire, Forties, Cromarty ...

The rhythmic incantation of the *Shipping Forecast* has entranced UK radio listeners for almost a century, with only one episode of radio silence during and after the Second World War. Broadcast four times a day on BBC Radio 4, it's a beloved national institution.

It has been mocked by Stephen Fry and read out by former Deputy Prime Minister John Prescott. In 2008, it featured in the closing ceremony of the Beijing Olympics. Four years later, in 2012, it featured in the opening ceremony of the London Olympics. It's turned up in music, art, literature, poetry, films, television and even video games. In 1995, plans to move it to a later slot on Radio 4 triggered a debate in Parliament and furious editorials in national newspapers. People have even named their pets after the shipping areas.

Typically done in 350 words or fewer the solemn forecaster needs to give out a gale warning summary, a general synopsis and sea area forecasts for over 30 sea areas from Southeast Iceland, at almost 65 degrees north, to Trafalgar off the coasts of Morocco, Spain and Portugal. A legion of dedicated listeners tune in to the weather bulletin in bed before they drift off into a meteorological-induced slumber.

But we often forget about the remarkable technology behind the reassuring facade and staccato intonation of "moderates becoming goods" and "occasionally severe gale nines". The forecast is not designed to be poetry for insomniacs; rather it's the cumulation of countless calculations collected by a network of computers dotted around the globe, with the ultimate goal of protecting property and saving lives.

One of these behemoths sits in a modern angular building in a leafy science park just off junction 29 of the M5 motorway in Exeter. The Met Office's supercomputers are capable of processing 14,000 trillion arithmetic operations per second. From the billions of weather observations from all over the globe, the service runs an atmospheric model, containing more than a million lines of code, which provides the information for the *Shipping Forecast*.

It's an astounding feat. The first known daily weather report from the Met Office, on 3 September 1860, was by Vice-Admiral Robert FitzRoy. Before this innovation, it was said that a frog in a jar could help to detect a coming storm. At the time, according to the BBC, the loss of life around the coasts of Victorian Britain was appalling. In just five years between 1855 and 1860, 7,402 ships were wrecked off the coasts, with the loss of almost as many lives.

FitzRoy had much less technology at his disposal – the first fully functional digital computer was many decades away – to help put together his bulletins. At first, he also had to contend with a rather cynical public. In voting on the creation of the Meteorological Department, of which FitzRoy would be its first head, one supportive MP, John Ball, said: "It is anticipated that within a few years, notwithstanding the variable climate of this country, we might know in this metropolis the condition of the weather 24 hours beforehand."[1] This statement was greeted with laughter in the House of Commons.

Now the four-day forecast of the Met Office is as accurate as its one-day forecast from 30 years ago. The organisation gloats that, in 2019, gale warnings were issued for over 95% of gales that occurred. The technology of today's weather forecast involves 'eye in the sky' satellites that orbit the planet at scarcely imaginable altitudes, and pulse-Doppler radars that can 'see' all manner of rain with radio waves. More and more we can see further and further into the future thanks to advances in AI. FitzRoy would be staggered at what today's technology lets us do.

The use of technology in the practice of law is at the cusp of a similar game-changing transformation. AI and big data will upend how we, as lawyers, manage and process our work. Regulatory changes and new working patterns, such as the increase in remote and hybrid working, will also have a great impact on how we do our jobs.

Of course, the purpose of the law is not to keep lawyers in business or technologists in their day jobs. Technology and innovation isn't something that lawyers should pursue as an end in itself.

Ultimately, it's here to serve us. It's here to help us be smarter, faster and better. It's here to move us away from frogs in jars, by giving us an array of smart tools so we can enhance what we humans do best. For meteorologists, technology helps them create the poetry of the *Shipping Forecast*. For lawyers? Well, that's for us to decide. This book shows us how.

We lawyers are a resilient and highly adaptable breed who are more than up to this challenge.

In the not-too-distant future, legal professionals will be doing things that are unimaginable to many of us now. There'll be bumps and scrapes along the way. Some things we'll get right. There'll be plenty that we get wrong.

In just over a decade, FitzRoy went from being a has-been (in the early 1850s), to having his work mocked in Parliament (in 1854) to being asked for advice by the Queen's Messengers (in the 1860s). Zero to hero in just over a decade.

He saw incredible changes.

We will too.

While this book is about our future and, in particular, looks at technology and innovation in its many guises, it's structured in the traditional way – it is a book after all.

Figure 1. How this book is structured

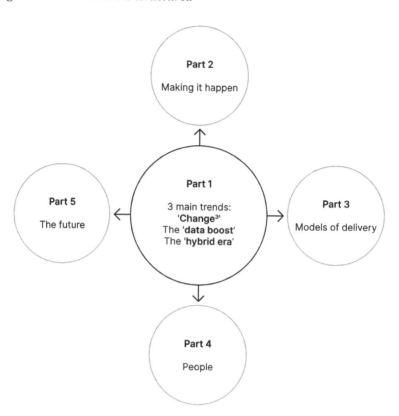

We've split the book into five parts:

- Part 1 looks at the three major trends which will impact everything in this book.
- Parts 2 to 5 look at the specific areas that will help lawyers navigate the future.

Each chapter gives an overview of the subject and is followed by a number of case studies and practical tips based on the authors' direct and actual experience. They set out the whos, whats, whens, wheres, whys and, most importantly, hows on thriving in this decade and beyond.

Above all, this is a practical book. The practical tips aren't regurgitated from textbooks or the product of theorising. They're what has caused the authors to lose sleep – literally in some cases – over our collective 75 years of operating at a junior and then senior level in both private practice and in-house.

Part 1: Trends
- Chapter 1 (Change3) looks at the change we face in more detail. In essence, change itself has changed: its pace, complexity and magnitude. This chapter helps the reader prepare for 'change cubed' so they can thrive.
- Chapter 2 (The data boost) considers the profound changes that the AI-powered data revolution is having, and will have in the future, on legal practice. Mining data and replaying it back to clients as insight will be game-changing for our profession.
- Chapter 3 (The hybrid era) examines how we'll need to be smarter, faster and better in how we look after our clients, who need to be at the heart of what we do. Do we have what it takes to put, and keep, them there and ensure they're delighted with our solutions? We also look at how our working lives have been transformed by events like COVID. Are we ready for the world of hybrid working?

Part 2: Making it happen
- Chapter 4 (Procurement) what do we need to know when buying technology and innovation? How do we move away from *ad hoc* procurement to aligning our procurement strategies to our strategies on technology and innovation.
- Chapter 5 (Collaborate to innovate) explores the serendipity of working together to create and deliver innovations which will propel us forward, perhaps in unexpected ways.
- Chapter 6 (Compliance, quality and risk) delves into what we need to think about to minimise risk, maximise quality and do all that we can to make the right compliance choices.

Part 3: Models of delivery
- Chapter 7 (New law models) deals with the many new ways that we can bring our expertise to the market. And it might not just be the current players who are eyeing up opportunities.
- Chapter 8 (In-house lawyer) reflects on the challenges that this growing sector of the profession faces (in the past 15 years alone the number of in-house lawyers has doubled). What can we learn from their success as partners in their businesses? What do in-house lawyers need to do to future-proof their careers and cement their roles as trusted and strategic advisers to businesses?

Part 4: People
- Chapter 9 (EQ ≥ IQ) is a reminder that, as good as tech is, it's not all about the unwavering logic that lies behind it. We have countless skills that can't and won't be replaced by technology. These will be needed more than ever. We will remain a human profession. This chapter shows us why.

- Chapter 10 (The aspiring and associate lawyer) studies the future of becoming a lawyer and what the profession is likely to need from the new blood that enters it. What do we need to do to attract the brightest talent? It also looks at associate lawyers. What challenges will they face in the 2020s and beyond? And, in a time when careers will look different to today, how do we keep associates fulfilled? How do firms embrace a profession for all the talents?
- Chapter 11 (The advanced lawyer) considers the part of the profession most able to bring about change. What do advanced lawyers need to do to stay ahead of the game?

Part 5: The future

- Chapter 12 (Horizon-gazing) concludes by looking at what's on the horizon and beyond to equip firms for the future. What things are going to impact the practice of law and the business of law in the years to come? If we want to thrive in the 2020s and beyond, this chapter is key to getting ahead of the game.

All of these parts and chapters are linked; some obviously; some less so. They don't sit alone. For example, those in society who are marginalised often live in communities where the demand for legal services is largely unmet. This 'Great Unmet Legal Need' (see Chapter 3) is something that technology and innovation might be able to solve in part, perhaps by lawyers collaborating with others (see Chapter 5) and using technologies that are developing, like AI (see Chapters 2 and 12). Other links are there for us to discover. And do something about.

In essence, this book is a call to action for the profession to look to the future and be excited by it. It's a call to devise goals and plans and the right strategies to achieve them.

Forget hiding. Forget just surviving – anyone can do that – the authors want lawyers to thrive.

It's a manifesto to be smarter, faster and better than previous generations; to leave our mark on this profession – our legacy – and make a difference.

In this book, the goal isn't to evangelise technology or advocate change just for the sake of change. This isn't a *Haynes Manual* for legaltech. We don't need to become world-beating experts in logic programming, ontological engineering and algorithmic biases to read what follows; after all, we don't need to know about cylinder head gaskets and poppet valves to drive a car.

But just as we 'get' how a car works and can see the profound change it has wrought on society since its inception – something that we now take for granted – what follows will help us understand what's in store for the legal profession. One day, we'll take all this for granted too.

A few final words before we press on.

This is a people-focused book. It's for people of all backgrounds, not just stereotypical 'techies'. The authors have looked for stories and examples across the spectrum and focused on writing it in gender-neutral language.

It's also a book in which the authors don't know all the answers. Or, let's be frank, all the questions. What follows is our contribution towards the important conversations that all lawyers need to be having.

It is also important to note what this book isn't.
- It's not a book that's binary in its approach to technology. In this book, the authors take a nuanced view. Technology is not a panacea; we have to focus on the bigger picture too. That's why this book focuses on the lawyers who use, and will use, the new technology we examine *and* the people who will benefit from it. Hence the mantra in what follows: technology is about people *and* tech, not people *or* tech.
- It's not a book which is only for senior lawyers. Although, for ease, lawyers (including in-house lawyers) and law firms are referred to throughout this book, it's not only intended for them, it's also for people who teach the business and practice of law; tech companies who work with lawyers; and anyone else who has an interest in how legal services or professional services more broadly will be affected by new technology and related disruptive forces, including students.
- It's not an academic book. Rather think of what follows as a call to action on the topics which follow. In particular, it focuses on the need to change our mindset in many areas. Shunning old ideas is often more difficult than embracing new ones. There are also many subjects to which the authors refer that are looked at in much greater detail elsewhere. This wealth of material is set out in endnotes.
- It's not a long book. 'I think the covers may be a bit too far apart' is a snarky quip that many book reviewers have deployed when faced with a needlessly large work. The authors have worked with great diligence to anticipate any such concerns: it's therefore a relatively short book, as these things go. Although it's meant to be read from start to finish, the reader may well want to dip in and out of it as they deem fit. That's fine too.

- It's not a book which is written in dense prose or legalese. The research is clear: the more complex the issue, the more people prefer plain English. As the Government Digital Service pointed out in 2014: "Those with the highest literacy levels and the greatest expertise tend to have the most to read."[2] And, of course, little time in which to read it. The authors hope that the reader finds it engaging, accessible and relatively jargon-free. A glossary of useful terms is also included after the conclusion.
- It's not a 100% unbiased book – what book is? The authors have written about what we've learnt and what we know, so most of the examples in the book relate to our lives as commercial lawyers in various full-service firms (both medium and large-sized in England) – also known as BigLaw. We've drawn from our in-house experience too.
- It's not a book that needs to be kept in pristine condition so don't feel shy about making notes in it.

As the writer and cultural historian John Higgs notes in his book *The Future Starts Here*, there was a time – the exact point of which is anyone's guess – when our attitudes flipped and we seemed to write off the future. We went from the utopia of *Star Trek* and the *Jetsons* – in the fictional cartoon series George Jetson was born in 2022 (feeling old yet?) – to the dystopia of *Mad Max*.

The narrative of constant progress, so embedded in Western culture, from the American dream to the Enlightenment, seems to have waned in recent years.

But all bad things must come to an end.

Enough of all the negativity!

What if, after all, there *is* a bright future for the profession?

Let's find out how ...

Notes

1   HC Deb 30 June 1854, vol 134, col 1006.
2   Mark Morris, "Guest Post: Clarity is king – the evidence that reveals the desperate need to re-think the way we write" (Government Digital Service, 17 February 2014), https://gds.blog.gov.uk/2014/02/17/guest-post-clarity-is-king-the-evidence-that-reveals-the-desperate-need-to-re-think-the-way-we-write.

Part 1: **Trends**

There are three key factors that will lead to the kind of seismic change witnessed in other sectors and industries. They're drivers that we see every day in our legal practice. In one way or another, they affect every one of us.

These key factors are:
- the pace, complexity and magnitude of change itself (the 'change3' effect), which is the focus of Chapter 1.
- the significance and value of data (the 'data boost'), often boosted by AI, which we explore in Chapter 2; and
- societal and attitudinal shifts to the way people want legal services and choose to live and work (the 'hybrid era'): we look at this in Chapter 3.

Figure 1. The three key trends

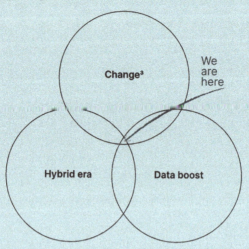

And there's a common denominator to each of these three factors: a force which is fuelling their impact, strength and speed. A force that is the underlying glue that binds them and intensifies their focus like a change-inducing laser. It has enabled and led to every major advancement and industrial revolution in history. Just as gravity holds our solar system in place, so this has become the force that dictates the order of life in this digital age. And, like gravity, it is all around us, constantly acting upon us, touching our lives. But unlike gravity, there's no escape velocity that allows us to move beyond its influence.

That force is technology.

This part (and indeed this book) doesn't seek to give the reader a precise prediction on how these trends will play out. In a complex world, there are far too many variables.

Others have tried in the past with mixed results. One top 30 firm in 2013, for example, predicted 25% fewer lawyers and 20% fewer firms by 2020. As it happens, according to the Solicitors Regulation Authority (SRA), there were over 160,000 solicitors with practising certificates in October 2022, about 30,000 *more* solicitors than in 2013.[1] But the firm was right to predict a fall in the number of law firms. In 2021, it dipped below 10,000.[2] The upshot? Making predictions is hard to do.

In the end, we need to think of these trends as being more like the climate than the weather. We can see what the climate might be like in the future; but we certainly can't see what the weather will be like on any given day a few years from now.

In the next chapter, we examine the first of these trends: change. In the chapters that follow in this part, we then look at data and, following that, the hybrid era.

Notes

1   "Population of solicitors in England and Wales" (Solicitors Regulation Authority), www.sra.org.uk/sra/research-publications/regulated-community-statistics/data/population_solicitors/.
2   "Breakdown of solicitor firms" (Solicitors Regulation Authority), www.sra.org.uk/sra/research-publications/regulated-community-statistics/data/solicitor_firms/.

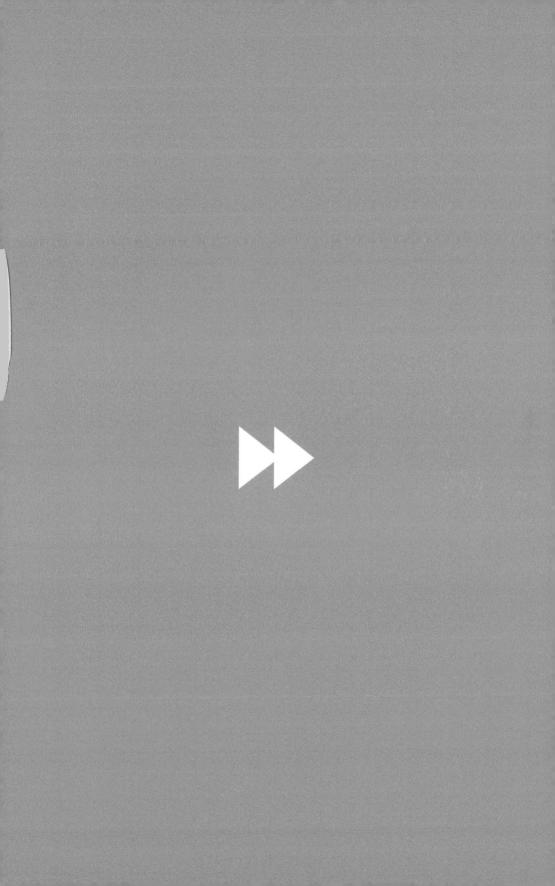

Chapter 1:
Change³

Change is the only constant in life.
Heraclitus of Ephesus

If you could change the world, what would you do?

Now there's a question: where do you even start?

The tyranny of choice over the changes we need to make means that we often end up doing little or nothing at all. Too many choices can be paralysing. Too often we give up. What's the point? Someone else can lose sleep over it. Change is a great idea – as this chapter shows, it's undoubtedly important – but perhaps it can wait for another day, when we've truly got the time to devote to it.

There are few things we humans are more committed to than resisting or delaying change. We're really quite good at it. We like to know what the new narrative is before we close the book on the old one. In other words, we want to defy physics and peer into the future to see what's ahead. But of course we can't. Not really. We might be able to see a suggestion of the first metaphorical bend in the road, but after that the twists, turns and bumps fade into the mist. The far distance is just a haze – if we can make it out at all. Both the journey and the destination are uncertain.

But there's no getting away from it – change is everywhere, all of the time.

It's basic science – the relentless loss of order is hardwired into our world. In the end everything slides towards disorder. Buildings crumble, cars rust and, as every small child learns, even the most lovingly created sandcastles get flattened and washed away. Grain by grain, the sands of time always win.

Change is not the exception to the rule, it *is* the rule.

But we don't need to be despondent about this second law of thermodynamics. As psychologist Steven Pinker asserts, it is: "The ultimate purpose of life, mind, and human striving: to deploy energy and information to fight back the tide of entropy and carve out refuges of beneficial order."[1] Since the dawn of time, we've agonised over the meaning of life. You may or may not agree with Pinker, but one thing is certain: entropy doesn't mean that we just give up.

In other words, we *can* challenge and push back against this law of nature. As a profession and as individuals, we have the power to create some semblance of order and mould the world and profession that we want to see.

And there's no doubt that a lot of change is coming. Economists John Kay and Mervyn King (ex-governor of the Bank of England) talk of "radical uncertainty" and remind us that without uncertainty – an aspect which is inherent in change – life would not be worth living.[2] Others talk of "certain uncertainty"[3] or "predictable unpredictability" (a leader in *The Economist* in December 2021 referred to this unpredictable world as "the new normal", adding bluntly: "get used to it").[4]

But we lawyers do have a choice about how we manage, embrace and thrive on change and uncertainty in this 'polycrisis' (or 'permacrisis') era. We could, of course, bury our heads in the sand, but even that metaphorical sand will blow away and leave us exposed in the end.

Resisting change is futile. After all, without change our world would be in stasis. Lawyers wouldn't have any reason to exist. New laws wouldn't be created to deal with new problems. New contracts wouldn't be drafted to manage new relationships. Nothing would happen, so disputes wouldn't arise either (the horror!). We'd all be stuck 'in the now'. Forever. Without change, it'd be a dull world indeed, a quagmire of stagnation.

Therefore, change is a constant. Our lives are all about change; it gives them meaning.

In this chapter we look at:
- understanding 'change3' and:
  - the pace of change;
  - the complexity of change; and
  - the magnitude of change;
- understanding the changes in the profession;
- overcoming the barriers to change;
  - being sceptical;
  - being risk averse; and
  - being behind the curve; and
- accepting, managing and thriving on change.

We then finish the chapter with two case studies and some practical tips on dealing with change.

1. Understanding 'change³'

The bigger problem we're all grappling with isn't so much change itself, but the pace, complexity and magnitude of it – the 'change3' effect. Let's look at each of the three intersecting factors in Figure 1, in turn:

Figure 1. The nature of change

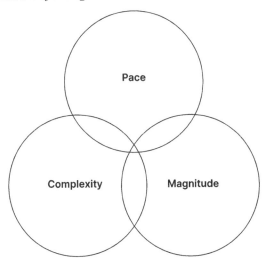

1.1 Pace of change

Human knowledge is expanding at a rate of knots. The upshot of this expanding knowledge is that everything feels a bit manic. Change approaches, quietly at first, but then it screams into view like a fighter jet banking low overhead. And then, like a squadron of jets, more change arrives. And then some more. We struggle to understand and manage yesterday's problems, let alone deal with today's and anticipate tomorrow's. We often can't see the wood for the trees.

Here are just four examples of the dizzying pace of change:

- The speed of technological change: dashing at full tilt is baked into what Big Tech does. Sergey Brin and Larry Page, the founders of Google, started the company so they could "instantly"[5] provide material to its users on almost every subject. Facebook's most well-known internal motto is to "move fast and break things".[6] (Alas, in 2014, it was changed to the much less quotable "move fast with stable infrastructure".)[7] The network effect of many tech companies means Big Tech has to build up their usership at breakneck speed.
- The speed of legal change: our institutions are struggling to keep up with all of this. As the government noted in a 2021 paper on digital regulation: "The challenge for government is to keep pace with the dramatic speed of technological change: unlocking the enormous benefits of digital technologies, while minimising the risks"[8] (see Chapter 12 on this 'pacing problem'). If keeping up with this change is going to be a challenge for the government, it will be something we lawyers will need to grapple with too.
- The speed of geopolitical change: we're living through the rise of China and the relative decline of the United States. Will there be a bifurcation of the global economy into blocs led by these two super-powers? Or a new Cold War? It's clear that events are happening at pace. Masses of troops crossing the border into Ukraine in 2022 resulted in Russia becoming the world's most sanctioned country almost instantly. According to compliance platform, Castellum.AI, sanctions that took about a decade to put into place, in the case of Iran, took about a week and a half in the case of Russia. International businesses pulled out of the country in their droves.
- The speed of financial change: the *Financial Times* noted in 2019 that even the volatility of volatility has started to spike[9] (now where do you even start with that one?).

Law firms are not sheltered from the strong winds of change:

- In October 2021, the 30th PwC Law Firms' Survey found that the third most common area of concern for firms in the top 100 is the speed of technological change (the top concern was cyber threats).[10]
- The SRA in its Risk Outlook 2021/2022 also confirmed that "there is no sign of the speed of overall change slowing".[11]

Dealing with the pace of change in these areas will challenge all firms. The SRA believes that larger firms will have an advantage in that they "can afford new systems and make use of their economies of scale", adding:

"those large firms that choose to list as public companies can access more resources and strengthen that advantage further".[12] As for smaller firms, they face a bigger challenge, having fewer resources, contacts and funds and less expertise to cope with the tsunami of change that they face.

1.2 Complexity of change

Digitisation; networked, cheaper and ubiquitous computers; and changes in business models and industry norms: these have upended how our world and profession works in recent decades.

- Macroeconomic complexity: China might become the largest global economy during this decade, overtaking the United States. (The country is currently on its Fourteenth Five-Year Plan (2021–2025) in which technology and innovation is core.) What people throughout the globe need and want will challenge even the most competent of our leaders, in a world where the gap between the haves and the have-nots in many places is widening; populism and nationalism is on the rise; and trade wars are threatened in many parts of the world.
- Microeconomic complexity: COVID and conflicts overseas have meant many states and businesses have switched their mindsets too, concentrating a bit more on resilience and a bit less on efficiency. At first sight, these sorts of mindset flips can seem innocuous, but they can have complex repercussions. Preferring a 'just-in-case' and less 'just-in-time' approach means nation states are likely to be more guarded and less open: from supply chains to tougher screening of foreign investment. In the end, businesses will need to adapt to such changes, with the help of their lawyers.

For lawyers, a complex world means complex laws:

- In 2021, Lord Justice Haddon-Cave worried that: "we labour under the heavy yoke of a lot of law and a lot of dense, complex law at that", adding that: "complexity breeds complexity and a downward spiral to yet more complexity".[13] This isn't good. There are many reasons for this development including – the authors' favourite – the "tyranny of cut-and-paste".[14] In 2013, the Office of the Parliamentary Counsel published a review entitled *When Laws Become Too Complex*. Sir Richard Heaton, who wrote the foreword to the OPC report, estimated in a TEDx talk that the statute book contained about 50 million words.[15] The 'good law' initiative was launched to tackle this complexity.[16]
- The common law has become more complex. More law reporting has been one contribution to its growth. Lord Justice Haddon-Cave notes: "You can find authority for pretty much any proposition."[17] In the past, the common law was supposed to be a "self-simplifying mechanism: elegant Common Law principles would grow tall in the

forest and fall like great redwood trees clearing away the under-growth".[18] Instead, the undergrowth seems to be spreading like giant knotweed.

There are now so many laws that we struggle to keep track of them. For example, there's no settled answer to the question: how many criminal offences are there? The maxim 'ignorance of the law is no excuse' starts to look frayed in a world where governments have a tendency, almost by default, to 'overcriminalise' much behaviour. For highly regulated busi-nesses, this is a worry.

1.3 Magnitude of change

More people in the world means more wants and more needs. Mid-way through this century the world population could be 9.7 billion, according to the United Nations, although others, such as Ipsos, talk of a 'population bust' with the world population heading up to 8.5 billion before dropping back again. Whoever gets this right, there'll still be anywhere between half to a few billion more humans stranded on this small rock in space, trapped by gravity and trying to make the best of things. It means more cities, more towns and more businesses. Every one of us has complex wants and needs so there'll be more challenges, opportunities and problems to solve. And this cumulative complexity is likely to increase the magnitude and the pace of change. And all this in a world where the climate is becoming more volatile too.

Various laws – more rules of thumb if truth be told – can help us make sense of the size of the change we see. Some of the most well-known include:
- Moore's law:[19] this revised famous rule of thumb on computing power (the death of which is announced regularly) is still just about holding on in there. This observation-cum-prediction is that the pro-cessing power of computers doubles every two years as transistors get ever smaller. At some point soon, however, the laws of physics will catch up with it and the law will have nowhere to go. Until then there may be some clever workarounds, such as new transistor designs. We can't write off the continued increase in computer power just yet. Ultimately, more computing power means people can do more things, meaning more technology and more innovation.
- Wrights' law:[20] this rule of thumb, from aeronautical engineer Theodore Wright, is said to be marginally more accurate than Moore's law. In essence, it's a learning curve. Wright noted that when aircraft manufacturing doubled, the need for labour dropped by 10 to 15%. And costs fell. (The exact figure for other goods can differ.) Put simply, by doing things we learn. By doing more things, we learn even more.

- Amara's law:[21] the adage of futurologist Roy Amara states that, in the short term, we have a tendency to overestimate the effects of a technology but, in the long term, we do the opposite: we underestimate it. But one thing is clear: the magnitude of change may look big now, but if a technology is successful, it could be off the scale in the not-too-distant future.

For us lawyers, more change also means more rules and more people to help us manage the influx of change:

- The scale of the law: the number of laws has boomed and, according to the House of Commons Library, the average number of pages per Act has risen fourfold, from 21 pages per Act in the post-World War II period (1950 to 1980) to 85 pages per Act in the period from 2000 to 2010.[22] In recent decades, we've also seen the introduction of new legislation and guidance in many areas, nationally and globally. Some of these new laws also have extra-territorial effect. To muddy the waters further, sometimes having to comply with some of these laws can mean breaching others: for example, the US Foreign Account Tax Compliance Act (FATCA) is thought to be incompatible with aspects of the EU GDPR. You can't do right for doing wrong, as they say. What is clear, however, is that many lawyers will be needed to navigate the interplay between the increasing number of laws we'll see in a world where, in the words of *Actuarial Post*, "extraterritorial compliance becomes [the] 'new normal'".[23]
- The scale of available experts: from data analysts to multimedia gurus, from businesses specialising in decision trees to start-ups offering software development tools in no-code, lawyers are going to need to work with all manner of new people in the years ahead. *The Lawyer* noted in a stark headline in September 2021 that: "soon lawyers will be a minority group in law firms".[24] Put simply, lawyering will involve more than just lawyers and we shouldn't default to the old thinking that, somehow, non-lawyers are subordinate to the legal talent in a firm. Just two years ago the authors' firm didn't have a social media team, an audiovisual/multimedia team or data analysts. Today, we have all of these. What's more, they're busy and in high demand.

2. Understanding the changes in the profession

Let's now look at change in the profession in more detail.

We know that it smacks of hyperbole to say everything is changing. After all, everything's been changing for years. Mancunian pop group *Take That* sang about it in 1993 so, in fairness, no one can say we weren't warned.

Societal change and technology has transformed the profession. In 1967, the percentage of women solicitors was 2.7%.[25] There are now more women on the roll than men. As for tech, people in the late 1960s would struggle to believe the gadgets we use today: mobile devices where, on a whim, we can access information on almost anything and do almost anything we want, at any time, from almost anywhere. In effect, the world is in our pockets.

If the pace of change is quickening, it isn't always that obvious to us. Does the document that you're working on today in Word look that different to one you were drafting a decade ago? Or even two decades ago? Reassuring and enduring, the warp and weft of our work can seem timeless. But change will continue to accelerate as the increase in ever-more powerful tech revolutionises what it means to be a lawyer, and diversity and inclusion transforms who our colleagues and clients are (see Chapter 10).

This is the bigger picture, but there are also many other specific drivers that are impacting the profession.

Professor Richard Susskind in the second edition of his book *Tomorrow's Lawyers* (2017) referred to the "perfect storm"[26] of three distinct developments which were transforming the legal world. These were the three 'mores' of *more* liberalisation, *more* tech and clients demanding *more* for less:

- More liberalisation in the profession will continue. This is certainly happening through, for example, reforms in 2019, which allow solicitors to practise in unauthorised entities and as freelancers. But despite this and other liberalising developments over the years, the CMA still doesn't think that the market is working well.[27] There are lots of opportunities, but will they be seized by enough players to make a difference? If so, when?
- Technology will revolutionise legal practice and who would dispute this? (Much of this book addresses this in detail.)
- Clients will continue to want more for less. Why wouldn't they? In these difficult economic times, many client budgets have been slashed, even though regulation has increased. Something has to give. (But this isn't a new phenomenon and is unlikely to have the seismic impact that some suggest. For example, survey after survey reveals that, for general counsels, price is important, but it ranks relatively low on the list of considerations for determining which legal professional to instruct. Perhaps more important is value for money.)

The authors substantially concur with these aspects of what Professor Susskind predicted. However, with the benefit of the passage of time since

Professor Susskind's book (as updated) and the authors' collective 75+ years' experience in legal practice, we take a different tack. Our view is that the three biggest factors that will lead to disruption in our industry over the next 10 years are those we identify in the introduction to this part, namely:

- the 'change3' effect (the focus of this chapter);
- the 'data boost' (the focus of the next chapter); and
- the onset of the 'hybrid era' (the focus of the last chapter in this part).

This disruptive trinity will be turbo-fuelled by technological change and shape the practice of law for years to come.

Some of the most illustrative shifts we see as a result of these dynamics include:

- the move, catalysed by COVID, to a more agile and remote workforce spread further geographically than ever before, but supported to work closer than ever thanks to collaborative technologies which optimise team working and efficiencies;
- a shift in client engagement activity: the way we engage with our clients reflects a shift to fewer physical meetings and more virtual meetings, which are ever-more reliant on collaborative software tools to support that virtual working;
- the desire of every board and C-suite to 'build back better' following COVID and which permeates every function in the business, including (in the case of in-house lawyers) the legal team;
- we lawyers being more adept with technology: we're typically better at tech than we think hence, at many firms (including the authors'), the IT team received far fewer requests for support during lockdown. This is because we'd all spent the three months of the first lockdown mastering from home all those systems we couldn't really be bothered to get to grips with when in the office (and, in many cases, surrounded by personal assistants who would sort it all out for us). Lawyers are, at last, stepping, blinking, into the 21st century;
- a change in mindset of many lawyers meaning that we need to offer more flexible working arrangements to retain and attract the best talent;
- the explosion and endless development of new data-rich tech specifically designed for lawyers (particularly AI). This is freeing up the law to be delivered in a fundamentally different way: faster, at lower cost and – lawyers always like this – more accurately. Given the massive unmet demand for legal services, among other things (see Chapter 3), it's likely that the next decade will be one of growth, not contraction;
- the emergence of the legal operations industry as a recognised internal (and external advisory) function in its own right. At the same

In these difficult economic times, many client budgets have been slashed, even though regulation has increased. Something has to give.

time, conference organisers and the legal media have been quick to recognise this is now a newsworthy subject;

- the deregulation of certain legal practice areas in the United Kingdom, allowing non-legally qualified staff to provide legal services and own such businesses;
- the increasing propensity of corporate clients to undertake legal panel reviews. This is not only forcing firms to distinguish themselves through innovation, but it's also opening the door to NewLaw providers to pitch against established players (see Chapter 7);
- the ever-important role that data plays in every part of business and personal life. We need to capture this precious data as we work on matters and ultimately feed that value back to clients (see Chapter 2);
- the amount of spare cash sloshing around the world economy given interest rates were so low for so long (although this is changing at the time of writing). The result? Investors are champing at the bit to plough their uninvested pounds, dollars, euros and yen into legal-tech; and
- the opportunity that canny firms have seen to expand into consultancy and connected services businesses.

The good news is that we're allowed to be excited by these changes. It's something we can be passionate about, even if 'excitement' and 'passion' don't feature in our professional conduct rules (the authors have checked).

In the next section, we look at change and why it is often so difficult to put into practice.

3. Overcoming the barriers to change

In 1997, Apple launched its *Think Different* campaign, at the heart of which was a TV advert featuring the heroes of Steve Jobs: Gandhi, Dylan and Einstein, among others. These were creative and risk-taking people who ultimately did things differently throughout their lives.

Some of the advert was written by co-founder Steve Jobs himself. The commentary exhorted viewers, in poetic prose, to "think big". It started with the well-known phrase "here's to the crazy ones"[28] and went on celebrate those who dislike rules and don't settle for the way things are done. Like them or loathe them, the advert made it clear that you certainly can't ignore them. The advert ended by saying that the crazy ones are geniuses because "the people who are crazy enough to think that they can change the world, are the ones who do".[29]

As Jobs recalled, this text was all about being creative. It had nothing to do with computer specs or memory size or processing speed. The advert wasn't just for customers; it was for employees too. It was a rethink of what Apple was all about, and a fundamental repositioning of its brand. It turned out to be a game-changing moment for the tech giant.

While Jobs didn't like much of the initial text of this commentary, berating it for being the 'bull' that comes out of advertising agencies, he soon came around to it. And it's a good thing he did. This call to arms transformed the fortunes and fate of what is now one of the most valuable companies on the planet. It ushered in the arrival of the Apple we all recognise today: the Mac, the iPhone, the iPod – all these products can arguably trace their origins back to this seminal "crazy ones" call to action.

The story of Jobs and Apple is well documented and their impact on the world around us is undeniable. Is it possible to replicate Jobs' passion-fuelled desire to make an impact and effect change in the legal world? What can we learn from it?

However, before rushing to compare the Apple experience with the opportunities within our own profession, it's important, first, to recognise some fundamental differences, most notably the psychology of the legal profession and other barriers to change.

3.1 Being sceptical
We lawyers are trained to be sceptical. Study upon study demonstrates that we have particular personality traits, which make us highly susceptible to cynicism and suspicion. We're trained to look at situations through curious eyes and this skill can sometimes leave us resistant to the kind of rallying call that worked so effectively for Apple in its *Think Different* campaign.

Dr Larry Richard reminds us of the most common words people who work with lawyers use when describing who we are. It's a thesaurus of misery: "sceptical", "pessimistic", "negative", "critical" and "cynical".[30] For us lawyers, it's not an edifying situation. "By both our nature and our training, lawyers focus on what can go wrong, on what's broken, on what possible problems exist", Richard says.[31]

What's more, some lawyers even try to wear their lack of imagination with pride – as if it were some sort of badge of honour.

This has to change. It's time for us to think different. Richard, for example, suggests having a chief mindset officer (CMSO). This is likely to be a step too far for most lawyers, but we do need to get better at recognising when we need to change our ways of looking at things so that we can each realise our firm's potential.

3.2 Being risk-averse

As lawyers, we're pretty risk-averse. We also tend to resist change if we perceive that the risks to ourselves are big, while the benefits only go to a few.

But being wary of risk doesn't mean doing nothing. If someone is standing in the middle of the road and a lorry is speeding towards them, most people in their right minds would leap to the side rather than do nothing. And yet, faced with a juggernaut of increased competition bearing down on us, many of us aren't doing much, if anything.

Where has this inaction come from? Scepticism? Risk aversion? Or perhaps even arrogance?

It's difficult to say. Many lawyers can be like rabbits in the headlights, not knowing where to move rather than not knowing that they must. Perhaps some of us are living in the vain hope that someone else in our firm, or in the broader sector, will scoop us out of harm's way at the eleventh hour.

3.3 Being behind the curve

The legal profession has also been relatively slow in adapting to change and technology compared with other professional services businesses. (We still wear wigs made of horsehair, a habit many people stopped when William Pitt introduced a tax on hair powder in 1795.) For centuries lawyers were the only professionals engaged in providing legal services. Our only competitors were other lawyers, and there was, more or less, enough work to go around so, frankly, why innovate?

This changed significantly with the coming into force of the Legal Services Act 2007, which created alternative business structures. With ever-increasing competition from NewLaw businesses, the Big Four and others, the size of the market may no longer sustain all the suppliers (see Chapter 7). We lawyers face true competition for the first time: a pivotal moment in our profession's history.

Can we overcome these barriers and change? As the next section shows, we can. But not only that: we *need* to change.

Recent history has seen many sobering examples where those who ought to have been best placed to triumph, during a fundamental shift in their industry, have failed to chart a new course.

4. Accepting, managing and thriving on change

Recent history has seen many sobering examples where those who ought to have been best placed to triumph, during a fundamental shift in their industry, have failed to chart a new course.

Some, in the face of such overwhelming change, worked night and day to preserve what they always had – Kodak and Blockbuster are notable examples. In the end, they failed: Blockbuster applied for bankruptcy protection in 2010. Kodak did the same two years later.

Others took the opportunity to decide what they actually wanted to be after the change. They reinvented themselves, remained relevant and emerged stronger. They thrived by understanding the change that was coming and responded proactively by using the momentum of that change in direction to slingshot themselves to even greater heights.

Despite the most intense competition, for example, Apple has continued to develop and offer innovative products and services that have led the market where others can only follow. And they haven't done this merely by having deep pockets. They've consistently shown an ability, not only to know what the public wants but, more radically, to offer the public things that they didn't know they wanted.

There's no doubt that the challenge for us lawyers is a daunting one.

Even with some firms now being listed on the stock exchange, most of us don't have the deep pockets of the Big Four or Big Tech. We don't have the huge R&D teams of major corporates in other sectors. But what we do have is much more relevant: the experience and capability to be creative and to have the ideas to offer the public what they want and, indeed, things that they don't even know they want. And we have the experience and ingenuity to breathe life into our own innovative ideas in the same way that we do on behalf of our clients day in and day out.

As lawyers, we can watch other sectors impacted by change and we can learn from them and from their mistakes too:

- Why did Netflix create its online streaming entertainment service? Why didn't the movie industry, instead, identify the potential growth in streaming and come up with a snazzy new platform for its customers to access their products?
- Why was it Amazon that created the Kindle e-reader? Why didn't global publishers see the impact of digital print consumption and changing reader habits?

- Why did a computer company, Apple, create iTunes, forcing the music industry to completely reinvent its business model?

There are plenty of recent examples where entire industries have been upended by businesses from outside those sectors.

We'd be arrogant in thinking that law is any different.

We're already seeing huge change impacting our traditional business lines, a notable example of which is the emergence of the contract lawyer model operated by the likes of Lawyers on Demand and Axiom. These have given lawyers greater flexibility and clients access to experienced lawyers at a lower price point. Put simply, technology has made this possible and this phenomenon is only set to continue. Multinationals like LexisNexis and Thomson Reuters are creating new business solutions too.

It's clear that we can't hide from change and, what's more, the pace, complexity and magnitude of it is increasing.

The key is how we accept, manage and thrive on that change.

Although we lawyers are already experts at helping our clients deal with change, we perhaps need to be better at dealing with it ourselves. We can no longer defend the *status quo*. We'd be fighting a futile battle. But we can choose what we'll be and lead the change, rather than being consumed by it. In the years ahead, we can, and must, re-imagine how we do law – to be the narrators of our own story. We have to think harder about what value we bring to the people who buy our services – how do we do that for them in a digital age?

Author and motivational speaker Simon Sinek makes the point that we need to be prepared to blow up our own business (metaphorically, of course) and rebuild it from the ground up.[32] Blockbuster wasn't brave enough to do that. But Apple successfully disrupted itself when it moved from the iPod to iPhone. And Kodak *almost* succeeded, having invented a digital camera, but then failed to do much about it. It was reported that the management's reaction was: "that's cute – but don't tell anybody about it".[33]

5. Case studies

5.1 Case study 1: Dealing with the short-term issues arising out of a crisis

At the beginning of January 2020, the BBC reported on a "mysterious viral pneumonia"[34] in the city of Wuhan, China for the first time. Just a few weeks later, officials locked down the city. By February, experts were warning of many storm clouds bubbling up on the horizon, and not just in China, but our attentions were elsewhere. Like SARS in 2002 to 2004, it would blow itself out surely?

It didn't. In March 2020, the virus crashed into our lives. Aside from war, it was one of the most shocking and immediate change agents in this country for over 100 years. There were no vaccines or specific treatments. For too many, it had tragic consequences as loved ones fell ill, some went on to develop long COVID; others passed away before their time.

For the legal sector, COVID was, and remains, a stark example of the 'change3' effect in action.

Figure 2. The nature of change: the COVID pandemic

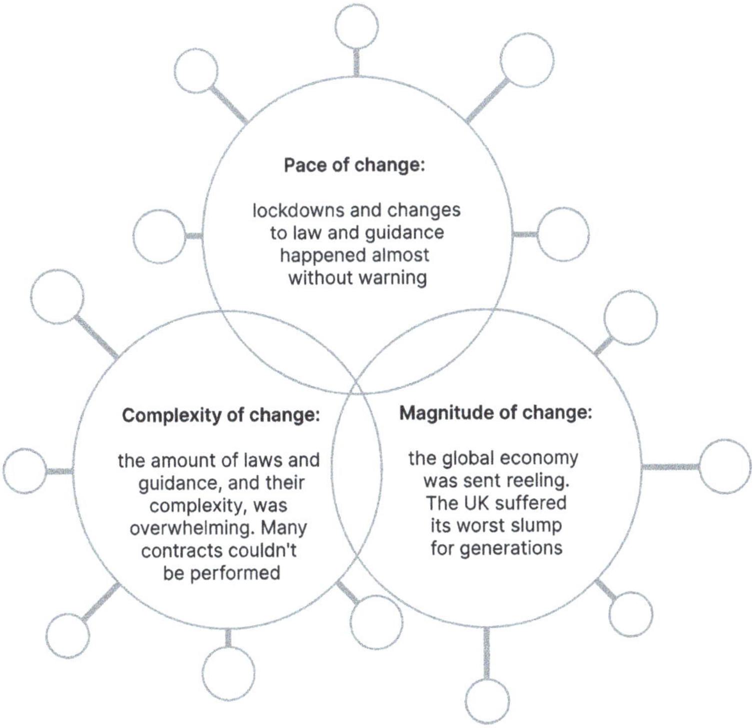

Pace of change:

lockdowns and changes to law and guidance happened almost without warning

Complexity of change:

the amount of laws and guidance, and their complexity, was overwhelming. Many contracts couldn't be performed

Magnitude of change:

the global economy was sent reeling. The UK suffered its worst slump for generations

As the crisis struck in March 2020, firms across the United Kingdom had to decide how they were going to respond. How would the virus affect their people and their clients? In particular, how would their businesses:
- deal with the immediate effects of the crisis?
- emerge from the tunnel, blinking into the light at the other side?

But as we now know, the other side (at the time of writing) hasn't arrived. The virus hasn't gone away. COVID has turned out to be, so far, like a mountain road with a series of tunnels – Alpha, Delta, Omicron and so on – each of which gets a bit shorter and relatively less difficult to navigate as the journey progresses. There have been plenty of unexpected twists and turns and we keep arriving at interim destinations that we weren't quite expecting. As for the end destination, this won't be a duplicate of the 'old normal'. It can't be: like most things in life, there are too many things that can't be undone. The *status quo ante* won't be our final stop.

However, most firms have accepted and managed this series of tunnels. And they've done well – perhaps much better than they expected in many cases.

Typically, firms have two options when dealing with this sort of shock:
- they can preserve what they've always had: the *status quo*; or
- they can hit the 'reset' button and decide what they will be: to reinvent, remain relevant and emerge stronger.

Forced to hunker down, most firms resolved to take the more challenging but optimistic second route and seize the opportunity to accelerate positive changes in their businesses. They sought to emerge from the crisis stronger than before. If we thought that firms were resistant to change, COVID has told us in the bluntest possible way: think again.

Let's briefly consider each element of 'change3' in the context of COVID:
- Pace of change: in the 2021 annual law firm survey by financial and professional services firm Smith & Williamson, in collaboration with *The Lawyer*, almost half of respondents (47.4%) said that change in their firms – not just technological – had been accelerated by between two and three years. Almost one in 10 respondents (9.6%) said the acceleration was more than half a decade.[35] The Law Society was even more optimistic, saying in July 2021 that according to some there was "5.3 years of digital transformation in the last year".[36] Quantifying qualitative change always seems to throw up these sorts of rather precise figures; even so, the direction of travel is clear: change has been turbocharged for a significant number of firms.

- Complexity of change: complex and rushed coronavirus laws and guidance resulted in complex legal advice. During COVID, hundreds of statutory instruments were promulgated to deal with it – and not only in the sphere of public health. The effect of the virus on the wider economy also meant far-reaching changes in many other areas of law, from tax to insolvency. Firms had to react with almost no notice.
- Magnitude of change: in most firms, productivity was affected by COVID to varying degrees. The financial impacts of COVID have been of a short-term nature, such as working out how to get all staff working remotely at the beginning of the pandemic in March 2020, to those of a medium- and long-term nature. And the nature of the change depends on where firms sit in the marketplace. The picture is complex. In October 2021, the 30th PwC Law Firms' Survey noted that the largest 25 firms experienced increased chargeable hours across almost all grades during the period of the survey (with full equity partners in the largest 10 firms going up by 10%), while the next 25 were flat.[37] After those firms, the next 50 firms saw reduced chargeable hours with falls of an average of 4%–5%. (It's unclear why the top 10 largest firms in particular did so well – perhaps it was because they got the biggest mandates arising from COVID and its fallout? Or perhaps, being London-based, they benefited most from the dispensing of commuting time.) For all firms, there continues to be a lot to unpack and learn from COVID.

Some change is expected: we have time to prepare for its impact, but other change has the power to blindside us. The luxury of preparing for it fully is simply something we don't often have. But most firms have done better than they and others expected at managing change. As the SRA noted: "The legal sector came through the challenge of COVID relatively well, demonstrating again its ability to survive and even thrive in extraordinarily challenging times."[38] On a further positive note, it added: "As ever, legal firms will be a key source of advice for people and businesses. They will help the economy and society recover from the impact of COVID and adapt to the challenges of the future."[39]

However, we shouldn't be complacent and rely on revenue growth as proof that no further change is necessary, such as investing in legaltech. The catalyst for technological and innovative change is here now, provided we look beyond the latest short-term financials for our firms, however good they may be. COVID brought about much-needed change, but it won't be the last event to do so.

5.2 Case study 2: Dealing with the long-term issues arising out of a crisis

This second case study looks at a medium- to long-term strategic project coming out of COVID: the 'New How'.

It wasn't long into the first lockdown before many businesses were not only coping well with the logistical aspects of their worlds being turned upside down, but they were beginning to realise the potential benefits of doing things differently. Necessity is the mother of invention, as they say. And the mantra that soon began to echo among countless boardroom Teams, Zoom and Webex meetings around the globe was 'build back better'. Very quickly, major corporates were starting to divert some of their best C-suite brains away from the fire-fighting stage of early lockdown and into thinking strategically about how the lessons from enforced agility could be applied to continued good effect, well after COVID ceased to feature in daily headlines.

Two of the authors, David Jackson and Tony Randle, were quick to see the trend and the opportunity that it presented to a law firm to offer a platform for clients to discuss and share their experiences. They were keen to capture people's willingness to think about doing things differently. But this was not to be just an opportunistic talking shop born out of the zeitgeist. Jackson and Randle had a very clear concept of what they wanted to create for clients. As Jackson expressed it at that time:

> *Every business we speak to wants to emerge from this crisis better than before. Most major businesses are already devoting a lot of management time to ensure that the future looks better than the past. There's a lot to be done. What businesses offer to their customers may not fundamentally change. But it is abundantly clear that how it is done will. How is up for grabs. The New How is how your business could – and should – be doing things now.*[40]

In May 2020 the 'New How' was launched. The launch itself employed its own 'new how' – how to get the attention of, and engage with, a large cohort of clients, all working remotely; and at a time when they were being flooded with countless online messages offering updates and webinar invitations (it was amazing how quickly Zoom fatigue became part of the national corporate malaise). How did Jackson and Randle plan to cut through the noise? They did so by using techniques that are fast becoming *de rigueur* for law firms now, but which back at that time (although it was not that long ago) were seldom employed:

- They created a YouTube animated video (they had to move fast, so the video was produced in three weeks from concept to launch). It was vital to be clear on messaging and a short, engaging video seemed the perfect medium through which to convey what they wanted to say.

- They devised a social media campaign, including dynamic ways to attract eyeballs on LinkedIn.

These creative devices worked. The launch did indeed cut through the noise and the concept resonated with clients. From their strong engagement with the launch campaign and with subsequent events that the firm held, it was obvious how eager clients were to explore how they could achieve what they still needed to achieve but do so smarter, faster and better.

This wave of demand then sparked another idea in the minds of Jackson and Randle – to create a suite of new solutions that would offer clients clever new ways of meeting their needs. And so they set to work again. In March 2021, they launched Shoosmiths8: a suite of non-legal connected services offering affordable new solutions to help clients do what they need to do. Some of the solutions were based on technological solutions, including AI; others involved blending legal and non-legal services in a new way to offer holistic solutions; and yet others involved partnering with third-party providers to offer easy access to their products, supported by Shoosmiths.

The 'New How' launch was enthusiastically received by clients, to the extent that in the year following its launch in 2021, the firm:

- was named "Legal Tech Team of the Year" (*Legal Business*);
- was selected as "Best Strategic Reimagination" (*Managing Partners Forum*);
- had two of its new legaltech solutions ranked in Band 1 of *Chambers LawTech Guide 2022*;
- had one of its products named "Best New Solution for Clients" (*Managing Partners Forum*); and
- had one of its clients named "Most Transformative In-house Team of the Year" (*Legal Business*) based on the use of Shoosmiths' products.

This case study goes to show the benefits that law firms can derive from being aware of the changing needs and priorities of clients in a time of 'change3', and of having the strategic leadership and prioritisation of resources within the firm to move quickly to adapt to new opportunities. It also shows how not all solutions fit within the stereotype of what lawyers offer their clients (we explore this new paradigm and 'legal practice matrix' in Chapter 3).

Add change to the agenda. Are you prepared to embrace and thrive on it? Is there a cultural mindset to embrace change and, in particular, innovation?

6. Practical tips on change

We set out below some practical tips on change.

These tips are split as follows:
- creating a change culture;
- understanding change;
- deciding on change;
- implementing change;
- consolidating change; and
- empowering others on change.

6.1 Creating a change culture
- Add change to the agenda. Are you prepared to embrace and thrive on it? Is there a cultural mindset to embrace change and, in particular, innovation? Is change or inertia the default setting? Do those in charge have the relevant experience and vision?
- Do more than just talk the talk: is change actually happening? You can have all the strategies you want, but if you don't have the right culture in place, you're fighting an uphill battle.
- Put the right structures in place. Is change reflected in your firm's strategies, visions and related aims?
- Speak to your peers in other firms: is your firm less progressive in dealing with change?

6.2 Understanding change
- Keep up to date: read articles on change and innovation. Join industry initiatives (national and local) which are focused on innovation and legaltech.
- Be prepared to remove elements: change doesn't always mean adding more elements to improve something (humans have a tendency to do this, which is why red tape and workloads always seem to increase).
- Remember that change isn't always steady. It often comes in fits and starts.

6.3 Deciding on change
- Put change high on the agenda: empower and support those who are going to drive change. Give them the mandate they need.
- Base change on empirical data, where appropriate. Guesswork, anecdotal evidence or educated guesses may not get you to where you need to be.
- Drive change through visionaries who really understand the business and its people (see the archetypes in Chapter 11).

- Involve your best people: people need to earn their place. Would the Manchester United football manager put people on the pitch merely because they want to play, or would the manager choose the best players?
- Reward change: create a system under which great ideas are both encouraged and rewarded.

6.4 Implementing change

- Craft narratives which act as compelling rallying calls: "we get to narrate our story" as we say in the preface to this book. Stories spark our imaginations and stir our emotions when facing and implementing change, but they can be basic and closed. Narratives, on the other hand, are open-ended: they imply that we need to get involved. The end has yet to be written. Compare Nike's battle cry "Just Do It®" (a narrative) with what Nike could've said: "Just Did It" (a story).
- Build the right narrative: people need to connect emotionally with change. Tell them what's in it for them. Case studies help. Lawyers can be control freaks, so reinforce the message that any change is their servant and not *vice versa*.
- Choose who will deliver the messages: presentations by someone charismatic and with high EQ can achieve a lot more than by more senior managers who are not great 'people' people.
- Consider if there are any champions within your team who can convince their peers that change is a good thing.
- Identify those for whom change will be hardest: ensure they're supported. But don't give any truck to those who are idealistically opposed to innovation and change and wear it as a default badge of honour.
- Play to people's strengths: change doesn't mean homogenisation. Any good change programme will recognise particular individuals' strengths and weaknesses, not seek to pretend that those differences don't exist. Play people to their strengths and don't expect people to become what they are not.
- Treat people fairly and consistently: inconsistency in the treatment of one team compared to another team may lead to resentment. Change causes enough stress in people as it is, without compounding it with resentment on top.
- Talk to people who have done this before: ask the views of those who have journeyed with a particular solution before you.
- Consider a pilot: initial implementation with a smaller number of people not only allows time to resolve any glitches but also allows you to point to the positive outcomes that have been achieved from the pilot.

- Listen to your associates: they may have valuable feedback as they're at the coal face and less able to control how the change impacts on them.
- Consider 'nudging' when implementing necessary change. The Behavioural Insights Team (BIT) – also called the Nudge Unit – was set up in 2010 within the Cabinet Office. BIT shows how even small changes can have significant outcomes, often at little cost. Every firm arguably needs a few easy wins to get people on board.

6.5 Consolidating change

- Lead by example: people in senior positions must stick to the new way of doing things and be seen to do so.
- Be consistent: ensure everybody adheres to any change consistently. Don't tolerate people who don't follow the new way of doing things.
- Check how things are going: regularly check back with people to see how they're finding any change. Don't assume that if there are no problems during the first two weeks then you can assume that all will be well from there on in.

6.6 Empowering others on change

Help those who are in less senior positions so that they can:

- Make suggestions: those in senior positions don't have the monopoly on good ideas.
- Voice their views: whether positive or negative, presented constructively, junior team members' views are important and the senior lawyers ought to welcome them.
- Earn themselves a place at the table: savvy partners will not just involve people because they are enthusiastic, but also because they have a lot to add.
- Be helpful: senior team members may appear to achieve things with the effortlessness of gods, but they have challenges. If junior team members can help with any of these aspects, they'll be grateful.
- Be a champion: help them to make change a success in your firm.
- Put their hand up so that they never miss an opportunity to get involved if they're given one.
- Talk to their contacts: knowing what is happening in other firms and in clients' businesses keeps them informed and in a better position to get involved in their own firm.

Notes

1   Steven Pinker, "2017: What Scientific Term or Concept Ought to Be More Widely Known?" (Edge), www.edge.org/response-detail/27023.
2   John Kay and Mervyn King, *Radical Uncertainty* (The Bridge Street Press, 2021), pxxix.
3   Lucinda Cameron, "Living with 'certain uncertainty'" the new norm in pandemic, says psychiatrist" (*Evening Standard*, 27 December 2021), www.standard.co.uk/news/uk/people-scotland-royal-college-of-psychiatrists-gps-b973930.html.

4   "The new normal is already here. Get used to it" (*The Economist*, 18 December 2021), www.economist.com/leaders/2021/12/18/the-new-normal-is-already-here-get-used-to-it.

5   "2004 Founders' IP Letter" (Alphabet Investor Relations), https://abc.xyz/investor/founders-letters/2004-ipo-letter/#_ga=2.165626872.610004439.1532311821-929489725.1521479135.

6   Steven Levy, "Mark Zuckerberg on Facebook's Future, From Virtual Reality to Anonymity" (*WIRED*, 30 April 2014), www.wired.com/2014/04/zuckerberg-f8-interview.

7   *Ibid.*

8   Department for Digital, Culture, Media and Sport, *Digital Regulation: Driving growth and unlocking innovation* (6 July 2021), www.gov.uk/government/publications/digital-regulation-driving-growth-and-unlocking-innovation/digital-regulation-driving-growth-and-unlocking-innovation.

9   Robin Wigglesworth, "'Volatility: how 'algos' changed the rhythm of the market" (*Financial Times*, 9 January 2019), www.ft.com/content/fd01e061 1110 11c9 a81-4ff/84045240.

10 "Facing the future with confidence, PWC Law Firms' Survey 2021" (PwC, 2021), www.pwc.co.uk/industries/law-firms/law-firm-survey-report-2021.pdf. Although in PwC's survey in 2022 macroeconomic volatility was the top worry for many firms, with the speed of technological change not featuring as a key area of concern ("Annual Law Firms' Survey 2022: Agility through turbulent times" (PwC, 2022), www.pwc.co.uk/industries/legal-professional-business-support-services/law-firms-survey.html.

11 "Risk Outlook 2021/2022" (Solicitors Regulation Authority), www.sra.org.uk/sra/research-report/risk-outlook-202122/.

12 *Ibid.*

13 Lord Justice Haddon-Cave, "English law and descent into complexity" (Gray's Inn Reading at Barnard's Inn given on 17 June 2021), www.judiciary.uk/wp-content/uploads/2021/07/ENGLISH-LAW-AND-DESCENT-INTO-COMPLEXITY-1.pdf.

14 *Ibid.*

15 TEDx Talks, "Good Law: Richard Heaton at TEDxHousesofParliament" (27 June 2013), www.youtube.com/watch?v=p8GUG0S9esU.

16 Cabinet Office and Office of the Parliamentary Counsel, *Guidance: Good Law* www.gov.uk/guidance/good-law. (This is not to be confused with the campaign organisation Good Law Project, founded by Jolyon Maugham, QC.)

17 Lord Justice Haddon-Cave, "English law and descent into complexity" (Gray's Inn Reading at Barnard's Inn given on 17 June 2021), www.judiciary.uk/wp-content/uploads/2021/07/ENGLISH-LAW-AND-DESCENT-INTO-COMPLEXITY-1.pdf.

18 *Ibid.*

19 "Moore's law" (Wikipedia), https://en.wikipedia.org/wiki/Moore%27s_law.

20 "Experience curve effects" (Wikipedia), https://en.wikipedia.org/wiki/Experience_curve_effects.

21 "Roy Amara" (Wikipedia), https://en.wikipedia.org/wiki/Roy_Amara.

22 House of Commons Library Briefing Paper, "Acts and Statutory Instruments: the volume of UK legislation 1850 to 2019", CBP 7438, 4 November 2019, https://researchbriefings.files.parliament.uk/documents/CBP-7438/CBP-7438.pdf.

23 "Extraterritorial Compliance Becomes 'New Normal' for Financial Institutions" (Actuarial Post), www.actuarialpost.co.uk/article/extraterritorial-compliance-becomes-%E2%80%98new-normal%E2%80%99-2661.htm.

24 Matt Byrne, "Soon lawyers will be a minority group in law firms" (*The Lawyer*, 30 September 2021), www.thelawyer.com/soon-lawyers-will-be-a-minority-group-in-law-firms/.

25 "75 years of women solicitors" (BBC News, 19 December 1997), http://news.bbc.co.uk/1/hi/uk/40448.stm.

26 Richard Susskind, *Tomorrow's Lawyers* (2nd edition, Oxford University Press, 2013), p3.

27 Stephen Mayson, "Reforming Legal Services: Regulation Beyond the Echo Chambers" (Centre for Ethics and Law, University College, June 2020), www.ucl.ac.uk/ethics-law/publications/2018/sep/independent-review-legal-services-regulation. The review was in response to the CMA market study into the provision of legal services in England and Wales which was published in 2016. Overall, the Competition and Markets Authority report (*Legal services market study final report*, 15 December 2016) found that: "the legal services sector is not working well for individual consumers and small businesses", https://assets.publishing.service.gov.uk/media/5887374d40f0b6593700001a/legal-services-market-study-final-report.pdf.

28 "Steve Jobs: 20 Best Quotes" (ABC News, 15 August 2011), https://abcnews.go.com/Technology/steve-jobs-death-20-best-quotes/story?id=14681795.

29 *Ibid.*

30 Dr Larry Richard, "Resilience and Lawyer Negativity" (*What Makes Lawyers Tick*, 19 September 2012), www.lawyerbrainblog.com/2012/09/resilience-and-lawyer-negativity/.

31 *Ibid.*

32 Oli Ballard, "Simon Sinek famously said: 'blow your business up before the market does it' – but what if you don't?" (*Business Leader*, 14 March 2019), www.businessleader.co.uk/simon-sinek-famously-said-blow-your-business-up-before-the-market-does-it-but-what-if-you-dont/.

33 Claudia H Deutsch, "At Kodak, Some Old Things Are New Again" (*The New York Times*, 2 May 2008), www.nytimes.com/2008/05/02/technology/02kodak.html.

34 "China pneumonia outbreak: Mystery virus probed in Wuhan" (BBC News, 29 September 2020), www.bbc.co.uk/news/world-asia-china-50984025.

35 Tess Waddington, "Evolving at a 100 miles per hour: change is the new normal for law firms" (*The Lawyer*, 5 October 2021), www.thelawyer.com/smith-williamson-law-firm-survey-executive-summary-2021/.

36 "Lawtech and ethics principles report" (Law Society, 28 July 2021), www.lawsociety.org.uk/topics/research/lawtech-and-ethics-principles-report-2021.

37 "Facing the future with confidence, PWC Law Firms' Survey 2021" (PwC, 2021) www.pwc.co.uk/industries/law-firms/law-firm-survey-report-2021.pdf.

38 "Risk Outlook 2021/2022" (Solicitors Regulation Authority), www.sra.org.uk/sra/research-report/risk-outlook-202122/.

39 *Ibid*.

40 See www.shoosmiths.co.uk/insights/legal-updates/the-new-how.

Chapter 2:
The data boost

Black gold, Texas tea, fossilised sunshine: whatever you call the trillions of litres of hydrocarbons under our feet, the yellowish-black substance has transformed our world.

In our thirst for petroleum – literally 'rock oil' – we've drilled holes deep into the Earth's crust. People of the future will look in astonishment at the way we lived: how we transformed our cities with oil-guzzling motor vehicles; how we let liquid hydrocarbons change the wars we fought and even modify the climate of the planet we lived on. They'll marvel at how we learnt to escape the gravity of our earthly home too: in 1957, highly refined crude oil propelled the first satellite, 'Prosteishiy Sputnik' ('PS-1'), into space, panicking the West and igniting the Space Race with the Soviet Union. Today, we live with the spin-off technologies from this geopolitical one-upmanship, from the GPS in our smartphones to data-rich weather forecasts from weather satellites orbiting far above our heads (Robert FitzRoy[1] would be astounded by what humans have done).

If the history of the industrial revolution is about another hydrocarbon, coal, the history of the modern age is all about oil.

And it's everywhere. But unless we're in a petrol station forecourt holding a fuel nozzle and staring at the price on the electronic counter tick up at a distressing speed, we scarcely register it's there. It's the bright blue stripe in some toothpastes (known as 'brilliant blue' or E133). It's in the synthetic fibres in the clothes we wear (polyester, nylon and elastane to name a few). It's even in some of the food we eat.

Oil is, beyond doubt, a valuable resource and the world's most traded commodity. It has made many countries rich beyond their dreams. On the other side of the North Sea to the United Kingdom, one of Norway's sovereign wealth funds – the Government Pension Fund Global – is worth about a trillion pounds at the time of writing: almost £200,000 for every Norwegian. (In contrast, the United Kingdom's sovereign wealth fund is worth £0. We never set one up.)

Put simply: in our world, oil is king.

For now. But is it about to be overthrown?

In 2017, *The Economist* published a (now famous) article accompanied by a cartoon of offshore platforms with digital plumes of ones and zeros pouring out of their flare stacks. It declared that "the world's most valuable resource is no longer oil, but data".[2] So are the black arteries of the world economy going to disappear altogether?

Not quite.

Oil has powered our societies and made them prosper. It will continue to do so, despite the well-known environmental costs. But change is afoot. Data is a resource that will power our society and our profession more and more. *The Economist* is definitely on to something.

Compare in the figure below, for example, the revenues of two groups of companies over the past two decades:
- 'Big Tech': Facebook (now Meta), Amazon, Apple, Google (now Alphabet) and Microsoft; and
- 'Big Oil': BP, Chevron, Eni, ExxonMobil, Shell, TotalEnergies and ConocoPhillips.

Despite the ups and downs in the price of oil, the revenue growth of data-powered Big Tech in the long term is clear: it's on the up. And many others based in Silicon Valley and the UK equivalents (Silicon Roundabout, Silicon Fen etc) are doing well too.

Figure 1. Big Tech v Big Oil: revenue in $ billions

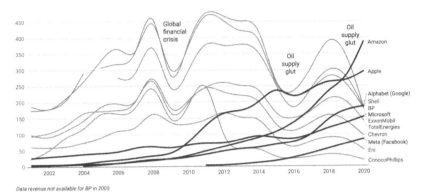

Data revenue not available for BP in 2005

Source: Based on data from CompaniesMarketCap.com, created with Datawrapper.

Of course, data being the new oil is a metaphor. Oil isn't the same as data, but the impact of data is as profound as the discovery of crude oil a few generations ago.[3]

From the authors' experience, we're not sure that many in the legal profession fully appreciate where we are right now: at the cusp of a great data- and AI-powered change. We lawyers sit on piles of unused data. It's everywhere: over the years we've stockpiled data often without thinking about it and, like the oil in our day-to-day lives, we usually don't see it. It's hidden in plain sight.

But the resource has so much potential. To give just two examples:
- It'll add significant value to the advice we give and differentiate those of us who use it from our competition. Think of visual heatmaps of contractual risk, using dynamic, real-time, AI-enabled insight. We're not just talking pretty colours here: this is the sort of powerful data-driven analysis that can help our clients understand and minimise risk, close deals quicker and even avoid potentially catastrophic events.
- It'll be the fuel that powers and trains AI solutions. As we examine later in this chapter, accurate AI and machine learning relies on copious amounts of reliable data. The better the data, the better the AI-powered solutions built on it.

Just as future generations will marvel at life in the 2020s, they'll also be fascinated to see how we dealt with the challenges of this coming transformation. How did we come to make the decisions we made? Who were the winners? Who were the losers? Did lawyers finally bite the bullet and start taking data seriously? Did we take full 'first-mover' advantage? Or were we led kicking and screaming into this new data world?

At present, we're like the visitors at the 1889 Exposition Universelle in Paris – the event at which Eiffel built his eponymous tower – looking over the new oil fields in the Oil Panorama attraction. At that time the organisers predicted that oil was going to play a big part in the industry of the future. And so it has.

And in the oil rush that followed, it wasn't just the oil companies who made money. The businesses which made the rigs cleaned up too!

In effect, we're the first cohorts of legal data prospectors. And legaltech companies are the producers of the rigs, which will help us explore more of the hidden depths.

But – and here's the great news – unlike oil, data isn't a finite resource. Compared to oil, it's almost infinite in its creation. *Forbes* reported in 2018 that 2.5 quintillion bytes of data were being created every day.[4] Two years later, market intelligence company IDC reckoned there'd be more than 59 zettabytes (ZB) of data in 2020 (although, if truth be told, these statistics are fiendishly difficult to prove or disprove).[5]

The upshot? We don't have to do as much as we think. We're already sat on much of the data that can transform how we work and the services we can offer our clients.

It's an exciting time to be in practice.

In this chapter, we look at this data transformation:
- first, we look at the bigger picture of data itself, including the need to change the culture in attitudes towards data and why now is the time to start our data journey; and
- we then set out how to use the data which we have (and often fail to use), including working with others so we don't have to start from scratch.

We then look at AI:
- again, this is about understanding AI in general and where the profession is now with it; and
- we then set out how we can use AI in our businesses and work with others to achieve this.

After this, we reflect on how we can be better at dealing with data and how we can prepare for potential future developments. We also look at costs. Finally, we include a few case studies and practical tips on 'doing data'.

Figure 2. Chapter contents

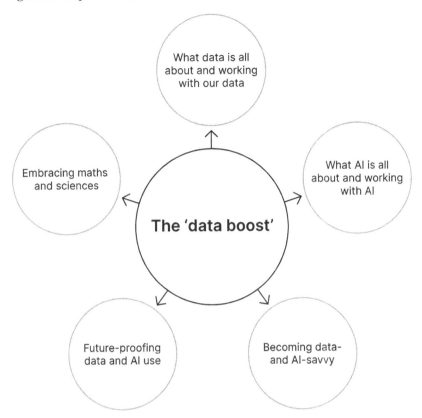

In what follows, you'll see that the right data analysed, often turbocharged by AI, and turned into insight will be crucial to the success of lawyers in the digital age. This data, as 'refined', will help us harness our 'collective clever' and provide clients with amplified insight the like of which has never before been possible.

More and more, this refined data will be the fuel that powers 'the machine': our firms.

Let's see how.

1. Understanding data: the bigger picture

It's become clear to us, over the years, that the profession needs to do two fundamental things before it can really start to take advantage of data and AI: (1) understand data more than we do now; and (2) spark a renaissance – a permanent culture change – in how we use it. We need to get these two ground rules right before we jump in at the deep end:

- First: understanding data. Not grasping the power of data and the upcoming transformation is like visiting a foreign country where you don't speak the language: helpful asides and informative remarks go over your head. But just as not understanding the global language of business, English, isn't an option, this is increasingly the case with data too. We can't afford not to be fluent, or at least conversant, in this new language. And, as this chapter shows, it really isn't that complicated (we lawyers are pretty bright after all).
- Second: using data. We deal with many matters every day, and yet, once completed, too much of the data in them goes into storage or is deleted. Much of this vast treasure trove of data is overlooked or downplayed. Surveys back this up: in one study only about one in five lawyers "agree" or "strongly agree" that their firms are capturing data "effectively".[6] We're data-rich, but analysis-poor: we do nothing with so much of our data – apart from paying to store it. Why not make it work for us? We need to change our mindsets and seize the data opportunities more. *Carpe diem*, or more precisely, *carpe data!*

Many other sectors have already discovered the power of data. Farmers, for example, are putting wearable trackers on their cows to calculate how many times a day each cow is chewing the cud. They can then work out how free from disease, happy and thus milk-producing she is.

Football clubs are also successfully using data. Winning, of course, means prize money and other lucrative income streams. Liverpool Football Club, in particular, has embraced data to an astonishing degree. So much so that, when considering who has what it takes to be the next manager, the *Daily Mirror* says the question won't be "can they manage the team?", rather it needs to be: are they "clever and aware enough to embrace the Data Science department and use the weapons they are currently developing?".[7] As Trevor Watkins, Head of Sports at Pinsent Masons, says: "You can't underestimate the value of data and analysts."[8] It's as far from 'jumpers for goalposts' as you could imagine.

The future of lawyering is increasingly about data too, as we show in this chapter. And while putting wearable technology on our clients to unlock insight is unlikely to be an easy sell; there are plenty of other exciting things that are open to us. (In fairness, we'd be fascinated to see what would happen if we were to give eye-tracking technology and a pile of contracts to our clients. What provisions do they really care about? Are they the ones that we care about? But we digress.)

So what's stopping us? Legal exceptionalism? Or is it something more prosaic?

1.1 Overcoming the barriers to using data: changing the culture

There are plenty of reasons why our treasure troves of data and other data sources are routinely ignored or devalued:

- hearing the word 'data' and switching off;
- not understanding how powerful data is;
- understanding how powerful data is in theory – and the remarkable insights it can bring – but not knowing what to do with it in practice;
- not having the right tech to collect and process data;
- having data in different formats – data is often 'siloed' – so it can't 'talk' to other data (ie, not having data standards);
- worrying about the data governance and legal framework. A survey by the European Company Lawyers Association, in partnership with Osborne Clarke, in June 2022 found that legal and regulatory worries are the biggest obstacles for data-driven businesses by a country mile (although the authors wonder if, in a report by lawyers, the response biases of respondees mean that they tend to say what we lawyers want to hear? Perhaps, but we still shouldn't discount these concerns);[9]
- worrying about getting hacked and other cybersecurity issues; and
- not having a data vision or strategy, which sets out a firm's aims, its approach to data, its appetite for risk, whether it's open to 'open data' (see later), and so on.

According to surveys, however, the profession needs to up its game and it knows that it needs to do so. For example, in 2020, a survey by information services provider Wolters Kluwer found that:

- about three-quarters of legal professionals believe the increasing importance of legaltech – much of which is powered by data – will be the trend that will affect their businesses over the next three years,[10] yet only just over a quarter were ready; and
- two-thirds of corporate lawyers say predictive analytics and big data will transform their work during the same time period. But, again, only a quarter understood it very well.[11]

We're still behind the curve.

One solution to this is to change our cultures: firms need to have a stronger culture of being bold, of "daring to dare", as poet Maya Angelou once said. In a time of 'change3', the mantra should be: 'go and try new stuff'. Embrace data and embrace innovation!

In some firms, partners work well together, trust each other and find themselves pushing against open doors with new ideas. In other firms, the push back is stronger. In the more innovative data-driven firms, the authors have spotted the following over the years (many of these apply to AI too – see later):

- Using data is a team effort, the vision of which needs to be led from senior management.
- The approach to data is strategic and not *ad hoc*, from the use of technology itself to, say, procuring the right technology (see Chapter 4).
- People have the space, autonomy and budget to try new things and, implicit in this, to make mistakes from time to time.
- There's a recognition that not all projects will succeed or work as expected: two steps forward and one step back is still progress. Projects are complex and full of uncertainties.
- Compliance isn't an afterthought and is built in at all stages of a project (see Chapter 6).
- Partners know that they'll keep each other in the loop and they'll find the balance on what the others need to know about projects involving data: overreporting can be as unhelpful as underreporting.
- Once there's a track record of success, partners are more inclined to trust in innovation and to try more new things: there's a virtuous circle of data innovation.
- Timescales are realistic and aren't underestimated. Most projects don't come readymade or 'out of a box'. They don't overpromise and underdeliver.
- These firms know that the R&D cycle doesn't typically (and conveniently) fit into an annual cycle. Resources are allocated to longer-term data projects notwithstanding the pressures of the annual distribution of profits to partners.
- Data, and the solutions it powers, are humanised. These firms tend to shy away from overusing abstract terms like 'data'; it's a pretty dry and off-putting Latinate word. These firms know that it's the alchemy of analysing raw data and turning it into *insight* that matters. It's this refined data – insight – which lawyers connect with better. (After all, giving insights to clients is what lawyers do every day.) The authors' firm, for example, humanised the data-powered contract review tool it developed (see the case study in Chapter 5) by not obsessing about the data, but referring more to how it can work in practice ('go make a brew and we'll do the review'). The firm also gave it a humanoid name: 'Cia'.

Figure 3. From data to insight

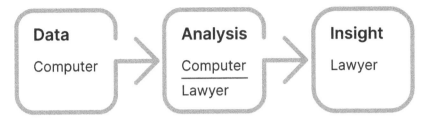

- There's a recognition that data-driven insight has a deeply human touch. While analysis of data can be done by machines (with the help of humans), they know that it takes legal *and* human expertise to convert that analysis into insight. Data can tell us *what* is happening, but it usually struggles to tell us *why* something is happening. This is where the lawyers come in: they understand the relevant markets and the context. They know the nuances and the way people think and behave. It's this human-focused, data-driven insight – or 'data boost' – which will take these lawyers to the next level of lawyering. As co-creator of the iPod and the iPhone, Tony Fadell, notes, "the majority of our decisions are typically 'data-informed', not 'data-made'".[12]
- Data projects for clients are client-focused (see Chapter 3). When developing data solutions they look to walk in the shoes of their clients. They use surveys and talk to their clients. They value user-centred design (UCD) and user experience (UX).[13] These firms begin by looking at things through clients' eyes and responding to them, as opposed to taking a purely lawyer-centric approach and potentially getting the wrong end of the stick. After all, clients typically speak in numbers: they respond better to statements like 'EBITDA has increased by 30 percentage points' as opposed to vague statements like 'the business is doing really well this quarter'.
- They know that moving to a data-driven world can be bumpy and full of surprises. Despite the benefits of a lot of technology, people can still be attached to the old ways: wet signatures on paper contracts is a good example. People attach meaning to rituals and may need help to move onto new ways of doing things. This is why hybrid solutions are often created (see Chapter 3).
- They always keep a keen eye on developments (see Chapter 12).

But too often we wait to see what others are doing. And we risk losing out.

1.2 Waiting for the data tipping point
Like much in life, things can take time to come to fruition.

Take oil as an example. One of the largest offshore oilfields in the world was discovered in the North Sea in 1969, but it wasn't until 1990 that the Norwegians set up their sovereign wealth fund to invest some of the surplus oil revenues. At the time of writing, the fund is now worth about £1 trillion.

It's easy to say "let's wait", but the earlier we start to sow the seeds of this data transformation the quicker we can start to reap the benefits. (The Norwegian fund could have been even bigger had it been set up earlier.) Ultimately, lawyers need to be at the forefront of this profound change in how we use data, leading and not following, choosing the direction that suits us, and not, say, Big Tech, which has the money and the resources to do almost anything that it wants if it were to decide to take a greater interest in our sector. And it's not just Big Tech. What about big data analytics companies like Palantir Technologies? Or the tech giants coming out of Beijing's tech hub, Zhongguancun or Shenzhen? In the future, the BATX tech giants in China (Baidu, Alibaba, Tencent, and Xiaomi) might take an interest in the legal sector globally. The disruption might even come from smaller players: perhaps some of the businesses with which firms collaborate now may become competitors?

We need to shake things up before someone else does.

Lord Heseltine, a cabinet minister in Margaret Thatcher's government, said that he regretted not setting up a wealth fund for oil revenue in the 1980s when the opportunity presented itself.[14] Our profession is now at a similar sweet spot in its data journey. Many exciting opportunities are now presenting themselves. Can we afford to miss out and make a similar mistake? What are our excuses if we decide not to do anything now?

What's more, many government departments, regulators and other bodies are also prodding us to get a move on:
- Various government bodies, from the Department for Digital, Culture, Media and Sport to the Government Office for Science, are pleading for businesses generally to be more data-savvy.
- In July 2021, LawtechUK published a report in which it said there should be "no sacred cows" and that simply "tinkering around the edges" won't cut it.[15] Put simply, it said our analogue world has to go. And this doesn't mean just sprinkling a bit of digital gold dust over existing processes either. LawtechUK called for extensive change in which managing and using data is key. To this end, it published its *Legal Data Vision* in March 2022 which called for an ecosystem of

legal data which will, among other things, "drive innovation" and "fuel growth and productivity".[16]

- The Legal Services Board (LSB) published its 10-year strategic direction in March 2021. One of its priorities is to focus on data, which it said will power our profession more and more. The LSB said using data more will give our clients: "fairer outcomes", "stronger confidence" and "better services".[17] Data will also shine a mirror back at us to ensure we're serving our clients well.

We're at the tipping point. And the message is clear: we need to get on with it.

2. Using data and turning it into valuable insight

Data is everywhere, but the key is to start using it in a measured way. We shouldn't be too keen and try to use it all at once.

Start somewhere and start small. If some of us are new to using data, the key is to be prudent before going all in.

2.1 Laying the data foundations
If there is a need to be solved and we have the data, we should start by thinking about our 'data points'.

What about a typical legal question that clients ask like: how standard is this indemnity?

To this end, there are many data points in contracts, from the names of the parties to how the contract is executed, but a lot of these data points won't help in answering our question. We need to home in on the data that really matters. (Talking to our clients also helps when working out the right data points, as they might include ones that we think are unimportant, but which are vital to them!)

Here are some examples of the data points in contracts relating to indemnities.

Table 1. Data points in contracts

Type of data	Data points
Indemnities (supplier)	• general breach of contract; • IP rights breach; • data breach; • property damage; • personal injury; • upstream breach; • IT security breach; • TUPE breach; or • tax liability.
General liability cap (supplier)	• less than 100%; • 101% to 150%; • 151% to 200%; or • 201% or more.
General liability cap (customer)	• less than 100%; • 101% to 150%; • 151% to 200%; or • 201% or more.
Property damage liability (supplier)	• within the general cap; • £0 to £5 million; • over £5 million to £10 million; • over £10 million to £15 million; • over £15 million; or • uncapped.

However we choose them, data points are the building blocks for the analysis, and then insight, that we give to our clients. Getting these right is key.

2.2 Analysing data for insight

Once we have our data points, the real fun begins. The data points are analysed to give the client valuable insight that they typically don't have now. This could be: 'our data analysis of these types of x contracts shows that a data breach clause is now found in x% of these types of contracts and that the average cap is £x. We can't justify not including an indemnity in the contract. This isn't market practice'.

Figure 4. From data to insight: indemnity example

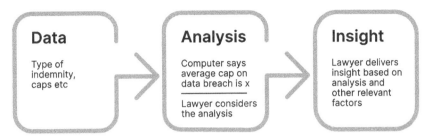

But, it doesn't end there. In processing all of this data, there's still something that computers usually can't do: understand the context in which the data is analysed. This is where technology and people truly complement one another.

In our example, the lawyer can, for example:
- explain why an indemnity matters. For example, in the context of data protection, the largest maximum fine under the UK GDPR is £17.5 million or 4% of the total annual worldwide turnover (whichever is higher);
- explain where the indemnity might not work, even though it's included in a contract; and
- perhaps most importantly ensure that the client has understood the analysis and its implications.

Using the data in our day-to-day practice can not only give our clients greater insights like this, but it even can:
- start to influence broader market practice if applied on a large enough scale; and
- create new business streams for the law firms offering this insight.

2.3 Working with your own data

What do we need to do to start taking greater advantage of the data we have and where do we start?

Typically, it means looking at:
- the data we have (and may not be using); and
- the data we need to have (and may not even have thought about using).

It also means working with others inside and outside our businesses, both lawyers and non-lawyers (see below).

Data itself is also categorised in many ways. First, we can look at data from a time point of view. This is roughly what this looks like:

Figure 5. Categorising data by time

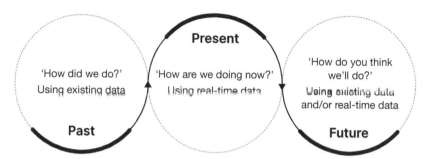

Another way to look at data, and understand what it can do, is to split it as follows:

Figure 6. Categorising data by type

The challenge with understanding all this data is also, in many cases, wading through the sheer volume of it (hence the term 'big data'). It can be daunting, but, as the authors say, the key is to start somewhere and start small.

And we don't always have to poke around in the obvious places. COVID, in particular, has shown insights from data can be found in the most unexpected of places: the United Kingdom and other countries, for example, put in place monitoring programmes to spot outbreaks of the virus early via wastewater. Where there's muck, there's data.

What about we lawyers? What insights can we get from our data?

Here are two examples:
- In the practice of law: litigation analytics data can give the percentage probability of a case winning or losing based on data. To date, lawyers have relied on statements like, "we think it's unlikely you'll win this case", but data has the potential to offer us more precision. Clients can be told: "You have a 37% chance of winning this case. What do you want to do?" While research commissioned by the LSB and SRA in March 2022 found that a majority of clients aren't yet persuaded by this technology,[18] the authors suspect that this will change once clients become more aware of what it can do and what safeguards are in place.
- In the business of law: a client once asked one of the authors: "What about giving fee quotes based more on data and less on gut feelings?" He suggested that there are often wide discrepancies in prices for instructions that are essentially the same. This 'noise' in human decisions can affect the effectiveness and consistency of fee quotes. Are our fee quotes 'noisy'? Can data help us be more consistent and more profitable?

There are countless other examples: from using data to bring down a firm's insurance costs to analysing and streamlining a firm's IT service desk. There's so much untapped data: structured and unstructured (and too often stuck in Word or Excel files).

2.4 Working with others
Working with data also means working with others. For most firms, it's almost inevitable.

This is because others typically have the things that we need to turn our data into insight:
- the technology (software etc);
- the expertise (data analysts and data scientists etc);
- the data; or
- a combination of all three.

We will look at these in turn.

(a) Technology
As a rough rule of thumb: starting from scratch with a data solution can mean that we're on a hiding to nothing, and an expensive one at that.

Remember how, during the pandemic, the government tried to create its own contact-tracing app, but then ended up using the technology developed by Apple and Google? It turned out to be quite an expensive detour. Working with data doesn't have to mean reinventing the wheel. Typically, others have already had the sleepless nights and sleep-deprived days getting the technology to where it is now. They have the products and know how to show for it. If the software they've developed fits the bill, for most intents and purposes, we should use it!

Take a data project which uses AI (which we look at in more detail later). In most cases, it makes no commercial sense for firms to create an AI platform. Businesses who specialise in AI are already working in the legal sector. They've already spent time and money training their AI on various data points. This means that firms can piggyback on a lot of the work done to date and only have to throw their energies into the 'last mile' or so. For example, when the authors developed Cia (see the case study in Chapter 5), we sent the technology company with which we collaborated, ThoughtRiver, wish lists of what we wanted the AI to analyse. They came back with a red-amber-and-green (RAG) list which set out where they thought they could, might and couldn't help us. There was a lot that they could help us with straight out of the box.

(b) Expertise

Many firms have also started to use data analysts or data scientists (or both). They help to make data more digestible and unearth the unseen things that are just there under the surface. As the volume and complexity of data increases, the profession will need to use data analysts and data scientists more.

While the terms are often used interchangeably, it's worth noting that they do differ:
- Data analysts focus on analysing data. They answer questions; spot patterns and trends; and give insights. Ultimately, they look to understand datasets.
- Data scientists focus on creating and organising datasets. They create statistical models and algorithms.

That said, we need to be careful to use experts at the right time. The authors' experience is that, initially at least, some work can often be done internally, such as by retraining existing staff. Blowing the budget on data experts and watching them twiddle their thumbs as we catch up to the point when we can best use their skills isn't money well spent. (The authors' firm has, though, now recruited a data analyst and more will inevitably follow.)

(c) Data

We often don't have all the data we need. We may need external data too. Where this happens, there are an increasing number of options to fill the gap, such as using third-party datasets or publicly available data; or the services of data aggregators or research institutes.

Don't forget: sometimes our clients and contacts can help us if we're missing some key data too (this is a resource that we all too often overlook). As lawyers, we're great at putting deals together for our clients but, when it comes to our own businesses, we aren't always anywhere near as canny. More's the pity. We typically know a lot of people in our wider communities. (It stands to reason: we've helped many of them.) Therefore, if we need some data, why not contact our clients? They may have data that might be of use. Perhaps a joint venture with them might benefit both parties in some way, and it might be cheaper than buying the data in.

(d) Open data

Open data may be another significant source of insight for firms too. The Department of Business, Energy and Industrial Strategy (BEIS) wants more smart data schemes, like Open Banking, to encourage data sharing with authorised third-party providers at a customer's request. The government anticipates that this will "deliver new innovative services, stronger competition … and better prices and choice for consumers and small businesses".[19] At the time of writing, the Data Protection and Digital Information Bill is proposing a framework for such schemes, which includes provisions on how to ensure the confidentiality of business data and customer data.

Others, such as LawtechUK and the LSB, are as keen as BEIS to open up the profession's data vaults. The LSB told the authors that it wants "an open-by-default data ecosystem" where data is "as openly available as possible". It also wants "everyone within the sector" to "reflect on the role that they can play in driving the collection and use of good quality, open data".[20]

A smart data scheme for 'open lawyering' could mean that firms release some of their data to create new and innovative legal services. In 2022, for example, Norton Rose Fulbright, Ashurst, Vodafone and the SRA ran a proof-of-concept in this area, in which these firms uploaded and analysed sample or redacted liability clauses in SaaS agreements. Aggregated statistics and insights were then shared by the parties. Given the paramount importance of client confidentiality, LawtechUK is working with the Regulatory Response Unit to allay concerns and ultimately see if industry standards can be introduced.

In the European Union, the proposed Data Act and Data Governance Act will regulate, for example, non-personal data and the sharing of it. The Data Act, in particular, is due to open up the open data market further. In the United Kingdom, if these proposed EU laws are successful they may influence the United Kingdom's approach, although, at present, the United Kingdom seems to prefer a sector-by-sector approach.

Whatever happens, law firms need to be alive to changes in the United Kingdom and the European Union and be prepared to pivot quickly. However, the big questions remain: what data will firms share? And how can firms who have already spent a lot of money building up large databases, at great cost, be persuaded to share the data in them? (Unless they are forced to open them up.)

In the authors' practical experience, data is inexorably linked to AI. We say this because capturing, processing and analysing vast quantities of data requires AI, and the accuracy of AI depends on it being trained with data.

We think AI is going to be *the* most disruptive tech in firms over the next 10 years. Just as email transformed the way firms communicated two decades ago, AI will be an increasingly powerful, data-hungry tool that will transform how firms work in a profound way. In the next section we look at this remarkable, game-changing technology.

3. Understanding AI: the bigger picture

> "AI argues for and against itself in Oxford Union debate"
> BBC News headline.[21]

Making sense of AI isn't easy. Like the Oxford Union debate referred to above, the arguments for and against it seem to flit between it being a 'brave new AI world' and 'it's the end of the world as we know it' (and not in a good way).

There's also nothing the press loves more than sensationalised reporting on the subject together with clichéd images of creepy humanoids and outstretched robotic hands:

- "AI to bring 'mankind to edge of APOCALYPSE' – with robots a bigger risk than NUKES";[22]
- "ROBOSTOP Facebook shuts off AI experiment after two robots begin speaking in their OWN language only they can understand";[23] and
- somewhat morbidly: "The AI that can tell you when you'll DIE".[24]

Another alternative is that AI turns out to be stupid: in December 2021 *New Scientist*'s stark headline declared that "human brain cells in a dish learn to play Pong faster than an AI".[25]

The reality is that AI is already in our lives: from the smart speakers in many of our homes to the fraud detection software used by banks to minimise false declines (those annoying times when a transaction is declined, usually at the worst possible moment).

There are also many businesses in the legal sector which are using AI in their solutions, including, but by no means limited to:
- in the business of law: Thirdfort: a tech company regulated by the Financial Conduct Authority (FCA) which uses AI, together with facial recognition, to help cut fraud in anti-money laundering checks;
- in the practice of law:
  - Frontier Labs: which has helped Weightmans develop a product, MatterLab, which uses AI to predict costs in personal injury matters;
  - Kira and Luminence: which offer comparative analysis across high volumes of documents, for example, they can analyse thousands of leases or corporate due diligence documents in a staggeringly short time;
  - Solomonic: a litigation analytics company which analyses judgments, orders and other court materials to help answer questions like: "what are our chances?", "how long will it take?" and "how much will it cost?";[26] and
  - ThoughtRiver: which is the AI platform that powers the authors' firm's contract review tool, Cia.

One of the three main strategic priorities of the SRA for the period up to 2023 is to "support the adoption of legal technology and other innovation",[27] including AI. It's inevitable that there will be many more AI businesses to come in the legal sector.

It's also clear, however, that the profession needs to understand AI better and foster a culture in which AI can be championed and used more, without the fear factor that seems to have tagged itself to this technology.

3.1 Overcoming the barriers to using AI: changing the culture
As with data, it's time to dare with AI.

Therefore, what's stopping some of us from using it? The barriers are similar to those of using data generally (see earlier), but given that this technology is newer, the hurdles are often higher.

From the authors' practical experience, these are:
- fearing AI generally, such as ChatGPT and similar chatbots;
- not understanding the value of what AI can do;
- not understanding how AI works (see the glossary for explanations on many key terms);
- not having the skills to use AI;
- waiting for the AI tipping point to arrive; and
- not having an AI vision or strategy, which sets out a firm's aims, its approach to AI, its appetite to risk and so on.

But one of the biggest barriers we come across is firms saying that AI means that junior lawyers no longer get to learn their craft by undertaking the more basic legal tasks (such as reviewing simple commercial contracts), because this'll all be done by AI. On the face of it, this seems a compelling concern. However, in our practical experience:
- a junior lawyer doesn't need to go through, say, a thousand contracts to become an expert in them (far fewer will do); and
- AI can teach junior lawyers and be a highly effective training aid; and it's more accurate!

Most of the actions needed to change the culture around data (set out earlier) apply equally to AI. But the moral panic around AI – think *The Terminator* or HAL 9000 in *2001: A Space Odyssey* – hasn't helped AI's cause either.

Many AI experts are pleading for us to stop thinking of AI as being in a constant battle with humankind where there's only one winner or believing that AI develops almost of its own volition, like a runaway train which we can't control, and where human desires and our deepest values aren't relevant (ie, the "I'm sorry Dave, I'm afraid that I can't do that" moment in Stanley Kubrick's film).

In other words, we have agency with this new resource.

On a more practical level, AI is key to churning through much of the data which firms will generate in the future. And the technology is developing quickly and starting to have a significant impact. Other sectors are using AI in significant, life-changing ways. Moderna, for example, used AI to help speed up the development of its COVID vaccine. Lawyers need to understand and engage with this powerful technology. We can't afford to be ignorant or to ignore it.

On a deeper level, we also need to use the agency we have to understand AI more than we do now. AI is challenging us to think about what it means to be a lawyer. We need to be part of this important discussion too.

3.2 Waiting for the AI tipping point
So where are we now?

Many firms are already using AI. But it's difficult to work out whether the AI tipping point in the profession has been reached. As it turns out, answering the question: 'where are we on the AI curve?' is like asking 'how long is a piece of string?'

Two major reports have tried to shed some light on where we are:
- In January 2022, a research consultancy, Capital Economics, authored a report for the Department for Digital, Culture, Media and Sport entitled *AI activity in UK businesses*.[28] It found that the two sectors with the highest rates of adoption of AI (out of 13 surveyed) were the IT and telecommunications sector (at 29.5%) and, perhaps to some lawyers' surprise (including the authors), the legal sector at 29.2% – not far off a photo finish for the top spot.
- Another report, *Technology and Innovation in Legal Services*, prepared for the SRA in 2021, noted that 84.6% of firm respondents were not planning to use, for example, data analytics with AI (that said, AI is used in some of the other technologies referred to in the report, where adoption is higher).[29]

The authors' experience is that many reports on AI adoption seem to leave more questions than answers.[30] In the first report above, for example, there's talk of an increase in the adoption rate of AI by the legal sector of 28.8 percentage points by 2040. To us, this feels like a substantial underestimate: it's a bit like someone in 1995 saying "only about 60% of people will be using email in 2015". The key is to take these sorts of findings with a pinch of salt. A report in 2020 by economic consultancy, London Economics, *AI for Services*, noted that there is "significant uncertainty over future trends".[31]

The current legislative vacuum also just adds to the uncertainty and potentially impedes adoption, with a list of initiatives trying to plug the gaps. One academic study in 2019 counted tens of available tools and methodologies.[32] Which ones matter? Which ones don't? The *Law Society Lawtech and Ethics Principles* matter. But what about the *Asilomar AI Principles*? The *OECD Principles on Artificial Intelligence*? The *Responsible Machine Learning Principles* from the Institute for Ethical AI & Machine Learning? Or should we follow what Big Tech is doing by using Google's *Objectives for AI applications*? Or the *Microsoft responsible AI principles*?

But it's time to get on board, not make excuses. For now, the AI regulatory framework could be much clearer, but, as the best lawyers say: "we are where we are". AI is here now and there is nothing stopping more and more lawyers from embracing the technology.

AI is here now and there is nothing stopping more and more lawyers from embracing the technology.

4. Using and training AI to turbocharge your data

Before we explore in more detail how AI works, let's quickly remind our-selves what this technology is and what it isn't as it's easy to confuse AI with sophisticated algorithms:

- What is AI? As it turns out, there's no settled definition for it. At its most basic, AI uses computers to mimic the way humans solve prob-lems and make decisions. In more complex form, AI can apply processes and work in ways that no human brain could ever manage, through sheer computing power and memory size. But don't worry: we're not at the stage where AI is as or more intelligent than humans (see 'ANI' in the glossary). Even so, this technology is nonetheless doing remarkable things, to the extent that, in 2021, Professor Stuart Russell said he was "spooked"[33] by the successes that AI has had. The technology is developing quickly.
- What isn't AI? Algorithms are sometimes badged as being AI. For example, many chatbots just look up answers from a database or take the user through a decision tree of varying complexity, after a keyword has been typed in. This sort of tech doesn't use AI at all.

For the purposes of this chapter, however, we focus on AI for the reasons set out earlier.

So where is AI used in the legal profession now?

According to the 2020 report *AI-assisted lawtech: its impact on law firms* by Professor John Armour, Professor Mari Sako and Dr Richard Parnham, the most popular AI-assisted technology in firms (and the respective adoption rates) according to their survey were:[34]

- legal research at 25.0%;
- due diligence at 18.2%;
- eDiscovery, eDisclosure and technology assisted review at 14.0%;
- regulatory compliance at 12.3%;
- contract analysis at 10.2%;
- fee-earner utilisation analytics and/or predictive billing also at 10.2%;
- the rather vague "other" at 5.1%; and
- finally, predictive analytics for litigation at 2.1%.

And contrary to popular belief, it's not just BigLaw that can benefit from the rise of AI. The use of data with AI in the broader profession ultimately democratises the experience, knowledge and expertise which is currently locked up in the heads of individual, experienced lawyers. If this data and AI gets applied ubiquitously across the sector, all of a sudden those who don't have such experience in their heads, now have it at their fingertips. It has the potential to level the playing field.

4.1 Teaching your AI

It's important to remember that AI does need some work to get it going.

Many believe that AI works exactly as desired as soon as you get it 'out of the box'. Sometimes this is the case. However, some AI platforms are nowhere near as educated or trained as we might initially think and the level of pre-training of AI products shouldn't be assumed. It may be less than we expect.

Put simply, an AI platform is like a very intelligent child: the potential is huge, but they need to learn before they can achieve their potential. Therefore, for AI to be reliable it usually needs to be trained with lots of data. The mantra that the authors use is 'train like an athlete'.

This means firms need to:
- identify the right data to collect in the first place;
- collect it (if it hasn't already been collected);
- check that it's accurate and valid for use in training; and
- then use that data for training.

Let's consider, by way of example, Cia. This contract review tool is a good example of a day-to-day product, which is changing how lawyers work in a profound way.

The authors' firm developed this AI-powered tool to review and make amendments to commercial procurement contracts quicker than a human (see the case study in Chapter 5). As part of this project, ThoughtRiver, a software company which specialises in rules-based AI, became the obvious collaboration partner. Cia uses ThoughtRiver's AI platform and can power through a 100-page contract in around 90 seconds.

At the beginning, the platform was initially around 50% accurate, ie, it was 50/50 whether it was reaching the right conclusions when analysing the contracts. After two years of inputting data from commercial contracts, and telling Cia when it had got an answer wrong ("marking Cia's homework" as the developers called it), it's now about 94% accurate.

In other words, AI is typically more accurate than the average legally qualified associate. In a controlled study on AI software in the United States, lawyers' accuracy when not using AI on reviewing non-disclosure agreements was, on average, nine percentage points lower at 85%.[35]

Figure 7. Training of AI contract review tool Cia

At the start:
**50% accuracy:
half right, half wrong**

When the system
was applied 'out
of the box'.

Now:
**94% accuracy – better
than the average associate**

After training the system
with over 3,000 contracts
during two years.

For the remaining 6%,
lawyers get involved to
complete the analysis.

However, lawyers shouldn't read this and think they're out of a job! Despite this high level of accuracy, they still need to turn up every day and power up their laptops. For example:

- A human overlay adds more value: lawyers still need to consider the amendments that Cia recommends and make any further amendments that they deem necessary given the context which Cia is not designed to cover. The upshot is lawyers have more time to attend to the more complex and nuanced parts of a contract and to focus on understanding clients' needs and context; and thereby deliver better outcomes.
- PI insurers sometimes require a human overlay to ensure the quality of the technology platforms (see Chapter 6).
- From a cost–benefit point of view, the authors found that it simply wasn't worth pumping in all the data that we could get our hands on to reach 100% accuracy from the AI, even if it was possible. This is where the law of diminishing returns applies: to add each further percentage point of accuracy would require an increasing number of contracts each time, because each percentage gap requires teaching the AI about aspects in contracts that apply with increasing rarity. (That said, the more that Cia is used day to day with a human overlay, the more training that happens as a by-product in the background. The result is that the accuracy will continue to increase further.)

From the authors' experience of training Cia and elsewhere, we can see, in the starkest terms, that access to good data is crucial for lawyers to benefit effectively from AI solutions. (That is, unless we lawyers are to be beholden to others who come to hold that data in the future.) At present, justifying using AI is the norm. In the future – perhaps sooner than we think – justifying *not* using AI in many areas could well be the new norm. Failure to adopt AI will make a law firm uncompetitive for a large chunk of legal services. AI is moving from being a nice-to-have to a tool which is essential to continue to remain market competitive.

4.2 Working with others

'There's no "I" in team'; 'teamwork makes the dream work' ... feeling awkward yet with these painful clichés? Possibly. But one thing is certain: in the years to come, like with data, lawyers will need to work with other experts when creating AI-powered solutions to legal problems. Clichés are optional, but teamwork is inevitable.

This means that we lawyers need to get used to working more in teams from multiple disciplines (MDTs) with "allied professionals",[36] such as with data analysts and data scientists. This means a change of mindset, from managing these MDTs to rethinking and "adjusting professional boundaries of the legal profession".[37] If we don't work with others outside of the profession, it makes it almost impossible to see the bigger picture.

Getting this right is good for the bottom line: working in MDTs has been "associated with a higher rate of deployment of AI-enabled lawtech solutions".[38] And yet, in a legal operations survey carried out by Bloomberg Law in April 2021 over four-fifths of respondents thought that MDTs could only consist of lawyers.[39]

It's time to bust this myth if we really want to create game-changing AI solutions.

5. Working out how much it all costs

What's the cost of all of this? This is the first question for many lawyers.

Since we're focusing on oil in this chapter, let's use it as an analogy one final time.

Many years ago, the profits to be made in oil were extraordinary. There was much more oil around and it was in easy-to-drill places. It ranked high on the 'energy return on investment' (EROI) index. We got a lot of bang for our buck. As the years have passed, however, finding oil – a finite resource – has become more difficult. Its EROI has declined.

$$EROI = \frac{energy\ delivered}{energy\ (and\ money)\ needed\ to\ deliver\ that\ energy}$$

Unlike oil, however, data-driven insights are getting easier and cheaper to extract. What's more, data is an almost infinite resource. If there were an 'insight ROI' (IROI) index, it might look something like this:

$$IROI = \frac{insight\ delivered}{effort\ (and\ money)\ needed\ to\ deliver\ that\ insight}$$

Thanks to increases in computing power and developments in AI, the amount of insight delivered to our clients and teams within our firms will increase and, at the same time, the cost and effort of getting it is likely to decrease. Some legaltech companies are starting to show up front the ROI that their products can deliver. AI-powered document review start-up Della, for example, includes an ROI calculator on its website to show estimated cost savings. Others might well start to take a leaf out of this start-up's book too.

While there are usually up-front costs in investing in the relevant technology, in both time and money, many lawyers would be surprised to learn both that:

- the relevant technology doesn't need to cost the earth; and
- when the IROI is taken into account, the investment becomes a no-brainer. And the ROI can also include other less tangible returns such as reputation gain, internal motivation, avoiding losing clients to new-entrant providers, increased client conversations, among others.

6. Being data- and AI-savvy

We know that the world of data-driven 'change3', often powered by AI, can be daunting. There's also a cost in changing mindsets: new data-derived facts are already upending the sacred work of many sectors and industries. In many areas, what was once taken as settled knowledge is being exposed as just a belief.

For example, in 2020, World Commerce & Contracting (previously called IACCM), published a report on the terms which are negotiated in contracts. It analysed the most negotiated, the most important and the most disputed terms. The theory should be that these three aspects are strongly aligned. In other words, we spend most of our time negotiating the most important terms and, if all goes wrong, these are the terms likely to be disputed. However, WCC's analysis indicates that this is often *not* the case and "priority is given to terms dealing with risk consequence, rather than risk prevention".[40] This means, as WCC notes, "contracts and negotiations are designed to deal with failure, not to facilitate success".[41] Here is a stark reminder, through data analysis, of our tendency as lawyers to focus on the worst-case scenario. Sometimes, this may be appropriate, but sometimes it may not. Data can help us understand these dynamics better and create better contracts as a result.

As we show in this chapter, basing what we do on data-rich fact and not data-poor folklore will make us better at what we do. It will also help our clients make better decisions and be better at what they do.

To have a nuanced understanding of data, we need diverse and inclusive teams to spot biases and give more perspectives: after all, not everyone thinks the same.

Figure 8. From data poor to data rich

The old ways: data poor	• Anecdote • Conjecture • Folklore • Gut feeling • Settled ways ('we've always done it this way')
The new ways: data rich	• Evidence and proof through facts

But in this 'data boost' for us and our clients, we must never lose or out-source our critical thinking faculties when processing the relevant data. Like how politicians during the pandemic were keen on saying they were 'following the science', as though science is some sort of unquestionable force which can't be disputed, we mustn't find ourselves 'following the data' unthinkingly either. We still need to keep our wits about us.

Understanding data means not hoisting it onto a pedestal and forgetting about the human element in particular. Co-founder of Twitter, Jack Dorsey, in 2020 said that a "critical mistake"[42] that he made from the start of setting up his business was not hiring experts who understood how humans inter-act with each other (through data) in the service.

As lawyers we're good at spotting holes in arguments, so we need to do the same when looking at data.

In particular, the authors find it useful to remind ourselves of the following:
- Data can easily hoodwink us into thinking a pattern or trend exists where one doesn't. We can so easily make 2 + 2 = 5. Correlation does not necessarily imply causation. Law student Tyler Vigen set up a website *Spurious Correlations* when at Harvard Law School. In it are gems such as the divorce rate in Maine and the consumption of mar-garine per head have a correlation of 99%.[43] Is there a link? Probably not. As scientists often say (following Carl Sagan), "extraordinary claims require extraordinary evidence".
- Data needs to be of good quality otherwise it risks being 'RIRO' (rubbish in, rubbish out) or, in US English, 'GIGO' (garbage in, garbage out).
- Data needs to be accurate. We need to avoid biases, such as confir-mation bias where we mine data for points to prove our position. We need to be led by the evidence.
- Data is *not* the preserve of one group to collect, interpret and use. Data needs to involve everyone. An article in the *Sunday Times* in

December 2021 referred, for example, to various men who were "the smoking-hot data crunchers" of the pandemic.[44] The *i* newspaper helpfully pointed out a few days later that there are plenty of women who crunched data during the pandemic too.[45] To have a nuanced understanding of data, we need diverse and inclusive teams to spot biases and give more perspectives: after all, not everyone thinks the same.

- Data takes us to many places, but it doesn't, by itself, always get us to our final destination – not without a bit of effort from us too. For example, data can tell us where the best restaurant in London is. The map apps on our smartphones can give us detailed directions and likely travel conditions and weather *en route*. But the data can't decide what we fancy for dinner when we finally arrive and are handed the menu. Similarly, taking the examples we use earlier:
  - Using litigation analytics: data can't make the actual decision on how a client should proceed. We need to ask: "Are you happy to spend your time and money on this case given you've only a 37% chance of winning?" "If you are, what makes your case different?"
  - Should we use algorithms to help decide our fees – in whole or in part? How much would the policy be to stick 100% with what the computer says? What if there's a fact that you can't input into the system, but it ought to have an impact on price? Or if a client wants to chip down the price? How much leeway is there?

7. Future-proofing data and AI

Who knows what the future holds?

We can hazard one guess though: transparency in the use of data and AI will become more important. We've already seen this, in the UK GDPR, where data subjects have rights to see how their data is processed.

AI still needs to do a lot to catch up, however.

The more we use AI and the more clever it becomes, the less we seem to know how we've got to where we are. If there's a mistake in how we use AI (perhaps we've used some biased data in error), we struggle to work out what happened, so then we also struggle to fix it. We go from A to C, but when asked what happened at B, we don't have an answer, like when we're asked to recall a car journey we've just taken.

Transparency in how systems arrive at their decisions means that we can 'work out our journey' and understand why we are where we are, and try to fix the systems if things go wrong. This matters because human biases, in particular, can easily translate into AI biases. A sexist or racist dataset, for example, is likely to result in a sexist or racist AI outcome. This is why non-profit organisations such as WEandAI is building a Race and Artificial Intelligence Toolkit to explore what people can do to avoid such outcomes. There's also a lot of potential 'noise' (ie, meaningless or irrelevant data) that can creep into AI solutions too.

As we use AI more, we need to keep a keen eye on developments; follow guidance on AI from relevant regulators such as the Information Commissioner's Office (ICO); and always consider to what extent we can futureproof our projects by keeping material on the 'journey'. Why have we developed our AI in the way that we have? Can we 'lift the bonnet' so others can have a good look at what's going on underneath? Should we avoid developing 'black box' systems (ie, systems where we don't know what's happening in them internally)? Even if the law doesn't yet demand this, our clients might.

In a world where AI will do more, more questions will be asked. We need to be ready to answer them.

8. Embracing maths and the sciences

We also need to prepare ourselves to be more maths- and science-savvy.

In January 2022, the Master of the Rolls, Sir Geoffrey Vos, declared that "major developments are imminent. They will mean that every lawyer will require familiarity with the blockchain, smart legal contracts and cryptoassets".[46] "Require familiarity": the Master of the Rolls chose his words carefully. He didn't say 'become an expert in', but equally it's clear that a better understanding of STEM subjects (ie, science, technology, engineering and mathematics)[47] is vital. These subjects increasingly underpin so much of what goes on in data and AI and the subjects Sir Geoffrey mentioned (see Chapter 3).

The traditional cultural gap between humanities, including the law, and STEM hasn't helped matters. In 1959, novelist and chemist CP Snow gave his famous 'two cultures' talk in which he lamented the country's intellectual life being split into two separate camps: LLBs and BAs on one side, BScs and BEngs on the other. A chasm of ignorance loomed between the two. Snow saw lost opportunities and breakthroughs stuck "in a vacuum", "because those in the two cultures can't talk to each other".[48] Not that much has changed since.

This split may explain why the badge of honour (for some) that 'lawyers don't do maths' has stuck around for so long. The authors spoke with

Edward Smith, ex-General Counsel at Telefónica UK (O2), who thinks that this approach is no longer sustainable. As Smith told the authors, this sort of behaviour "demeans the value of our voice around the table where a solid grasp of the numbers is crucial". "Saying that you 'do' words, not numbers, is a sure-fire way to lose credibility", he continued, adding "we all need to take more pride in the fact that we can 'do' numbers as well as words".

Now, more than ever, the profession needs to step up to:

- Understand maths more. We don't need to be experts like Pythagoras, Archimedes or Muhammad ibn Musa al-Khwarizmi (the word 'algorithm' derives from the ninth-century polymath's name). But we think we do need, as a profession, to open our minds more to the subject and stop the knee-jerk reaction of 'I don't do maths'.
- Understand technology more: Elon Musk, Richard Branson and Jeff Bezos aren't rocket scientists, but they understand what rockets can do and why they matter. We need to make sure that we're on top of technological developments and what they can do; and we aren't the ones who say "what rockets?" to any new or widely adopted technology.

STEM subjects are key to understanding the threats and opportunities in our data-driven world, which we look at in this chapter and elsewhere in this book. We can no longer afford to sideline them.

From the certainties of faith to the uncertainties of knowledge (and where it might take you), data-driven change can be unsettling. And like the stages of grief – denial, anger, bargaining, depression and acceptance – lawyers need the space and time to come around to new ways of thinking and doing things. This is all part of the process.

Figure 9. From the certainty of faith to the uncertainty of knowledge

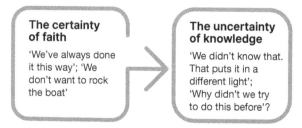

Although it might not feel like it at times, we're lucky to be practising at a time when so much is changing. It's a time of opportunities, not only to use data in our firms, but also develop new practice areas to advise our clients on the areas covered in this chapter, such as AI.

In the end, we think the 'data boost' is something which we'll be well placed to drive forward, not in spite of, but because of, the challenges. (After all, we lawyers love a good challenge.)

9. Case studies

9.1 Case study 1: Using data to provide insight of great value to clients

We lawyers are so attentive to the details of the work we're doing for our clients while a matter is live. But after it's completed, we hardly ever look at the details again, unless a specific reason to do so arises.

It occurred to the authors' firm that analysing all this collective data could be of tremendous value to its clients in so many ways. For example, this could be by:

- giving a client insight into where the main commercial risks lie in their portfolio of commercial contracts or other documents, from leases to equity investments;
- showing clients what the market norm is on various risk positions in such documents;
- offering clients insight into areas for improvement by comparing their portfolio's risk profile against the market norm; and
- giving visibility to clients of how their risk profile is improving over time if they address those areas where there is room for improvement.

Initial discussions with clients on the idea were enthusiastically received: it was clear that not only would clients value this type of insight greatly, but also it would distinguish the firm from its competition, who, we were told, had never had this type of discussion with their clients. Therefore, having established that the concept was strong, the firm assembled a multi-disciplinary team to map out what would be required, including:

- Identifying the best analysis platforms: this meant finding the most appropriate means of quickly and reliably analysing large volumes of data – an 'off-the-shelf' machine (into which the above documents could be fed and that would then deliver the analysis) didn't exist. The team identified a shortlist of AI platforms and reviewed in detail the specifications of each before selecting a preferred platform.
- Testing the platforms: the firm intensively tested the preferred AI platform to establish how accurately it could identify the relevant datapoints within the documents that were fed into it. This was a time-consuming exercise and (as has been its experience on previous AI-powered solutions) the initial level of accuracy was around 50%. However, after some 24 months of continually feeding in documents and 'marking the AI's homework', it had increased its accuracy to a workable level.

- Identifying where humans were better at analysing data: the team also realised that there were certain datapoints (such as, contra-intuitively, numerical values of limits of liabilities) where it would be more efficient for a human to analyse that data (until the AI software develops further). But even for these aspects, the AI could nonetheless reduce the amount of human time required by directing the individual to the relevant clause in a document rather than the individual having to scan numerous pages to find the relevant clause.
- Showing the results: the firm also had to work on identifying the best means of displaying (or 'surfacing') the results of the analysis to be most easily and quickly digestible to clients. There are several tools available to achieve this, such as Microsoft's Power BI and Tableau.
- Working with a pilot group of clients: the firm then liaised with a limited and carefully chosen cohort of clients in a pilot to test the solution based on each client's portfolios. As well as testing that the system worked in a live environment, it also allowed them to gather feedback on system features, user interfaces and user experience.

At the time of writing (the pilot having been successful), the firm is in the final stages of product design before making it available generally to its clients.

9.2 Case study 2: Adoption of AI in legal and accountancy firms
Adopting AI isn't typically a case of buying it and switching it on. The odd solution might have a 'plug-and-play' option, but these are rare. This means that firms need to manage their adoption of this technology.

To this end, the NextGenPSF Project, headed up by Professor Tim Vorley from the Oxford Brookes Business School, brought together professional service firms (PSFs) in accounting and law, academics, regulators and others to bridge the gap between AI and its adoption. The focus of its work was principally on AI in mid-sized firms. Many larger firms or their spin-off companies worked on the project including DWF Ventures, DAC Beachcroft, Lewis Silkin, Mishcon de Reya and the 'legal engineers' at Simmons Wavelength. The authors' firm also participated in a number of the workshops to test and refine the methodology in the toolkit.

The project, which is now formally complete, produced various free documents and tools which PSFs, including law firms, can use. These include:[49]

- An AI readiness toolkit: this resource features a methodology, referred to as the "design sprint", where users can explore the options for using AI in their businesses. Firms can work through 17 methods to create an innovation roadmap. In the end, firms ask themselves: "now what? What actions are sensible and achievable? What might happen if we don't act?". They can then engage in a reflective conversation about the learning outcomes. All of this can help firms shape AI aims and an AI vision and strategy.

- A landscape report: this document includes an overview of the legal services landscape (focusing on law firms with a turnover of £10 to £20 million).
- A report on AI in the professions: this document looks at AI adoption in the context of mid-sized firms in particular. It examines what's happened to date and then looks at the risks and challenges which firms are likely to face.
- A scenarios report: this report gazes into the future and looks at three possible scenarios about what the world might look like in 2030. These scenarios are designed to help lawyers "explore the strategic implications" of each of them and to test their own firm's strategies against them.
- A white paper: this paper brings all the above together and looks at some of the general themes of the project.

Although the focus was on mid-sized firms, there's much that firms above and below this cohort can take from these resources.

Alas, despite the many materials which are now available, 'AI readiness' is still to be found wanting in much of the profession. The authors spoke with Professor Tim Vorley. He told the authors:

> The legal services sector has not universally embraced the prospect of accelerating digital transformation. As a profession steeped in tradition, and with many long-established norms, the adoption of AI and other advanced technologies has been slow to occur, and in some instances actively resisted. As digital technologies become more pervasive, the legal profession will need to evolve or face being disrupted from outside.

He went on to say:

> Our research has highlighted that organisational culture and professional norms are in fact the biggest challenge to the adoption of new technologies. Through our delivery of design sprints we have been working with law firms to demystify AI and increase what we have come to refer as 'AI readiness'.

As always, however, you don't have to go all in. The project also makes the important point that modest change is better than no change at all.

10. Practical tips on data

We set out below some practical tips on data.

These tips are split as follows:
- creating a data culture;
- understanding data;
- being strategic with data; and
- using AI.

10.1 Creating a data culture
- Add data to the agenda: is there a cultural mindset to embrace the insights that data can bring? Is data innovation, or inertia, the default setting? Do senior team members have the experience and vision?
- Do more than just talk about data, act on it: what's the direction of travel? Is change in how you use data actually happening? The US-based Association of Corporate Counsel (ACC) has created a useful model which you can benchmark against.[50] By doing so, you can see whether you're at the early, intermediate or advanced stage of using data and can then plan accordingly.
- Put the right structures in place: is data reflected in your firm's strategies, visions and related aims?
- Sort out becoming a data-driven organisation internally first, before focusing on external elements.
- Speak to people you know in other firms: are others preparing for the 'data boost' future more? Consider participating in initiatives such as *Reshaping Legal Services* from the LSB and learning from others.
- Don't fixate too much on projects that have gone wrong in the past: put them in context.
- Remember that change is continuous: 'change3' means that change is not a one-off event. There is no end point to data change.

10.2 Understanding data
- Try to bridge the divide between humanities and sciences. Apple's Steve Jobs put it simply when he said: technology together with the liberal arts and humanities yields "the results that make our hearts sing".[51] Many law firms are looking to connect this divide too. Clifford Chance, for example, offers tech-focused training contracts under the name 'IGNITE'. Another firm, Allen & Overy set up a shared space innovation lab, Fuse, in 2017.
- Remember that we're not the only profession to struggle to use data to its best advantage. Others struggle too. See what their successes are and learn from them.

- Make more of an emotional connection with data: concentrate more on the human stories connected with data, as opposed to fixating on data itself. If we concentrate too much on the abstract, we'll struggle to fire our imaginations about what data can do for us as lawyers, our clients and society in general.
- Learn about data: understand and get involved in the nuts and bolts of structuring the systems and procuring the tools that your firm needs. From the tools which capture the datapoints, through to feeding that data into a database, and then analysing and presenting the analysis, there's a lot to do. Don't underestimate the value that you can bring to the process, both in understanding the significance of the data involved and in appreciating exactly what your clients will find most useful to derive from that data.
- Read any relevant guidance with care. Consider, for example, the *Law Society Lawtech and Ethics Principles* and others that will be published in the future. Ask: who is issuing it? Is it mandatory? Is it best practice? What is the status of any other guidance referred to in it?

10.3 Being strategic with data

- Stop waiting: waiting for the time to be right; waiting for someone in IT to start the process; waiting for colleagues to start the process; waiting for anyone to start the process. You could well be sitting on a rich seam of data, sat idle and ready to be mined, but you just don't know it yet because you've not looked.
- Get some wins under your belt: if you don't, you're an unknown quantity to the people who matter and who may decide whether your project gets the go ahead or not. For example, quick wins in the use of data can help bring and keep people on board. And sometimes the odd new whizzy feature can spark interest too. Making people (and senior leaders) wait for months or years for some data-driven solution means that they might soon lose interest. And you might lose their support. A drip feed of quick wins can help keep engagement at the required level.
- Work out how you will sell data to people in your firm: how will you measure the benefits so you can show others in the firm how data projects are, for example, improving profitability or client engagement?
- Identify why you're looking at the data in the first place: start with a problem. Consider what's the end point? Is there a client need? Is there a business need?
- Ask: what is the minimum critical data that is needed to provide the insight required (you might be surprised – it might be a lot less than you think)?

Identify why you're looking at the data in the first place: start with a problem. Consider what's the end point? Is there a client need? Is there a business need?

- Recognise now the value of data: how will it add value to your clients and distinguish your firm from the competition? There will come an inflection point in the future when the business of law becomes a lot more about data than about practising law as we know it now. Many of your fellow colleagues may well have concluded their careers by that time; but you may still be in the thick of it. Don't take any apathy on their part as a lead that you should follow. Equip yourself now for the future in which you will play a part.
- Use your position as senior staff to prioritise data projects: this includes making investment and giving your people the headspace and time to deliver those projects.
- Understand the ownership of, and right to use and retain, data: ensure, in whatever structures you put in place to capture, analyse and use data, that you own the data or have the right to use and, where necessary, retain it:
  - This may involve changes to standard client engagement letters or specific terms being put in place relating to individual projects.
  - If your firm has access to a data room for the purposes of a potential transaction on behalf of a client, check carefully whether you can deploy that data outside that narrow purpose. (In the authors' experience, most data room terms will prevent such use. Even if your client proceeds with the transaction such that the data then belongs to your client, do your terms of engagement with the client allow broader use of the client's data without their express consent?)

Remember, data is a completely new asset in the business of law! Therefore, when using data:

- Don't presume that someone has done something before: you might be more ahead of the game than you think.
- Gather the critical data: consider how to gather the data that you need. Can data be downloaded from public sources (perhaps through APIs), such as Companies House?
- Work out what the minimum critical data that you can justify collecting at any particular point is. Do you need to ask for all the data you need up front? Can you wait for some data to arrive at a later date? When collecting data don't ask for more information than you need: asking for enough data for a particular purpose means that it's easier to get the information you need. (Think of all those red asterisks in online forms and how frustrating it can be when you need to give data which isn't critical. Don't be that online form.) That said, you can still offer clients value-added solutions which encourage them to provide you with data that's unrelated to the matters on

which you are acting. In this case, you repay them with insight and analysis based on a larger data pool.

- Use personal data with care as data protection laws will apply. Consider data protection laws from the start of the project: reverse-engineering compliance can be tricky, if not impossible. Can you sidestep certain obligations by anonymising or pseudonymising certain data?

- Be green: collecting data also has an environmental impact. All that data needs to be stored somewhere and there is a financial and environmental cost in doing so. Greening your data processing can help you fulfil any corporate and social responsibility (CSR) and environmental, social and governance (ESG) requirements.

- Store wisely: for decades storage costs have become cheaper. However, future improvements in storage costs per byte of storage media may be slower in the future than in the past. Distinguish between data that is a nice-to-have and data that is a must-have.

- Do a post-project review for each project: this isn't an easy ask as there's often a lack of time and typically people move on to the next urgent project. But lessons learned and analysing the value of a project are important. Again, it's about selling stories: 'this is the value of this project' and so on.

10.4 Using AI

- Learn about AI: if you don't understand how AI works in the context of data, organisations like Tech Nation provide useful guides to AI, including an AI glossary and suggestions on the best books, podcasts, and news and blogs sites on AI too.[52]

- Recognise the importance of data in training AI platforms to get to the level of accuracy that you need: the majority of lawyers have no idea that this is the case and think that if they want to introduce AI into their business functions or client offerings, they can simply buy it and it'll work straight out of the box. The AI brain needs to be trained: if you don't have that data, you'll be left behind those that do.

- Remember that not all AI solutions work straight out of the box. Challenge suppliers on the accuracy of their AI brains and establish how much work you may have to do to get the AI to a useful level of accuracy. And think whether you have the data and the time to do it,

- Remember that training AI takes a lot of time and effort. This should be built into the calculation of ROI, which might make the result look a little less rosy!

- Be accurate and consistent when training AI: if more than one person is training the AI it is essential that they all are completely consistent in the way that they mark the AI's 'homework'. For example, if one of the trainers has wrongly told the AI to ignore a particular phrase within a contract that the AI thinks is relevant, it could well be that the other trainers will never have the opportunity to correct that mistaken teaching unless they then happen to spot that the AI is ignoring that phrase in the future. The old adage of 'rubbish in, rubbish out' applies just as much to the training process as it does to the data that is input in the first place.

- You may need to limit those who train the AI.
- When designing the best way to collate and analyse data, don't assume that technology will do the whole job and that there's no requirement for humans to have a role in that process. Certainly, technology allows us to deal with vast quantities of data much quicker and more accurately than a human. But in the authors' experience there can be nuances in certain aspects of data identification and analysis that it would take an inordinate amount of time to teach an AI platform, given the state of the art of technology currently available in the market. (One of the case studies in Chapter 5 gives an example of this.)
- When buying a licence for the use of an AI platform from a tech provider, check who will own the IP in any enhancements that you make as a result of the training that you undertake to increase the platform's accuracy in particular areas on which you want to deploy the technology. If you're going to be undertaking extensive training then you may want exclusive ownership of that IP and will want also to prevent the tech provider from benefitting from those enhancements for the benefit of its other customers. However, in other cases you may be content for the learning from your training to go back into the AI platform to benefit all future users of the platform. (The authors have entered into both types of arrangement as appropriate to the circumstances – one size does not fit all.)

Notes

1   "Robert FitzRoy and the early Met Office" (Met Office), www.metoffice.gov.uk/research/library-and-archive/archive-hidden-treasures/robert-fitzroy.
2   "The world's most valuable resource is no longer oil, but data" (*The Economist*, 6 May 2017), www.economist.com/leaders/2017/05/06/the-worlds-most-valuable-resource-is-no-longer-oil-but-data.
3   For example, oil is finite, for example, whereas data is far from finite. The oil price is quoted in the news, whereas data's value varies and derives from its context: every 'barrel', as it were, could have a different price.
4   Bernard Marr, "How Much Data Do We Create Every Day? The Mind-Blowing Stats Everyone Should Read" (*Forbes*, 21 May 2018), www.forbes.com/sites/bernardmarr/2018/05/21/how-much-data-do-we-create-every-day-the-mind-blowing-stats-everyone-should-read.
5   "IDC's Global DataSphere Forecast Shows Continued Steady Growth in the Creation and Consumption of Data" (*Business Wire*, 8 May 2020), www.businesswire.com/news/home/20200508005025/en/IDCs-Global-DataSphere-Forecast-Shows-Continued-Steady-Growth-in-the-Creation-and-Consumption-of-Data.
6   R Parnham, M Sako and J Armour, "AI-assisted lawtech: its impact on law firms" (University of Oxford, December 2021), www.law.ox.ac.uk/sites/files/oxlaw/ai_final1097.pdf. The report presented the outcomes of a research project, which ran from 2019 to 2021: "Unlocking the Potential of Artificial Intelligence for English Law" (University of Oxford), www.law.ox.ac.uk/unlocking-

potential-artificial-intelligence-english-law. See also M Sako, J Armour and R Parnham, "Lawtech Adoption and Training: Findings from a Survey of Solicitors in England and Wales" (University of Oxford, March 2020), www.law.ox.ac.uk/sites/files/oxlaw/oxford_lawtech_adoption_and_training_survey_report_18_march_2.pdf.

7 David Maddock, "Inside Liverpool's data team judging Steven Gerrard's suitability to replace Jurgen Klopp" (*Mirror*, 11 December 2021), www.mirror.co.uk/sport/football/news/inside-liverpools-data-team-judging-25668499.

8 Justine Harper, "Data experts are becoming football's best signings" (BBC News, 5 March 2021), www.bbc.co.uk/news/business-56164159.

9 *Data-Driven Business Models* (European Company Lawyers Association), www.osborneclarke.com/system/files/documents/22/09/30/DDBM_Study_20220930.pdf.

10 *The 2020 Future Ready Lawyer Survey: Performance Drivers* (Wolters Kluwer), https://know.wolterskluwerlr.com/2020-Future-Ready-Lawyer.

11 *Ibid.*

12 Tony Fadell, *Build* (Bantam Press, 2022), p64.

13 Good design is good for business: it gets us closer to our clients emotionally so they want to engage with us and the products and services we offer. It's key to clients actually wanting to use them. Research backs this up. In 2018, management consulting firm McKinsey launched the *McKinsey Design Index* or *MDI* in short. The index tracked 300 listed companies over a five-year period in various countries and industries. After combing through 2 million bits of financial data and 100,000 'design actions' the firm found a strong correlation between businesses that care about good design and strong business performance.

14 www.thisismoney.co.uk/money/news/article-5050243/Michael-Heseltine-Build-wealth-fund-UK.html.

15 LawtechUK, *The LawtechUK Report 2021 – Shaping the Future of Law* (July 2021), https://technation.io/wp-content/uploads/2021/07/LawtechUK-Report-2021-Final.pdf.

16 LawtechUK, *The Legal Data Vision*, https://resources.lawtechuk.io/files/legal-data-vision.pdf.

17 Legal Services Board, "Reshaping Legal Services" (March 2021), https://legalservicesboard.org.uk/wp-content/uploads/2021/03/Strategy_FINAL-For-Web.pdf.

18 Legal Services Board, "Social acceptability of technology in legal services" (March 2022), https://legalservicesboard.org.uk/wp-content/uploads/2022/05/Acceptability-of-technology-in-legal-services-research-report-FINAL-March-2022.pdf.

19 Department for Digital, Culture, Media and Sport, "Data Protection and Digital Information Bill Impact Assessment" (6 July 2021), https://assets.publishing.service.gov.uk/government/uploads/system/uploads/attachment_data/file/1091814/Data_Protection_and_Digital_Information_Bill_Impact_Assessment.pdf.

20 The LSB told the authors in connection with the Reshaping Legal Services strategy for the next decade: "One of the priorities in the strategy is a need for more, and better quality, open data. The benefits of good quality, open data are widespread – from enabling legal professionals to understand how consumers are using their services and identify service improvements, to regulators understanding how the market is operating, and whether interventions are needed."

21 Jane Wakefield, "AI argues for and against itself in Oxford Union debate" (BBC News, 17 December 2021), www.bbc.co.uk/news/technology-59687236.

22 Tom Fish, "AI to bring 'mankind to edge of APOCALYPSE' – with robots a bigger risk than NUKES" (*Daily Star*, 12 July 2018), www.dailystar.co.uk/news/latest-news/ai-artificial-intelligence-autonomous-weaponry-16872452.

23 James Beal and Andy Jehring, "ROBOSTOP Facebook shuts off AI experiment after two robots begin speaking in their OWN language only they can understand" (*The Sun*, 1 August 2017), www.thesun.co.uk/tech/4141624/facebook-robots-speak-in-their-own-language/, although see this useful analysis of this chatbot story: Chris Baraniuk, "The 'creepy Facebook AI' story that captivated the media" (BBC News, 1 August 2017), www.bbc.co.uk/news/technology-40790258.

24 Cheyenne MacDonald, "The AI that can tell you when you'll DIE: Stanford reveals 'startlingly accurate' system to predict the end of life for hospital patients" (*MailOnline*, 18 January 2018), www.dailymail.co.uk/sciencetech/article-5285811/The-AI-tell-youll-DIE.html.

25 Michael Le Page, "Human brain cells in a dish learn to play Pong faster than an AI" (*New Scientist*, 17 December 2021), www.newscientist.com/article/2301500-human-brain-cells-in-a-dish-learn-to-play-pong-faster-than-an-ai/.

26 'Overview' (*Solomonic*), www.solomonic.co.uk/overview.

27 "SRA corporate strategy 2020 to 2023" (Solicitors Regulation Authority, 20 March 2020), www.sra.org.uk/sra/corporate-strategy/.

28 *AI Activity in UK Businesses* (Capital Economics, January 2022), https://assets.publishing.service.gov.uk/government/uploads/system/uploads/attachment_data/file/1045381/AI_Activity_in_UK_Businesses_Report__Capital_Economics_and_DCMS__January_2022__Web_accessible_.pdf.

29 Mari Sako and Richard Parnham, *Technology and Innovation in Legal Services* (University of Oxford, July 2021), www.sra.org.uk/globalassets/documents/sra/research/full-report-technology-and-innovation-in-legal-services.pdf?version=4a1bfe.

30 The Capital Economics report refers, for example, to "nearly 18,000 firms currently using AI".

However, there are currently just under 10,000 regulated by the SRA. Furthermore, given that the adoption figures are based on surveys, the authors question whether, for example, some firms use technology which incorporates AI, but they don't realise it (using the virtual assistant on their smartphones, for example, means using AI). How does this impact any survey results?

31 *AI for Services* (London Economics, 2020), https://ktn-uk.org/wp-content/uploads/2020/09/AI-for-Services-full-report-2020_KTN-green_Final-1.pdf.

32 Jessica Morley, Luciano Floridi, Libby Kinsey and Anat Elhalal, "From What to How: An Initial Review of Publicly Available AI Ethics Tools, Methods and Research to Translate Principles into Practices" (*Science and Engineering Ethics*, December 2019), https://arxiv.org/abs/1905.06876.

33 Nicola Davies, "'Yeah, we're spooked': AI starting to have big real-world impact, says expert" (*The Guardian*, 29 October 2021), www.theguardian.com/technology/2021/oct/29/yeah-were-spooked-ai-starting-to-have-big-real-world-impact-says-expert.

34 R Parnham, M Sako and J Armour, *AI-assisted lawtech: its impact on law firms* (University of Oxford, December 2021), www.law.ox.ac.uk/sites/files/oxlaw/ai_final1097.pdf.

35 Kyree Leary, "The Verdict Is In: AI Outperforms Human Lawyers in Reviewing Legal Documents" (*Futurism*, 27 February 2018), https://futurism.com/ai-contracts-lawyers-lawgeex.

36 Colin S Levy, "Bill Henderson: Thoughts on the Evolution of the Legal Profession" (Colin S Levy, 3 February 2021), www.colinslevy.com/post/bill-henderson-thoughts-on-the-evolution-of-the-legal-profession.

37 R Parnham, M Sako and J Armour, "Augmented Lawyering" (European Corporate Governance Institute – Law Working Paper 558/202, December 2021), https://papers.ssrn.com/sol3/papers.cfm?abstract_id=3688896.

38 R Parnham, M Sako and J Armour, "AI-assisted lawtech: its impact on law firms" (University of Oxford, December 2021), www.law.ox.ac.uk/sites/files/oxlaw/ai_final1097.pdf.

39 Francis Boustany, "ANALYSIS: Lawyers – Consider Expanding Your Multidisciplinary Team" (Bloomberg Law, 22 April 2021), https://news.bloomberglaw.com/bloomberg-law-analysis/analysis-lawyers-consider-expanding-your-multidisciplinary-team.

40 "TASK/Ask the Expert: Optimizing Contract Terms with the Insights from the 2020 Most Negotiated Terms" (World Commerce & Contracting, 9 October 2020), www.worldcc.com/Resources/Content-Hub/View/ArticleId/9937/Optimizing-Contract-Terms-with-the-Insights-from-the-2020-Most-Negotiated-Terms.

41 *Ibid*. But in defence of the lawyers, our job has always been to anticipate what might go wrong and to allocate those risks, with the theoretical optimal allocation being to the party who is best able to manage the risk, but quite often with price and negotiating strength being the overriding determining factors. Moreover, don't forget that many contracts do include provisions on, generally, the use of best practices and, more specifically, sometimes including practical method statements detailing how one or more of the parties will ensure performance (the latter, though, usually falling to the client or their technical advisers to lead on).

42 Lauren Jackson, "Jack Dorsey on Twitter's Mistakes" (*The New York Times*, 7 August 2020), www.nytimes.com/2020/08/07/podcasts/the-daily/Jack-dorsey-twitter-trump.html.

43 James Fletcher, "Spurious correlations: Margarine linked to divorce?" (BBC News, 26 May 2017), www.bbc.co.uk/news/magazine-27537142.

44 Ed Cumming, "Phwoar! Look at the vital statistics on these lads" (*The Times*, 19 December 2021), www.thetimes.co.uk/article/phwoar-look-at-the-vital-statistics-on-these-lads-d2k3l8cx3.

45 Kasia Delgado, "The female 'data lads' crunching Covid numbers and keeping us informed throughout the pandemic" (*inews*, 21 December 2021), https://inews.co.uk/news/long-reads/female-data-scientists-lads-crunching-covid-numbers-pandemic-1362875.

46 Michael Cross, "Every lawyer will require familiarity with crypto, says MR" (*Law Society Gazette*, 11 January 2022), www.lawgazette.co.uk/news/every-lawyer-will-require-familiarity-with-crypto-says-mr/5111085.article.

47 Alas, the evidence for lawyers embracing STEM subjects remains shaky. The argument whether lawyers should learn how to code computers, for example, continues to rumble on – some say the debate may well have been superseded, to an extent, by no-code and low-code platforms, which means that lawyers can now build apps with little or no coding expertise. The authors remain unconvinced by the commercial merit of this argument.

48 CP Snow, "The Two Cultures" (*Leonardo*, vol 23, no 2/3, The MIT Press, 1990), 169–73, https://doi.org/10.2307/1578601.

49 *AI Readiness Toolkit* (NextGenPSF), www.nextgenpsf.co.uk/ngs-toolkit.

50 *Legal Operations Maturity Model* (Association of Corporate Counsel), www.acc.com/maturity/metrics-analytics.

51 Horace Dediu, "Steve Jobs's Ultimate Lesson for Companies" (*Harvard Business Review*, 25 August 2011), https://hbr.org/2011/08/steve-jobss-ultimate-lesson-fo.

52 https://technation.io/resources/guide-to-ai/#understand-the-impact.

Chapter 3:
The hybrid era

EM Forster isn't an author who naturally springs to mind when thinking about the future.

Born in 1879, Forster is foremost in many people's minds with the popular Merchant Ivory period dramas based on his novels, such as *A Room with a View* and *Howard's End*. But Forster was also an essayist and writer of short stories.

In recent years, one of his works, *The Machine Stops*, has been rediscovered by a new generation. First published in 1909, this science-fiction short story is set in a future where people live atomised lives underground (*A Room Without a View?*). They communicate with one other remotely and all creature comforts are provided by "the Machine". They never have to leave home.

For many, unearthing this short story is a bit like finding out that Emily Brontë wrote *The Matrix*.

As it happens, much of what Forster predicted didn't come to pass, but over 11 decades after he wrote this story, aspects of his imagined world ring true.

We can, for example, all avoid contact with people by using the Machine –

the internet – and nowadays there are plenty of ways to do this. For example:

- During lockdown, almost all of us significantly increased our online shopping while most high-street shops were closed for business. (Many of us have seen, during virtual meetings, participants leaving their seat momentarily to answer the door to their latest delivery from Amazon.)
- Netflix and other online streaming services give us a bewildering choice of home entertainment at the press of a button. Fifty years ago, to have a choice of which movie to watch in the evening involved visiting a cinema. Forty years ago, it involved visiting the local Blockbuster. Now it involves no physical contact with the outside world at all.
- Takeout-delivery businesses like Deliveroo Editions have opened up 'dark kitchens' which only produce food for delivery. For its customers, there's no more phoning the restaurant and asking for a table next to the window. There's no window. Or table.

Author and broadcaster Professor Noreena Hertz calls this the "Contactless Age".[1] While, from time to time, we need to withdraw from the world to recharge our batteries and have our private moments, this "institutionalisation of contactless living"[2] through technology has the potential, if we're not careful, to isolate and disconnect us from our fellow humans in an echo of Forster's dystopia.

It's something that is starting to concern policymakers. In 2018, the government wrote that: "... as we continue to make the most of new technologies, ways of working and delivering services, we need to plan for connection and design in moments of human contact."[3] The then-Prime Minister, Theresa May, worried that "the warmth of human contact risks receding from our lives".[4]

The businesses mentioned above have a vital role to play to help those who are, say, isolating or shielding. They include human touchpoints in their services. People can also use the above services for profoundly social reasons such as preparing a meal for friends and family.

But, we're a profoundly social species and we should take great care not to lose the human elements of life that spark joy and foster a sense of belonging. We can't afford to overlook people in the race to 'out-tech' our competitors. Our clients, and the need to connect with them, should be at the forefront of our minds. As Table 1 shows, this is what this 'hybrid era' is all about.

Table 1. The contactless versus the 'hybrid era'

The contactless era	The 'hybrid era'
Tech *or* people	Tech *and* people
Emphasis or obsession with tech: tech for tech's sake	Emphasis on finding the sweet spot between tech and people
Tech replaces people where it's more efficient. It may replace them altogether	Just because tech can replace people doesn't necessarily mean that it should. People appear in person, remotely or using new tech in some other way (or there's, at the very least, an option to contact a person)
All or mostly contactless	Human contact points built in

And as we all become increasingly accustomed to a world that offers convenience at our fingertips, the way in which we lawyers engage with our clients and deliver our services is thrown into stark contrast (even nowadays legal service is often not so much akin to Netflix, than one of its period dramas).

Times have changed, and so must we. We're already seeing exciting examples of this hybrid-era world:
- Hybrid concerts: in 2022, the four band members of pop group ABBA started to perform as avatars, alongside a 10-piece live band, in a purpose-built arena in East London where thousands of fans were able to enjoy the deeply social experience of attending a concert together. (And the best thing? Technology like the 'ABBAtars' is immune to both ageing and COVID.)
- Hybrid workouts: keep-fit businesses already offer fitness classes where people can join a class remotely or in person. Ericsson conducted a survey in 2021 in which four-fifths of people reckon gyms will have augmented or virtual reality treadmills by 2030.[5] Peloton, and its internet-connected treadmills and bikes, is another example of a hybrid technology.
- Hybrid medicine: apps such as Livi and VideoGP (from Lloyds

Pharmacy), already offer consultations with a GP using a smartphone. Prescriptions can also be ordered on the NHS app and through other apps developed by the private sector. But people still need to be poked and prodded from time to time. And bad news is still better delivered in person and not by text message.

The authors see a similar hybrid world for our profession where lawyers use a blend of technology and human contact to get the best out of both worlds and bring innovative and people-led solutions to our firms and clients.

In this chapter we examine this hybrid world and the two main elements of the 'hybrid era' for lawyers:
- First we look outwards and focus on client-facing solutions. We look at the 'legal practice matrix' and how to bring hybrid solutions into the legal market. The challenges of regulation where there isn't a level playing field for all are also discussed. We also examine the need for a hybrid mindset so that we can drive our hybrid solutions forward and how hybrid solutions themselves need to be hybrid. One-size-fits-all, cookie-cutter approaches to the problems we face won't cut it.
- We then look inwards and focus on our businesses and hybrid working. Given how much of our working lives we spend working, the people side of our working lives is something that we need to get right. The opportunity to create a hybrid working model that works for all, as part of a people-first culture, is there for the taking. It's no less important than our steely focus on clients.

After this, we reflect on at what training we need to make sure that our people are ready for the exciting challenges set out in this book. Finally, we include a few case studies and practical tips on the 'hybrid era'.

Hybrid lawyering means technology *and* people working together in whatever combination works best. It means not defaulting to an approach of 'tech knows best'. As this chapter shows, hybrid lawyering is about being hybrid in a myriad of ways:
- it's about being a lawyer and, say, an entrepreneur;
- it's about combining lawyers and technology; and
- it's about balancing working from home with a physical presence in the office.

Ultimately, it's about practising law in a time of accelerated change, messy complexity and nuance, where a binary approach to what we do won't work in many cases.

Figure 1. Chapter contents

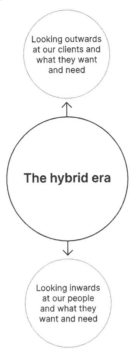

A client-centric, agile and hybrid mindset is our passport to a future in which we're much better placed to seize the opportunities that come our way.

1. Embracing the 'hybrid era' for clients

In 2019, YouGov undertook a survey of 28,663 people on the legal needs of individuals in England and Wales on behalf of the Law Society and the LSB.[6] It asked how satisfied people were with the services they received:
- 50% reported being "very satisfied";
- 35% were "fairly satisfied";
- 5% were "fairly dissatisfied";
- 2% were "very dissatisfied"; and
- 8% didn't know.

As far as legal user experience goes, this isn't bad, but there's room for improvement. If, for example, you were to let a family member know you were 'fairly satisfied' with their attempt at cooking Sunday lunch, you might find yourself wearing parts, or perhaps all, of your lunch in some way. "Fairly satisfied" isn't damning with faint praise, but it's not far off it.[7]

In 2021, a similar, smaller survey of over 3,500 consumers by the Legal Services Consumer Panel found that consumer satisfaction with the service

A client-centric, agile and hybrid mindset is our passport to a future in which we're much better placed to seize the opportunities that come our way.

given by their lawyers was at 83%. The only three options in this survey were "satisfied", "unsatisfied" and "neither satisfied nor unsatisfied".[8] Again, there's not much room for nuance there.

On the other hand, businesses like Amazon have higher ambitions and speak of "delighting" their customers. In 2017 founder and ex-CEO Jeff Bezos remarked that: "Customers are always beautifully, wonderfully dissatisfied, even when they report being happy and business is great."[9]

So, according to Bezos, even when people say they're satisfied, they're not?

Confused?

There's a lot of work that we still need to do. While 'delighting' customers may sound a little hyperbolic – is anyone in the United Kingdom ever 'delighted'? 'Quite pleased' sounds more the ticket – we can't be complacent. In this 'hybrid era' where we need to be much more client-centric and agile in what we do, can we risk our clients being anything less than 'very satisfied'?

In writing this section, just out of interest, the authors did a Google autocomplete check for the term 'my lawyer is'. The results, alas, were surprisingly poor:
- *my lawyer is working against me;*
- *my lawyer is taking too long; and*
- *my lawyer is not doing his job.*

A similar autocomplete search for 'solicitor' was even worse with a common search being "my solicitor lied to me". Not a single positive search was suggested in the initial drop-down menu.

We need to do much more to focus on client satisfaction. This situation can't continue.

The YouGov survey looked at satisfaction with services that had actually been given. But there's also a significant unmet demand for legal services in England and Wales:
- A LawtechUK report published in July 2021, *Shaping the Future of Law*, put the unmet legal needs of SMEs and consumers at a staggering £11.4 billion (the 'Great Unmet Legal Need' as the authors call it).[10] And if they are met, further research by LawtechUK in October 2021 noted that "across the board, the main frustration for SMEs is that getting legal issues resolved is costly and time-consuming".[11] As a result, many SMEs try to resolve issues themselves – often with unsatisfying results.

- The Small Business Commissioner in December 2021 asked what kind of legal services do SMEs need, suggesting that their needs were not being fully met ("The last thing anyone wants to do is end up in court to resolve a dispute. It's too costly in time and money").[12]
- According to *The State of Legal Services* report from the LSB in 2020, every year 3.6 million people had an unmet legal need involving a dispute.[13]

How satisfied should our clients be with this gaping hole? If clients are at the heart of everything that we do, we still seem to be collectively ignoring many of their needs. We're not even offering solutions, let alone hybrid ones. We perhaps shouldn't be surprised at this unmet need. A survey of 2,023 people carried out in May 2021 by Bolt Burdon Kemp found that six out of 10 people were uncomfortable approaching solicitors.[14] Contrast this with how happy people are to buy from businesses like Amazon.

None of this is good enough. We lawyers need to catch up fast. Imagine if all these figures for unmet needs were repeated for healthcare.

But taking a client-centric approach is still a challenge: in 2017, LexisNexis published a report which found "not a single client interviewed was satisfied with what law firms provide".[15]

The headlines of the YouGov survey referred to above suggest that we're doing well on client satisfaction, but it's clear that if we peek under the surface and look not only at what the profession is doing, but also at what it *isn't* doing, things don't look quite as rosy. If we proceed on the basis that all is well, it won't be long before all is not well. In this 'hybrid era':

- non-traditional and more agile legal providers may take work from firms and offer their own hybrid solutions; and
- we're also missing a massive opportunity to do more work servicing the Great Unmet Legal Need with the clever use of technology and innovation and creating hybrid solutions in this area. There's a massive opportunity, which is there for the taking.

As technology and 'change3' shift the expectations of customers, lawyers aren't and won't be sheltered from the winds of change. If Big Tech businesses like Amazon won't make do with "fairly satisfied", why should we?

1.1 Embracing a hybrid worldview

Before we look at how we move to a more client-centric and agile approach to what we do, we need to be aware of, and challenge, our tendency, at times, to think in binary terms.

The problem is that a binary worldview is reassuring. We love a compelling story: good versus evil; superheroes versus baddies. Over the years, a fair amount of popcorn has been dropped onto cinema floors as cinemagoers perch on their seats fretting over such existential battles. Oversimplifying and generalising things into, say, yes/no, right/wrong, good/bad or win/lose does have its place: these shortcuts mean we can digest and process large amounts of information without being overwhelmed. But complexity is baked into our world.

We wonder whether legal practitioners, despite interpreting and advising in a nuanced world, day in and day out, are often too willing to think of *themselves* in solely binary terms? Take the term 'lawyer' or, more precisely, 'solicitor'. At first glance, it looks binary: under the Solicitors Act 1974 either (i) you're a solicitor (and have been admitted as such); or (ii) you're not. But there's nothing to stop lawyers being something *more* than just a solicitor.

In the 'hybrid era', we need to also think of ourselves more as hybrid, 'yes-and' lawyers: yes, we're lawyers *and* we're many other things too.

Each of us might be, for example, a solicitor *and*:
- a start-up founder;
- a scale-up entrepreneur;
- a data analyst;
- a thought leader;
- an app developer;
- a social media guru; or
- an activist.

The combinations are as long as our imaginations (and the limits of any professional conduct rules).

Professor Stephen Mayson, whose review of the regulatory framework for legal services was published in June 2020, takes it further. In 2021, he said the best way lawyers can prepare themselves for the future is "probably to stop thinking of themselves as lawyers", saying that there's a lot of baggage in the term.[16] Mayson makes a good point: we need to move on from the things which are holding us back. We need to conceive of ourselves differently.

(a) Client versus consumer
The language we use frames our perspectives too. Take the terms 'client' and 'customer' – the two words that sum up well the dichotomy of next-generation lawyering. If the person to whom we're giving legal advice is a

'client' our approach to them might differ than if they're thought of as a 'customer'. The medical profession has itself grappled with similar issues with 'patient', 'client' and 'consumer' for years.

Aren't the terms 'customer' and 'client' mutually exclusive? With a binary hat on, it'd be easy to bang the table and declare "Yes! The people for whom we work are clients and always will be. Customers? We're not selling widgets you know!" That said, the Solicitors Regulation Authority (SRA) on its homepage asks. "are you a customer?" when speaking to the general public, but uses the term "client" when talking to lawyers.[17]

Why does this all matter? This isn't mere semantics: the authors think this mentality is affecting how we think as lawyers working in the business of law as suppliers of legal services. Where appropriate, a more customer-led approach, or a blended customer/client approach is likely to be the better way forward. We discuss this 'legal practice matrix' below.

Of course, there's no suggestion that, in taking a less stereotypically client approach, we're doomed to offer an inferior service. On the contrary. A hybrid approach will help drive the profession to higher levels of client satisfaction if we let ourselves think differently.

1.2 Embracing the legal practice matrix

In what we do for our clients, we're likely to be sitting somewhere along the legal practice continuum between:
- a client or service mindset at the one end; and
- a customer or product mindset at the other.

At times, we may be much more towards one end than the other. Or we may be bang in the middle. In the future, we lawyers will offer more products alongside our more traditional services. The legal practice matrix below is a more fluid way of looking at what we do whether we work in a larger firm or smaller specialist firm. If we stick to a fixed, traditional mindset, the benefits and opportunities of the 'hybrid era' may well be lost on us.

In Table 2 we set out some, but by no means all, of the characteristics of these two mindsets from the authors' experience in practice. Some of these are stereotypes; some are not. Most, if not all, are subject to exceptions. But, putting these caveats aside for a moment, the general categorisations are useful to get us thinking in a more nuanced way.

Here's how they look in practice:

Table 2. Mindsets

Traditional client mindset	Traditional customer mindset	Traditional view	How things are changing now
Service	Product	We offer services and not products; suppliers of goods offer products and not services.	Increasingly, we offer products that complement our bespoke legal services, eg, SaaS solutions, document automation, self-serve AI contract review solutions.
Lawyer-centric	Customer-centric	The supply of lawyers is less than the supply of the providers of most goods. This typically leads to the balance of power in the relationship lying with the lawyer. Contrast that with the relationship between customers and providers of goods, where customers can usually shop around.	Increasingly, we're regarded as a commodity. Clients can pick and choose who they want in an increasingly competitive market. Customer service is still vitally important and yet Amazon receives better satisfaction scores than the legal profession (testament, perhaps, to the fact that technology is increasingly paramount to customer satisfaction in all areas of life).

continued on next page

Traditional client mindset	Traditional customer mindset	Traditional view	How things are changing now
Stronger, long-term relationship	Weaker, short-term relationship	We establish long-term relationships with clients, and, even now, individual relationships matter, with client partners who are responsible for maintaining those relationships. Contrast that with the supply of goods, where customers will generally shop around.	Many consumers now have a longer relationship with Amazon and Netflix than they do with a single lawyer or firm.
Formal	Informal	For many reasons, not least regulatory and to do with insurance, the interactions with our clients are largely formal in nature. Although a customer might be met with a similar level of formality when purchasing, say, a tailored suit, in most cases buying a product involves little or no formality.	From recent studies, it seems that the formal nature of legal services puts many consumers off going to a lawyer, even when they need one. Customers want to be treated efficiently, respectfully and to experience professionalism, but they don't appreciate formality as a barrier to be overcome, either when on-boarding or in the way work is conducted for them. We need to work harder at finding new ways of interacting with our clients.

continued on next page

Traditional client mindset	Traditional customer mindset	Traditional view	How things are changing now
Vocation	Business	As a liberal profession, practising law is often seen as a vocation or calling: a chance to serve the common good. The training and qualifications required have also limited who can be a lawyer, unlike suppliers of products (who often require no qualifications). Being a successful lawyer is often associated with being good at the law, whereas it's traditionally accepted that to be successful in selling products has required more business acumen than technical ability.	More than ever, we need to develop our business skills far more than we need to develop our technical legal skills.
Fees	Price	Professional services are mainly sold on a time-and-materials basis whereas the vast majority of goods are sold at a fixed price.	Increasingly, we're under pressure to offer a defined scope of legal work for a fixed price using alternative fee arrangements whenever possible.

continued on next page

Traditional client mindset	Traditional customer mindset	Traditional view	How things are changing now
Inputs	Outputs	We typically speak of options and actions to be done, rather than focus on an end result. We can sometimes sit on the fence or show too much of our thought processes. Suppliers of products supply an end product and the customer is, in most cases, not interested in how that is achieved.	Most people (whether buyers of professional services or products) just want their suppliers to deliver what they need: the output (ie, a solution). The inputs into achieving that are just as irrelevant whether they need goods or professional services. We need to focus on the needs of our clients and how to meet those needs in clever ways that make the outcome for our clients as good as possible.
Data-poor	Data-rich	Although most lawyers (in private practice) measure data on their work in progress, hardly any of us analyse our client databases or capture data on the work we're doing.	As Chapter 2 shows, we must wake up to the importance of data capture and analysis, both of our client databases and of the work we do. This is, however, still nascent in our profession.

continued on next page

Traditional client mindset	Traditional customer mindset	Traditional view	How things are changing now
Guarded front door	Open front door	In both physical and metaphorical senses, we're hard to access. Gone are the days, in the main, when someone could saunter into a lawyer's office without an appointment to make an enquiry. Only high-end jewellery shops and nightclubs tend to put up a similar barrier to entry. In that sense, seeing a lawyer is more analogous with seeing a doctor or dentist than it is with simply getting something that you need. And that physical barrier adds to the disinclination that people feel about seeking legal advice, even when they need it.	Increasingly, the marketing and provision of legal services is now through virtual, rather than physical, means. We advertise through websites, podcasts, webinars, videos, LinkedIn etc. We provide our services by email, video conference, telephone, web-based collaboration platforms etc. Despite this, there is still a distinct difference in accessibility between Amazon and the average firm. Regulatory requirements notwithstanding, there's still an unnecessary gap that we need to close if we're to tap into the Great Unmet Legal Need that is out there.
Non-instant	Instant	Very few services that we provide can be delivered instantly. Nor are they pre-made, stacked up on a shelf ready for someone to take them away the same day.	More types of product are being developed which are capable of instant delivery. For example, AI contract review services can deliver results practically while-you-wait.

continued on next page

Traditional client mindset	Traditional customer mindset	Traditional view	How things are changing now
Local	Global	The vast majority of firms are not global, but domestic to their own countries. And each country has its own laws and requirements to practise law. In contrast, the majority of goods are capable of supply across a multinational marketplace.	Innovative models may well be capable of deployment internationally, possibly with modification for other countries. For example, AI contract review tools are adaptable for different legal systems and languages. Furthermore, the opportunity for future international sales might make the business case for the initial investment even easier. What's more, legal work may move from expensive areas to cheaper ones. Witness legal process outsourcing (LPO) to offshore locations and northshoring in the United Kingdom.

continued on next page

Traditional client mindset	Traditional customer mindset	Traditional view	How things are changing now
Personal	Non-personal	In all but a small number of practice areas (such as conveyancing, debt collection and other high-volume work types), our clients are serviced by a limited number of lawyers within a firm who are known to them. People speak (sometimes with pride) of 'their' lawyer. Contrast this with the provision of goods where customers don't care whether or not they're served by the same person at the shop counter and, indeed, they may be just as happy being served by a website as by a human.	This is the area where we need a nuanced approach going forward. We certainly need to focus more on efficiency and on making services accessible without thinking that each one of us is personally indispensable. At the same time, if we're going to prevail over purely technology-based legal service providers in the future, we must understand what aspects of what we do for a client are truly valued for being personal. EQ will be such an important part of being a successful lawyer in the future (see Chapter 9).

To see how the legal practice matrix works in practice, it helps to play a game of 'if lawyers did x'. For example, we could ask ourselves what the outcome would be 'if lawyers did Google'. Following the more traditional client mindset, this might mean that a search would:

- cost between, say, 10p and £10;
- involve paper signatures for the terms and conditions in order to access the site; and
- use far too much jargon ('an exception has occurred during the search submission').

The above is, of course, an exaggeration, but only just. Would the answer be any different if a less traditional mindset and hybrid-era approach were to be taken? Absolutely.

There's always a potential conflict between the customer never being wrong and us acting in their best interests. After all, a client may do something they think is 100% right, but this doesn't mean it's in their best interests.

1.3 Understanding the scope of regulation and engaging with the regulator

A quick word of warning, however, our professional conduct rules also mean the rough customer/client rule of thumb in the legal practice matrix doesn't work for all aspects of what we do, particularly for those aspects which touch upon regulation in some way.

If, for example, we adopt a 'customer/product' mindset and declare 'our customers are always right' how do we square this with the SRA standards and regulations?

We can't. That is because there's always a potential conflict between the customer never being wrong and us acting in their best interests. After all, a client may do something they think is 100% right, but this doesn't mean it's in their best interests.

There's no doubt that non-regulated businesses have more room for manoeuvre in what they do.

We therefore need to keep a watchful eye on the regulatory regime (see Chapter 6). The SRA is ambitious to help lawyers in the technology and innovation arena. It isn't averse to partnering with others to further its approach, including to help SME law firms more; and also consumers of legal services. Some would like to see the SRA, for example, identify technology platforms, and possibly even certify them; publish guidance on adopting technology; and bring people together in forums.

1.4 Creating a hybrid mindset

A hybrid mindset is one where technology is embraced, but people are never forgotten.

When we think of 'hybrid solutions':
- We need to think of *people first*: our clients and the people in our businesses. What do they want? What do they need?
- We then think of tech: how can technology or innovation help us be smarter and more agile for our people and our clients?

In more detail, this means:
- People first: it may be a hackneyed line, but in this 'hybrid era' people are at the heart of what we do.
- Technology: the 'hybrid era' also means we need to be more agile in how we use technology and implement innovation. In a 'change3' world, we can't afford to move at a glacial pace. Alas, 'agile' is a bit of a loaded term.[18] Aside from its specific use in project management circles, the term is well known enough to mean, roughly, being smarter, faster and better.

In this book, and this chapter in particular, when the authors refer to being 'people-first', 'client-centric' and 'agile', this is what we mean. These are the base elements of the 'hybrid era'.

1.5 Understanding the nature of hybrid solutions

Finally in this section, we need to remember hybrid solutions themselves are often hybrid: they involve people and technology to different degrees. This simple fact is easily overlooked.

- Hybrid solutions in firms are rarely as simple as a 50/50 tech/people split.
- Further options and adjustments may be necessary in different contexts.

This means:

- Any given hybrid solution for our clients involving technology will fall on a continuum with 'tech' at one end and 'people' at the other. (If a solution falls squarely at either end, then it's not a hybrid solution!) Some hybrid solutions have a bigger tech element; some have a bigger people element.
- Despite this book enthusing about technology, we must never forget that not everyone can or wants to use technology. Research commissioned by the LSB and SRA in March 2022 found that, generally, those who are comfortable using technology in their lives aren't fazed by legaltech.[19] But what happens with our clients who are technophobic or technosceptic? Although research shows that lawyers underestimate their clients' willingness to use legaltech, we shouldn't overestimate their willingness either. And even if they're willing, they might not have access to the relevant technology. *Essential Digital Skills* data, collected by Ipsos MORI for Lloyds Bank, noted in 2021 that 19% of the UK population is either digitally excluded in whole or in part.[20] In some areas the figure is higher (27% in Wales).[21]

We can unpack these two concepts using a quick example:

- a firm is developing a website where clients write a will by answering a series of questions;
- at the end of the process, the website gives a client the option to talk to a solicitor:
  - online via the chat function;
  - via the telephone; or
  - through a face-to-face appointment offline; and
- a solicitor can also be contacted, if needs be, throughout the process too using the same contact details above.

How hybrid is this solution?

- The self-serve functionality means that in most cases most of the work is done through the site (such as through FAQs). Typically, we might say that this hybrid solution has an 80/20 tech/people balance. It *isn't* 50/50.
- But hybrid solutions themselves are also hybrid: not everyone is comfortable with using the firm's website; some are vulnerable and disabled; others just dislike the idea of creating a will online. In such cases, the hybrid solution itself needs to be hybrid in order to comply with legislation such as the Equality Act 2010. This means that some users may be able to use aspects of the site; some may not be able to use the site at all; but both cohorts are likely to need more personalised help where lawyers can give eye contact and provide a reassuring voice.

As this example shows, and we lawyers know more than most, the world is usually more hybrid and nuanced than it seems at first sight.

Finding the sweet spot between the two ends of the scale for our clients, or types of user, is the key to developing the exciting new technology and innovation that will propel our firms forward.

We mustn't forget the simple truths: that the resilience of humans – and our society – is nurtured and boosted by social contact (COVID has surely taught us that). More often than not, our clients need this resilience to get them through their legal problems. Every encounter with another human makes us, and them, more human. Not every bit of legal work needs this human touch, but we exclude it at our peril. We need to think of the solutions we develop like good WiFi: the stronger the connection, the stronger the experience.

2. Embracing the 'hybrid era' for people in our firms

In September 2020 an advert for the cleaning brand Dettol appeared on Tube billboards. Office workers were returning to their desks after months working from home. The advert praised office life and included such 'joys' which they missed, such as "proper bants", "hearing buzzwords" and "those weird carpets".

It didn't go down particularly well: the virus-destroying bleach went viral itself with the campaign threatening to destroy the hard-earned reputation of one of the United Kingdom's top antiseptics – among some sceptical commuters at least. Did the owners of the brand fail to read the room? During lockdowns, who missed the things mentioned in the advert, like plants made of plastic? Or using a lift? Or indeed accidentally replying-all to an email, which, as it turns out, we learnt we could do equally as well from our desks at home? This advertising copy – cobbled together as though the writer had 60 seconds to name all of the features of office life during an elimination round of a gameshow – was a 'celebration' of a past world. One that is unlikely to return in full.

But the jury is still out on how we organise our working lives in the future.

Much of the debate boils down to: how effective is working from home? Two main camps do a lot of the shouting:

- The 'not-effective' camp: In October 2020, government ministers scolded workers, telling them to get off their Pelotons and "get back to work".[22] Companies like Goldman Sachs have been notable in their desire to get everyone back at their desks and chatting around the watercooler.
- The 'effective' camp: the old ways of doing things were stifling. Take commuting. It was often said that travelling long distances to work was bad for the soul and productivity. Research on inventors indicates that there may be truth in this assertion. In one study on patents, every increase in the distance travelled by six miles (10 kilometres in the research) was linked with a 7% decline in the quality of the patent.[23] However, surely we didn't really need this research? It's obvious. Standing on train platforms and travelling on a packed Tube takes up valuable time and energy that could (and has been) spent better.

However, in the middle are those who can see both sides of the story. This ongoing debate is a nuanced one, one in which firms, and not politicians and policymakers, need to decide what is best for them.

A mindset which says we don't need to meet up anymore and we can all work virtually is unlikely to work for most. People value the work/life balance of working from home (WFH), but, according to the ONS in June 2021, they often struggle to collaborate when working remotely.[24] Networking, supervision, team building and serendipity, to name but a few, are difficult to facilitate virtually. But going back to presenteeism with coats on the backs of chairs to indicate fake productivity is not something that most of us want to see return.

Enter the world of hybrid or blended working. Put simply, it's the obvious desire to take the best from both worlds. The future for most workers is likely to be not fully WFH or WFA (working from anywhere, perhaps in a co-working space) nor fully RTO (returning to the office), but a combination of remote and office-based working.

Figure 2 illustrates what our working and personal lives will increasingly look like.

Figure 2. Overview of our work and personal lives

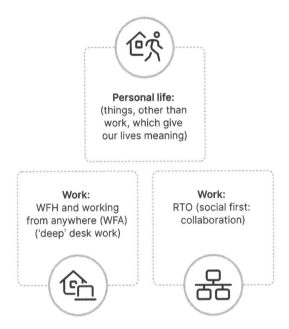

'Deep work' is done remotely and more social work at the office. Some talk about going to the office for the four c's: connect, collaborate, create and celebrate. In particular, RTO helps to reinforce a firm's culture, provide personal and professional development and to foster team spirit. There's also a recognition of the wider context: that we all have private lives too.

For the majority of complex legal work, clients can't effectively be served without human interaction. But how this happens is changing. A fundamental part of lawyering in the future will be to determine how we find the right balance to keep our clients happy.

These interactions in the graphic above will be driven by a combination of:
- efficiencies and ways of working that both clients and firms have enjoyed during lockdowns and the benefits of them continuing as businesses become more agile; for example:
  - fewer face-to-face (and often superfluous) meetings;
  - less travel;
- each of us and our clients, as individuals, having preferences on how we work in the future and the extent to which the policies of our

respective businesses permit or restrict us exercising these preferences. All of this needs to be balanced against what's good for each of us, which may not be the same, and what is good for the others with whom we work:

- junior staff, for example, need to be nurtured, taught, supervised and managed. This can't all be done remotely (even in the unlikely eventuality that anyone would want to do it all remotely);
- but equally, we can't allow inflexible partners who can't or won't supervise remotely to dictate that everyone has to be in the office simply because of that partner's lack of talent and adaptability. Nor can we tolerate partners spending all their time in their comfortable home offices when their juniors don't have the same level of luxury; and

- broader societal impacts that may significantly influence the two factors above, such as: the desire to keep city centres alive; how enticing those city centres will be, balanced against the commute to get there; government policies on restricting and taxing traffic; investment in improved and affordable public transport, and so on.

There are many debates on how these different, but related, influences will ultimately balance out now COVID restrictions have been relaxed. They range from some businesses insisting on a full-time return to the office to others declaring that staff will have the full freedom to choose. Most firms, however, seem to fall somewhere between those two extremes: at the time of writing, they're still trying to find that sweet spot between the buzz of the office and the benefits of WFH (and also trying to avoid the counterintuitive position of their staff commuting for hours only to sit in isolation on Teams meetings all day).

We all also hear messages that the cities *must* return to the *status quo ante*, often advanced by those with a partisan and understandable interest in seeing activity return to pre-lockdown levels – not least of all metropolitan authorities and interest groups; and those in the commercial real estate sector.

The simple fact is that we don't yet know how all this will pan out. But what we can be pretty certain about is that those of us in the business of law will need to be ready to:

- meet the needs of clients, whether or not their preference is physical meetings or virtual meetings or (more likely) a combination of the two;
- meet the preferences of our talent to work in the way they want to work, with the working assumption currently being that offering as much flexibility as possible will retain and attract the most and best talent; and

- run our businesses effectively while those needs and preferences are being met and do so in a way that significantly increases our own efficiency so that we can continue to compete with alternative legal services providers (see Chapter 7).

A tall order? Well, yes. But perhaps not as daunting as that prospect would have been before every business on the planet was forced to accept new circumstances and, to various degrees, adapt to them at the speed of light.

So now, a tall order? Yes. But not a problem. Rather, a really exciting opportunity!

2.1 Adopting the right kit and environment
Our working environment, where all the tech we use sits and stares at us dispassionately, is something that many of us don't think about too much.

Experimental psychologist Professor Charles Spence, author of *Sensehacking* reminds us how the physical world around us, and the environments we work in, can affect us in ways that we are only just beginning to understand. People who sit around a round table, for example, are more likely to strike a deal compared to those seated at a rectangular or square one: the former "primes a need to belong" whereas the latter "primes a need to be unique".[25] Even the height of a ceiling can affect the way in which we think.

As we embrace and build hybrid working models, are we aware of the many ways to gain a competitive advantage? Do we know, for example, what a proper environment means in practical terms for the future of lawyering?
- It means well-equipped, well thought out and safe home-working environments and systems. Broadband glitches and fuzzy cameras may have been tolerated when COVID started, and may even have added a healthy bit of empathy during lockdowns, but there's no excuse going forward. What's more, while some staff may have home offices, we mustn't presume that this is the case for all. For some lawyers, WFH isn't much fun at all.
- It means using the right technology; although, at the moment, there isn't much tech specifically designed for lawyers which enables them to work better in a hybrid environment. Most available tech is still rather generic. Even with the tech we use, there are many questions:
  - Can it facilitate hybrid meetings, with some people gathered physically and others remotely? This isn't as easy as it looks.
  - Have we thought through the advantages and disadvantages of the tech we use in a methodical way? For example, tech like Zoom and Teams have allowed us to do some things better than

There are other developments on the horizon. A hybrid working world demands that we continue to be agile in our thinking on these too.

in a physical meeting, such as screen sharing. But what happens when people have too many video calls? In December 2021, *The Guardian* lamented the tired "zombie-like survivors of back-to-back Zoom meetings" or "Zoombies".[26] Do we need to try to limit the amount of such calls? Should we at least require a 10-minute break between them?

- • How do we avoid stilted online or hybrid meetings? What training do we need to be collaborative? For example, on video calls people seem to be more ready to leave someone hanging without responding to them – a lonely experience. How do we cope with the sense of talking into the void?
- • How do we use the technology in the best way from a client's perspective: hence the debate between using a corporate background (professional, but sterile?) versus a home background (authentic, but a bit messy)?

- It means offices that people want to come into, not actively avoid. At the authors' firm, we'd already started the process of fitting out our offices before COVID. In Manchester, for example, the firm created break-out spaces for large teams to come together; huddle spaces for smaller teams; and quiet pods for when lawyers need a quiet space to make a call. The library contains books – to be expected – but also framed pictures of local celebrities, such the character Vera Duckworth from Coronation Street and Olympic-winning cyclists Sir Jason Kenny and Dame Laura Kenny. The fit out of the new London office, done during the pandemic, contains a state-of-the-art recording studio and has an even greater focus on being a hub for collaboration and social interaction. It makes people want to come into the office.

2.2 Being agile in hybrid working

There are other developments on the horizon. A hybrid working world demands that we continue to be agile in our thinking on these too.

For example, in January 2022, the *Law Society Gazette* in its daily email to subscribers asked: "Hybrid working is so last year – time for a four-day week?" The catch (for employers)? It's on five days' pay. The email noted that a culture of presenteeism and the billable hours model makes this four-day working week a tricky ask for many firms, but firms shouldn't close their minds to the potential benefits. The United Kingdom and other countries are running major trials to see if it could work for them. Consilia Legal, based in Leeds, introduced a four-day week in 2021 and found there was no adverse effect on productivity. Nor did they find that condensing five days' work into four was leading to unduly long days – people were just more effective with their time during those four days.

As we examine in this part of the chapter, it's likely that hybrid working (and an agile approach to adopting and maintaining it) will be the approach that the majority of firms adopt. A world without tech just isn't feasible: we can't uninvent the wheel or undiscover antibiotics. Laptops and the modern workplace's spaghetti of cables are with us now, and they're not going anywhere. As with most things in life, it's about nuance and balance, which is probably why 85% of those surveyed by the ONS in April and May 2021 want to use a hybrid approach to working.[27]

2.3 Learning about the world to come

Training in the subjects set out in this chapter and elsewhere in this book is vital and ought to be a key part of a firm's continuous learning programme. As well as wanting flexibility in their training, the best talent will also want to learn effectively. A scattergun approach to training, hoping that some of it will hit, certainly won't get us to where we need to be. As with other subjects in this book, we need to plan and be strategic in this area too.

Training helps lawyers deal with 'change3', take advantage of the 'data boost' and – the focus of this chapter – learn how to become much more agile in what we do.

In March 2020, in a survey of 353 solicitors, nine out of 10 said that they would need training in at least one legaltech area. The most common training needs according to survey were:[28]
- data analytics (71%);
- legal issues raised by use of AI/technology (65%);
- software packages used by the respondent's employer (61%);
- ethical issues raised by use of AI/technology (48%);
- digital literacy (45%); and
- innovation techniques (44%).

The least common training need was for software coding at around 20%.[29] Mindset training in how we approach technology is vital too.

Training can take place in many ways. As well as all the usual training formats with which we're all familiar, new formats are increasingly being used such as podcasts, videos and hackathons where people get together to work through and solve an intractable problem or two, and learn as they do so. It doesn't matter really, as long as it works. And none of these have to be bland affairs. Spice them up a bit. Add some humour and perhaps some gamification?

Moving to a more hybrid world is certainly doable – large-scale transformation of a sector has been done before – and an exciting prospect. We're not suggesting that lawyering is currently a disaster zone; if anything, our legal sector is one of the most successful globally. Paradoxically, it might be that very success itself that is leading to complacency or resistance to change (or both). But many of us do need to change our attitude to technology and innovation in our sector more than we're doing now.

Those of us in leading roles need to help raise the status of technology and innovation and hammer home its vital role, but do so in a way that recognises that people are at the heart of all of this. In this 'hybrid era', we can't afford to offer our clients and people the 'same old, same old'. We need, dare we say, a few *enfants terribles* to shake things up.

3. Case studies

3.1 Case study 1: Getting closer to your clients
Nowadays, clients expect us to not just be good lawyers, but also great communicators. Only a few years ago, the vast majority of what lawyers created was just the written word. Nowadays, there is an ever-growing number of ways to get the attention of clients and communicate with them.

And getting the attention of clients isn't easy. Like us, our clients are busy. They're swamped with emails, texts, direct messages, group chats, meetings, telephone calls, video calls, notifications and the traditional desk drop-by (for those not WFH). It's so much information to process, with one major consequence: as political scientist and pioneer in the field of AI, Herbert A Simon, noted way back in 1971: "The wealth of information means a dearth of something else … a poverty of attention."[30] If only he knew how much worse it would get.

But we can help our clients (and prospective clients) to notice us by being more agile in how we communicate with them.

These are the trends that the authors are seeing:
- More online collaborative platforms, such as HighQ from Thomson Reuters. The authors' firm has used this platform to create its own, *LiveWorking*, which allows clients to interact with the firm online in real time.
- More blogging. Attention spans aren't what they used to be: consider how long-form blogging has been superseded, to a large extent, by micro-blogging sites like Twitter. In particular, micro-blogging site Passle is used by many firms to create bite-size insights to

demystify legal developments. It also allows lawyers to show their human side a bit and offer opinions on legal and commercial issues of the day.

- More video content – and shorter content at that. Video is a powerful way to get a message across. Time will tell how the typically longer-form videos of YouTube will be impacted by the shorter-form videos of TikTok (according to cloud services company Cloudflare, TikTok was the world's most popular web address in 2021). In short, keep it short.
- More podcasting: podcasts are particularly popular among younger listeners. In 2020, 18% of adults in the United Kingdom were podcast listeners, with the figure rising to 27% among 25 to 34-year-olds.[31] 44% of podcasts are listened to while travelling or driving.[32] Mishcon de Reya is a good example of a firm that has embraced the medium through its *Jazz Shapers* series, where presenter Elliot Moss interviews entrepreneurs – "business shapers" – who have "defied convention and gone on to achieve great success".[33]
- More QR codes (QR stands for quick response). The pandemic has seen an explosion in the use of such codes. They have even been woven into the carpets in some hotels! By scanning a code with a smartphone camera, users can be directed to a relevant website. It can be used for marketing too.
- More webinars. Three years ago, webinars were a minority activity. Nowadays, lawyers almost have webinar fatigue. However, on the right subject they can be a popular means of law firms sharing information with clients and getting noticed.
- More gamification. As the UKIE (the trade body for the gaming sector in the United Kingdom) notes, "games are the culmination of creative and technical innovation, fusing the best of the arts with revolutionary technology".[34] There's a surprising amount that firms can learn from a more 'gamified' approach to engaging with clients. Wharton Interactive (at The Wharton School at the University of Pennsylvania), for example, is developing "game changing learning" – good pun there – through "Alternate Reality Courseware" using the latest teaching techniques.[35]
- More originality. Nothing seems to be off the table. At the University of Western Australia Law School there's a Comic Contracts Team that uses comics to explain how aspects of contracts work. The authors have colleagues who've started to use simple animations to humanise podcasts and make them a little bit more fun and therefore engaging.
- More networking online. COVID forced all networking online – at least for a while. And much of it found itself on LinkedIn.

(According to Passle in 2021, the average firm in the UK top 100 has 26,910 followers on LinkedIn.)[36] Networking is likely to remain hybrid for a while, and sites like LinkedIn are vital in keeping within the radar of our clients and contacts.

Firms need to be aware of how their clients consume information and adapt the above accordingly. The 'hybrid era' means that we can't presume that all of our clients are online. On the other hand, we need to shy away from dismissing technology out of hand by asserting 'x' technology is 'only for kids'. Sometimes they can spot trends before we do!

There are some useful tips to bear in mind when using these new methods of communicating:
- Think like your client. Why does this matter? (The 'so what?' test.)
- Why should our busy clients listen to us? Less is often more: fewer words often have greater impact. More firms are adopting tone of voice and brand guidelines.
- Craft a narrative if you can. You need to win hearts and minds.
- Write for the ear. Reading what you've written out loud is an underrated trick to understand how your writing works for others.
- Get statistics on who's read what you've published and adjust accordingly. Otherwise, you risk shouting into the wind.
- Think like a website designer: write for the web. People read webpages in a different way to how they read on paper. Research suggests that over three quarters of people scan webpages as opposed to reading materials word by word. GOV.UK have published guidance on how to get this right.[37]
- Talk to your clients, not over them; favour 'you' and 'your' over third-person constructions like 'our clients'.
- Show people. Putting pictures of people on your site – even just one – is a well-known way of increasing engagement with it. People like to see people.
- Be modest: don't show off and shy away from technobabble. Don't use big words all the time. People know that lawyers are good with words. Don't labour the point.
- On social media in particular:
  - Put the social into social media: mention people and tag them in, where appropriate.
  - Include an image if you can. A relevant picture adds more colour to posts and brings them to life. From a technical perspective, a post with a picture takes over more of a user's screen, so there's more chance of it grabbing someone's attention.

3.2 Case study 2: Adapting to an agile working environment but also using it to your advantage to communicate better than before

Few lawyers used virtual meeting platforms regularly before 2020. Fast-forward to the first few weeks into lockdown, and most of us were not only able to convene and hold virtual meetings; but we could change our virtual backgrounds; add multiple screens to our laptops; share those screens at will; and do all this while drinking a double expresso and answering the door to receive our Amazon deliveries.

From zero to tech hero in a few weeks. Lawyers throughout the country learned quickly – we had to – and we coped incredibly well with these 'new' methods of communication, despite being thrown into a highly adverse situation, with almost no notice.

There were certainly some aspects of virtual meetings that were no substitute for getting together in 'IRL' (in real life) in 3D. But there were other features that enabled us to do things better than meeting in person, such as:

- each virtual participant could take control and share their screens without having to shuffle seats and take turns to plug their laptops into a large meeting room screen; and
- firms could host virtual training sessions for hundreds of attendees without any of the usual room and seating logistics; or worrying about handing out name badges and putting coats into cloak-rooms.

And that's not to mention the time savings and environmental benefits of not having to travel to the office. It was clear to most lawyers that there would be a long-term place for virtual meetings after the pandemic.

This type of meeting isn't, of course, a wholly new phenomenon: video-conference facilities have been around for decades. But they were expensive and often difficult to use. In recent years, the quality and functionality of them has increased dramatically and the cost of the systems has reduced too. And, more fundamentally, now everyone with a laptop can join in from the comfort of their home, as opposed to having to head into an office where all the requisite video-conference hardware is installed. Alongside this, the scope for combining physical and remote attendees in a meeting at the same time also became clear. Many law firms have now equipped their meeting rooms with cameras and screens to allow virtual attendees to join a physical meeting.

Had the state-of-the-art in multi-site meetings reached its zenith? Two of the authors, David Jackson and Tony Randle, thought there was still more that could be done to take full advantage of newly available technology – and of the new-found enthusiasm of lawyers to embrace what new tech can offer.

Enter *The Studio*. This is a fully purpose-built, hybrid communication space, based in the authors' firm's new London office. *The Studio* has been designed to go beyond traditional video-conferencing:

- it incorporates large touchscreens and advanced presentation software (Prezi): this enables more dynamic and interactive presentations than is usually possible when using software such as PowerPoint;
- it includes two linked but independent screens: this means two people can present at the same time. The transitions between them are far slicker and seamless: images and videos can be 'thrown' from one screen to the other with the mere flick of a finger;
- it uses dynamic cameras: whatever the audience present in the room is watching can also be broadcast to remote attendees using sophisticated cameras, which can track the positions of the presenters as they move around the room;
- it's flexible on what's shown: the broadcast can either show the presenter standing in front of the touchscreen (like a television weather forecast) or it can just show remote attendees the content of the screen without the distraction of the presenter

And, of course, the presentations can be recorded so those who missed the live show can watch it on catch-up.

All this adds up to us lawyers now being able to give live, virtual and hybrid presentations the quality of which far exceeds what any firm still relying on PowerPoint can offer. (Dare we say we lawyers have even exceeded what the Big Four accountants can currently offer? No doubt we have just opened ourselves up to receiving comments from them if they read this book – the authors hope they do!)

But *The Studio* isn't just a state-of-the-art, hybrid-era presentation suite. It's also a powerful tool for working on client matters. For example:

- the touchscreens can be used for collaboration in negotiating and marking up documents, drawing diagrams and capturing notes (among other things);
- all these working documents and thought processes can be recorded to refer back to, or to share with anyone who was not able to attend the meeting; and
- content on the screen can be emailed out to third parties directly using the touchscreen.

The aesthetics of *The Studio* were important too. It was designed to be inspirational – to make people want to collaborate and have great ideas when they're in it. It can be used as a 'mission control' when completing deals or for holding away-days and hackathons.

The Studio is an ongoing experiment too. As we all settle into the future of hybrid working, inevitably working preferences and patterns will change. New technologies will arise. Others will have ideas that we have not thought of. Therefore, Jackson and Randle are committed to using *The Studio* as a testbed to constantly try out new things and new ways. Their firm also wants to make it available to its clients as well – not just for deals and away-days, but so they can learn from what the firm has done (and from any mistakes that have been made along the way) before they make decisions on investing in similar facilities in their offices.

4. Practical tips on the 'hybrid era'

We set out below some practical tips on thriving in the 'hybrid era'.

These tips are split as follows:
- Evolving from a purely traditional lawyering mindset in the 'hybrid era';
- Looking after our people in the 'hybrid era'; and
- Finding the balance between tech and people in the 'hybrid era'.

4.1 Evolving from a purely traditional lawyering mindset in the 'hybrid era'
- Be acutely aware of the perception gap between law firms and clients: most law firms want to provide high-quality legal advice. Most clients want affordable solutions to their problems. As technology increases in power and general availability it will facilitate the shift away from traditional advisory services towards productisation. Rather than holding out as long as possible before being forced to accept that change, start to implement changes in areas where your firm is obviously lagging behind your competitors.
- Talk to your clients: don't take anything for granted or assume what your clients want – talk to them and ask them. Do they want more accessibility to your services through online platforms? What needs do they have that they are currently not able to solve on a cost-effective basis? If they had a magic wand, what problem would they want someone to take off their desk tomorrow?
- Don't confuse productisation with commoditisation: new ways of delivering high-value and highly specialist advice will develop alongside new ways to handle the more routine support that clients need.

(An example of this in the authors' firm is supporting clients on the automation of privacy compliance – a highly specialist area. Contrast that with automation of the review of large volumes of documents as part of a due-diligence exercise, or of low-value debt recovery operations.) But make no mistake, there is a place for both. (One of the authors recalls a senior partner in a relatively large law firm saying recently that there's no place for technology in 'quality law'. He couldn't be more wrong.)

- Innovating to keep up in the 'hybrid era' is not a nice-to-have: put it high on your agenda or you will soon be out of step with the market. Most law firms are currently doing well and there is no burning platform impelling them to evolve from the traditional model. Forward-thinking firms are taking the opportunity to begin investing in innovation while times are good, rather than waiting for a downturn in the economy, when not only will they be less able to invest but also they will be coming to the innovation party behind the curve.
- Lead from the top and win hearts and minds with examples: relay examples of how changes being introduced by other law firms are obviously leading to improvements for clients, for the firms and for their people. Everyone is a winner if the right innovation is implemented in the right way and if everyone understands what's in it for them!

4.2 Looking after our people in the 'hybrid era'

- Find the right balance: locating the sweet spot between giving people maximum working flexibility and setting parameters within which they must operate cannot be generalised. Don't think, because other firms are taking a more directive or a more flexible approach than you, that your approach is wrong. If your approach is working for your people, for your clients and for your firm then it is the right approach. None of us can claim to have the single right formula. And every firm, and their people and culture, is different. Whatever approach you adopt, regularly take feedback soundings and keep it under review. Be prepared to pivot – you won't be losing face but rather continuing to evolve in a highly fluid environment.
- Don't forget to set some rules for your partners as well: in addition to considering whether to direct associates and support staff on hybrid working patterns. There's no room for allowing senior staff to display a resolute unwillingness to move with the times, whether it be those who refuse to come into the office or those who refuse to consider any home-working. Staff should not have their choices compromised simply because senior people can't adapt to allowing others to work on a hybrid basis. Consider having, for example, monthly team 'anchor days' during which everyone comes in at the same time.

- Equip your people to work efficiently, safely, compliantly and comfortably from home: from the lessons we've learned over the last two years, this tip alone could form the subject of an entire book in itself! In the interests of brevity, investment made in each of these aspects is, ultimately, not optional but a necessity. (Inevitably, in the long term that investment will be more than recouped by the reduction in office space that many firms will be making over the coming years.)
- Equip your people to work efficiently, safely, compliantly and comfortably from the office too: if you do ask associates to come in, ensure that the facilities they have when they are in the office are at least as good as those they have set up at home (eg, at home they'll have taken care of their keyboard, monitor and mouse, so ensure that every workstation is kept in full working order for when they come in. It is frustrating to have undertaken the commute into an office only to find that when you arrive the hot desk you've booked has a wonky chair and someone has taken the mouse because theirs was not working.)
- Be aware that everyone is different, both in personality and in their home circumstances: those who seem to be thriving by working predominantly from home may nonetheless not be developing their skills (or their contacts within the firm) as much as if they were coming into the office more. Sometimes a considerate intervention may be appropriate in the interests of those unwittingly falling into an unhealthy comfort zone.

4.3 Finding the balance between tech and people in the 'hybrid era'

- Remember the fundamental human element of lawyering: as one senior in-house lawyer once said to one of the authors, "lawyering is a contact sport". People will always be the fundamental element in a successful legal services business. Technology will simply help those people achieve more for our clients than ever before. Even if a technological solution to a particular process or problem presents itself, always consider whether, by retaining a human element in the solution, the outcome or experience for the client will be enhanced. (In the authors' experience, this has invariably proved to be the case.) This is incredibly important, not just to ensure the best outcomes for the client but also to reassure our people that their jobs are not going to be taken over by machines!
- Consider the extent of human involvement: if you are exploring using technology and find that it can only get you so far towards providing a full solution, don't abandon the technology without considering whether the missing aspects can be undertaken by people. The chances are that whatever you are looking at presently is probably performed 100% by people, so even if you only achieve

improved efficiency in 50% of that process, it is still worth doing. Any improvement is better than none! Also, even if the technology can, with further development, be enhanced to perform 100% of the solution, the cost of enhancing the technology to that extent might be prohibitive compared to the cost of people performing that part.

- Trial the solution: whatever hybrid solution you're proposing to offer clients, trial it in beta with a few open-minded clients first. There is no better acid test of the required tech/human balance in a solution than to hear the views of your clients having used it 'in anger'. Again, the authors' experience is that this will always give rise to very helpful suggestions from the clients on where the additional human contact in any particular aspects of the solution can enhance the output or the user experience or both.

- Be considerate of the roles that you are assigning to people in a hybrid tech/human solution: it might be most efficient to recruit a paralegal to repeatedly perform a particular task in a process, but you may find that the rate of attrition in paralegals for the role is high because it is boring and not developing or challenging them. Alternatively, could the task be one that you assign to trainees or junior associates on a rotation basis, so that each of them will see it as gaining valuable experience in next-generation lawyering, but in the knowledge that it is only a small and temporary part of their job.

Notes

1   Noreena Hertz, *The Lonely Century* (paperback, Sceptre, 2020) p71.
2   *Ibid*, p73.
3   Department for Digital, Culture, Media and Sport, *A connected society: a strategy for tackling loneliness* (October 2018), https://assets.publishing.service.gov.uk/government/uploads/system/uploads/attachment_data/fil e/936725/6.4882_DCMS_Loneliness_Strategy_web_Update_V2.pdf.
4   *Ibid*.
5   "10 Hot Consumer Trends 2030" (Ericsson), www.ericsson.com/en/reports-and-papers/consumerlab/reports/10-hot-consumer-trends-2030-the-everyspace-plaza#trend8-the-nev erending-store.
6   YouGov plc, "Legal needs of Individuals in England and Wales", https://legalservicesboard.org.uk/wp-content/uploads/2020/01/Legal-Needs-of-Individuals-Technical-Report-Final-January-2020.pdf.
7   To be fair, the gradations of satisfaction in the YouGov survey weren't that nuanced: in reality, it's a big jump between being "very satisfied" and "fairly satisfied". (Why isn't there, for example, a simple "satisfied" between these two answers?) What's more, the younger the person surveyed, the more likely they'd say they were dissatisfied with the service, with 32% of those people aged 18–29 years old falling outside of the "satisfied" brackets.
8   Legal Services Consumer Panel, *Legal Services Consumer Panel Tracker Survey 2021* (June 2021), www.legalservicesconsumerpanel.org.uk/wp-content/uploads/2021/07/LSCP-2021-How-consumers-are-using-FINAL.pdf.
9   Kali Hays, "Bezos Says Customer 'Delight' at the Heart of Amazon Success" (WWD, 12 April 2017), www.com/business-news/technology/bezos-says-customer-delight-heart-of-amazon-success-10866159.
10   LawtechUK, *The LawtechUK Report 2021 – Shaping the Future of Law* (July 2021), https://technation.io/wp-content/uploads/2021/07/LawtechUK-Report-2021-Final.pdf.
11   Community Research Limited, "Qualitative research into SMEs' legal needs and adoption of lawtech" (October 2021), https://resources.lawtechuk.io/files/Lawtech_SME_report_FINAL.pdf.
12   Small Business Commissioner UK (@SB_Commissioner), "I've been asked to think about the kinds of legal service small firms need. It would be great to have your thoughts before mid-Dec. The last

thing anyone wants to do is end up in court to resolve a dispute. It's too costly in time and money. What would help you?" Twitter, 1 December 2021, https://twitter.com/sb_commissioner/status/1466081179204046849?s=11.

13 Legal Services Board, *The State of Legal Services 2020*, https://legalservicesboard.org.uk/wp-content/uploads/2020/11/The-State-of-Legal-Services-Narrative-Volume_Final.pdf.

14 Jemma Slingo, "Six out of 10 people 'not comfortable' approaching solicitors" (*Law Society Gazette*, 8 October 2021), www.lawgazette.co.uk/news/six-out-of-10-people-not-comfortable-approaching-solicitors/5110098.article.

15 LexisNexis, "Amplifying the voice of the client in law firms", www.lexisnexis.co.uk/pdf/3799_LN_VOTC_Online.pdf.

16 "Images of the Future Worlds Facing the Legal Profession 2020–2030" (Law Society, 28 July 2021), https://cdn.worktechacademy.com/uploads/2021/06/Law-Society-Future-Worlds-2050.pdf

17 "Welcome to the Solicitors Regulation Authority" (Solicitors Regulation Authority), www.sra.org.uk/.

18 Some love it. Some hate it. Writer and journalist Dan Lyons says it's morphed into something that's almost religious; hence it so often being capitalised ('Agile'). A slew of articles have appeared, first celebrating and then castigating the term ("Agile Ruined My Life", being a favourite hyperbolic headline of ours). But most of us probably don't care much one way or another.

19 Legal Services Board, *Social acceptability of technology in legal services* (March 2022), https://legalservicesboard.org.uk/wp-content/uploads/2022/05/Acceptability-of-technology-in-legal-services-research-report-FINAL-March-2022.pdf.

20 "Essential Digital Skills" (Lloyds Bank), www.lloydsbank.com/banking-with-us/whats-happening/consumer-digital-index/essential-digital-skills.html.

21 *Essential Digital Skills Report 2021* (Lloyds Bank), www.lloydsbank.com/assets/media/pdfs/banking_with_us/whats-happening/211109-lloyds-essential-digital-skills-report-2021.pdf.

22 "Conservative conference: Get off your Pelotons and back to work, says Oliver Dowden" (BBC News, 5 October 2021), www.bbc.co.uk/news/uk-politics-58804607.

23 Hongyu Xiao, Andy Wu and Jaeho Kim, "Commuting and innovation: Are closer inventors more productive?" (*Journal of Urban Economics*, Volume 121, 2021), https://doi.org/10.1016/j.jue.2020.103300.

24 "Business and individual attitudes towards the future of homeworking, UK: April to May 2021" (Office for National Statistics), www.ons.gov.uk/employmentandlabourmarket/peopleinwork/employmentandemployeetypes/articles/businessandindividualattitudestowardsthefutureofhomeworkinguk/apriltomay2021.

25 Charles Spence, *Sensehanking* (Viking, 2021), p22.

26 "Polyworking and Zoombies: welcome to the new home office jargon" (*The Guardian*, 13 December 2021), www.theguardian.com/business/2021/dec/13/polyworking-and-zoombies-welcome-to-the-new-home-office-jargon.

27 "Business and individual attitudes towards the future of homeworking, UK: April to May 2021" (Office for National Statistics), www.ons.gov.uk/employmentandlabourmarket/peopleinwork/employmentandemployeetypes/articles/businessandindividualattitudestowardsthefutureofhomeworkinguk/apriltomay2021.

28 M Sako, J Armour and R Parnham, "Lawtech Adoption and Training: Findings from a Survey of Solicitors in England and Wales" (University of Oxford, March 2020), www.law.ox.ac.uk/sites/files/oxlaw/oxford_lawtech_adoption_and_training_survey_report_18_march_2.pdf.

29 The authors think that, on balance, this is a good thing. We should stick to what we are expert at doing and let others who are experts in coding get on with it. The existence of low or no-code solutions doesn't change this as, in the main, we think that we'll still get non-lawyers to use such technology. None of this, by the way, means that lawyers can't have an appreciation for what code is and what it does!

30 HA Simon, "Designing organizations for an information rich world", in Martin Greenberger, ed, *Computers, communications, and the public interest* (1971), pp37–72.

31 Department for Digital, Culture, Media and Sport, *Digital radio and audio review* (21 October 2021), www.gov.uk/government/publications/digital-radio-and-audio-review/digital-radio-and-audio-review.

32 *Ibid.*

33 "Jazz Shapers" (Mishcon de Reya), www.mishcon.com/jazzshapers.

34 "The voice of the UK games industry. Our story, our beliefs, our people" (UKIE), https://ukie.org.uk/about.

35 ARC.platform (Wharton Interactive), https://interactive.wharton.upenn.edu/learning-platforms/arcplatform/.

36 "The Top 10 UK Law Firms by Number of LinkedIn Followers" (Passle, 7 June 2021), https://blog.passle.net/post/102gzvu/the-top-10-uk-law-firms-by-number-of-linkedin-followers.

37 "Content design: planning, writing and managing content" (Government Digital Service, 25 February 2016), www.gov.uk/guidance/content-design/writing-for-gov-uk.

Part 2:
Making
it happen

COVID has shown us how technology can bring us together in a time of social distancing. Apps such as FaceTime, Zoom and Teams enabled us to stay connected with colleagues, friends and loved-ones, whatever our level of tech savviness. At the beginning of the pandemic, communities came together through technology, to offer lifelines to the most vulnerable in them. People made it happen. They had to.

Take the community centre Hub at Henley in Warwickshire – a microcosm of the impact that technology has on people.

Its chairman, Peter Crathorne, told us that he was concerned about Henley's elderly residents who were starting to self-isolate at the beginning of the pandemic. He received messages "out of the blue" from worried relatives overseas, including from one based in the US: "My 99-year-old mum is isolating on her own. She's never used a computer and I've sent her an iPad so she can see me on calls. Would you mind popping round to talk her through using it?" Crathorne visited the soon-to-be centenarian, setting up her FaceTime while sitting on the grass in her front garden after she'd passed the tablet through her front window. After a few lessons delivered through the window, mother and daughter were reconnected. They could see each other on their respective devices, despite being an ocean apart. Crathorne had made it happen.

This part of the book looks at the background to what law firms now face. It looks at what to do to make it happen. It focuses on making people-centred technology and innovation work for firms by:

- procuring the technology and implementing the innovation in firms so that they can do what they do smarter, faster and better (see Chapter 4);
- creating exciting products and services for the people they advise by collaborating to innovate (see Chapter 5); and
- ensuring that firms get the regulatory, quality and risk aspects of technology and innovation right (see Chapter 6).

Chapter 4:
Procurement

A few years before the turn of the millennium, writer Bill Bryson moved to the country of his birth, the United States, for a while. While 'over there' he wrote about his new life: from the delights of diners to the remarkable number of lawyers in the country (more than the rest of the world put together).

One of the stories which resonated with many buyers of technology was his piece on buying a bit of new tech – a PC – making sense of it and, most important of all, trying to set it up. He said that his new computer was configured to use "higher processors running at 2,472hz on variable-speed spin cycle".[1] His wry turn of phrase as he tried to understand his fictional "Anthrax/2000 Multimedia 615X Personal Computer with Digital Doo-Dah Enhancer"[2] spoke to a universal truth: few of us have the faintest clue about what it all means.

Here's a quick experiment: go online, Google 'laptop' and check out the results.[3] Do you know what, say, an "11th Generation Intel® Core™ i5-1135G7 Processor" is? Do you know what it actually does and how it might make your working life better? Or what it means when a hard drive specification is as follows: "256GB M.2 PCIe NVMe Solid State Drive"? (Aside from the fact that anything 'solid state' has to be impressive, surely?) What about "300 nits of brightness"? And should you be worried about them spreading?

It's not as though Bryson was being obtuse. In his biggest-selling popular science book of the 21st century, *A Short History of Nearly Everything*, he talks about black holes, the Higgs boson and the poetically named Öpik-Oort cloud. For this work, he won the Descartes Prize for Science Communication. Bryson knows his stuff or, as an experienced writer and journalist, he knows where to find the answers to some of the most taxing of questions. He might be self-deprecating, but if the best-selling author can explain many of the deepest secrets of the universe, and yet can't make head nor tail of the way a lot of technology is described, as his gentle mocking suggests, then arguably something isn't quite right.

Procurement of technology can, too often, feel like entering a black hole out of which little or no hope can escape. How can we hope, for example, to understand what's hiding behind all of these acronyms and initialisms? What does it all mean? Where are the definitions? And what is a "M.2 PCIe NVMe" anyway?

The problem is we lawyers don't like to look as though we don't know what we're talking about. As analytical creatures, we're apt to flick on our suspicious, 'don't-bother-me-now' switch if we fail to understand the basics of what we are looking at within a minute or so. It's bad enough trying to find the time to get our heads around a new statute or 150-page judgment, let alone some new legaltech app.

The result of all this? Many of us aren't engaging with procurement like we need to. It feels like it's for someone else in the firm to worry about. Or perhaps some of us do have the IT departments to deal with these sorts of things and the numbers on a computer spec aren't the biggest problem? Instead, the challenge is for things we think we do understand, such as document automation systems or document checking software, where there are still innumerable features and differences between the available systems. So the tyranny of choice rears its head: the fear of making the wrong decision becomes so overwhelming that paralysis sets in and we end up buying nothing.

This chapter helps the reader navigate the universe of procuring technology, avoiding getting near to a black hole in the first place. And even if readers find themselves slipping into a vortex of techno-babble and impenetrable jargon, they shouldn't give up. There is a way out. There is hope. If Stephen Hawking reckoned that there could be an escape route out of a black hole, then procurement doesn't have to be a one-way street into confusion and techy mumbo jumbo. Senior lawyers need to push their suppliers and internal teams to make sense of what really shouldn't be a painful subject.

From the authors' experience, we know that procurement, done properly and with passion has the ability to transform a business.

In fact, for many firms, it's more important than that. Procurement isn't just a nice add-on. While the death of the billable hour has been announced more times than we'd care to remember, alternative fee arrangements (AFAs) are nonetheless increasingly common, including value-based pricing. More often than not, such arrangements demand more efficiency to deliver them within budget (and they require reliable data to arrive at the appropriate fee arrangement). Legaltech and innovation have a key role to play in turbocharging such efficiencies and procurement has, in turn, a key role in getting legaltech and innovation into firms in the right way.

Procurement: the hidden weapon in a firm's armoury? Undoubtedly. It's time to plan, be strategic, and be smarter, faster and better in how we buy the technology our teams need.

In this chapter, we examine:
- the tendency to focus too much on previous bad procurement experiences and the need for a more positive mindset;
- developing a procurement vision and strategy and tying this into other firm visions and strategies (and considering regulatory issues too);
- working out what technology to invest in; and overcoming the typical hurdles to investment;
- working out a procurement budget;
- having a procurement process;
- sharing procurement know-how; and
- working out what innovation to invest in.

The chapter then goes on to consider some case studies and set out practical tips so that the reader can make the right procurement choices.

1. Dealing with the bad news and moving ahead anyway

First, the bad news: procurement can go spectacularly wrong if we take our eyes off the ball. IT projects, in particular, have a notorious track record.

Tens of billions of pounds of public sector money have been wasted over the years on failed IT systems. Plenty of private sector companies have gone bust due to IT disasters and had their reputations sullied. The human cost of the Post Office scandal, where 736 sub-postmasters were wrongly convicted of offences such as theft and false accounting because of a faulty IT system, is a stark reminder of what happens when we continue to operate a procured system, even though the red lights are flashing to turn it off.

First, the bad news: procurement can go spectacularly wrong if we take our eyes off the ball. IT projects, in particular, have a notorious track record.

The National Audit Office (NAO) in a report in 2006 on delivering IT-enabled business change set out the eight most common causes of failure in IT-enabled projects. It's a sobering list of errors. And, by looking to do the opposite, it can also be used as a handy checklist on how to get things right. But we also need to stand back and ask ourselves: how common are these types of failure? How many projects *have* succeeded in the public and private sector? They don't seem to make the news anywhere near as much.

Despite our best intentions, the nature of news, including news on procurement and project management, is that we tend to home in on the bad news stories. The availability bias of such stories, where we focus too much on the information available to us, as opposed to what is more representative, sometimes darkens our views on things like IT procurement. We're rarely told about the successful tech projects. For every single failed IT project in a firm, there are many more which are quietly successful, but guess which ones stick in our minds? Once bitten, twice shy? This is too often the case.

But procurement drives businesses forward. In 2020, McKinsey surveyed 265 businesses. It found that, in the half decade after the 2008 financial crisis, the total return to shareholders for those businesses with procurement capabilities in the top quartile was 42% higher than for those businesses whose capabilities were in the bottom quartile.[4] And it's clear that many law firms are doing remarkable things with procurement too. From the authors' experience, for example, Slaughter and May's procurement team is hugely impressive in terms of how well-resourced and developed it is and, in particular, how well it runs procurement processes and debriefs afterwards. (Legaltech awards also regularly showcase great work in this area too.)

The bad news is that there's not enough good news. Firms need to ensure that they don't go into any procurement with a mindset of 'IT procurement is a nightmare'. This is where a focused technology vision and strategy, with clear and measurable aims, is key.

2. Having a technology vision and strategy

> *The Romans did as all wise rulers should, who have to consider*
> *not only present difficulties but also future, against which they must*
> *use all diligence to provide.*
> Niccolò Machiavelli[5]

Machiavelli understood the need for a strategy: to plan and to look forward; to pre-empt problems; and to spend less time firefighting. He noted that problems are easy to fix before they occur, but once they arrive, they are "easy to recognise but impossible to cure".[6]

Technology is a key area where vision, strategy and clear aims are needed. According to a report by HSBC in 2019 (produced in collaboration with *The Lawyer*), 81% of the firms which they surveyed think that technology is the "most important area of strategic development activity"[7] for them.

2.1 Changing the procurement mindset

Procurement teams have often been accused of not being strategic enough, meaning that these teams can be overlooked or just left to get on with it without the management of the firm being closely enough involved. To state the obvious: procurement is far more nuanced than buying and investing in stuff a firm needs or negotiating discounts off suppliers. A general change in mindset is required.

During the pandemic, many firms were cornered by the unexpected speed of the first lockdown and had to procure a lot of technology quickly. Doing it strategically was the last thing on their minds. Now that the worst of the storm has passed, firms need to be much more strategic in how they source tech. For some, it's time to develop and implement a robust tech vision, strategy and aims to achieve this; for others, they need to re-evaluate and update what they have in place now.

The following questions need to be asked: how does any technology, whether used in the firm itself or passed through to clients, tie in with, for example:
- where the firm is in the market;
- the work which the firm does;
- the vision, strategy and aims of the firm;
- the firm's branding and unique selling proposition (USP); and
- the R&D cycle of the firm, which is often on a different timescale to the profit distribution cycle.

2.2 Considering regulatory issues when procuring

The procurement of technology also needs to comply with the SRA Standards and Regulations. Its guidance on technology needs to be considered carefully, including its compliance tips for solicitors published on the SRA website.[8] (For more on compliance generally, see Chapter 6.)

The SRA expects firms to understand the legal framework which underpins the technology they use, "in particular that [for] AI". The SRA says that a firm's governance frameworks should be "fit-for-purpose".[9] It further notes: "To ensure there is senior leadership and oversight, we would expect as a minimum that the Compliance Officers for Legal Practice (COLP) to be responsible for regulatory compliance when new technology is introduced. Board oversight both of purchasing and ongoing use are also highlighted as critical in managing the risks of technology failure."[10]

2.3 Considering any accreditation requirements

In some cases, a specific strategy on procurement of technology is expected from a third party. For example:

- The quality mark for legal practice, Lexcel, which is run by the Law Society and split into three versions, gives guidance on what accredited firms need to think about when setting their strategy, including identifying resources and then any gaps which need to be addressed. Technology is also a principal resource to consider. It also mentions finance, facilities and HR – three areas in which the procurement of technology can also have a big impact.
- The B Corp certification was set up in 2006 with the mission of business being a force for good. Anthony Collins Solicitors, Bates Wells, Brabners and Radiant Law, for example, are certified under this scheme. Such firms' procurement strategies and processes need to be in line with B Corp standards.
- ISO standards such as ISO 20400 give guidance to organisations who are looking to integrate sustainability with their procurement processes (see also ISO 26000 on social responsibility).

3. Knowing what technology to procure

There's a lot of legaltech on the market. And a lot of noise about it too. In 2021, we saw the first IPOs in legaltech on the NASDAQ:

- LegalZoom (a legal document creation company) in June 2021;
- Intapp (a cloud software solutions company focusing on professional services firms), also in June 2021; and
- CS Disco (a legaltech company offering, among other things, eDiscovery solutions and given the apt stock code of 'LAW') in July 2021.

In the same year, two legaltech businesses also achieved 'unicorn' status; that is, they were valued at more than $1 billion:

- Everlaw (an eDiscovery software company); and
- Clio (a law practice management company).

However, the majority of legaltech providers don't have stock codes or lavish market open ceremonies But big or small, there are many types of legaltech out there. Tech.law.stanford.edu is one of the most recognised directories of legaltech. It splits legaltech into the following nine categories:

- analytics;
- compliance;
- document automation;
- eDiscovery;
- legal education;

- legal research;
- marketplace;
- online dispute resolution (ODR); and
- practice management.

However, no one agrees on exactly how legaltech should be categorised. Tech.law.stanford.edu shows just one way of doing this. Others take a different approach. For example:

- Legaltech Hub (LTH) refers to use cases instead, of which it has listed 18 types of legaltech (at the time of writing); and
- Legal Geek has taken a different approach, which splits legaltech into four main categories (to do with managing the business; managing and doing work; doing work; and consumer-focused matters) and then it lists legaltech subcategories under these.

Other directories include Dealtech and LawSites (and particularly its legaltech start-ups list). As an alternative, tech directories often allow users to search for legaltech businesses and solutions.

It's hardly surprising that knowing what technology to procure can therefore be a daunting prospect. Which one or more of the above categories does a firm need to concentrate its energies on?

That said, many firms find it of interest to see what other firms are focusing on – or indeed not focusing on – in the round. The 31st *PwC Law Firms' Survey* published in 2022[11] found that improving the use of technology was the top priority for the firms surveyed, with data analytics about halfway up the list of priorities; and reducing cyber risk – joint third in the list of priorities – no surprise given how working remotely has increased such risks since the pandemic.

In no particular order, PwC reported that the top three priority areas for future tech investment by law firms in 2021 were in:

- document management systems;
- collaboration tools; and
- matter management.

And it's in these three areas that most firms have already invested. But current investment in more avant-garde technologies, according to the 30th *PwC Law Firms' Survey* (published in 2021),[12] was more subdued:

- contract lifecycle management at 28%;
- robotic process automation (RPA): this can be used, for example, to automate back-office operations, such as processing invoices also at 28%; and

- expertise automation (where lawyers' experience and know-how is shared much better among their teams, often through no-code or low-code applications and powered by AI) sits at 21%.

It seems clear that firms are currently investing in obvious and immediately practically useful technologies, such as document management systems and virtual data rooms, whereas more advanced technologies, such as expertise automation and RPA, are still receiving less attention even though these are the areas which may ultimately have the biggest impact for the profession. Even now, the reports indicate that the immediate future focus will be on practical tools and not on the clever stuff like RPA. Those firms that get ahead of this trend will potentially steal a march.

What's more, investing in one or two large prestige legaltech projects doesn't have to be the only way forward. Vodafone, for example, takes a "thousand flowers"[13] route to legaltech R&D. As Rosemary Martin, Group General Counsel and Company Secretary at Vodafone, explained to *Artificial Lawyer*, Vodafone likes to invest in a lot of small projects as opposed to a small number of large projects. While its IT team (who'd rather not deal with lots of different systems) isn't always fond of such an approach, it does mean that the legal team can be nimble, learn from a larger number of projects and, all being well, produce better solutions.

3.1 Overcoming hurdles

As with almost all things in life, there are hurdles to be negotiated. Table 1 highlights some of the most common hurdles that the authors have seen and what firms can do to overcome them.

Table 1. Hurdles and how to overcome them

Legaltech seller perspective	Firm buyer of legaltech perspective	Authors' view
Legaltech suppliers perceive that it's hard to sell efficiency tools to firms while the predominant client-billing structure is still based on time spent! What's the incentive for lawyers to reduce that time?	Firms know they have to modernise. But in the absence of clients insisting on change as a priority, what's the imperative to make any changes quickly?	Firms which are waiting for clients to complain before making efficiency changes will pretty soon lose their clients to more enlightened firms.

continued on next page

Legaltech seller perspective	Firm buyer of legaltech perspective	Authors' view
The partnership model doesn't lend itself to large investments that are recouped slowly over time.	Firms know they need to invest. But, equally, their next partnership drawings will be directly affected by whatever investments they make today.	Recouping big investments over the mid- to long-term can be a challenging proposition in the partnership structure. However, significant advances can be made without huge expenditure, and the investment can be recouped relatively quickly.
In some cases the tech being offered is considered by firms not to be good enough.	In many cases the tech being offered simply isn't good enough.	Firms should be clear in knowing what their minimum requirements are before commencing procurement. It's true that some legaltech products seem somewhat underdeveloped before they've been launched in the market. However, suppliers are usually keen to hear feedback and to improve their products so that they are fit for purpose. But there's no doubt that firms need to test products carefully before buying them. Insist on a trial of the product before buying.
In some cases, the IT departments of firms want the lawyers to use existing systems before seeking new suppliers.	Many firms will be guided by their IT teams.	The authors' experience is that, in some cases, a universal solution can work for several use cases. But, more often, a universal solution can be far too generic or isn't sufficiently intuitive to use in a particular use case. A best-in-breed solution for every use case is typically the best way to go, particularly for cloud-based SaaS solutions that don't involve much IT team input.

continued on next page

Legaltech seller perspective	Firm buyer of legaltech perspective	Authors' view
The legaltech sales cycle can be long, ie, the time taken for a firm to say "yes" to a product and sign on the dotted line.	Firms often find legaltech sales personnel to be somewhat unrealistic in the time it takes to make a considered decision to commit.	Firms won't be rushed into quick procurement decisions where there's no burning requirement to do so. Also, most lawyers are conservative when it comes to selling their own services to clients and so they don't take kindly to overly pushy legaltech salespeople. Legaltech suppliers need to accept that it's always going to be a slow burn, particularly at the current relatively nascent stage of adoption in the legal sector.
Lawyers may have been scarred by a bad tech procurement experience previously.	Many firms may well have made a wrong decision in the past and whoever was responsible won't be in a hurry to risk making a mistake again.	Firms need to learn from past experience to ensure it doesn't happen again. But they equally shouldn't use that experience as a reason not to procure solutions that can help in the future. If the previous experience has scarred key people too deeply to remain objective, they should let someone else lead the next procurement.

continued on next page

Legaltech seller perspective	Firm buyer of legaltech perspective	Authors' view
Firm IT departments are too busy to provide their input into the procurement process.	Many firms are reluctant to procure legaltech without the IT department by their side and so are dependent on the scheduling of the project within the IT department's overall workload.	Resource can, of course, be an issue, particularly where all legaltech procurements are IT-led. The authors' experience is that many legaltech solutions (particularly cloud-based SaaS solutions) require only minimal input from the IT department as long as the rest of the procurement team have the requisite procurement and project management skills. The authors' firm tends to lead legaltech procurements through its project management team, but the firm includes at least one experienced technology lawyer in the procurement team so that the required IT department input can be minimised and brought in at the right time in the process.

4. Working out a procurement budget

The cost of much technology has dropped dramatically over the years. In 1985, the standard rate of a call from the United Kingdom to the United States was £2.05 a minute, about £5 a minute in today's terms (a half-an-hour call would cost, at this rate, almost £150 in today's money). Nowadays, a business can use software which means that such calls are free.

However, we shouldn't be fooled by this fact; a substantial amount of a firm's finances is spent on technology, both software and hardware:

- According to the HSBC report above, "leading UK headquartered"[14] firms typically expect to invest about 4% to 6% of their revenue in technology, which for most firms is likely to include a lot of IT infrastructure. This investment, according to HSBC, tends to be cyclical between new technologies and those which deal with business-as-usual matters.
- According to the PwC survey referred to above, the average outlay on

legaltech in the top 100 firms – a narrower term than above – is between 0.5% and 0.9% as a percentage of fee income. Larger firms tend to have their own procurement processes and teams to manage legaltech and other types of procurement. These teams can also keep up to date with the latest developments.

As for R&D, 43% of the firms surveyed by HSBC in 2019 put aside a ring-fenced pot of cash just for R&D projects, with about half of firms including R&D in their IT budgets.[15] Ring-fencing cash for R&D can play an important part in helping firms foster a more corporate approach to long-term investment in technology, particularly if it's tailored to the realities of the R&D development cycle, as opposed to the annual profit distribution exercise. What's more, with inflation increasing and the era of cheap money drawing to a close firms will need to be much smarter in their investment strategies.

5. Having a procurement process

The procurement process has its own life cycle: from project cradle to project grave, procurements take on a life of their own, particularly larger ones. The key is to nurture them throughout their existence so that at the start they don't go off the rails like an unruly teenager or, to stretch the analogy, have a mid-life crisis later on. In the end, we need to learn from each project when all is done and dusted.

The procurement lifecycle itself doesn't have an agreed number of steps. (The Chartered Institute of Procurement and Supply's (CIPS) procurement and supply cycle, for example, has 13 steps, although this may be a bit too detailed for small-scale procurements.) That said, the authors' experience is that a lifecycle typically includes the following:

- Considering the regulatory and procurement frameworks that apply or might apply to the procurement process:
  - the regulatory framework: the SRA notes that firms "should have appropriate governance, systems and controls to ensure [they] are using technology responsibly".[16] This includes, but is not limited to, "undertaking risk and impact assessments". Other important laws to consider include data protection laws (eg, undertaking data protection impact assessments); and
  - any procurement frameworks (internal or external): for example, the Institute for Ethical AI and Machine Learning publishes its *AI-RFX Procurement Framework*, which is designed to ensure best practice in the use of machine learning systems.
- Working out what the firm needs or wants, or both. What's the business case and budget? As many IT teams ask themselves at the

beginning of a project: "Do we buy it?" "Do we build it?" "Do we rent it?" (If it's the latter, what are the licensing terms?) How does it fit in with any relevant visions, strategies and related aims?

- Considering whether a project management methodology is required. Do people understand each other in the project, from IT teams to the partners who are looking to procure the tech? Are project managers needed to help manage and 'translate' communications between these two cohorts and any others?
- Considering any non-tech alternatives:
  - is a tech solution needed or is it more trouble than it's worth? Are there any feasible non-tech solutions? From the authors' experience, this isn't always a question that is asked; and
  - for client-facing IT: what options are there for clients who can't or won't use legaltech? For example, as the SRA notes: "Not everyone will be able to or will wish to use legaltech. Give them other options to work with you."[17] It goes on to ask: "Do consumers have a choice over whether to use lawtech-based services or not? Is there any convenience or cost detriment if they do so?"
- Working out a potential list of suppliers. There are increasingly curated (non-exhaustive) directories of legaltech providers which can help law firms source products, such as the AL 100 Legal Tech Directory (from *Artificial Lawyer*); Crafty Counsel, which directs users to suppliers via its (A)LSP Circuit Board; Global Legal Tech Directory; LTH; and the directories mentioned above. The Stanford CodeX Center for Legal Informatics also curates a list of "companies changing the way legal is done".[18]
- Agreeing to work with a supplier and doing due diligence on them, including any relevant credit checks. This may also involve meeting with the supplier. Due diligence is also required in order to comply with SRA standards and regulations.
- Working out what testing may be required and working with both technical team members and intended users of the system (and, where appropriate, clients) to test, trial and gather feedback.
- Working out the terms and conditions and understanding the extent to which they can be negotiated. This is where firms should factor in any input from the procurement team (and not just on price!). What KPIs are required?
- Determining what security is in place. In 2018, the Law Society and the National Cyber Security Centre (NCSC) published a paper on the steps firms can take for the safe use of technology.[19] This paper gives a good overview of best tips in using IT safely (although, given the date of the paper, further security developments will have taken place since that date and should be considered).
- Monitoring on an ongoing basis. Is this done as a matter of course?

The SRA notes that it expects the "monitoring and evaluation impact of ... technology to avoid unintended consequences".[20]

- Learning from the whole process. After the procurement is done, is there anything that could have been done better? Was there anything that went particularly well? We also need to get better at shouting about our successes, both for internal and external purposes!

A procurement process should also ideally set out how to make the transition from any old systems to new ones following any 'digital hygiene' processes too. As noted in Chapter 1, change can be difficult for people to deal with, so any procurement needs to factor in any resistance to new tech. Training is likely to be required in many cases.

For public-sector organisations, there are also specific procurement laws and guidance (eg, the *Data Ethics Framework*) that must be followed, including sector-specific rules, such as the Office for AI's *Guidelines for AI Procurement*. At the time of writing, the Procurement Bill was also passing through its parliamentary stages.

In developing a procurement process, the following may also be relevant:
- In July 2021, the Law Society published a model process for the procurement of legaltech in its *Lawtech and Ethics Principles*.[21] It's aimed at firms who are less familiar with legaltech and who may not have the internal support to help in the procurement process. In its guidance on using legaltech in firms it also contains helpful checklists such as on semi-automated online legal services. But these resources aren't maintained, so it's worth checking the date of publications: things move quickly in IT procurement.
- Lexcel is light on procurement, but it does give high-level guidance on strategy, which should ensure that the relevant firms think about what procurement processes they have in place.
- CIPS publishes its *Global Standard for Procurement and Supply* (currently on version 4).[22] In Segment 3.3, it expects that managers know and understand developments in technology when procuring.
- Other organisations such as the Buying Legal Council, "the international trade organisation for legal procurement", has best practice guidance in buying legaltech, although it tends to concentrate on helping businesses buy legal services as opposed to firms buying tech.

Ultimately, firms need to ensure that their processes are robust and contribute to furthering the firm's vision, strategies and aims.

Ultimately, firms need to ensure that their processes are robust and contribute to furthering the firm's vision, strategies and aims.

6. Sharing procurement knowledge

In September 2019, the Law Society published its report on *Technology, Access to Justice and the Rule of Law*. In it, it recommended that "the advice sector and private practices should share information on the adoption and application of legaltech within their organisations, as well as any evaluation of these projects".[23] At the time of writing, we're not aware of any widespread system in place where such sharing of know-how takes place. There's also been much talk about a register of trusted, available tech.

Could firms who've been through the pain of legaltech procurement perhaps contribute to a curated database for the benefit of other firms? This might not only list exactly what the tech does in a highly nuanced form, but also show how good it is at doing those things. From this, all could benefit from the huge amount of due diligence that other firms have already done on the tech. This could, if done well, save the legal profession collectively a significant amount of time and money.

The amount of due diligence that firms currently need to undertake should not be underestimated. At the time of writing, one of the authors had attended his fifteenth internal meeting on adopting a proposed piece of software. The group had already eliminated at least three suppliers because it was obvious, from even a cursory examination, that their systems simply couldn't do what the firm needed (and, indeed, couldn't do what the tech purported to be able to do!). Of the two remaining suppliers, one system appeared to be incapable of keeping documents formatted in the way the group wanted. The other had such a long time lag when using it that it drove the relevant team to distraction. Each of these products purported, on the face of it, to offer fantastic functionality and user experience. None of them did. This sort of know-how has immense value, but it is rarely shared.

And if larger firms, with lots of resources, find this tricky, what chance do small firms have? This may be why almost all of the small firms in an SRA compliance officers conference at which one of the authors spoke raised their hands when asked if they would value information on procuring new tech.

The SRA is keen to do more in this area. If it has the resources to be as proactive as it would like, and has the support of the profession, it might be in a position to offer 'tech assurance', such as guides, checklists and flowcharts on using specific technologies, but this is all still aspirational at the time of writing.

7. Knowing what innovation to invest in

So far, we've concentrated on the procurement of technology, but we mustn't forget about other forms of innovation too. As we mention in this book, change doesn't always involve a technological solution.

Innovation isn't something which can be plucked off a supermarket shelf or cobbled together in a few minutes on a couple of Excel spreadsheets. Rather, it is more of an innovation mindset that firms need to develop (as this book sets out). And some mindsets are tricky to budge. Legal strategy consultant Eric Chin (who is thought to have coined the 'NewLaw' moniker) says lawyers should be particularly concerned, for example, when they hear people say: "we have always done it this way".[24] Chin often refers to this as the seven most costly words in legal practice. As Chin notes, this sort of passive attitude can ultimately lead firms down costly routes – and no doubt costly cul-de-sacs too from time to time.

In recent years, we've seen the concept of legal operations or 'legal ops' used increasingly in the context of both firms and in-house legal teams. Legal ops analysis can help firms, and in-house teams, understand where to best deploy improvements and innovation. Corporate Legal Operations Consortium (CLOC), for example, has created the 'CLOC Core 12' to categorise the work of legal departments into 12 core functional areas. Any one of these areas, from business intelligence (BI) to training, from knowledge management to the organisation's financials, can see innovation make a real difference.

Firms and in-house teams can learn from this categorisation when working out the improvements and innovation that can be introduced into their practices, either by trying to make changes themselves or by engaging external consultants to help them do so.

And, as always, people shouldn't be sidelined in this process.

The authors' firm, for example, has created a six-step programme for in-house teams, called 'Hexagon'. The point of the programme is to help optimise in-house legal ops. It can also be applied to help firms identify improvement and innovation opportunities in their businesses:
- start with an exploratory session with senior leaders to establish current challenges in the business;
- hold exploratory sessions with key business stakeholders to establish current requirements;
- hold team workshops to report on the exploratory sessions; review data; and engage in a collaborative discussion to identify improvement and innovation opportunities;

- create a strategy plan: this would bring together the threads from the exploratory sessions and workshops in a comprehensive strategy with operational recommendations, deployment guidance and indicative ROI;
- manage the deployment of the agreed strategy and implement any new improvements, innovations, policies and procedures; and
- finish by holding periodic check-in workshops to analyse longer-term success and any areas for recalibration over time.

Some other large firms and the Big Four also offer legal operations services, along with a number of independent specialists.

The subject of legal operations could take up a whole book. As a result, the commentary on this subject in this work is brief, but there's no doubt that, through legal ops, firms can streamline what they do. And people in these firms will see the benefits of this, which, in turn, can make it much easier to embed a culture of innovation into their firms.

8. Case studies

8.1 Case study 1: Procurement of a best-in-class document automation system

More and more law firms are using document automation systems to speed up document production and ensure that their firm's output is as consistent as possible. Typically, a lawyer will fill in a questionnaire in which they answer a series of questions. These can range from 'what are the parties' names?' to questions of a more legal nature, such as: 'do you want to include a confidentiality clause?'. In theory, they take the pain out of creating the first draft of documents. But not every system is the same; they are surprisingly difficult to get right. The principle sounds easy enough; the execution often isn't.

For several years the authors' firm had been using a third-party document automation platform to enable it to produce client-facing documents. Although the system had a high degree of technical functionality, there were aspects the firm wanted to improve, namely:
- the process of automating existing Word templates wasn't intuitive and required the firm to engage a number of coders for this purpose;
- the user interface wasn't user-friendly and, although regular users who were familiar with it coped well, new users took some time to get to grips with how it worked; and
- the licensing terms from the tech supplier allowed only the firm to use the system. It precluded the firm from allowing its clients direct

access to use the system themselves, unless they each purchased their own licence (which was too expensive to make that feasible).

The firm was conscious that, since it originally procured its chosen platform, several new document automation systems had been released in the market and it was keen to explore whether any of these might address the three areas of concern above, while still meeting the firm's technical requirements and, last but not least, being affordable.

In running a procurement exercise to explore whether a replacement system would serve the firm better, it adopted the tips and practices set out in this chapter. Of particular note:

- The procurement team included not only procurement, project management and IT expertise but also:
  - users of the current platform, who were well placed to both observe differences between the current system and others; and also to test the functionality and user interface of the alternative systems in absolute terms;
  - two commercial partners who were keen to extend document automation capability beyond merely internal use, so that they could also offer to automate clients' templates for their own internal use. Having discussed this with clients, they felt this would be a compelling offer, given that it gives them all the advantages of having their own document automation platform but without: (a) having to go through an extensive procurement exercise themselves; and (b) without clients having to purchase their own licences to use the document automation platform; and
  - a representative from the compliance, quality and risk team, to address aspects such as:
    - could the firm offer a document automation service to clients given that it's an SRA-regulated body? SRA Innovate was extremely helpful in helping to answer this;
    - would the firm's insurance cover such an activity and what requirements would the insurers have? The firm had discussions with its brokers to establish the answers;
    - what residual risk would the firm be taking on as a result of the tech supplier limiting their liability to it to a level much lower than the minimum level the firm is required to offer to its clients under SRA rules? The conclusion was that there would be a gap, but that risk would be managed by: (a) extensive testing of the accuracy and reliability of the platform with periodic human spot checking; (b) being careful to pass the ultimate risk of checking the documents produced to the client; and (c) insurance cover in any event; and

- ensuring that the use of the document automation platform by the firm's clients would not unwittingly put it in breach of conflict of interest rules. Having considered this, the procurement team ensured that the tech supplier blocked the firm from having any access to any data being entered onto the document automation platform by clients. The team also proposed an end-user licence agreement directly between the tech provider and the client to cover data protection responsibilities between them directly.

- The procurement team identified a long list of four suppliers, in addition to the incumbent, who (from their marketing material) appeared to offer the functionality that the firm needed. It became clear from just a cursory examination that, in fact, two of those five were simply not fit for purpose because they couldn't maintain document clause numbering and font type as part of the automation process (which, for legal documents, is a pretty basic requirement).

- This left the firm with a shortlist of three: the incumbent and two new suppliers. As the procurement team was already fully familiar with the functionality of the incumbent, it tested the two newcomers intensively for two months and identified that:

  - each of the two new systems was easier to code and had a more intuitive user interface than the incumbent;

  - each of the two new systems had equal functionality with each other, but neither had the extensive degree of functionality of the incumbent that was needed for producing the most complex documents;

  - but each of the two new systems offered licence terms that *would* allow the firm's clients to use the system themselves (unlike the incumbent).

From this, there was one key takeaway: the team concluded that, in fact, it wasn't going to find a single platform that would be suitable both for the firm's own internal use and for the use of clients directly. Therefore, it decided to retain the incumbent for internal use and procure one of the new systems for client use. (This demonstrates that a best-in-class multiple solution approach is often right, because otherwise by choosing just one single system the firm would either compromise its internal functionality or have to abandon offering a document automation service to its clients.)

- This left the firm to decide which of the two new systems to adopt for client use. Given that the two systems were highly comparable, in the end that decision was made based on the fact that one had ISO27001 accreditation and the other did not.

- Having decided on the preferred client-facing solution the firm then approached a small number of forward-thinking clients to

trial the offering for three months. That process was invaluable to:
- identify additional functionality that clients would find useful. The supplier welcomed the feedback and was keen and able to build that additional functionality in a matter of days; and
- verify the benefits that the offering gave to clients, including:
  - time saved in producing documents;
  - increased consistency in the documents produced;
  - increased ease of non-lawyers producing documents; and
  - better control of risk by allowing more complex and protective documents to be produced even by non-lawyers.

At the time of writing, the new document automation offering has completed its beta phase and is about to be launched for general use by clients.

8.2 Case study 2: Procurement of best-in-class document checking software

As well as producing first drafts of thousands of documents each year (a process which, as mentioned above, can be made vastly more efficient through document automation), law firms also have to check every document when they're in their proposed final forms before signature. Getting this right is key to good client service. Misspelling a client's name or getting their address wrong, for example, means they often start to doubt the quality of the rest of the document: "what else have they got wrong?"; "how can I trust that they've got all the 'legals' right?" If what we lawyers do is all about attention to detail, not attending to such detail is unforgivable.

Usually, documents are checked after the document has been through several rounds of negotiation and numerous draft versions. All sorts of gremlins can unwittingly creep into the document as it passes between lawyers and parties, so a final pre-signing check is both routine and important. To date, most firms have undertaken this checking manually, deploying trainees or junior associates to perform this task.

Software is now available that can vastly reduce the time it takes a person to check a document, including, among many other clever things:
- directing the checker to contract particulars (names, addresses, amounts, dates etc) so they can be checked quickly rather than having to scour the entire document for them manually (and risk overlooking some);
- identifying any terms in clauses that purport to be defined but for which no definition has been included;
- identifying definitions that have been included but which are not used anywhere in the document; and
- verifying clause numbering and cross-referencing.

By adopting document checking software there is, therefore, the obvious potential to:

- reduce considerably the time it takes a trainee or associate to check a document, thus releasing extra capacity to undertake other productive work;
- allow a faster turnaround of the document, thus giving a faster service to the client; and
- increase the accuracy of document checking given that, with the best will in the world, human eyes will never be able to spot all the potential mistakes in a 100-page contract, the vast majority of which (if not all) the software will pick up with effortless accuracy.

A procurement team in the authors' firm embarked on the procurement of a suitable system, once again adopting the guidance in this chapter. Of particular note:

- It identified three products that, in their marketing material, purported to do what was needed. The team arranged an initial demonstration by each of the three suppliers to see what their software offered. Each of them seemed, on its face, to be able to perform the tasks that were needed. The team then arranged with each supplier to undertake more detailed assessment of their product in a two-month trial (undertaken by professional support lawyers from each of the firm's legal disciplines).
- It identified a preferred supplier relatively quickly, because:
  - one of the three systems simply took too long to load, making the user interface fiendishly frustrating and compromising considerably the potential time savings that the firm wanted to achieve;
  - the remaining two systems were highly comparable in functionality and user interface. However, one distinguished itself by having a feature that the firm hadn't originally specified: it allows the user to click on a definition and the software will automatically open a pane in which all clauses containing that definition can be viewed easily. It quickly became clear that, not only is this a function that assists with a final check of a document, but also (more generally) it allows lawyers to review long, complex documents more easily on screen by quickly navigating the lawyer to all the relevant parts of the contract that contain a particular definition. The team realised that this could deliver several benefits over and above those which it was originally expecting for a document checking system:
    - many lawyers still print off hard copies of contracts to review them, preferring the ability to flick quickly between the pages with their fingers to navigate the document. This software not only allows a lawyer to have several viewing

panes open at the same time on screen, but – fundamentally – also directs the lawyer to those parts of the contract which are related to each other. This functionality means that it's so much easier to review long documents on screen, potentially greatly reducing the amount of printing the firm does (thus both reducing costs and being more environmentally sustainable);

– given that almost all of the firm's lawyers now work from home at least part of the time, this also reduces the need to provide and maintain home printers; and

– because fewer documents need to be printed at home, there's less need for shredding documents at home and a reduced risk that any hard-copy documents might not be disposed of securely at home.

For all of those reasons, the team decided to make that tech provider the preferred supplier. This goes to show that, even in the best run procurements, things can arise – good and bad – that weren't originally anticipated; in this case luckily it happened to be a good thing that arose!

• Document checking systems have the potential, given the huge volume of documents that law firms produce, to deliver huge benefits. Equally, these systems are not inexpensive and require a considerable commitment of budget to purchase a licence. To secure that budget within the firm, the team had to submit a strong business case based on robust data to demonstrate the anticipated return on investment. Accordingly:

· as well as the procurement team making its own estimates of potential time and cost savings, it asked the supplier to provide it with (anonymised) data on the savings achieved by other firms using the system (which aligned very closely with the firm's own estimates);

· the team agreed with the supplier to initially roll out the system to one-fifth of the firm's lawyers for a three-month period for a relatively low licence cost. If, at the end of the three months, the firm is content that it's deriving the benefits that it anticipates, it can then proceed to extend the licence to more users at an increased cost that (the firm can be certain) will deliver a ROI at least as strong as had been initially projected.

9. Practical tips on procurement

We set out below some practical tips on procurement.

These tips are split as follows:
- considering your need for the tech;
- taking the first steps;
- understanding the nature of the technology;
- understanding the nature of the suppliers;
- implementing the solution; and
- considering after-purchase matters.

9.1 Considering your need for the tech
- What's the business case for the technology? What need or issue does it address? Never procure a tech solution for tech's sake: always start with your needs or those of your clients.
- Consider the extent to which it will improve your working life. How will it make you better at what you do?
- For in-house teams, consider how does it increase your value and that of your team? Does it help you be a stronger partner to your business?
- Have any internal solutions been considered? Is some tech being used elsewhere in your organisation that might be repurposed for what you need?
- When looking to procure solutions to meet a need within your firm, always consider whether that need also exists for your clients and whether your procurement can be applied for the benefit of clients as well. (Considering this at the outset will ensure that your subsequent procurement process always has in mind that client-centred use case as well as your principal internal use case. But be sure not to compromise the solution you are procuring for your own use – that was the primary purpose, after all).
- Beware of building your own bespoke solutions in-house. A good third-party solution may already exist. Do not underestimate the time, cost and expertise involved in developing your own tech solution. And if you do, there is a good chance that someone else may come up with a superior solution in just a few years' time. There may be exceptions to this general rule:
  - if you wish to monetise the solution by selling it to other users and not merely using it to meet your own needs. Owning the IP in your own system is an advantage in that case;
  - if what you build makes your output better than everyone else's;
  - if your need is very particular and a ready-made solution is just not available.

If you're intent on building the solution, you can get quotes from external developers. But also consider whether you could collaborate with an existing tech provider (see Chapter 5).

- Don't be put off doing something now! Technology is constantly evolving and new and better solutions will always come along later, but you could end up just waiting and doing nothing.

9.2 Taking the first steps

- Speak to your friends and contacts in other firms to ask them whether they have identified a similar need and if they have procured a tech solution and how they have found it. This could save you months of work.
- Assemble the right team with the right expertise for the procurement in question. Procuring legaltech successfully involves so many elements that might be relatively new to your firm's mainstream procurement team (such as dealing with regulatory aspects, gathering users' and clients' input, negotiating with tech start-ups, developing new user interfaces etc). The team might be somewhat wider in expertise and involve more people than has historically been the case in your firm.
- Identify early on whether the policy of your firm is to procure a best-in-breed solution or whether the preference is to establish whether existing solutions or suppliers can be extended or modified to the need in question. Although there are schools of thought that businesses should have a limited number of tech solutions, and try to apply them as broadly as possible, the authors' experience is that best-in-breed solutions work best and that a more limited approach leads to suboptimal solutions. (A good example is document automation. One solution might be needed internally for highly complex documents. On the other hand, you may just want a more basic and intuitive system for making simple document automation directly available for use by clients.)
- Be clear on your specification for the solution from the outset. It should be written in terms of the outputs that it needs to deliver. Inevitably the specification may need to include some technical language; but your guiding light must always be what the tech needs to achieve for you and not the nuts and bolts (or rather, the coding and algorithms) of how it achieves that behind the scenes.
- Don't ask for the moon on a stick when deciding on your specification! The authors have had countless discussions with lawyers who, when offered a great solution that will dramatically improve their efficiency, will then pause for a minute and ask, 'but can it do x, y and z as well?' Better is better. Don't fall into the trap of allowing the pursuit of perfection (or, in procurement terms, unnecessary scope

creep) to get in the way of significant improvement. After all, 80% better is better than 0% better.

9.3 Understanding the nature of the technology

- Try before you buy. There may well be a cost associated with this, but that may be negotiable, particularly with start-up tech businesses that want to gain early customers and market share. What's more, most legaltech suppliers recognise that you will need to satisfy yourself that the solution works for you. Give yourself a realistically long time to undertake a meaningful examination of the solution the supplier is offering.
- Ensure the solution is easy and intuitive to use: even the most powerful technology will be hard and expensive to implement if people find it difficult to use or if it requires a lot of training (or both). Look for software that's designed specifically with lawyers in mind or, even better, designed by lawyers for lawyers.
- Consider the cost-benefit analysis and ROI. Ask the tech providers if they can give you an indicative ROI for the solution you're looking at. Some providers are starting to give this sort of information on their websites. Others will give you data they have compiled from firms actually using their system.
- How many people know how it works? One in-house lawyer the authors spoke to said buying something esoteric might be appealing at first, but if the technology isn't well known in the marketplace and highly specialised staff are required to run it, what happens if those staff become unavailable or leave? The firm ends up, potentially, with a risky single point of failure.
- Find out the weaknesses in systems: there will always be some. And some may be so fundamental that, unless the supplier can rectify them quickly, you'll need to go with another supplier. Be wary about accepting promises to rectify errors – even contractual promises – rather than finding an alternative product that does not have errors in the functionality that you need.
- If there is a shortfall in what the tech solution can deliver, consider whether a human overlay could close any shortfall in the tech's functions rather than seeking to close the gap with more tech. The additional marginal costs of getting tech to a level of near 100% accuracy (if this is even possible) might outweigh the benefits.
- Consider what level of configuration to your requirements is required. You may be surprised in some cases by how quick and easy this can be. In other cases, it can be incredibly time consuming and costly and require a lot of your resources to achieve. Always find this out before committing to the system.

- Consider its installation: bear in mind that web-based solutions will require less input from your IT teams because they don't need to be installed on your IT systems (the IT team will, of course, still rightly want to investigate the security aspects of any web/cloud-based system).
- Ensure that whatever data you input into a tech platform can be easily exported to a new platform when it (inevitably) comes along.

9.4 Understanding the nature of the suppliers

- Don't assume that you'll get a better service from long-established tech providers than from new start-ups, who are often hungrier for business and less complacent about customer satisfaction.
- Always ask about the product development roadmap and establish what degree of influence you as a customer will have on that.
- Often the terms of supply offered by the supplier will be negotiable to an extent. That extent may be greater for relative newcomers to the market. Also, consider whether you can negotiate a discount in return for offering a case study or quote in support of the product – many new suppliers that are keen to establish a credible client base will entertain that idea.

9.5 Implementing the solution

- Consider the onboarding process: check how much time, cost and resource it's going to take.
- Roll out a pilot with a small cohort initially so you can iron out glitches before firm-wide application. The easiest way to get a tech project to fail is for people to lose confidence in it the first time they try to use it.
- Ensure your internal support teams work with the lawyers when selecting and trialling tech solutions: involving end users will ensure that the user experience is put at the forefront.
- Always ensure there is going to be a benefit to lawyers in using tech when procuring tech that is going to be used by them – otherwise the only way they'll use it is with you applying a stick. Carrots are much more effective.

9.6 Considering after-purchase matters

- Check the level of support you'll receive after purchase.
- Ensure you can and do monitor usage. If take up is lower than you wanted, find out why and do something about it.
- Seek regular feedback on what you have implemented – always ensure your users still like the solution and that the initial flush of enthusiasm is not then overtaken by a more negative reception.
- Ask your users for potential improvements in the system and

suggest these to your suppliers to see if they are on their development roadmap or can be added to it.

- Always be aware of new products emerging on the market. In any event, in good time before your solution approaches its end of licence or renewal date, put in place another procurement exercise to test the market to see if there is now a better alternative available. The legaltech market is developing so quickly that this is entirely possible.

Notes

1   Bill Bryson, "Bryson's America: Congratulations. You are about to be driven insane" (*The Independent*, 29 November 1999), www.independent.co.uk/arts-entertainment/bryson-s-america-congratulations-you-are-about-to-be-driven-insane-1129608.html.
2   *Ibid.*
3   The authors found the Dell Inspiron 15 2-in-1 laptop, hence our query on what's an 11th Generation Intel® Core™ i5-1135G7 Processor?
4   Tarandeep Singh Ahuja, Yen Ngai, Sukrut Kharia and Harkanwal Singh Sidhu "Reimagining procurement for the next normal" (McKinsey & Company, 26 August 2020), www.mckinsey.com/capabilities/operations/our-insights/reimagining-procurement-for-the-next-normal.
5   Quoted in Jonathan Powell, *The New Machiavelli* (The Bodley Head, 2010), p171.
6   *Ibid*, p172.
7   "Legal tech analysis" (HSBC, 2019), www.business.hsbc.uk/-/media/library/business-uk/pdfs/hsbc-2019-legal-tech-report.pdf.
8   "Compliance tips for solicitors" (Solicitors Regulation Authority), www.sra.org.uk/solicitors/resources/sra-innovate/law-firms/compliance-tips-for-solicitors/.
9   *Ibid.*
10   *Ibid.*
11   *Annual Law Firms' Survey 2022: Agility through turbulent times* (PwC, 2022), www.pwc.co.uk/industries/legal-professional-business-support-services/law-firms-survey.html.
12   *Facing the future with confidence PWC Law Firms' Survey 2021* (PwC, 2021), www.pwc.co.uk/industries/law-firms/law-firm-survey-report-2021.pdf.
13   "The Legal Sector R&D Gap: 1% vs 5% Average" (*Artificial Lawyer*, 26 July 2021), www.artificiallawyer.com/2021/07/26/the-legal-sector-rd-gap-1-vs-5-average/.
14   "Legal tech analysis" (HSBC, 2019), www.business.hsbc.uk/-/media/library/business-uk/pdfs/hsbc-2019-legal-tech-report.pdf.
15   *Ibid.*
16   "Compliance tips for solicitors" (Solicitors Regulation Authority), www.sra.org.uk/solicitors/resources/sra-innovate/law-firms/compliance-tips-for-solicitors/.
17   *Ibid.*
18   "Discover Legal Technology" (Stanford Law School), https://techindex.law.stanford.edu.
19   *The cyber threat to UK legal sector* (National Cyber Security Centre), www.ncsc.gov.uk/files/the_cyber_threat_to_uk_legal_sector_NCSC_2.pdf.
20   "Compliance tips for solicitors" (Solicitors Regulation Authority), www.sra.org.uk/solicitors/resources/sra-innovate/law-firms/compliance-tips-for-solicitors/.
21   Law Society Lawtech and Ethics Principles (Law Society, July 2021), https://prdsitecore93.azureedge.net/-/media/files/topics/research/lawtech-and-ethics-principles-report.pdf?rev=f85012d16bf142a78fc222352a98d5aa&hash=3AB88DE062F031E736157CB8142C6F24.
22   "Global Standard for Procurement and Supply" (CIPS), https://globalstandard.cips.org/.
23   *Technology, Access to Justice and the Rule of Law* (Law Society), https://prdsitecore93.azureedge.net/-/media/files/topics/research/technology-access-to-justice-rule-of-law-report.pdf?rev=7e0b66965a484682828cf0636ec55980&hash=FE6B57256242EB420046FFF0505A02FA.
24   "Interview with Eric Chin, the man who coined the phrase 'NewLaw'" (*Josef*, 9 April 2019), https://joseflegal.com/blog/interview-with-eric-chin-the-man-who-coined-the-phrase-newlaw/%3E/.

Chapter 5:
Collaborate to innovate

Wasei-eigo are 'English' expressions used in Japan which are loosely based on a combination of various English words, or parts of them. To English-speaking ears these innovative linguistic collaborations are often meaningless. Consider, for example, the *wasei-eigo* nominee for buzzword of the year in 2013: *furaingu getto* (or 'flying get'), which means to purchase something ahead of its official sales launch, like a new video game or pair of trainers. Sounding like a term of Cockney abuse, this linguistic mashup is still, by all accounts, popular and figuratively flying off the shelves in Tokyo and Osaka. To English-speakers, it just leaves us scratching our heads.

To many lawyers, innovation can seem like an impenetrable, made-up foreign language. It feels like an area full of jargon, buzzwords and terms almost as nonsensical as *furaingu getto*.

However, as this chapter shows, innovation and working together in a common endeavour is something that we humans have been doing since time immemorial. We're hardwired to do it. It's an activity that's fundamental to our species and is key to flourishing in the legal world of the future.

In this chapter, we explore:
 • understanding the importance of collaboration;

- collaborating to create the 'magic'; and
- getting the timing right.

The chapter then goes on to look at some case studies and set out practical tips to help the reader before, during and after a collaboration project.

1. Understanding the importance of collaboration

Our understanding about human evolution is, like the process itself, evolving. Why are we the way we are and how have we managed to be so successful? Because we're violent? Caring? Clever? Or are we just impressive hunter-gatherers? In recent years, many academics have taken a more cross-disciplinary approach, plundering the fields of genetics, neurobiology, psychology, anthropology, archaeology and palaeontology, to try to work out what the secret to our success is.

Biological anthropologist Agustín Fuentes believes he has the answer. In *The Creative Spark* he says that the "cocktail of creativity and collaboration distinguishes our species".[1] In other words, our imagination and ability to work with each other has powered us to do remarkable things. Fuentes reminds us, while the creative spark is in all of us, it isn't a solitary pursuit. The "interconnections of ideas, experiences and imagination"[2] are the wellspring of, and key to, creativity. And thus innovation.

At times, however, the temptation is to become more risk-averse and hunker down – to stick to the 'natural ways'. Researchers call this 'threat rigidity'. We can almost visualise the stiff, caught-in-the-headlights demeanour of business people who have to deal with unexpected threats to their livelihoods. The world is full of volatility, uncertainty, complexity and ambiguity – VUCA for short – and this is increasing year on year. At times, creating a new innovative product might seem superfluous: a nice-to-have, if not decadent.

But perhaps it is time for VUCA 2.0: "vision, understanding, courage and adaptability".[3]

Research on the 2008 financial crisis indicates that collaboration – in the spirit of VUCA 2.0 – leads to sustainably higher commercial performance. In one firm studied, "the most highly collaborative workers – the top 10% – grew their business during the crisis and continued that upward trajectory afterward".[4] They expanded their networks and worked with more people. They pursued new opportunities "even when it meant getting less personal glory on a project-by-project basis".[5] On the other hand, the research showed that the revenue generated by the least innovative groups in the firm contracted and still hadn't recovered five years after the end of the recession.

In the VUCA-laden (and often recessionary) years ahead, thinking and acting creatively and working with others will be key to lawyers thriving in the profession.

2. Collaborating to create the 'magic'

Following a chance meeting in 1957, John Lennon and Paul McCartney went on to form *The Beatles*, creating an icon of the 1960s that revolutionised music. Yet they were an unusual pairing.

It was said that McCartney was good at communicating whereas Lennon sometimes struggled to get his ideas across. McCartney wanted to smooth things over; Lennon wanted to shake things up. McCartney was polite; Lennon often wasn't. McCartney wasn't a fan of being criticised; Lennon was happy to hear what others thought. Writing the music was intense. Lennon called it "writing eyeball to eyeball".[6] But it worked.

What's more, they loved technology. They were innovators, using all manner of (then) unconventional recording techniques. They would try new things and if they didn't work they'd scrap them. They were always pushing to do things differently.

The band didn't just influence music, it also inspired many businesspeople. Steve Jobs, part of one of the most famous collaborations in tech history (with Steve Wozniak) and whose corporation – Apple Computer – had been in litigation with the band's record company, Apple Corps, said in an interview that his model in business was *The Beatles*. He liked how, together, they found an equilibrium and that collectively the musical team was bigger than the sum of its parts: "great things in business are never done by one person, they're done by a team of people", Jobs said.[7]

The dynamics of legal innovation are no different to that of Apple Computer or Apple Corps: a common purpose and each contributor bringing different but complementary attributes to the party to create something amazing that can't be achieved alone.

So what 'bottles' can the contributors to a legaltech collaboration typically bring to the party?

'Bottles' that the authors have seen in our collaboration projects include:
- identifying a genuine need that doesn't currently have an effective solution;
- identifying an existing solution that can be made much more efficient, accurate, faster, cheaper, accessible etc;

The dynamics of legal innovation are no different to that of Apple Computer or Apple Corps: a common purpose and each contributor bringing different but complementary attributes to the party to create something amazing that can't be achieved alone.

- an idea for the adaption of an existing technology in a new context (ie, applying that existing tech to a new 'use case');
- specialisms that are vital to delivering the new solution or use case;
- know-how or previous experience of doing something similar;
- relevant data (see also Chapter 2);
- resources, which include the people to develop, support and market the innovation;
- routes-to-market to commercialise and exploit the innovation;
- credibility (eg, legaltech 'designed by lawyers for lawyers' generally carries more credibility, with lawyers anyway);
- money for product development and sales; and
- sheer creativity (of course, lawyers aren't or often do not see themselves as being creative; we're trained to look at things with sceptical eyes. We need to be able to work with people who can bring creative 'bottles' to the party. We can't always be trusted to do it alone).

3. Getting the timing right

No wonder *The Beatles* sung that they'd been "working like a dog". The band worked prodigiously. But hard work only gets you so far. Timing is often overlooked, but is crucial too.

In the case of *The Beatles*, their manager, Brian Epstein – sometimes referred to as the 'fifth Beatle' – had a key role to play in the timing of *The Beatles*' success, finally managing to get the group signed to EMI's small Parlophone label in 1962. As former *Rolling Stones* manager Andrew Loog Oldham recalled, their music "was the sound of the future".[8] During a torrid winter of mourning in the United States, after the assassination of John F Kennedy in November 1963, the playing of *I Want to Hold Your Hand* on Washington DC radio station WWDC in December of that year caused a sensation. It was the right time for the sound of the future.

Studies have shown that timing is one of the most important factors when assessing business success. Take Airbnb: its exponential growth was due to its timing. Launched during the 2008 financial crisis, the rental business fulfilled a vital need as homeowners wanted, and often needed, to lease out space in their homes to supplement their income.

Put simply, are people ready for what you're offering? Timing is tricky. In Silicon Valley, it's often said that "being early is the same as being wrong". There's even a name for this predicament: the 'Collingridge dilemma'. This quandary, coined over four decades ago by an academic at the University of Aston, David Collingridge, in a book about assessing technology, explains why understanding and acting upon new technologies and innovation is so tough. It goes like this:

- The consequences of using a new technology or innovation are usually only fully understood when they're in use. We often don't know in advance what the tech will ultimately look like, how it will be deployed in practice and, most importantly, whether customers will love, hate or be indifferent to it.
- But by the time it's in use, it's difficult to change course. It might not work as expected or there may be unforeseen consequences. But the proverbial genie is out of the bottle.

Lawyers operate in a fiercely conservative sector. Inevitably, many will dig in their heels as long as they can. The upshot is that opportunities may be lost. Finding the Goldilocks principle – when it's not too soon to act, but not too late either – isn't easy.

When fast timing is everything collaborating can have the benefit of bringing something to market much more quickly. For example, the authors have experienced this where:

- they've re-purposed an existing tech product to a new use case, rather than building it from scratch, which would've take much longer;
- less time was needed to beta test a new product to ensure it worked because it was based on an existing platform that was already tried and tested;
- internal approvals to proceed with projects are typically more quickly and easily granted than otherwise would be the case, because the risks and costs are much lower in a collaboration than when going it alone; and
- the broad and deep collective experience of the contributors avoids making many of the mistakes a less wary sole venturer may make.

In the long run, forward-thinking, innovative lawyers who spot interesting possibilities and act on them are the ones likely to come out on top.

4. Case studies

4.1 Case study 1: Collaborating to bring a new legaltech product to market

The authors' firm has close connections to the in-house legal community, with a lot of its commercial work coming from in-house teams. Many of the firm's commercial lawyers have themselves worked in-house. In discussions with in-house lawyers in 2016, it became apparent that, unlike those in private practice firms who time-record on matters, in-house legal teams had no means of capturing and managing all the work they were doing for their internal clients.

Two of the authors involved in this project found that, generally speaking, in-house legal teams had no means of accurately keeping track of:
- instructions from their internal clients;
- how busy their internal lawyers were;
- volumes of the types of legal support they were providing;
- what instructions were being put out to external firms; and
- whether those firms were completing that work on time, on budget and providing great client service.

At best, in-house teams were typically using manually compiled Excel spreadsheets to try to keep on top of this information. They were crying out for a slicker, technology-based solution.

Therefore, the firm set about obtaining quotes from developers to build a solution from scratch. The cost was prohibitive and the senior management of the firm would never have approved the spend required. Undaunted, the authors (convinced of the demand that existed) thought again. Following a eureka moment (in a meeting at the offices of the world's most recognised football club) it occurred to them that the situation of an in-house legal team within a business is analogous to that of an IT helpdesk:
- the team sits at the centre and users in the business contact them when they have a problem that requires help from the team;
- when a request for help has been received, that request has to be allocated to available and appropriately experienced team members;
- sometimes the team needs to bring in outside help to resolve the matter (when additional resource or particular skills are required).

Although there were no bespoke solutions available for in-house legal teams, there were many software systems to assist IT helpdesks to manage their work. They therefore went on a search for an existing IT helpdesk software business with which to discuss the opportunity. They applied certain criteria to narrow down that search, in that the potential suitor had to:

- have been in operation with its product for over 10 years (to ensure the system was tried and tested);
- have a large and growing customer base (including very large household names that will have run a rigorous test on the product and supplier before becoming a customer); and
- have a single, entrepreneurial shareholder, so that it would be easier to reach agreement on the terms of a collaboration than if multiple owners or third-party investors were involved.

Applying those requirements quickly narrowed down the field to identify a suitable candidate: Deskpro.

When they approached Deskpro with the idea, it became obvious what 'bottles' each contributor could bring to this particular party:

Shoosmiths:

- a strong use case that would enable Deskpro to realise the potential of its existing technology platform in a way they hadn't previously considered;
- existing contacts with a large client base and a route to market;
- credibility for the product in a legal context;
- marketing support and collateral;
- practical experience and knowledge of the use case and client base to be in a better position to ensure that the product would be intuitive and fit for purpose for its target (in-house lawyer) market; and
- the means to continually gather ideas and feedback for future product enhancement.

Deskpro:

- an existing technology platform which avoided the need for significant platform-build costs, and which offered a tried-and-tested platform that would be reliable and ready to launch quickly;
- resources to modify and develop the existing platform for the new use case;
- hosting and ongoing technical support; and
- ongoing technical development for future product enhancements.

It took just six months for a product, matters+, to be developed, from the initial proposal to collaborate to the product being launched on the market.

The product has been well received:

- it is now in daily use in several large household-name businesses around the United Kingdom;
- in September 2021, matters+ client, Scania, won "Most Transformative In-House Team of the Year" at the Legal Business Awards, having used matters+ to transform their in-house function;
- at the same awards the firm was named "Legal Tech Team of the Year"; and
- matters+ is, at the time of writing, top ranked in *Chambers LawTech Guide 2022*.

4.2 Case study 2: Collaborating to further develop an existing tech platform

Most in-house legal teams have a huge demand to review business-as-usual commercial contracts but:

- they often don't have the resource to do so; and
- they usually can't afford to outsource this work to external firms based on traditional fee structures (even heavily discounted hourly rates or fixed fees render the cost unaffordable).

A completely new method of reviewing and marking up commercial contracts was needed. The authors' firm decided to develop an AI contract review service to identify key risks in contracts and suggest corrective actions through the 'comment' function in Word.

The firm had already developed a playbook which enabled relatively inexperienced paralegals to undertake contract reviews and mark up contracts. This was done with appropriate supervision by following a defined process and undertaking a kind of spot-the-difference exercise. After time, it was thought that if that playbook could be applied by technological means, rather than by a human, then not only could it save the cost of four (or more) human hours in the process for each contract review, but it could also deliver the end result to the client far quicker, and potentially with higher accuracy levels. It could even be offered to the client on a self-serve basis.

By offering this new solution, the firm wasn't seeking to cannibalise the work it already had, but rather:

- it was looking to increase market share; and
- find clients that could now afford to review contracts that otherwise might well have gone unchecked.

The solution would also lead to an improved risk profile within the client's business which, in turn, would reflect well on the client's general counsel. In turn, this would strengthen the relationship between the firm and the general counsel.

An existing AI technology business, ThoughtRiver, was identified, which had a suitable natural language processing (NLP) AI platform that could be deployed for this purpose. The firm worked with ThoughtRiver to take its AI platform and train it to create a 'Shoosmiths brain' using the firm's playbook and legal expertise. ThoughtRiver was keen to work with the firm because, as well as generating licence fee income from the use of its platform, it also offered an excellent example of how this tech company could undertake collaborations with other firms that could think of other new use cases to which to apply the platform.

Both Shoosmiths and ThoughtRiver brought 'bottles' to the table:

Shoosmiths:
- an existing highly developed playbook for commercial contract reviews (which was tried and tested, having been applied many times by humans) and which would lend itself well to the introduction of an NLP platform to replace 90% of the required human input;
- many real-life contracts to provide the data with which to 'train' the existing ThoughtRiver platform;
- resources to enter data to 'train' the existing ThoughtRiver platform on the correct application of the playbook;
- an existing client base with which to test the proof of concept;
- contacts with the proposed client base and a route to market;
- credibility and brand in the legal sector; and
- marketing support and collateral.

ThoughtRiver:
- an existing NLP platform with a good level of existing functionality relevant to the use case;
- credibility as an acknowledged leader in NLP platforms;
- contribution to joint promotion of the resulting new product; and
- ongoing product improvements and developments.

The collaboration took the form of a contractual licensing model. Favourable licence rates were agreed. ThoughtRiver also worked to develop interfaces that would enable the product to be particularly user-friendly: this was essential as the product was to be offered to clients on a self-serve basis as well as on a supported basis. ThoughtRiver continue to own the platform whereas Shoosmiths own the 'brain' created as a result of its training and use.

The authors spoke to Tim Pullan, CEO of ThoughtRiver, on what he took from this collaboration. He reminded us about George Bernard Shaw and his comment that "all progress depends on unreasonable people – by which he meant people who see the world differently and possess the capability and character to act on that vision". The key for Pullan is to work with professionals "who are willing to challenge received wisdom whilst remaining measured and grounded". He continued, "for me as an early-stage technology disrupter in law, this relationship has been fundamental to delivering our mission. I would encourage technology founders in all domains to nurture these vital early collaborations. Of course, this is useful for market access but also for new ideas and thinking".

The resulting product:
- has won numerous awards including "Best New Solutions for Clients" by the Managing Partners' Forum (MPF);
- is, at the time of writing, top ranked in *Chambers LawTech Guide 2022*; and
- has received plaudits from clients, such as this one:

Well worth a try! It's like a magic trick. Cia helps contracts disappear from your inbox, then reappear Marked Up.

Saying abracadabra is optional, but recommended ▢ #LegalTech #Magic

4.3 Case study 3: Collaborating on an R&D contract review software

The value of R&D to communities by higher education and research institutions can't be underestimated. The authors spoke to James Muscat-Sharp, Business Engagement Partner at the University of Birmingham (UoB). He told us:

> *University-industry collaboration isn't a new phenomenon, but it is one that is becoming increasingly important to boosting innovation. This is particularly true in countries like the United Kingdom and United States where government policy is ever more focused on facilitating interconnectivity between industry, policy and academia to leverage returns greater than the sum of their parts.*

Muscat-Sharp also told us this "Triple Helix" approach to innovation and growing mandate for collaboration:

> *is ushering in new opportunities in sectors less traditionally associated with joint university R&D, in particular business, professional and*

financial services where rapidly changing business and consumer needs are compelling leaders to think differently – and urgently – about how to most effectively harness the power of emerging technologies.

UoB has also invested in sector-leading business engagement professionals, who, as Muscat-Sharp noted, are "uniquely positioned to drive the University's innovation strategy in partnership with industry and government bodies". UoB, "as with the sector at large", is eager to expand what it does "to reach new heights through collaborative R&D". Put simply, "the door to university-industry collaboration is wide open".

In this spirit, the authors' firm and UoB decided to collaborate on the many R&D contracts that UoB needs to review and amend each year. Having developed Cia (see case study 2 above), it occurred to the authors' firm that an AI platform could similarly be trained to be applied to these types of R&D contracts. However, for Shoosmiths to train the AI brain for application in the context of R&D contracts would require a considerable resource commitment. Furthermore, before making such a commitment, the firm would need to have confidence in the appetite for such a solution within universities such as UoB and of the volume of such contracts that potential university clients might need to review.

The firm approached UoB to discuss the potential use case. Immediately UoB could see the potential value of such a solution for its own use. There could also be the opportunity to monetise any such AI tool developed in collaboration with Shoosmiths by offering the solution for use by other higher education and research institutions on a commercial paid basis.

Both Shoosmiths and UoB brought 'bottles' to the table:

Shoosmiths:
- the use case concept;
- existing methodology for the development of AI contract review products;
- prospect of enabling UoB to use technology to help service its own requirements for R&D contract reviews;
- prospect of enabling UoB to participate in the subsequent commercialisation of the product with other higher education and research institutions;
- legal experience, expertise and resource to develop the playbook;
- law firm credibility and brand;
- marketing collateral and materials; and
- the opportunity for UoB staff and students to gain hands-on experience of developing legaltech.

University of Birmingham:
- large existing database of R&D contracts, providing the data vital to training the AI brain in this new context;
- resources to enter data to train the existing AI platform on the application of the playbook;
- academic credibility;
- contacts with proposed higher education customer base and route to market for commercialisation; and
- contribution to joint marketing.

Following initial discussions on the concept, the firm and UoB decided to run a proof of concept to establish:
- how much training of the AI brain would be required for the use case;
- whether the trained brain would be accurate in undertaking the required R&D contract reviews;
- the reception of senior and experienced UoB staff to the concept.

This was an early example of collaboration between the higher education and private sectors to develop legaltech, which aligned closely with regional strategic priorities for the advancement of professional services tech, led through the regional Local Enterprise Partnership.

5. Practical tips on collaborating to innovate

We set out below some practical tips on collaborating to innovate.

These tips are split as follows:
- thinking about and starting the collaboration;
- undertaking the collaboration; and
- finishing the collaboration (and key milestones).

5.1 Thinking about and starting the collaboration
- Don't collaborate just for the sake of it: ensure there are compelling reasons for a collaboration in the first place so you don't unnecessarily involve another party and thereby dilute your control and ownership of the product.
- Find the right collaborator: search out a party with whom it'll be easiest to reach an agreement. For example, an organisation having a single shareholder may be easier to negotiate with than where there are multiple shareholders to be persuaded of the opportunity.
- Ensure the collaborator has capacity: do they have the resources they need? Check what other projects they have on the stocks that may compete for priority.

- Use the experts you have: enlist the experts in your firm to help with structuring the collaboration (eg, IP experts on the ownership of IP; corporate experts on joint venture vehicles, commercial experts etc).
- Agree heads of terms early on: it's vital that each party understands, at least in outline, all the key commercial considerations of the collaboration before considerable time and intellectual investment is made on starting to develop the product.
- Agree contributions: be very clear on what (if any) capital commitments each party is to contribute. You need to cover both anticipated costs and what happens if unanticipated costs arise that need to be funded.
- Agree aims: be clear what each party anticipates from the collaboration, including considering exit and what happens if you disagree on the direction the venture is taking.
- Protect confidentiality: always have in mind that any tech aimed for use by clients of law firms must protect their confidential information to the highest extent possible. Some tech businesses may be familiar with the protection of personal data but not necessarily in protecting confidential information more broadly. They won't be under the same obligations as a firm regulated by the SRA. In this respect, consider the following:
  - whether the tech business has all the security accreditations your clients want to see (such as ISO 27001, Cyber Essentials, Cyber Essentials Plus, SOC2 etc);
  - on what basis the tech business engages its personnel (eg, some may engage staff on a call-off contract basis, but with minimal documentation in place to impose confidentiality obligations on the worker);
  - sometimes workers may be based overseas: having them work on the project may be a breach of data protection laws or lead to undue security risk;
  - on the other hand, it may be that the tech company already operates in a highly sensitive subject area (they may have even more ideas on security than you do);
  - remember, law firms are disciplined in terms of maintaining client confidentiality. If your tech collaborator does not appreciate that, then they're unlikely to be a partner with whom you can work; and
  - bear in mind that damage to your reputation is unlikely to be compensated appropriately through even the best-drafted collaboration documents. Identifying and managing the risks is the safest way to address them.
- Think about IP: if you've chosen a tech partner on the basis that they give you access to an existing platform that they own, check the

rights they have and ensure that you'll have licensed rights to access that IP. Also, agree how the IP developed through the collaboration will be owned. When it comes to legaltech (or any tech), the IP rights are absolutely crucial and unless the parties are clear and agreed on the issues early on, much time and effort can be wasted.

- Agree all other key points: consider all the other 'good stuff' that would normally appear on a joint venture checklist (distribution of profits, assignment, termination etc).
- Think about insurance: consider if the collaboration requires its own insurance cover. Check with your CQR team.
- Involve your CQR team early (see Chapter 6): as well as commenting on insurance, they can see whether there are any regulatory aspects to be considered (such as the need to make clear to your clients any interests you have in the product or any commission received from its sale to them etc).
- Think about technical support: be clear on what technical support is needed after the product is developed and is being sold to clients. As lawyers, you'll probably be heavily dependent on the tech partner for ongoing support.
- Make a project plan and get all parties to buy into it: keep up the momentum in meeting deadlines. An issue for some firms might be that this project is regarded like a nice-to-have but shouldn't take priority over the day job; nothing is more likely to lead to the failure of the collaboration than lack of prioritisation. Before embarking on the collaboration ensure that the most senior management of your firm have bought in to the fact that this project has to be delivered with just as much priority as if it were an instruction from a client.
- Pick a relatively simple project for your first collaboration: learn your lessons from that one before trying anything more ambitious.

5.2 Undertaking the collaboration

- Meet the team early on: don't start going too far down the road until you believe you'll be able to work with them. Remember, collaborations don't end when the contract is signed: they only just begin.
- Remember that you might not speak the same language: the parties are likely to have much in common: they are both highly intelligent, well-qualified, experienced, commercially astute and already successful. That's a great starting point. However, be aware that the other party may not have the same experience in the areas where you're strong and *vice versa*.
- Understand the processes your prospective collaborator needs to follow and the way they make decisions: this is particularly the case if you're collaborating with a party in the public sector or higher

education sector. If you don't personally have experience in their sector, enlist someone from your organisation who does.

- Listen to what your collaboration partner is telling you: if your collaboration partner makes a good suggestion in an area you're leading, don't dismiss it simply because they aren't supposed to be leading that aspect. Be open-minded and be ready to pivot if needs be. Don't be dogmatic on what the best solution looks like.
- Let the tech experts be tech experts: unless you have a degree in coding and several years' practical experience in software development, chances are that your tech partner knows more about coding than you do. Never assume that everything you want the product to deliver is easy (or even possible) to deliver from a technical perspective. And always ask how hard it would be to change it later, so that your initial design allows for the most flexibility for enhancements in the future.
- Keep the 'bottles balanced': once a product has been developed, don't expect your tech partner to rush to create further enhancements and new releases before there has been some commercial success in selling the product.
- Debrief at the conclusion of every stage of the project (both internal and with the other party): this means that you can establish what might be improved in future stages and/or the next project.

5.3 Finishing the collaboration (and key milestones)

- Celebrate your successes: congratulate yourselves on completing the various project milestones. Ensure you have a bottle of champagne together (or your favourite equivalent) when you sell your new product to your first customer. Enter submissions for awards and take a table at the awards dinner. Enjoy what you have achieved together!
- Involve your clients: get feedback regularly on how they are finding the product. *Never* assume that silence means satisfaction. Involve them in suggesting future updates so you know where to prioritise future investment.
- Stay ahead: keep abreast of potential new entrants and competitor products.

Notes

1 Agustín Fuentes, *The Creative Spark* (Dutton, 2017), p2.
2 Agustín Fuentes, "Creative Collaboration Is What Humans Do Best'" (*The Cut*, 22 March 2017), www.thecut.com/2017/03/how-imagination-makes-us-human.html.
3 Bill George, "VUCA 2.0: A Strategy For Steady Leadership In An Unsteady World" (*Forbes*, 17 February 2017), www.forbes.com/sites/hbsworkingknowledge/2017/02/17/vuca-2-0-a-strategy-for-steady-leadership-in-an-unsteady-world/#7b2474fe13d8.
4 Heidi K Gardner and Ivan Matviak, "7 Strategies for Promoting Collaboration in a Crisis" (*Harvard Business Review*, 8 July 2020), https://hbr.org/2020/07/7-strategies-for-promoting-collaboration-in-a-crisis.

5   *Ibid.*
6   David Sheff, *Last Interview* (Sidgwick & Jackson, 2000), p137.
7   "Steve Jobs on '60 Minutes' (video roundup)" (CNET, 5 October 2011), www.cnet.com/news/steve-jobs-on-60-minutes-video-roundup/.
8   Quoted by *Rolling Stone*: "How the Beatles Took America: Inside the Biggest Explosion in Rock & Roll History" (*Rolling Stone*, 1 January 2014), www.rollingstone.com/music/music-features/how-the-beatles-took-america-inside-the-biggest-explosion-in-rock-roll-history-244557/.

Chapter 6:
Compliance, quality and risk

In 2020, our lives were upended and micromanaged to a striking degree. Barrister Adam Wagner, a leading expert on the coronavirus laws, tweeted in January 2021 that never in his "wildest imaginings"[1] did he expect to be interviewed by the team at ITV's *Good Morning Britain* about whether it was illegal or not to sit on a park bench.

It seemed nothing was off the table, or potentially on it. For example, was a Scotch egg a substantial meal? At the time of this debate, the relevant regulations only allowed alcohol to be served in a 'tier-two' area where it was part of a 'table meal'. Pubs had to pull down the shutters unless they could serve more than a token meal. *The Sun*'s headline quipped "10 pints of lager and a scotch egg please".[2] *The Telegraph* reported "overzealous" police were arguing with landlords about whether a Scotch egg was a substantial meal and, on occasions, throwing customers out once they'd finished eating.[3] *The Daily Mail* punned it was "beyond a yolk".[4]

In December 2020, one keen academic studied more than 300 rulings from various councils to try to unearth some basic rules on this legal conundrum. He discovered a bowl of crisps, nuts or olives didn't constitute substantial food (according to Brighton and Hove Council) but high-end crisps with elaborate dips did (Westminster City Council). It all depended on the "'class and calibre' of the nature of the establishment and the clientele".[5] It'd be amusing if it wasn't so serious.

And despite all of the hand-wringing in the press and on social media about 'covidiots' and 'pandemic fatigue', the public weren't given the credit that they deserved. The ONS reported in April 2021 that "overall, compliance was high"[6] (aside from in certain central government offices, but that's a different story, as we know).

The pandemic, and the rules that we were told and asked to follow, showed that people typically want to do the right thing, but they don't always know where the right side of the line is. They *want* to comply, but they aren't always sure *how*.

Those who are responsible for compliance in firms, in all of its various guises, will be familiar with this dynamic: where to draw the line and how to navigate the ever-expanding library of statutes, statutory instruments, case law, regulatory decisions, guidance, codes of practice and the like. And how to do all of this without bumping into any Scotch-egg-type problems.

And it's easier said than done. Compliance is tough. It's complex. And, in the round, it's unlikely to get less difficult any time soon, despite the best intentions of policy makers. The interplay of law and guidance, in particular, can make the most phlegmatic of lawyers break out into a nervous sweat. Sometimes known as 'hard law' and 'soft law' – and often deliberately conflated by those making the rules – working out how these work together feels like trying to unscramble an omelette.

Regulators aren't letting up either. In June 2022, the Legal Services Board (LSB) remarked on the "difficult ethical questions"[7] that in-house and commercial lawyers face between the pressures of running their firms or departments and complying with their professional obligations. The LSB had "very significant concerns" that they aren't getting it right and expressed concern that "certain parts of the sector may not consider themselves to be under the regulatory and supervisory spotlight".

Lawyers are going to have to buckle up and brace themselves for a lot more hard and soft compliance law in the years to come, including on legaltech[8] and other innovation. Regulators will continue to shine their lights on us.

What's more, as technology and innovation is raised on the agenda within law firms, lawyers will, in future, want to offer new products and provide new services. As a result, compliance, quality and risk (CQR) teams are going to find themselves having to think more deeply on many of the new questions that will start to land on their desks in the future.

In this chapter, we examine:

- changing the CQR mindset to make it more future-ready;
- having a CQR vision and strategy, backed up with clear and measurable aims;
- understanding how the use of technology and new ways of working affect CQR;
- understanding regtech;
- focusing on quality and risk (we look at each in turn);
- dealing with external stakeholders; and
- considering the impact of regulation.

The chapter then goes on to look at some case studies and sets out practical tips to make the right compliance choices.

1. Changing the CQR mindset

As we note in Chapter 8, some in-house lawyers have an unfair reputation as being in the 'Department of No' or the 'Business Prevention Department'. If such a department existed, it would still come with risks: a default "no" to every query would stop business and result in staff contriving questionable work-arounds to the issues they face. Of course, this is hyperbole. No one says "no" to everything. But reputations are difficult to shake off.

In many ways, CQR teams find themselves in a similar situation to in-house lawyers. Common complaints over compliance can include:

- "you're getting in the way of business"; or
- "other firms don't seem to have these gold-plated requirements".

Difficult laws with severe criminal sanctions, such as anti-money laundering checks, don't lend themselves to easy, one-size-fits-all answers.

Compliance is a price we pay for being in a profession. It's a fundamental part of how we build trust with our clients and how we play our part in society. But at a time of accelerated technological change, CQR teams need to embrace the 'hybrid era' and think more creatively than they do now. CQR teams are specialists in compliance law and guidance, but, to an extent, they're also enablers.

Table 1 shows some, but by no means all, of the stereotypical characteristics of a more traditional mindset of a CQR team versus the mindset that the authors anticipate is required in the years to come. Every firm has a different culture and many of these may be unfair or unrepresentative of the reality 'on the ground' for many of them. Even so, they help us to set the scene for what we need to do next.

Table 1: Stereotypical characteristics of a traditional mindset

Traditional mindset	Future mindset	Traditional approach	How things are changing
Negative	Positive	CQR teams are risk averse, or are (unfairly) perceived to be, hence the unfortunate moniker 'Department of No'. Generally speaking, the team risks being seen as a blocker.	CQR teams need to be, and be seen to be, the 'Department of Let's-See-What-We-Can-Do'. Sometimes the answer to a query may, of course, be "no", but a more can-do attitude can usually find ways through seemingly intractable problems, including where the law and guidance isn't clear. In the main, the team is seen as an enabler.
Risk avoidance	Risk management	Only a few people in the firm put their minds to risk and managing it, such as the CQR team. (This is a 'them-and-us' model.) The roles in the CQR team are often narrowly drawn: the culture of risk avoidance means that people are unwilling to step outside of their roles. Compliance can be more of a game of box ticking and, as a result, the system itself can often be 'gamed'.	Everyone in the firm is responsible for spotting and managing risk (a 'risk- partnership' model). Technology can also help to identify, assess, manage and monitor risk. The CQR team acts as the focus for supporting this. The roles in the CQR team are still delineated, but the people in this team look to be more dynamic in their approach to the matters before them. The culture isn't focused on formulaic form filling (indeed, we're likely to see tech used to streamline a lot of this in future).

continued on next page

Traditional mindset	Future mindset	Traditional approach	How things are changing
Passive	Active	CQR teams deal with queries as they come in. Often, there's a lot of last-minute firefighting: dealing with matters reactively and against tight deadlines.	CQR teams keep their ears to the ground and seek to manage issues proactively. The culture is one where lawyers contact such teams as early as possible to discuss ideas and manage matters. As new laws and guidance around the use of tech in law emerges, the modern CQR team gets on top of it early, including making informed representations in consultation exercises with law makers and regulators if possible.
Data-poor	Data-rich	CQR teams, in the main, are not big users of data-powered solutions to help them in their work.	The legal regtech market is likely to develop much more. Products and services, often powered by AI, will help CQR teams do their work smarter, faster and better (see below), so they can focus their minds more on the really difficult matters they need to deal with.[9]
Guarded front door	Open front door	CQR teams nominally have an open-door policy, but they still seem to be somewhat invisible in the firm. The 'Department of No' stereotype means that people can be reluctant to knock on the team's door.	CQR teams need to build relationships within the firm, winning hearts and minds. They need to be helpful, friendly and straight-talking. Supportive members of CQR teams should be available with a true open-door policy. (The future may well see easy queries dealt with by CQR chatbots too.)

What does this mean in practice for a typical member of the CQR team?

In the round, a typical CQR team member of the future will need to:
- be comfortable with:
  - 'change3' and the challenges of the legal and regulatory system constantly trying to play catch up with technology and innovation, which outpaces our ability to deal with it;
    using data much more, not only in the firm in which they work, but also in the CQR team itself. After all, the boost that data gives applies to both the practice *and* the business of law; and
  - the 'hybrid era', including dealing with the implications that increased remote working throws up, as well as with new products and services that don't fall neatly within the traditional menu of what services have been offered by law firms within the regulatory regime (see Chapter 3);
- be keen to use technology and innovative solutions, wherever they can add value and make the CQR team more agile in what it does (this doesn't mean deploying and using tech or innovation for the sake of it);
- be used to dealing, and building relationships, with people at all levels and roles in the firm, from lawyers to those in other teams – some of whose titles will be named after things we've not even thought of or invented yet. The President of Microsoft (and lawyer) Brad Smith reminds us that "every company in part is becoming a tech company";[10]
- maintain integrity and continue to uphold the highest standards in the face of the change that is coming. The 'Department of Let's-See-What-We-Can-Do' isn't a default 'Department of Yes'. From time to time, defending the values of our respective firms and those of our profession will have a cost, and sometimes a financial cost at that. What's more, the values which we defend aren't just those of our profession, but they are increasingly the values we set out in our CSR agendas and ESG programmes;
- be proactive, dynamic and strategic: this fast-paced environment is not one in which standing still is an option. Using initiative is important too;
- be resilient: there's a lot in the above list. But equally, CQR team members need to be fulfilled in what they do too. If their firm respects the work that they do and values it, then CQR team members can really make a difference in a world turbocharged by technological change;
- be familiar with the regulation of legaltech and where to find it. For example, the SRA notes that, if things go wrong "you must be clear about your responsibilities and have explained them to your client

when they are using the technology to access your services".[11] These sorts of requirements are often not found in one place and can be hidden in the detail. CQR team members need to be good researchers. There are many other requirements that typical CQR team members will need in their roles, particularly if they are also an MLRO, COLP or COFA. (This is not the book, however, to examine these roles in detail.)

2. Having a CQR vision and strategy

As we note in Chapter 2, having a technology vision, strategy and related aims are important, but so is having the same for the CQR team. This can help it mitigate risk for the firm, while also helping the business keep on the right side of the law and regulators.

The questions that may need to be asked include:
- What are the team's goals in the short, medium and long term? What sort of team do we want to be? Perhaps set out some principles and key performance indicators (KPIs).
- What new laws and guidance are on the horizon? (See Chapter 12.) What do we need to do generally to comply with them?
- What laws do we comply with now? What do we need to do generally to continue to comply with them?
- What technology and innovation will we use? What processes will we have to evaluate and adopt them?
- What new risks are there in the firm that need to be managed? How will we do so?
- What is our risk appetite? Does it vary depending on the matter in question?
- What policies and procedures do we have to help us fulfil the vision, strategy and aims?
- What training is required?
- To what extent will we highlight our compliance best practice to clients? Other businesses in other sectors often showcase their commitment to, say, health and safety and data protection. Should we do the same for our compliance efforts and drive it as a competitive advantage?
- What support do we have internally for this? Can we get a board sponsor, or even the CEO to help launch it?
- How often should the vision, strategy and aims be looked at and any amendments made to them in light of developments?

A CQR strategy needs to align with all other strategies and aims of the firm; and its overall vision too.

Long-term trends mean that cybersecurity threats are likely to grow, particularly in light of the invasion of Ukraine by Russia. And the threat from inside firms – whether accidental or malicious – shouldn't be forgotten either.

3. Understanding how the use of technology affects CQR

Technology is capable of both good and bad. And it is often the latter that can gift CQR staff sleepless nights and fretful days.

Cybersecurity, in particular, is a growing area of concern. In September 2020, the SRA did a thematic review of cybersecurity. It found that three-quarters of the firms visited by the regulator (30 out of 40) had suffered a cyberattack. In 23 of these cases, cybercriminals stole a total of more than £4 million of client money. These firms were able to claim £3.6 million on their insurance policies, however, the remaining £0.4 million had to be repaid out of the relevant firm's own monies.[12]

And it's often not the technology itself that causes issues, but the people that use – or indeed don't use – the technology at their disposal. Most firms visited by the SRA recognised the power that their people have to open their firms up to risk, but also to be their firm's first line of defence. As this book notes throughout: technology is about people and tech, not people or tech. The same applies in this chapter. Technology can do extraordinary things, but if the people in our firms aren't using it or updating it as intended, the compliance risks are likely to give even the best-run firms costly headaches. The reputational risks can also be significant.

Long-term trends mean that cybersecurity threats are likely to grow, particularly in light of the invasion of Ukraine by Russia. And the threat from inside firms – whether accidental or malicious – shouldn't be forgotten either. In a 2018 report the National Cyber Security Centre (NCSC) noted that the threat level to the legal sector is significant.[13]

We set out below some examples of particular threats firms face.

3.1 Fighting hacking

Hackers typically seek to 'own' a computer system ('own' is hacker-speak for 'completely control'). They may do so with criminal intent or out of boredom, curiosity or even the bragging rights they get from hacking a tricky target. Finding ingenious ways to attack a business' weak spots is their *modus operandi*.

Firms act for all manner of clients, many of which are in the limelight. Confidentiality is at the heart of what we do. But with just one hack, it can all be lost. Reputations are extremely difficult to build back. And the attack doesn't have to be too complicated: in June 2022, the SRA noted that four out of five cybercrime reports to it involved email.[14]

Consider the *Panama Papers* hack: a leak of 11.5 million legal and financial records in 2016.[15] The leak of 2.6 terabytes of data,[16] which included details on hundreds of thousands of offshore entities,[17] led to an investigation about alleged ethical and legal wrongdoing in various offshore tax regimes. Mossack Fonseca & Co, the Panama-headquartered firm at the centre of the leak, was forced to close in 2018 (having traded for over 40 years) due to the financial and reputational damage inflicted by the hack.[18]

3.2 Fighting viruses and ransomware

Brad Smith, President of Microsoft – the operating system and word-processing software on which so many firms rely – reminds us that "in a world where everything is connected, anything can be disrupted".[19] The WannaCry ransomware attack is one of the most well-known attacks, which crippled parts of the NHS and other organisations globally.[20] *WIRED* reported in March 2022 that many ransomware gangs are run like businesses, with one of the largest even having a human resources department.[21]

The WannaCry attack was indiscriminate but be in no doubt that criminals have specific firms in their crosshairs. A notable example is when a cyber-gang stole data from US firm Grubman Shire Meiselas & Sacks.[22] The firm was an appealing target, instructed by numerous VIPs and celebrities. At first, the gang demanded $21 million from the firm, but it then doubled it to $42 million after finding files relating to Donald Trump; publicly releasing 169 emails which included the term 'Trump' in them.[23] To prove they had compromised the firm's systems, they also published on the dark web over two gigabytes of information, including details of Lady Gaga's contracts.[24]

In May 2021, the National Crime Agency (NCA), in its 2021 *National Strategic Assessment of Serious and Organised Crime*, noted that ransomware attacks had increased dramatically and were becoming more severe.[25] In June 2022, the SRA revealed that 18 firms had reported ransomware attacks to them in the previous year.[26] The regulator noted that ransomware "is likely to increasingly become fully automated, attacking any target with suitable weaknesses".[27] In August 2022, the Law Society also published further guidance on ransomware and what firms can do to protect themselves.[28]

3.3 Minimising the risks of hybrid working

The 'hybrid era' and hybrid working also brings new risks. Each home where someone is working remotely is now, in many practical respects, a branch office of the firm – 52 Acacia Avenue might be in some sleepy suburb, but the leafy surroundings don't matter to those who seek to compromise a firm's systems.

And working from home is an important reminder that not all risks are directly computer-based. Many lawyers, for example, print out documents at home to read, particularly if they don't have more than one screen. If every lawyer does this there are, in effect, hundreds of thousands of confidential paper documents distributed across tens of thousands of homes across the country. What can lawyers do with these confidential documents once they are done with them? Even if they are disposed of securely, how do they secure the papers when they're at home? And what's the environmental cost of all of this extra printing?

There are solutions to these types of (often) unexpected problems. One solution, in the example above, is a Word plugin, which allows better navigation of large documents by identifying and displaying related parts of the document to be viewed in different panes simultaneously. It avoids having to print off any documents in the first place – a powerful and simple solution to an extensive security issue.

3.4 Minimising the risks of the 'little' things

As this section shows, cyberattacks and continued, paper-based security threats are big issues that firms need to grapple with. It's relatively easy for CQR teams to concentrate their energies on these matters, particularly when they fill the legal press with tales of woe.

But the seemingly little things shouldn't be overlooked either, as they may often turn out not to be so little. Take emails, for example. How easy is it to accidently send an email to an autocompleted email address? In a word: 'very'. Often, these sorts of errors are quickly rectified. Sometimes, however, an email to the wrong recipient can change the whole course of a matter. And no firm ever wants to be on the receiving end of a claim for negligence or a complaint to the Information Commissioner's Office (ICO).

Firms therefore need to put their minds to the little things too; the sorts of things that can quickly explode into big things. In the example of emails, additional solutions, which often don't feature in the relevant software itself, can help to minimise the risks. There's software, for example, that challenges the user if it detects a possible incorrect addressee (based on that user's previous patterns of behaviour). This type of guardian software is evolving further (for instance, to flag up if an employee is potentially emailing large quantities of data to, say, a competitor). The upshot? Beware of ignoring the little things at your peril.

4. Understanding regtech in the legal sector

Regtech (technology that helps businesses deal with regulation) in the legal sector is still a somewhat underdeveloped market, but it's something that should interest CQR teams more and more. Perhaps the most *avant-garde* firms should start to develop regtech themselves (and sell it to others).

Some have said that the pandemic has been a watershed moment for regtech generally. A report from RegTech Associates in 2021 (in partnership with the City of London Corporation) referred to a "critical year"[29] for regtech. It talked about the story of a sector that wants to scale up, but it needs to "overcome [a] complex network of challenges" before it can do so. There is, it would seem, much work that still needs to be done before regtech truly breaks out.

But CQR teams need to keep a keen eye on this area. The benefits of regtech include, in particular, better and more agile:
- insights;
- management of risk; and
- systems (ie, they're more efficient and effective).

4.1 Understanding the legal regtech available now
Although the fintech sector is miles ahead of the legaltech sector generally, there are a number of areas where legal regtech has started to offer powerful solutions to firms:
- Regtech[30] can help firms to complete anti-money laundering (AML) checks. Such checks typically include customer due diligence (CDD), risk assessments and source-of-funds checks (including on crypto payments). Technology streamlines many of these checks, such as doing biometric checks on passports, and frees up time for CQR teams to deal with more complex cases. And getting AML right matters: the SRA's 2021–2022 business plan says the SRA is to increase the "proactive monitoring and regulating of anti-money laundering arrangements within the profession".[31]
- Data compliance: automated data-compliance tools can help firms comply with data protection legislation by automatically flagging up things like sensitive data, which needs greater protection, or finding where personal data is located for data subject access requests (DSARs) within the timescales laid down in such legislation.
- AI contract review tools: compliance teams often need to look at contracts to which their firms are a party to determine their risk profiles and to highlight areas of particular concern. (Confidentiality, disclosure and insurance provisions are a few of the most obvious examples of clauses in contracts highly relevant to our regulatory obligations.) AI-powered contract review software can help to speed up this process to raise red flags.

4.2 Dealing with the legal regtech to come

How, in the years ahead, will technology help with CQR?

It's likely that we'll see exciting developments in the products and services we set out above. However, for any new products and services, there are a number of things that we'd do well to bear in mind:

- To what extent will any tech or other innovative solutions be provided by SRA-regulated bodies, such as law firms? What protection is there if something goes wrong and the regtech provider is unregulated? Many solutions will be AI-powered. But we should never assume that AI works 'straight out of the box'. A lot of AI tools need to be trained by the firms which have purchased them, which can be time-consuming and costly (see Chapter 2). AI, and the collection of data, and personal data in particular, also poses a number of risks that CQR teams need to manage.
- Some solutions may involve new or relatively new technologies, which are likely to get us scratching our collective heads. These may be in areas where there is little or no regulation. For example, will firms start to accept cryptocurrency *en masse*? If so, which ones? In May 2022, for example, the stablecoin TerraUSD proved to be somewhat unstable and collapsed together with its sister token Luna.[32] In November 2022, the world's second largest cryptocurrency exchange (at that time), FTX, filed for bankruptcy in the US.[33] What are the consequences for lawyers and the risks in using cryptocurrencies? (And that's not to mention the ecological footprint of cryptocurrencies; how does this tie in with any environmental commitments?)

5. Focusing on quality and risk

In this section, we look at quality and risk.

5.1 Focusing on quality

First, what do we mean by 'quality'? The answer, as far as firms are concerned, isn't as clear-cut as it seems.

Research commissioned by the SRA in 2020, *Better Information in the Legal Services Market (Year One Evaluation of the Transparency Rules)*,[34] revealed that firms find answering this question difficult. There are quality marks, such as Lexcel, but in the absence of such marks, defining what quality means in practice isn't easy. 'We know it when we see it' is perhaps the unhelpful response. But we need to start somewhere, particularly if our firms are to become more client-centric in the 'hybrid era' (see Chapter 3). The research, which focused on the views of consumers and small businesses, found that these clients seem to measure the quality of firms in two broad ways:

There is still, however, a mismatch between firms' perception of what clients value in terms of quality and what clients actually want.

- information on credibility and trustworthiness: this includes a firm's expertise (including lawyer profiles); any reported success rates; whether it's regulated; and whether it has any quality marks. To an extent, they also look for the regulator's logo (such as the SRA clickable logo); and
- information on how they think they'll be treated and their needs satisfied by the firm. They might check client reviews and search for information on their rights and protections (including client-complaint procedures). To an extent, they may look for details on insurance cover and details of any redress schemes to the Legal Ombudsman.

There is still, however, a mismatch between firms' perception of what clients value in terms of quality and what clients actually want. We hear this when we speak to clients:
- law firms perceive that clients want advice, and high-quality advice at that. Too often this advice is over-engineered and gold plated;
- but what clients typically want is a cost-effective solution to their needs, covering the aspects they need to be covered, but not going beyond that.

The extent of this gap in perception is probably greater than most lawyers think. Here are two examples (one non-contentious and one contentious):
- A client gives a lawyer a low-value, business-as-usual commercial contract to review. An experienced commercial lawyer could well raise 200 or so points on it. However, if the client is only really concerned about 20 key commercial risk points, why would they pay for 10 times that number to be reviewed in detail? What's more important: 20 key points assessed with high accuracy? Or 200 points assessed with the potential for some of those 20 key points being missed or underrated? (This was the philosophy the authors applied when developing its firm's AI-powered contract review solution.) This is just one of many examples of how quality is becoming increasingly nuanced as new solutions emerge to meet client needs.
- The Master of the Rolls, Sir Geoffrey Vos, predicted in March 2022 that by 2040 disputes will be settled largely through automated systems. He said, for small disputes clients don't care much "whether the outcome is robust and dependable",[35] adding "AI-driven portals [will] provide a rough and ready resolution". The response of one legal journalist on Twitter to this was a simple "😮".[36] For other disputes and large disputes, "the parameters will be different, and the parties may be prepared to invest time and money in achieving a more just and perhaps objectively correct solution".[37]

All CQR teams need to be keenly aware how clients perceive quality and what the appropriate level of quality should be. This goes as much to the scoping and terms of reference of the work we take on as it does to the manner in which we undertake that work.

Turning many of the above factors into KPIs that can be acted upon and measured is tricky. One option is to take a leaf out of the book of tech businesses by using one of the customer satisfaction metrics which they commonly use. Given the change in mindset that is often needed when offering innovative products and services to clients (see the table on the legal practice matrix in Chapter 3), this is not an unwarranted step. Examples of these metrics include:

- non-propriety scoring methods such as the Customer Satisfaction Score (CSAT);
- propriety scoring methods, such as the Net Promoter Score® (NPS); and
- in the legal sector itself, surveys such as the *Legal 500 Client Service Survey*, which uses over a dozen criteria for its Overall Client Service Score.

These ways of scoring satisfaction, and many others, can help firms improve the quality of what they do by, for example, highlighting trends and showing whether clients would recommend a firm's products and services to others. After all, who would recommend a poor-quality product? Data analytics and the use of surveys can also give firms insight into client satisfaction: clients regularly tell the authors that they really appreciate being asked for their views and feedback. All we need to do is ask. Plus, from the authors' experience, there hasn't yet been one instance where we've asked a client and a new piece of useful information hasn't been discovered.

But this is all looking at matters after the event. CQR teams also need to look to embed quality into everything that firms do 'before the event'. To this end, firms can seek to:

- be accredited to, for example:
    - a standard such as ISO 9001 on quality management;
    - a quality mark such as Lexcel or the Conveyancing Quality Scheme (CQS); and
- take advantage of technology to improve what they do, such as:
    - document automation software;
    - document checking software; and
    - AI-powered contract review tools, which can free up lawyers' time to concentrate on what really matters to a client.

Ultimately, seeking to provide as high a quality product or service as is necessary (ie, not over-engineered) helps our clients build trust in us and our firms. They trust that we'll do a good job at the right level for them. In turn, this trust helps to minimise the risk of any claims or complaints and maximise the good things our clients say about us.

We cannot, of course, assume the trust of our clients; we have to earn it, just as other brands in the technology and innovation space have done. One key way of doing this, as this section shows, is to build a quality-assurance framework and to use metrics to see how we are doing. As firms offer an increasing amount of non-traditional products and services, this is something we'll see a lot more of.

5.2 Focusing on risk

Risk is the third key area for many CQR teams, but it is no less important for that.

For such teams, and firms in general, there are many ways of managing risk. For example:
- The SRA talks about a firm's risk management strategy in the context of COLPS and COFAs. As part of this strategy, many firms operate formal operational risk committees to help them deal with:
  - risks in the practice of law, including claims and complaints; and
  - risks in the business of law, including matters such as health and safety, data protection, business continuity planning etc. As technology and innovation develops, and is adopted by firms in increasing amounts, firms also need to consider carefully the risks in their use; and
- Standards like ISO 31000, which can help firms manage risk in a more formal and methodical way.

What sorts of risks are there? There are plenty. They include:
- Confidential client information going into a third-party software platform and then being stored in the cloud: from the authors' experience, our CQR team is having to consider the implications of this and to involve our IT team on security audits much more than a decade ago.
- An increasing amount of personal data being processed: the authors' CQR team now has someone who deals exclusively with the data protection risk aspects.
- Liability issues: many firms are caught in the middle between limits of liability that we offer to our clients, compared to the much lower limits that tech suppliers offer to us.
- Being used for money laundering: given how high this is on the SRA's agenda and the fact that firms are being visited or having

The insurance implications of new technology and innovation can present numerous challenges to consider and overcome. This can take time.

desk-based audits means the CQR team must ensure sufficient resource and expertise is available.

And we especially need to consider the risk in any new products and services we offer. The risks are growing as we offer more technological solutions and new innovations to our clients. If, as Microsoft's Brad Smiths says, we're all tech companies now – well, at least in part – what are we lawyers doing about the risks that manifest themselves in this new paradigm? How do we deal with emergent risks too?

Alas, it's impossible to set out here the risks in using specific technology and innovation. In practice, these can only be scrutinised on a case-by-case basis. But one big step that we can take, as we mention above, is to move from a mindset of risk avoidance to risk management. The fact is that not all risks can be avoided. As we mention in Chapter 1, without change everything would be in stasis. Nothing would happen. And so it is with risk too. 'Change3' and risk go hand in hand. Without risk, we can't move forward, for the only way of avoiding the risk of doing new things is to do nothing. But doing nothing itself creates business risks for law firms. To do nothing would be to watch our firms ossify and atrophy out of existence.

Therefore, we need to embrace and manage risk as the powerful but sometimes problematic ingredient that drives our increasingly tech-powered businesses forward. In this time of accelerated change, risk needs to be embraced, not shunned.

6. Dealing with external stakeholders

It's likely that lawyers will work more and more with others. CQR teams need to prepare for this.

The SRA said in its November 2021 to October 2022 draft business plan and budget that "strong stakeholder relationships and collaboration are central to our success".[38] As noted in Chapter 6, there's ample opportunity for lawyers to work with the SRA, and SRA Innovate in particular. The SRA says that it wants and needs to work with firms so it can "support the adoption of legal technology, and other innovation, that helps to meet the needs of the public, business community, regulated entities and the economy".[39]

Firms, however, also need to work with other stakeholders, including their insurers. The insurance implications of new technology and innovation can present numerous challenges to consider and overcome. This can take time. Although in many cases tech actually leads to less risk and greater consistency, insurers have a lot to get their heads around.

Insurers' approach to the use of AI, in particular, needs to be considered carefully. Often they'll require the manual supervision of aspects of an AI product or service, which may have an impact on any self-serve element of such solutions.

Insurance is often assumed to apply and is therefore overlooked until the last minute, so firms need to get into the habit of not only speaking with the CQR team early, but also their brokers and insurers. Insurance is also renewed annually on a claims-made basis so this needs to be considered too. (It is quite probable, if not certain, that you will end up having to explain to insurers on an annual basis all the weird and wonderful new solutions you are offering to your clients. This process can be challenging, but is necessary.)

7. Understanding the regulatory playing field

As more businesses enter the market, it's clear that law firms are at a regulatory disadvantage. Law firms enter the marketplace with one hand tied behind their backs. If, for example, a law firm creates a piece of legaltech and wants to sell it, the product needs to be backed up by professional indemnity (PI) insurance under the SRA Indemnity Insurance Rules and, in particular, the minimum amounts of cover set out in them.

There are also other gaps between the terms law firms must offer clients and terms that tech suppliers typically offer.

And let's not forget that law firms supplying such products will be bound also by confidentiality and conflict of interest obligations, which can act to limit the potential clients to which products can be supplied or affect the design of the products themselves. For example, if a law firm is offering document automation services to its clients, it has to ensure that it doesn't have access to any confidential client information that is entered by the client in the course of populating the details to produce a document using the automation service. An unregulated tech company providing such a document automation service isn't bound by any such constraints.

A Competition and Markets Authority (CMA) review published in December 2020 noted this gap in regulation for unreserved services. In general, consumers can purchase services from unauthorised legaltech providers with the result that they won't then receive regulatory protection under the Legal Services Act 2007. The CMA noted that "this leads to risks of different standards and levels of protection depending on who the provider is".[40]

There are over 160 regulated professions in the United Kingdom and over 50 regulators. Will their ranks continue to grow to include legaltech providers? Will we see more regulation generally? Put simply, the choice for policymakers is the question – to create a level playing field, do we:

- 'regulate up'? There's more regulation of the unregulated; or
- 'regulate down'? There's less regulation of the regulated.

At the time of writing, regulating down seems to be the more likely option of the two, as regulation becomes more outcomes-focused and policymakers are forced to prioritise their limited budgets. In June 2022, the LSB also rejected the creation of new rules for the unregulated sector.

In the end, it may be that there will be a bit of a fudge between the above two options. But whatever happens, we need to fight for as fair a regulatory regime as possible. If we don't, law firms could see themselves priced out of the market for innovative products and services by less-regulated competitors.

Ultimately, CQR teams can help firms:

- keep an eye on regulatory developments;
- liaise with regulators. Sometimes we work on projects where the regulation doesn't seem to fit or make much sense to the matter in hand. Initiatives like SRA Innovate, which often fall under the radar of busy lawyers, can help us navigate through regulatory issues. Sometimes even certain rules can be waived; and
- contribute to any consultations on reform.

In the years to come, there is likely to be more change. But, of course, this isn't new. As Sir Thomas Lund, Secretary-General of the Law Society, said just after the War:[41]

> *Standards of professional conduct change as time passes. What is entirely proper for one generation may be slightly irregular for the succeeding generation and highly improper for the next.*

8. Case studies

8.1 Case study 1: The fintech sector
Fintech has developed much more than legaltech. What can it teach law firms?

In the past, the legal profession has been less enthusiastic about tech than other industries and sectors. One reason is that the pace, complexity and magnitude of change, which has been forced upon the legal sector, has been less than that in the financial services (FS) sector. 'Change3' has turbocharged the adoption of technology and innovation in the FS sector:

- Pace of change: the FS sector often sees stark overnight change, such as the Big Bang, the day in 1986 when the FS sector was deregulated and electronic screen-based trading took over. The pace has not let up since.
- Complexity of change: a glance at the voluminous FCA Handbook alone is enough to make even the most skilled lawyer break out into a cold sweat. At the Bank of England, a report in 2019 noted that its supervisory teams "receive the equivalent of twice the entire works of Shakespeare of reading each week".[42]
- Magnitude of change: FS businesses have always needed to consider how very large volumes of regulated administration can be handled. In October 2021, Jennifer Clarke, Senior Editorial Manager at CUBE, lamented that in the first six months of 2021 there were 6,459 regulatory insights in the FS sector that were published, with 1,503 updates in March 2021 alone.[43] According to the Bank of England, its own "rulebook is longer than the Old Testament".[44] Enforcement is also changing. Proceedings against FS businesses have led to a surge in fines in the United Kingdom.

In the legal sector, there's not been the same amount of new regulation to get to grips with in how we practise our profession. Nor do lawyers see the level of fines that FCA-regulated businesses have to contend with, even taking into account the recent hike in the SRA's fining powers. Furthermore, a research paper for the LSB published in 2019 noted that the "incentive for entrepreneurs to enter the legal regtech industry is nowhere near that of the financial sector".[45]

All of the above, and other factors, explain why fintech has raced ahead of legaltech. It's had to. In 2021, according to the *Kalifa Review of UK Fintech*, the sector was worth an estimated £11 billion in revenue and it's thought that 71% of people in the United Kingdom now use the services of at least one fintech business.[46] The United Kingdom has an estimated 10% of global market share in this area.

What can we learn from this story of success?

- Changing mindsets works: FS businesses have embraced technology and innovation: it's now part of their business models. They understand their customers and use the latest UX techniques and UCD. Disruption is also at the heart of their models: the *UK Fintech State of the Nation* report by the Department for International Trade and HM Treasury in April 2019, for example, noted that 56% of traditional FS businesses have placed disruption at the heart of their strategies.[47]
- Embracing new business models is key: 'challenger banks' have sprung up which operate online or in-app, such as Monzo and Starling Bank. Others offer more specialised services, such as Revolut (peer-to-peer payments and currency exchange) and Wise (bank transfers). These virtual businesses have no 'bricks-and-mortar' branches, which typically means lower fees, 24/7 customer service and clearer and simpler products (after all, selling something complex online isn't easy).
- Market entrants include lots of SMEs: according to Deloitte, there are around 2,500 fintech businesses in the United Kingdom.[48] The fintech market in the United Kingdom includes numerous start-ups which have gone on to greater things.
- Improved access for the 'unbanked' and 'underbanked' and the potential for improved financial literacy (although views differ on how successful fintech will be on people's financial wellbeing).

From a compliance point of view:

- Fintech's success is built on strong legal foundations. The *Kalifa Review of UK Fintech*, published in 2021, noted the strength of the United Kingdom's reputation for regulation and the rule of law (and thus trust), but that it "must ensure that we build trust in this new wave of tech-enabled products and services".[49] Kalifa also made 15 recommendations to support the sector to grow further.
- Fintech is customer-focused. The FCA has reported that net satisfaction with regtech is high.[50]
- Change is happening all the while: in the future the whole system could have compliance built in through 'rules as code' (RaC). This 'compliance by design' isn't a new idea. In 2016, the FCA noted that such an approach "could significantly reduce the cost of change" and "help ensure greater consistency between the intentions of a regulation and its implementation".[51] It could also help to widen access to justice. The OECD, in 2020, pointed out, however, that it is still early days for RaC, nothing large-scale yet having been embedded in and across any governments.[52] Even so, are we ready as lawyers for this sort of shift?

But even the extensive use of tech isn't a panacea in a tough market. Despite innumerable plaudits, over six million customers and coming top of CMA-mandated customer satisfaction surveys, Monzo, for example, had to state in its 2021 annual statement that "material uncertainties cast doubt on our ability to continue as a going concern".[53] Using technology and embracing innovation doesn't mean the rules of the game no longer apply.

At the time of writing, a new Centre for Finance, Innovation and Technology is being set up. This is a new body the goal of which is to drive financial innovation in the United Kingdom. In 2022, LegalUK proposed the setting up of a National Institute for Legal Innovation. If this is set up, it might be just the catalyst the legal sector needs to help drive the legal-tech sector forward.

8.2 Case study 2: Lawtech and ethics principles

Guidance incoming! We need to brace ourselves for an increasing amount of guidance as lawyers use legaltech more in the years ahead.

Some has already been published, such as the Law Society *Lawtech and Ethics Principles* in July 2021. The *Principles*, developed over two years with some of the country's largest law firms, aim to help lawyers: "make informed decisions, engage in meaningful discussions with Lawtech providers, and take advantage of the opportunities Lawtech and digital transformation offer".[54]

It's important to note, however, that these *Principles* aren't mandatory. Nor do they amount to, for example, a practice note (even if these *Principles* were to be published in the future as a practice note, it would only amount to what the Law Society deems to be good practice, as opposed to guidance that must be followed). Whatever their status, now or in the years to come, it nonetheless looks likely that firms will follow the *Principles* to minimise any CQR risks. They are also designed to benefit legaltech suppliers, creating "a more stable and predictable environ-ment"[55] for them.

Given the speed at which technology and innovation is developing, it's hoped these *Principles* will be reviewed and, if necessary, developed further in light of lessons learned in their application and general practice in the sector. This will be vital as the *Principles* have already been misin-terpreted by some, with one article saying, for example, that clients should be "asked for consent before artificial intelligence (AI) is deployed"[56] (which is a simplification of what the *Principles* say).

The *Principles* inform the three d's of lawtech, namely, its:
- design;
- development; and
- deployment.

The five principles, which themselves are subject to an overriding principle of client care, are:
- Compliance: the three d's of lawtech "must comply with all applicable regulations".
- Lawfulness: the three d's of lawtech "should comply with all applicable laws".
- Capability: "lawtech producers and operators should understand the functionality, benefit, limitations and risks of the products used in the course of their work".
- Transparency: information on how the lawtech solution has been designed, developed and deployed (the three d's again) should be accessible.
- Accountability: "lawtech should have an appropriate level of oversight when used to deliver or provide legal services".

The *Principles* need to be read carefully. In particular:
- The definition of lawtech is wide. The *Principles* state that this is "technology which supports or enables the provision of legal services and dispute resolution systems. It is roughly synonymous with legaltech or legal technology".
- The *Principles* say that some types of client "may be less likely to want to be consulted on their solicitor's use of LawTech". Can we infer from this that it isn't best practice in all cases to seek a client's consent to the use of lawtech? Perhaps, in practice, this will depend on the extent to which AI is used and whether it's a core or incidental part of the legaltech offering?
- There's reference to the American Bar Association's (ABA's) "principles and ethics on the use of Lawtech" and the "European Commission's seven non-binding principles for Trustworthy AI", both of which are more explicit on certain points. These are "mentioned as they provide useful supplementary context". They are not, therefore, explicit Law Society 'good practice' for solicitors, rather they indicate best practice in other jurisdictions.
- A firm may be acting as a "Lawtech Operator" and there may be some use cases where a firm might fall into the category of "Lawtech Provider" (in which case a raft of different good practice rules also apply). Firms need to consider carefully the different capacities in which they may be acting.

In conclusion, when deploying legaltech you should ask, in particular:
- Should you apply what the Law Society regards as good practice (and others as best practice), even if it's not mandatory?
- What do your insurers expect on Law Society good practice or legal sector best practice? How does it affect insurance cover?
- What do your clients expect? Is it, in any terms of engagement, to use good or best practice in the delivery of legal services?

9. Practical tips on CQR

We set out below some practical tips on CQR.

Many of the tips for in-house teams in Chapter 8 apply equally for CQR teams in law firms.

These tips are split as follows:
- considering the product or service;
- understanding any tech issues; and
- working with others.

9.1 Considering the product or service
- Ensure that early consultation with the CQR team is a routine part of the product development process. For many projects, this will be critical to their success.
- It's all too easy to involve the CQR too late (or not at all), leading to delays at best, and, at worst, a lot of wasted time in developing a product in a way that isn't compliant. Typical questions you should expect to answer include:
  - What is the proposed product or service?
  - Do you think your firm can actually do what's proposed, given its SRA authorised and regulated entity status?
  - What are the risks?
  - What will be the reputational damage if a mistake is made?
  - Does your firm have the resources and competence to do what is proposed?
  - What sort of clients does it involve?
  - How many clients does it involve?
  - Are there any conflict of interest aspects to consider? Will you need access to client information in the course of them using the product, or can you avoid that to remove potential conflict issues?
  - Is there an international element to it?

Remember that every case is different: each one needs to be looked at by the CQR team on its merits, even if you've done something similar before. One slight change can make a big difference.

- The CQR team also needs to be aware if external products or services are being adopted by the firm even if they are not then advertised to clients as products or services in their own right. What happens, for example, where you adopt an AI solution to review client contracts, or to undertake bulk due diligence on a transaction for a client, but you don't want to publicise that AI is being used?

- Be wary of suppliers' marketing spiel: always undertake your own due diligence on what you're told by an external product or service provider. Your firm could incur a liability to a client for failure of that product or service without you having recourse against the supplier. Do your homework!

- Think about insurance and liability: consider:
    - Will what is proposed be insured? Have you contacted your brokers/insurers for any critical advice and quotes?
    - Must your firm offer a minimum liability of £2 million (for partnerships) and £3 million (for LLPs) to clients when providing the proposed product/service? If so, and you're relying on a supplier to provide you with the underlying technology, what's the level of liability offered to you by the supplier? (Almost certainly it will be considerably less than £2 million or £3 million!)

- Be an enabler (where possible): the CQR team is likely to receive more questions in the future that take it outside its current experience, knowledge and comfort zone. Don't default to putting these questions into the too-difficult box. Be the 'Department of Let's See What We Can Do Here', not the 'Department of No'.

- Embrace technology: do this to help make your own CQR function as efficient as possible. Matter tracking and case management solutions are available to assist with CQR queries, just as they are for enabling in-house lawyers to manage their work for their internal clients.

9.2 Understanding any tech issues

- Explore how technology can help to increase efficiency, improve quality, reduce risk and increase consistency in your firm (such as through document automation, document checking etc).

- Ensure tech is cost-effective: be aware that some compliance tech may simply not be cost-effective to adopt in the particular circumstances. In other words, beware of tech for tech's sake: do cost–benefit analyses. For example, the cost of a technology system to manage DSARs may be high compared to the number of DSARs you typically have to deal with.

- Speak to your insurers and brokers: if you have not done so already, the CQR team should be speaking to brokers or insurers (or both) about the insurance requirements for new products and services using new technology such as AI. For example, some insurers require any use of AI systems to include some form of human supervision.

9.3 Working with others

- Get to know SRA Innovate (they sometimes describe themselves as the best-kept secret in the SRA; but they don't want to be!): they're incredibly helpful as well as being passionate advocates for the greater adoption of technology among regulated firms.
- Keep up with all guidance and best practice notes as they are published (this includes any Law Society guidance, including on cybersecurity). Ensure that you don't consider the guidance in isolation within your team, but be sure to involve those in the firm to whom the guidance is likely to be relevant (eg, those who are using or proposing to use the particular type of technology that's the subject of the guidance).
- Reach out to others: small firms may well not have a separate CQR function (and it will be just one of the many balls being juggled by the sole partner on a daily basis). Reach out to your contacts in the compliance teams in bigger firms for some friendly guidance. The legal compliance community is a friendly cohort and are often willing to share war stories and to help out others when they can.
- Consider who is in the CQR team: do they need to broaden their outlook and have a modern, forward-thinking mindset? Should they speak with the SRA? What training should they do? How should any job specifications change?

Notes

1   Adam Wagner (@AdamWagner1), "Never in my wildest imaginings did I think I would find myself being interviewed on Good Morning Britain about whether it is illegal to sit on the park bench", Twitter, 11 January 2021, https://twitter.com/adamwagner1/status/1348609466187571201.
2   "Newspaper headlines: Tory revolt over tiers and Scotch eggs with beers" (BBC News, 1 December 2020), www.bbc.co.uk/news/blogs-the-papers-55139619.
3   Tony Diver, Hannah Uttley, Helena Horton and Martin Evans, "Overzealous police patrol pubs and argue with landlords over Scotch eggs" (The Telegraph, 3 December 2020), www.telegraph.co.uk/news/2020/12/03/overzealous-police-patrol-pubs-argue-landlords-scotch-eggs/.
4   "Newspaper headlines: Tory revolt over tiers and Scotch eggs with beers" (BBC News, 1 December 2020), www.bbc.co.uk/news/blogs-the-papers-55139619.
5   Jed Meers, "Is a Scotch egg a meal? I investigated more than 300 council rulings to find out" (The Conversation, 3 December 2020), https://theconversation.com/is-a-scotch-egg-a-meal-i-investigated-more-than-300-council-rulings-to-find-out-151320.
6   "Coronavirus and compliance with government guidance, UK: April 2021" (Office for National Statistics), www.ons.gov.uk/peoplepopulationandcommunity/healthandsocialcare/conditionsanddiseases/bulletins/coronavirusandcompliancewithgovernmentguidanceuk/april2021.
7   Nick Hilborne, "Oversight regulator 'very concerned' about ethics of commercial lawyers" (Legal Futures, 8 June 2022), www.legalfutures.co.uk/latest-news/oversight-regulator-very-concerned-about-ethics-of-commercial-lawyers.

8 The Law Society has started the ball rolling, having published its *Lawtech and Ethics Principles* in 2021. The SRA too has published compliance tips on using technology and is likely to add to its guidance as technology plays an even more important role in firms. More will follow, particularly on AI.

9 Examples of legaltech providers (mainly in the sphere of AML compliance) include, among others: AMLcheck, Clear View, FileInvite, Legl, NewBanking Identity, ML Verify ProcessGene and Verify 365.

10 Brad Smith, *Tools and Weapons* (Hodder, 2021), p197.

11 Compliance tips for solicitors (Solicitors Regulation Authority), www.sra.org.uk/solicitors/resources/sra-innovate/law-firms/compliance-tips-for-solicitors/.

12 "Cyber Security – A thematic review" (Solicitors Regulation Authority, 2 September 2020), www.sra.org.uk/sra/research-publications/cyber-security/.

13 *The cyber threat to UK legal sector 2018 report* (National Cyber Security Centre), www.ncsc.gov.uk/report/-the-cyber-threat-to-uk-legal-sector—2018-report.

14 "Reports on cybercrime and innovation set out the risks" (Solicitors Regulation Authority, 1 June 2022), www.sra.org.uk/sra/news/press/risk-outlook-innovation-and-cybercrime/.

15 Marina Walker Guevara, "ICIJ releases Panama Papers offshore company data" (Investigative Consortium of Investigative Journalists, 9 May 2016), www.icij.org/inside-icij/2016/05/icij-releases-panama-papers-offshore-company-data/.

16 Mar Cabra and Erin Kissane, "Wrangling 2.6TB of data: The people and the technology behind the Panama Papers" (Investigative Consortium of Investigative Journalists, 25 April 2016), www.icij.org/investigations/panama-papers/data-tech-team-icij/.

17 "About the investigation" (Investigative Consortium of Investigative Journalists), www.icij.org/investigations/panama-papers/pages/panama-papers-about-the-investigation/.

18 Nicola Slawson, "Mossack Fonseca law firm to shut down after Panama Papers tax scandal" (*The Guardian*, 14 March 2018), www.theguardian.com/world/2018/mar/14/mossack-fonseca-shut-down-panama-papers.

19 Brad Smith, *Tools and Weapons* (Hodder, 2021), p92.

20 "Massive ransomware infection hits computers in 99 countries" (BBC News, 13 May 2017), www.bbc.co.uk/news/technology-39901382.

21 Matt Burgess, "The Workaday Life of the World's Most Dangerous Ransomware Gang" (*WIRED*, 16 March 2022), www.wired.com/story/conti-leaks-ransomware-work-life/.

22 Catalin Cimpanu, "Ransomware gang asks $42m from NY law firm, threatens to leak dirt on Trump" (ZDNET, 15 May 2020), www.zdnet.com/article/ransomware-gang-asks-42m-from-ny-law-firm-threatens-to-leak-dirt-on-trump/.

23 *Ibid*; Davey Winder, "Hackers Publish First 169 Trump 'Dirty Laundry' Emails After Being Branded Cyber-Terrorists" (Forbes, 17 May 2020), www.forbes.com/sites/daveywinder/2020/05/17/hackers-publish-first-169-trump-dirty-laundry-emails-after-being-branded-cyber-terrorists/.

24 Catalin Cimpanu, "Ransomware gang asks $42m from NY law firm, threatens to leak dirt on Trump" (ZDNET, 15 May 2020), www.zdnet.com/article/ransomware-gang-asks-42m-from-ny-law-firm-threatens-to-leak-dirt-on-trump/.

25 *National Strategic Assessment of Serious and Organised Crime* (National Crime Agency, 2021), https://nationalcrimeagency.gov.uk/who-we-are/publications/533-national-strategic-assessment-of-serious-and-organised-crime-2021/file.

26 "Reports on cybercrime and innovation set out the risks" (Solicitors Regulation Authority, 1 June 2022), www.sra.org.uk/sra/news/press/risk-outlook-innovation-and-cybercrime/.

27 "Risk Outlook report: information security and cybercrime in a new normal" (Solicitors Regulation Authority, 1 June 2022), www.sra.org.uk/sra/research-publications/risk-outlook-report-information-security-cybercrime/.

28 "How we can help you in the fight against ransomware" (Law Society, 11 August 2022), www.lawsociety.org.uk/topics/cybersecurity/how-we-can-help-you-in-the-fight-against-ransomware.

29 The Global City, *2021: A Critical Year for RegTech* (City of London Corporation), www.theglobalcity.uk/PositiveWebsite/media/Research-reports/2021-A-Critical-Year-for-RegTech-final.pdf.

30 Terms like 'regtech', 'legal regtech' and 'fintech' are by no means clear-cut. The authors have come across, for example, sophisticated decision tree software. It can help to advise clients on the permitted content of financial promotions under the Financial Services and Markets Act 2000. Is this 'finpromtech'? Where do you draw the line? After all, even legal regtech for AML is by no means confined to lawyers, it is also used by financial institutions, other professionals, casinos and so on. The key is not to get too het up on the definitions.

31 "Business Plan sets out work for year ahead" (Solicitors Regulation Authority, 26 October 2021), www.sra.org.uk/sra/news/press/2021-press-releases/latest-business-plan-published-2021/.

32 Muyao Shen, "How $60 Billion in Terra Coins Went Up in Algorithmic Smoke" (Bloomberg UK, 21 May 2022), www.bloomberg.com/graphics/2022-crypto-luna-terra-stablecoin-explainer/.

33 Natalie Sherman and Joe Tidy, "Crypto giant FTX collapses into bankruptcy" (BBC News, 11 November 2022), www.bbc.co.uk/news/business-63601213.

34 "Better Information in the Legal Services Market – Year One Evaluation of the Transparency Rules" (Solicitors Regulation Authority, 15 October 2020), www.sra.org.uk/sra/research-publications/better-information-legal-services-market/.

35 Sir Geoffrey Vos, "The Future for Dispute Resolution: Horizon Scanning" (The Society of Computers and Law, Sir Brian Neill Lecture 2022, 17 March 2022), www.judiciary.uk/wp-content/uploads/2022/03/MR-to-SCL-Sir-Brain-Neill-Lecture-2022-The-Future-for-Dispute-Resolu tion-Horizon-Scannings-.pdf.

36 John Hyde (@JohnHyde1982), "Claimants, according to the *checks notes* master of the rolls, want quick fixes 'without much caring' if the outcome is robust and dependable", Twitter, 18 March 2022, https://twitter.com/johnhyde1982/status/1504816210671771656?s=11.

37 Sir Geoffrey Vos, "The Future for Dispute Resolution: Horizon Scanning" (The Society of Computers and Law, Sir Brian Neill Lecture 2022, 17 March 2022), www.judiciary.uk/wp-content/uploads/2022/03/MR-to-SCL-Sir-Brain-Neill-Lecture-2022-The-Future-for-Dispute-Resolu tion-Horizon-Scannings-.pdf.

38 Business plan and budget (November 2021 to October 2022) (Solicitors Regulation Authority, 25 October 2021), https://www.sra.org.uk/globalassets/documents/sra/consultations/draft-business-plan-2021-22.pdf.

39 Ibid.

40 Competition & Markets Authority, Review of the legal services market study in England and Wales (2020), https://assets.publishing.service.gov.uk/media/5fd9e53cd3bf7f40ccb335e1/Legal_Services_Review_-_Final_report.pdf.

41 Quoted by Iain Miller, "Client selection: The next frontier in the evolution of legal ethics" (Law Society Gazette, 9 March 2022), www.lawgazette.co.uk/commentary-and-opinion/client-selection-the-next-frontier-in-the-evolution-of-legal-ethics/5111779.article.

42 Huw van Steenis, Future of Finance (June 2019), www.bankofengland.co.uk/-/media/boe/files/report/2019/future-of-finance-report.pdf.

43 Jennifer Clarke, "922 regulatory insights a month: is it any wonder enforcements are on the rise?" (UK Finance), www.ukfinance.org.uk/news-and-insight/blogs/922-regulatory-insights-month-it-any-wonder-enforcements-are-rise.

44 Ibid.

45 Alison Hook, The Use and Regulation of Technology in the Legal Sector beyond England and Wales (Hook Tangaza, June 2019), www.legalservicesboard.org.uk/wp-content/uploads/2019/07/International-AH-Report-VfP-4-Jul-2019.pdf.

46 Ron Kalifa OBE, "Kalifa Review of UK Fintech" (2021), www.gov.uk/government/publications/the-kalifa-review-of-uk-fintech.

47 Department for International Trade, UK Fintech State of the Nation (April 2019), https://assets.publishing.service.gov.uk/government/uploads/system/uploads/attachment_data/file/801277/UK-fintech-state-of-the-nation.pdf.

48 Deloitte, "The UK Fintech Landscape", www2.deloitte.com/uk/en/pages/financial-services/articles/uk-fintech-landscape.html.

49 Ron Kalifa OBE, "Kalifa Review of UK Fintech" (2021), www.gov.uk/government/publications/the-kalifa-review-of-uk-fintech.

50 www.fca.org.uk/insight/future-regtech-what-do-firms-really-want.

51 "Call for input on supporting the development and adopters of RegTech", Feedback Statement FS16/4 (Financial Conduct Authority, July 2016), www.fca.org.uk/sites/default/files/publications/feedback/fs-16-04.pdf.

52 J Mohun and A Roberts (2020), "Cracking the code: Rulemaking for humans and machines", OECD Working Papers on Public Governance, No 42, OECD Publishing, https://doi.org/10.1787/3afe6ba5-en.

53 Annual Report and Group Financial Statements (Monzo Bank Limited, 28 February 2021), https://monzo.com/static/docs/monzo-annual-report-2021.pdf.

54 "Lawtech and ethics principles report" (Law Society, 28 July 2021), www.lawsociety.org.uk/topics/research/lawtech-and-ethics-principles-report-2021.

55 Ibid.

56 Dan Bindman, "Law Society: Solicitors must not use AI without clients' consent" (Legal Futures, 30 July 2021), www.legalfutures.co.uk/latest-news/law-society-solicitors-must-not-use-ai-without-clients-consent.

Part 3:
Models of delivery

Nowadays, it's become a bit of a trope to say that people are sick and tired of experts. In 2016, the then-Lord Chancellor and Secretary of State for Justice, Michael Gove, told Sky News: "I think the people in this country have had enough of experts."[1] But Gove's subsequent qualification – "from organisations with acronyms saying that they know what is best and getting it consistently wrong" – got lost in the cut and thrust of the debate. Most people remember the first part of his statement, but few recall the rest. That's politics for you.

With people feeling less deferential towards mainstream institutions and professions, it'd be easy to think that not only are people fed up with, but they've also given up on, experts. And this, alas, includes lawyers. But the fact remains that in a time of 'change[3]' people still need experts to help them make sense of a complex world. If anything, people need them more.

In the legal sphere, more information than ever is available on countless legal matters online. Some commentators have suggested that lawyers have historically been the self-anointed custodians of legal knowledge and that, by democratising this knowledge, by making it widely accessible, the need for lawyers reduces. But merely making knowledge available doesn't imbue the ability to process and apply it. It's like giving everyone a copy of the instruction manual for a helicopter and expecting them not only to fly it safely and within the regulations, but also to navigate it to where they want to be – and to do all this quickly enough to ensure that they're on time too. (Hyperbolic? Yes, but it makes the point.) The law is complex and is becoming more so. People still struggle to make sense of it all. Even we lawyers struggle to get our heads around some of it. More than ever, clients need our wisdom, experience and ability to make solid judgements to help them navigate their legal problems.

But the way in which we provide our services is changing. Some legal services may not need much involvement from qualified lawyers at all, but many others will continue to need lawyers to guide clients to where they want to be. In the end, the authors suspect that people aren't so much unhappy with experts, as the trope would have it, but they're unhappy with the way expertise is delivered. A haughty, take-it-or-leave-it, we-know-what's-best-for-you attitude is no longer acceptable (if it ever was!). People are increasingly railing against it. Perhaps it's this that Gove was trying to refer to?

Moreover, the digital transformation of the profession makes it more important than ever that we shake up how we deliver what we do. As Martin Gill, writing for Forrester Research points out:

> Digital disruptors are tearing up the rule books and no industry is immune. In response, firms must take a different approach to digital strategy, embedding digital capabilities into the heart of their business, rather than treating digital touchpoints as peripheral add-ons.[2]

But Gill was by no means the first to see the potential and importance of shaking up the traditional model of lawyering.

This part of the book looks at models of delivery, namely:

- how new law models like alternative business structures and alternative legal services providers, among others, are changing how the law is delivered (see Chapter 7); and
- how in-house teams are transforming the way in which they deliver their services to their businesses, using new digital tools, to become a department that the business wants to engage with (see Chapter 8).

In the future, people won't have had enough of experts, but they'll be much less tolerant with those experts who stick to the old ways of doing things.

Notes

1   Amy Hawkins, "Has the public really had enough of experts?" (*Full Fact*, 14 September 2016), https://fullfact.org/blog/2016/sep/has-public-really-had-enough-experts/.
2   Dr Jim Hamill, *Digital Disruption and Small Business in Scotland* (Federation of Small Businesses, 5 December 2015), www.fsb.org.uk%2Fstatic%2F6cf4a340-634a-4108-8a0a74286b0b2f4d%2 Digital-Disruption-and-Small-Business-in-Scotland.pdf.

Chapter 7: New law models

The digital transformation juggernaut is impacting industries that, in many cases and until very recently, remained unchanged for hundreds of years.

Take publishing, for example. The Statute of Anne (ie, the Copyright Act 1710), formed the basis of copyright law in the United Kingdom and is generally recognised as the first piece of legislation in the world to protect the interests of authors and publishers. In later years, in 1888, the United Kingdom was one of the main protagonists of the Berne Convention which provided the basis for the international protection of intellectual property (IP).

The UK newspaper industry can trace its origins back more than 300 years to the time of William of Orange. *Berrow's Worcester Journal* is said to have started life as the *Worcester Postman* in 1690 and was published regularly from 1709. It's believed to be the oldest surviving English newspaper. Yet, despite books and literary content having been published in physical form for hundreds of years, the last decade has seen profound change in this industry. It's barely recognisable.

The changing habits in how we consume content and the written word has meant publishing giants have been forced to radically overhaul their business models and fundamentally change how they deliver their content.

We are more connected than ever by technology. Our appetite for information hasn't reduced – in fact, we're consuming more of it now than at any other time in history. But how we consume content is fundamentally different from just 10 years ago. Physical print has seen a significant decrease in favour of digital consumption through devices like the laptops, tablets and smart-phones. Between 2012 and 2018, the number of hours spent globally on traditional media flatlined at about four-and-a-half hours per person daily, but the amount of digital media time increased from about five-and-a-half hours daily to six-and-three-quarter hours.[1] The figures are so high because many people 'second-screen', watching TV while tweeting about it at the same time. Put simply, we can't get enough information and entertainment. And these figures don't include the pandemic, when the shift to digital was even more pronounced.

This shift in public habits has forced corporate titans to dispense with the time-honoured processes of producing bulk print runs, to taking a more agile and bespoke approach of producing digital content and printing on demand – moving print production from large, dedicated factories to smaller remote printing sites, closer to where the reader wants their content.

Change is hitting the music industry too. Bruce Springsteen, David Bowie, Blondie, Whitney Houston and Bob Dylan (or their respective estates), among others, are selling their own music catalogues, or parts of them, for millions of dollars. In Springsteen's case it is for a reported half-a-billion dollars. Why? As *Rolling Stone* noted in January 2021, these artists don't know what the future holds. Will some technology come along to transform how artists make money from their work? Possibly. And if they can get an average multiple of "14.76x historic annual income"[2] now for their catalogues, it's a difficult proposition to turn down.

Therefore, if an industry as old as publishing is capable of such root-and-branch reform as it has seen in the past decade, and the music industry is changing too, it would be naïve to think that the legal sector were somehow immune to the digital transformation affecting other industries and sectors. In July 2022, LSB undertook a survey, which suggested, for example, that unregulated businesses have up to almost a 40% share of the legal services market serving SMEs.[3]

In this chapter we look at the changes in delivering legal services, particu-larly from businesses other than 'traditional' law firms. (Although we shouldn't write off law firms just yet. As we will show, there's a lot that law firms are doing to evolve.) We explore:

- ABSs (alternative business structures) and ALSPs (alternative legal service providers);

- what the Big Four, Big Tech and retail giants are looking to do;
- what NewLaw is and the impact this is having; and
- other growth opportunities.

We then look at two case studies and finish with some practical tips on new law models.

1. Setting the scene

We start this section with the word 'alternative'. It sounds pedestrian enough. But the moment we tack it onto another term, our choices increase. For regulators, from the CMA to the LSB via the SRA, choices are the rocket fuel that powers the profession. More choice leads, in theory, to better outcomes for our clients through greater competition.

In the practice of law, the word 'alternative' promises choices which are faster (alternative dispute resolution) or more flexible (the Alternative Investment Market). Outside of the law, alternative comedy allowed us to choose an edgier future in the 1980s; alternative rock, a more unconventional one in the 1990s. Time and again, 'alternative' is the hip and trendy sibling to the more humdrum '*status quo*'.

In the business of law, the profession hasn't been spared this adjective either, usually in the form of similar-sounding initialisms. ABSs and ALSPs, which we explore below, are terms which nowadays pop up in the legal press with unrelenting regularity. But what exactly are these free-spirited 'alternatives'? Aren't they just a bit too unconventional? Unproven? Unethical even? Or are they the future of legal services? After all, in 2015, SRA Chief Executive Paul Philip told a conference: "If you're starting a legal business today, why would you not adopt an alternative business structure?"[4] Are the 'alternatives' becoming the mainstream? Is it time to say 'goodbye' to the traditional law firm?

To answer these questions, we look at ABSs and ALSPs in turn to understand what they are, before we look at the impact that they are having in the digital age.

1.1 ABSs
ABSs allow non-lawyers to have an ownership interest in a firm and to participate in the management of it. We can think of ABSs being a 'law firm+'. But, as we explore later, they're not just for law firms.

From a legal point of view, the focus of an ABS is on ownership and management of a 'licensed body' (law firms which aren't ABSs are 'recognised bodies' or 'recognised sole practices'). ABSs apply only to legal businesses which carry out 'reserved legal activities' including:

- the exercise of rights of audience;
- the conduct of litigation;
- undertaking 'reserved instrument activities' (eg, preparing any instrument of transfer or charge for the purposes of the Land Registration Act 2002);
- probate activities;
- notarial activities; and
- the administration of oaths.

It's easy to think that ABSs are relatively new, but the history of ABSs is a long one. Here's a brief timeline:

- 2001: the Office of Fair Trading published a report on competition in the professions.
- 2003: the government called the regulatory system for legal services: "outdated, inflexible, over-complex and not accountable or transparent enough".[5] Sir David Clementi reviewed the sector and, in 2004, proposed the creation of ABSs.
- 2004: the government broadly welcomed the Clementi Report and the setting up of ABSs.
- 2007: the Legal Services Bill received Royal Assent.
- 2011: the legal 'Big Bang': the first ABS application was received by the Council for Licensed Conveyancers. In 2012, the SRA also began licensing ABSs.

Despite all of this legal hullabaloo, only about one in 10 regulated firms were ABSs in 2020.[6] By this date, regulators had authorised more than 1,400 ABSs.[7] At the time of writing, the figure stands at almost 1,900. (Over seven in 10 licences have been issued by the SRA, and less than one in five by the Institute of Chartered Accountants in England and Wales (ICAEW).)[8]

At the current rate of adoption, it'll take many decades until, in numbers alone, even half of all legal businesses are in the form of ABSs. However, in aggregate revenue terms, the impact of ABSs is quite probably somewhat greater.[9]

ABSs are used throughout the legal sector. These include, among others:

- Law firms: Irwin Mitchell was the first firm to receive multiple ABS licences in 2012. This enabled non-lawyers from PwC and KPMG to take up roles in the firm. Reed Smith converted to an ABS in 2019, saying that it was the first international law firm to do so.
- Listed law firms: Gateley was the United Kingdom's first law firm to go public in 2015. It needed to become an ABS in order to list on the Alternative Investment Market (AIM).

Figure 1. Growth in alternative business structures

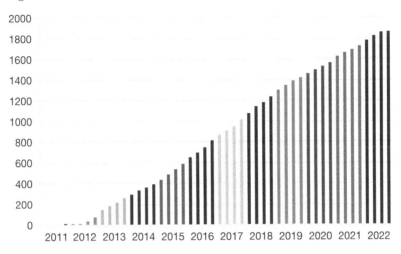

Source: Based on data from the Legal Services Board market structure dashboard.

- Private equity-backed legal businesses: In 2019, Kayne Partners invested $25 million in Elevate, which provides consulting, legal technology, and other services to in-house teams and law firms. Elevate was also the first law company to be granted an ABS licence in the US (from the Arizona Supreme Court).
- Retailers: Co-op (see below), which was one of the first to become an ABS in 2012.
- In-house lawyers: BT's in-house team set up an ABS in 2013 to deal with liability and claims matters. In 2019, it sold it to DWF.
- Accountants: the Big Four have all set up ABSs (see below). Deloitte was the last to do so in 2018.
- Local authorities: LGSS Law (now Pathfinder Legal Services) was set up in 2015 and is owned by four councils. It aims to be a "national leader for local government law".[10]
- ALSPs (see below): businesses like Farewill, which offers online will writing, probate and funeral services, set up as ABSs as they offer some reserved legal activities.

The question really ought to be: "where aren't ABSs used?". However, despite their growth the jury is still out on their impact. They do seem to be more innovative and no less ethical than non-ABS firms:

- In 2020 the LSB said that ABSs were "significantly more likely to have introduced service innovation (38%) compared to non-ABS firms (25%)".[11]
- The LSB also noted that the available data shows that ABSs "have no

worse a disciplinary record than other types of law firm, which suggests they have not lowered standards as was feared".[12]

As for ownership, Jonathan Molot, a founding member of litigation-funding business Burford Capital, said in 2020 that more and more firms will consider external ownership but "mass adoption of outside ownership is unlikely in the short term or even medium term".[13] Is this legal 'Big Bang' still a bit of a damp squib?

What's more, setting up as an ABS is no guarantee of success. They face the same pressures as other traditional law firms. Crispin Passmore, then head of strategy at the LSB, said in 2012 that firms need to focus on the substance, not the form:

> *I would encourage firms not to think that they should or shouldn't be an ABS. I would encourage them to think about who their customers are, what they want and how they, as lawyers, can best meet their needs.*[14]

As far as the authors are concerned, we think that this remains sound advice. For some firms converting to an ABS makes sense. For many others, it doesn't. Start with being client-centric and then see what works best.

1.2 ALSPs

Being client-centric is at the heart of many ALSP business models.

'ALSP' is a wider term which is used more and more in the legal sector, but, unlike the term 'ABS', it isn't defined in any law. Sometimes it's called 'NewLaw' (although see below) and the businesses are called 'new law companies' or just 'law companies'.

The focus of many ASLPs is on processes and tasks. For example, tasks that would be loss-making for a law firm to undertake itself, or some volume tasks in a firm, from, for example, document review to due diligence, can be outsourced to an ALSP, freeing up lawyers to concentrate on, say, more high-value work. But ASLPs can also offer *all* of the services which traditional law firms offer (and sometimes more), often through an ABS.

ALSPs are either:
- captive (owned by a law firm); or
- independent. Sometimes the Big Four are included as a separate category of ALSP.

ALSPs are used throughout the legal sector. Starting from the more traditional and moving to the more *avant-garde*, these include, among others:

- Legal services, including legal advice: this is provided by non-law firms, such as the Big Four (see below).
- On-demand legal support, including the supply of lawyers on a short-term basis. They include businesses such as:
  - Lawyers on Demand (LOD), which was established by Berwin Leighton Paisner but is now independent;
  - Axiom, which was co-founded in 2000 by an ex-associate of Davis, Polk & Wardwell; and
  - Vario (from Pinsent Masons).
- Managed legal services (MLS), including:
  - businesses which offer legal process outsourcing (LPO) using labour arbitrage, ie, using the lowest cost staff to produce goods or services. Although the use of that term is rare in daily legal parlance, the concept is very familiar:
    - 'northshoring': moving business processes and functions out of London and the south east of England for lower costs: from Baker & McKenzie in Belfast, Ashurst in Glasgow or BCLP in Manchester; and
    - offshoring: moving business processes and functions out of the United Kingdom for lower costs such as moving some legal processes from, say, London to Hyderabad. (If unsuccessful, they may be 'backshored'; also known as 'inshoring' and 'reshoring');
  - businesses which offer more sophisticated managed legal services. They may use data, legaltech and legal ops more in providing their services:
    - GravityStack, which Reed Smith set up in 2018. It says it "applies technology to solve critical problems". Its solutions are split into "litigation and investigations", "contract intelligence" and "business advisory solutions".
    - Konexo, which was established by Eversheds Sutherland in 2019. It uses analytics, automation and "innovative operational processes" to offer solutions in five main areas: legal services, legal resourcing, digital transformation, human resources services and financial services.
    - Riverview Law, which was launched in 2012, bought by EY in 2018 and then rebranded a year later. The business focused on fixed-price managed services for in-house teams and was one of the first to use an AI-powered virtual assistant powered by its 'Kim' technology platform.

Whatever we call this sector and the categories within it, we ignore it at our peril. In 2019 *The Lawyer* noted: "ALSPs have evolved from a relatively unknown phenomenon into a fast-growing segment that is an integral part

Since the turn of the century, we've witnessed two decades of the Big Four retrenching and then renewing their push into the legal arena.

of the legal services industry."[15] This segment continues to grow and develop quickly.

But there's no doubt that pinning down the exact scope of categories in this area isn't easy. The lines between them are grey, with many ASLPs offering a variety of services, which may fall within more than one of the above categories. More and more traditional law firms are also experimenting with new business streams and exploring how they can improve their internal processes to be smarter, faster and better.

In the next sections, we explore a few notable examples of how ABSs and ALSPs are changing the legal landscape. We start with the Big Four.

2. Waiting for the accountants

Who remembers the predictions of the early 2000s, when the accountants had their sights set on taking over the legal world? The Big Four (Deloitte, EY, KPMG and PwC) were at the door.

The legal press was full of headlines about how they were going to encroach on the Magic Circle and provide their impressive client lists with a one-stop-shop approach. As one expert on the legal profession put it, "clients don't have legal problems, they have 'problem problems'".[16]

The previously perceived concerns around conflicts seemed to be forgotten and the tricky conundrum of a corporate going to a firm to receive legal advice and then be audited by the same firm was seen to be surmountable.

Powered by the dot.com boom, the accountants fuelled the speedy increase in associate salaries that hit the market, leading to a fierce war for talent. But then the dot.com bubble burst and Enron happened. Arthur Anderson collapsed. All of a sudden it was curtains for this particular assault on the legal profession. The battle seemed lost.

But perhaps we shouldn't be too quick to write-off our bean-counting contemporaries just yet.

Since the turn of the century, we've witnessed two decades of the Big Four retrenching and then renewing their push into the legal arena.
- In 2014, all but Deloitte had secured licences from the SRA to operate as ABSs. Deloitte followed suit later. ABSs also made way for the possibility of multi-disciplinary practice, something the accountants have long courted as a business model.
- Deloitte Legal made its long-awaited debut in January 2019 by hiring

former Allen & Overy banking partner Michael Castle (who had spent 20 years at the firm) to lead its UK legal arm. In November 2020, Deloitte announced its significant expansion plan in a landmark transaction with Kemp Little, a well-respected City-based technology law firm. As well as adding 29 partners and many more lawyers, the deal marked a significant acceleration of Deloitte's plan to scale up its legal offering.

- Only a few months after Deloitte Legal took shape, EY acquired Thomson Reuter's managed legal services business Pangea3 to consolidate its NewLaw offering, following the earlier acquisition of Riverview Law from DLA Piper (who had set up that business in 2012 but struggled to gain traction for it in the market). EY combined both of those acquired businesses into a new MLS offering under the EY Law brand with the stated intention of helping clients to "increase efficiency, manage risk, improve service transparency and reduce costs of routine legal activities".[17]

- Similarly, KPMG Law and PWC Legal Solutions have each been ramping up its respective legal offerings in the United Kingdom with the aim of providing clients with that one-stop-shop panacea for professional advisory services.

And at the time of writing, late 2022, EY "blinked first"[18] and is the first of the Big Four to examine separating its audit function from its advisory offering in an attempt to reduce potential conflicts of interest that have held the Big Four back from fully realising their potential to offer the one-stop-shop to which they aspire. To move away from the long history of combining audit and advisory in a single entity surely signals louder than ever the strategic intentions of EY to make a much bigger play for legal mandates. If approved, the split probably won't be completed until the end of 2023 at the earliest.

One would, perhaps, have expected similar moves from the others of the Big Four; however, for now, Deloitte, KPMG and PwC have all ruled out splitting their businesses. In whatever way the Big Four approach this, they seem to share a common strategy: to fuse the traditional world of lawyering with their mainstay of consulting, managed services and tech-enabled professional services.

And it's a strategy that is not without merit. Doubtless, they'll be keen to replicate the penetration they have so deftly achieved in the auditing market, where their combined majority share in the sector is overshadowed by the statistic that together they act for around 97% of all FTSE 350 companies. In August 2022, *City A.M.* reported that the Big Four were capturing a larger share of the UK legal market.[19] Contrast this position of dominance with the key players in the legal world; no single law firm holds more than about 0.5% of the global market.

And the accountants have deep pockets to fund their aggressive investment-charged growth agenda. As the LSB noted in 2020: "The Big Four accounting firms all hold ABS licenses, and their scale and multidisciplinary approach holds the potential for disruption in the corporate market."[20] Could it be that the accountants will succeed in being the kind of digital disrupters that Uber, Deliveroo and AirBnB proved to be to their respective industries?

3. Understanding NewLaw

It's not just the Big Four who see the opportunity for shaking up the competition in the legal market.

Eric Chin, a well-known consultant to the legal sector, once said that the "seven most expensive words" in the business and practice of law are "we have always done it that way".[21] And it's hard to argue against this: just ask the former CEOs of Kodak and Blockbuster (see Chapter 1).

But Chin's claim to fame isn't limited to these seven prophetic words. In 2013, he tried to predict what the legal sector would look like in 2018. Chin described a model for the delivery of legal services; one that put labour arbitrage at its core. He called this model 'NewLaw'. The term took off. (Like many popular neologisms, it's short and includes the obligatory multiple capital letters in it, giving it the authoritative aura of 'the next big thing'.)

In the legal sector, NewLaw was used in the context of legal process out-sourcing (LPO) in particular, but Chin's vision of it was more sophisticated than merely leveraging workforce location. Fundamentally, it looked at the:
- type of people;
- basis on which they're engaged;
- tasks that they do;
- processes by which they do them, and
- scope of products or services sold.

In NewLaw these are all deeply different from the model most 'traditional' law firms operated, which hadn't changed significantly for decades (ABSs, for example, had only just been launched at that time). Chin was describing a new breed of legal services provider, the difference being in the 'engine' that produced the legal services. Chin's NewLaw model wasn't fundamentally designed to use legaltech – a surprise perhaps, given that it wasn't conceived that long ago – rather it was based on the smarter use of people and processes.

Since 2013, things have moved along at pace. Today, as commonly understood, the term 'NewLaw' can be pinned onto any ALSP. "NewLaw is now mainstream",[22] as Chin noted in 2019. He's not wrong. And it's a mainstream which is moving its focus from labour arbitrage to tech arbitrage.

So far, however, tech arbitrage – a nice way of saying 'software solutions' – isn't making too many inroads into how law firms produce their output or how that output is delivered to clients. That's not to say that firms and NewLaw businesses aren't adopting more and more technology (including legaltech) in their processes. But it *is* to say that tech arbitrage hasn't yet become the tool predominantly used by established law firms to conduct their business: they haven't fully evolved to be powered by a technology-driven engine. In other words, we're still at the stage of law firms doing a bit of legaltech; as opposed to legaltech firms doing law.

But law firms are evolving: several firms, particularly in BigLaw, have some form of NewLaw activity (in nature, if not in name) and are also applying legaltech to give clients new tech-led solutions for their legal needs.

What's in a name? As NewLaw shows, it's difficult to say. The jargon in this area has an uncanny ability to shapeshift at will. What's clear, however, is that business models are changing. According to HSBC in 2021, 58% of BigLaw firms think that their legal competitors using more tech-driven business models present them with the "greatest strategic change considerations"[23] (followed by non-law firm ASLPs at 34%). Arbitrage – labour or technological – will increasingly play a part. And in creating solutions which work for us and our clients we need to challenge the *status quo*. If we don't, someone else may well do so.

Therefore, rather than trying to categorise legal businesses as either 'traditional', 'NewLaw' or 'legaltech', it's perhaps much more useful for law firms (in particular) to consider the characteristics which differentiate them.

Table 1. Comparison between traditional law firms, NewLaw businesses and legaltech businesses

	Traditional law firm	NewLaw business	Legaltech business
How legal services are produced	People-based: Partners supervising senior associates supervising junior associates – mostly all legally qualified staff producing output in a pyramidal structure	Predominantly people-based; but more highly leveraged in terms of senior qualified lawyers compared to other staff, deploying more advanced processes for the types of legal services produced	Predominantly technology-based although a part of the process may involve human input and intervention
Nature of legal services produced	Full range	More limited in the nature of services that can be delivered within the processes and resources deployed	More limited still in the nature of services that can be delivered within the capability of technology currently available. (We anticipate that this capability will increase dramatically over the next 10 years)
Pricing of legal services	Still mainly time and materials (hourly rate), albeit some variants based on fixed fees	Predominantly fixed prices based on a clearly defined scope of output	Almost always fixed prices based on a clearly defined product specification

continued on next page

	Traditional law firm	**NewLaw business**	**Legaltech business**
Sales generation	Predominantly based on firm or partner reputation and relationships	Typically relies on existing parent law firm (or accountancy firm) contacts and brand. But has the potential to gain custom also through more usual commercial business routes to market (ie, through marketing and sales teams)	Almost exclusively through more usual commercial business routes to market (marketing and sales teams)
Business management	Typically, a partnership structure, where managers are also senior producers of output	Typically, a corporate structure, where management is not personally engaged in production of output	Typically, a corporate structure, where management is not personally engaged in production of output
Business ownership	Owners are the partners who work in the business (save for the tiny minority of firms that have listed)	Often at least part of the equity is owned by third parties who are not lawyers	Typically, a majority of the equity is owned by non-lawyers (although a former practising lawyer may have been instrumental in founding the business)

continued on next page

	Traditional law firm	**NewLaw business**	**Legaltech business**
Investment in innovation	Typically, no more than 1% of turnover (probably influenced by the owner-manager partnership structure where senior management have conflicting interests between the long-term benefit to the business and short-term reduction in profit distributed)	Likely to be greater than in a typical firm, given the reliance on process improvement and separation of management from ownership through a corporate structure	Higher than in both typical firms and NewLaw businesses, given the need for both initial and ongoing investment in technology
Regulation	Fully regulated by the SRA	Likely to be undertaking work that does not require to be undertaken by a regulated solicitor and therefore subject to lesser regulation (sometimes as an ABS)	Almost certainly won't be undertaking work that may only be undertaken by a regulated solicitor and therefore subject to lesser regulation than a firm or ABS. But activities may become increasingly regulated (particularly where AI is used with consumer clients or to make decisions carrying ethical implications) if regulatory policy is to 'regulate up' rather than to 'regulate down' or do nothing (see Chapter 6).

Inevitably, NewLaw businesses are also increasingly adopting more technology in their service production and delivery (research in 2019 by the International Bar Association, for example, suggests that "software solutions now actively compete with labour arbitrage as the primary mechanism for both companies and law firms to reduce legal costs").[24] But that's not to say that the direction of travel is, or should be, necessarily towards the last column on the right-hand side in the table above.

The authors' collective view is that law firms have the opportunity to evolve into something more powerful than mere purveyors of tech-led legal products. By combining the power of tech and the human skills of people, law firms stand to benefit from technical efficiencies and power like never before, while at the same time applying equal investment in their people to add value that technology simply cannot deliver. Law firms can be driven by technology and at the same time be more people-focused than ever before (see Chapter 9).

In doing so, we need to be aware of how the language used in this area, while it may not be familiar to us, can frame our approach – perhaps more than we appreciate. As John Croft, co-founder and President of Elevate has noted, the idea that his business is an ALSP "seems to ... imply that there is one 'proper' way of providing legal services", such as "going to a traditional law firm" and that "any other way is 'alternative' (ie, wrong/new/risky!)".[25]

And, of course, what is now seen as 'traditional' was often once, in its time, 'alternative'. For example, Cravath, Swaine & Moore, the firm which created the 'Cravath system' in the United States, was once pilloried for having created 'law factories'. However, by the 1960s, it was seen by many as the gold standard in how firms provided legal services,[26] including its pure lockstep remuneration system (which, in 2021, it changed to a modified lockstep system). Alas, change never stops!

4. Waiting for the retailers and Big Tech

'Tesco law' was supposed to be the future. At least it was when the regulators started to license ABSs in the early 2010s. The *Law Society Gazette* said that it was going to be the equivalent of the Big Bang in the City. But there were no bangs, "more of a muffled bump".[27]

Although Tesco never entered the market, others like Co-op did. But in 2018, a report for the SRA noted that "the expansion of services by Co-op Legal has not fulfilled expectations".[28]

Co-operative Legal Services was launched in 2006. By 2010, it was advertising its legal services in Co-op's thousands of supermarkets nationwide. Two years later, it was granted ABS status, but things soon started to go awry: the business had tried to run before it could walk. As the *Law Society Gazette* noted in 2014, after slumping £5.1 million into the red, "Co-op quickly realised the legal sector was not as easy as it first seemed".[29] Tough regulation, tough competition and changes in personal injury law "all made this a harsh landscape in which to take your first steps".[30]

The SRA looked at this market and concluded in 2018:

> *Some retail brands have entered the market but, overall, these have been fewer than expected, their influence has been less than expected and some have ceased trading; (positive and negative) expectations related to 'Tesco law' have not been fulfilled.*[31]

Since then, Co-op has turned its legal services fortunes around, making a profit of £5 million in 2021. But few would say that the retailers offering legal services ('Tesco law') have had a game-changing impact on the profession. Not yet anyway.

Perhaps the expectations were too high. Some suggested that buying legal services would be like buying a tin of beans off the shelf, but underestimated how tough putting beans on a shelf can be. If we think 'Tesco law' is a tough nut to crack, running a supermarket like Tesco is hardly a walk in the park either. Think of all of the supermarket brands which have disappeared from our high streets in recent years. What might look like a relatively simple business, certainly isn't.

Other well-known, large brands might still try to leverage their reputations and enter the mature and competitive legal market in the future. An SRA focus group with consumers pointed out "the greater trust that might be associated with a strong and reputable retail brand".[32] A well-known brand could also try to make a much-needed dent in the Great Unmet Legal Need (see Chapter 3). But it's likely to require patience, deep pockets and a robust risk appetite. At a time of economic uncertainty and (at the time of writing) flat store sales, entering new markets is a hazardous endeavour.

"Alexa, draft a contract."

Nowadays, some have started to talk about 'Amazon law' instead, but not quite in the sense of using the company's smart speakers to satisfy our every legal whim.

Amazon is big. It's one of the largest companies on the planet. But so far its entry into the legal market has been limited. Is its narrow approach the future for now? Specific solutions to specific problems? Or to use the retail analogy: a boutique store as opposed to a sprawling out-of-town hypermarket?

Amazon operates a limited boutique service for SMEs, *IP Accelerator*, so they can protect their IP portfolios while using the Amazon site. Work is done by vetted IP law firms at pre-negotiated and discounted rates. In the United Kingdom, these are Stobbs IP and Cleveland Scott York. The contract for this work isn't with Amazon, but with the law firms in question and, as its website notes, Amazon doesn't endorse any particular service provider or its services. At present, this is Amazon barely dipping its toe in the fountain at the far end of the supermarket car park.

That's not to say that Amazon won't look at legal services at some point. After all, Amazon tends to think of itself more as a technology company than a retailer so when tech arbitrage in the legal sector becomes more sophisticated, Amazon might well see an opportunity to jump in and make a bit of a splash. It could, for example, use its algorithms to tweak prices dynamically to gain market share. However, even with its corporate might, this may only get it so far: industries and sectors with a higher degree of service have tended not to have been as impacted by Amazon compared with those which don't, such as consumer electronics.[33]

Maybe the focus of Big Tech will be more on legaltech instead. In 2022, Gradient Ventures, Google's innovation fund, co-led an investment of $7 million into Legal OS. This product allows "lawyers, legal teams, and law firms to build and release legal services as software products".[34] Legal OS says that this can be done "in hours" and without needing to code. Whoever cracks user-friendly client-facing technology and links this in well with the data in firms, in particular, could be onto a winner!

5. Understanding other growth opportunities

But while we can speculate on the retail and Big Tech Goliaths entering the legal services arena, and the extent that they'll do so, there are already other players out there shaking things up.

A McKinsey report on US law firms in 2020 noted there are three main sources of growth for firms:[35]
- expanding the markets in which they operate;
- gaining market share from competitors; and
- acquiring another business.

Expanding markets, such as advising on new areas of law as they emerge in the future, will always be an exciting source of growth for many firms, provided that they take a long-term view. It can take time to build up experience and expertise.

On McKinsey's second source of growth, this can be trickier, but times are changing. Gaining market share from one's peers was traditionally difficult to do in the highly competitive legal marketplace, but technology and innovation are changing the fundamentals of this market. Firms which innovate are more and more likely to win market share from those which don't. At present, tech-driven competition in the sector is still developing, but as the market matures those tech-led businesses and forward-thinking law firms which entered the fray early will be in a stronger position to gain market share and drive their businesses forward.

On the last source of growth, however, there are now 'consolidators' in the market. Like beings from a higher plane, consolidators look to hoover up small rocks to build planets, forming much larger and efficient legal services businesses, with economies of scale, designed to be fit for 21st-century lawyering. However, at the time of writing, some, such as the Metamorph Group, have experienced difficulties in making this model work. In late 2022 and early 2023, the SRA intervened in a number of the group's businesses.[36]

Acquiring other firms can be an effective way to obtain growth, but like all such tools they do need to be wielded with care. As McKinsey noted, acquiring, say, a boutique firm typically creates more value than what it called 'bet-the-firm' mergers. And, of course, any M&A activity doesn't have to be confined to law firms. In 2021, ULS Technology, which is listed on AIM, bought a firm of licensed conveyancers, Amity Law. ULS (now called 'Smoove') did so in order to "build, pilot and evolve new products in a live environment"[37] and then refine them before rolling them out nationally.

It's often said, somewhat hyperbolically, that no matter what business you're in, including law firms nowadays, some VC-funded techie is scheming to destroy your company and steal your business. There's certainly a lot of activity going on, all designed to give existing traditional firms a run for their money. Eat or be eaten? It's probably not that bad, but law firms would do well to keep their wits about them in the years ahead.

6. Using trust

Trust is a remarkable thing. It's the 'glue of life' that enables us to get on. Being so ubiquitous, we rarely notice it – until it's been broken, so we need

Good lawyers have something which many of our competitors do not – the hard-won trust of our clients, often built up over years of hard work. And this is backed up by our obligations to our professional bodies.

to nurture it. Whatever NewLaw business models we use in the future, we need to remember how important (and fragile) trust is in these models, and enshrine this thinking in everything that we do. Without it, building robust client-centric business models will be like building a house on quicksand. One moment it's there; the next it's crumbling all around us.

Good lawyers have something which many of our competitors do not – the hard-won trust of our clients, often built up over years of hard work. And this is backed up by our obligations to our professional bodies. For example:

- We're obliged under the SRA Principles to uphold "public trust and confidence" in our profession and to act in our clients' best interests.
- The oversight of lawyers is also greater than ever. Any glance at the *Law Society Gazette* will highlight the misdemeanours – accidental or intentional – of those who practise as solicitors. A lot of these lead to fines for relatively minor technical breaches of accounts rules. Harsh as it might seem, the authors think this direction of travel is right. Regulators need to preserve (and demonstrably so) the integrity of the profession so that we can continue to distinguish ourselves and enshrine trust in everything we do.

Rather than seeing regulation as putting us at a competitive disadvantage, we need to proclaim regulation as a virtue. A strong bond of trust also means that lawyers will continue to be the go-to advisers when things go wrong (or, better still, we can help our clients avoid any unfortunate incidents in the first place).

But we mustn't be naive. If, according to the LSB, almost four in 10 SMEs are content to give their custom to businesses which don't come under SRA regulation,[38] it is not a far stretch to think that trust alone won't give lawyers the edge over any non-regulated competitors. But along with enhanced EQ and better tech, it'll certainly be an ingredient that'll help power us to where we want and need to be.

In 2015, SRA Chief Executive Paul Philip said: "I don't think we're moving to a world where there won't be any lawyers, but where they are business-people first and lawyers second."[39] Lawyers, as this chapter demonstrates, have certainly had to act in a more business-like fashion in recent years. Non-lawyers have joined the legal sector too.

There's little doubt that the regulatory regime will need to change in light of these trends and 'change3' transforming the tech landscape:

- The Ministry of Justice's spokesman in the House of Lords said in 2019 that there is "room to review" the legal regulatory regime in light of technological advances.[40]
- The final report of the Independent Review of Legal Services Regulation published in June 2020 also pushed for change and called for a single, sector-wide, regulator (the Legal Services Regulation Authority).[41]
- In September 2020, the CMA published its review of the legal services sector, following its 2016 market study. It said "the CMA is repeating its call for the Ministry of Justice to undertake a review of the Legal Services Act 2007".[42]

The last decade has seen ABSs and the rise of NewLaw (and ALSPs). There's no doubt that this decade will see more change too. Are our firms ready for these challenges ahead?

7. Case studies

7.1 Case study 1: Failure of hybrid legal software and law firm start-up, Atrium

Atrium Legal Technology Services Inc was launched in 2017. The Californian start-up had a promising future ahead of it. Atrium was "a new kind of law firm", which was "powered by proprietary technology".[43] One of its co-founders, Justin Kan, had earned his tech stripes, having co-founded Twitch, a video live-streaming service which was sold to Amazon for $970 million in 2014. Kan was looking for a new challenge. As a "power-user"[44] of legal services he was frustrated with the legal market and wanted to disrupt its prevailing orthodoxies.

The company developed a hybrid subscription-based pricing model. Membership ranged from $500 to $1,500 a month. It developed software in-house, which included a document management system and optimised workflows, among other things. But it struggled. In January 2020, the company restructured to focus more on the legaltech side of the business, but this also came to nothing. By March 2020, Kan threw in the towel and shut down the ailing company, saying that the firm hadn't worked out "how to make a dent in operational efficiency".[45]

In 2021, Kan reflected on Twitter what the "biggest lessons learned were"[46] from the failure of this start-up. In a world where people are invited to own their failures, it's still rare to see someone who does this and admits "I messed up". It's to his credit that he laid bare his mistakes and allowed others to learn from them.

Kan's biggest lessons were, in particular:

- "Start with the mission" (he noted that this is something that's difficult to fix once the horse has bolted).
- "Adding more money to a situation of lack of product market fit rarely works."
- "Should have asked 'who are we building for?' much more specifically and ruthlessly iterated for them." And: "We should have moved more quickly to a flat rate hourly model and iterated the business model."
- "There is no skipping of the R&D phase of a company." Kan went on to say that if you miss this stage "you miss the part where you are forced to develop something differentiated".[47]

Looking at each of the above in turn:

- The mission: get-up-and-go and enthusiasm for the product are key to driving a project forward. In a later YouTube video, Kan said that while "he loved learning about new industries", he was "barely interested in legal services and legal technology".[48] Was Kan being irked by the way legal services were provided – "I hated the experience"[49] – enough? At the time, TechCrunch said that "developing drab but useful software" was a "drastic shift" for Kan. It seemed to be a shift too far.
- Product market fit: this means, in the words of this term's creator, "being in a good market with a product that can satisfy that market".[50] Getting 'PMF' right is important:
  - a 'good market' is one where there's enough demand to turn a profit and the market is also big enough (after all, there comes a point where a low level of profit isn't worth going for); and
  - a good product is needed to satisfy that market. *Failory*, a site for start-up founders, notes that the legal sector seems to be a sector where products aren't easy to create. On its webpage discussing the failure of Atrium, it says that the legal sector is "highly relationship-driven" and that "one-on-one relationships are not scalable"[51] (in 2021, academics John Armour and Mari Sako similarly noted "'client-facing' aspect of service delivery still eludes complete automation").[52] Ultimately, to what extent can services be productised through streamlining processes? *Failory* wonders: "It might be the case that there is no market need for such a one-size-fits-all solution in law."[53]
- It's important to know your market and change the solution if it isn't working.
- R&D: investment into R&D in the legal sector is poor. In one legaltech survey, law firms surveyed spent at most 1% of revenue on R&D projects, compared to 5% on average across most parts of the economy.[54]

Atrium:

- also created most IT tools in house. As we explore in Chapter 8, creating software from scratch in house isn't always a cost-effective route.
- may have employed too many people too soon. It scaled up too quickly. And when it laid off lawyers towards the end, they took clients with them. Some clients ended up confused and unsure of their legal representation.

Selling streamlined workflows were also hard to sell into established legal practices where the leadership was more senior and the processes were entrenched.

Of course, with any start-up it's almost impossible to pin down the exact reason for its failure. Some you win and some you lose, as they say. What this example shows, however, is the concept of using tech arbitrage for sophisticated legal work is never as easy as it seems at first. The advice that may ring in many people's ears from Kan is: "Don't build a services company. It's more work to manage everyone and the reward isn't there at the end of the day."[55] A bit too pessimistic perhaps? The authors believe that this is another example demonstrating that the legal services market is a hard one to break into. Relationships matter and you have to be passionate about that market. It's far easier for an existing law firm to leverage tech than an outsider. (So far at least ...)

7.2 Case study 2: Moving from traditional lawyering, through new law and onto legaltech (or combining all three)

For many in-house teams it can feel that nothing can make a dent in all of the things that they need to do. From routine, business-as-usual matters to transformational 'bet-the-bank' deals, the typical team has innumerable demands on their time. It can all be overwhelming. In-house teams require an experienced general counsel or head of legal at the tiller to prioritise how their team's limited resources are applied. But, even then, some things are often overlooked.

The problems are well known:

- Lack of capacity: relatively low-value procurement contracts, in particular, are often relegated to the bottom of the to-do list as they take a disproportionate amount of time to review (from around three to five hours per contract), compared to their relative importance to the business and the other demands being made on the legal team's time. These often don't get reviewed as quickly or thoroughly as the business would like. In many cases, they don't get reviewed at all.

- Law firms may have capacity, but in-house teams can't afford them: using a law firm to do, say, contract reviews, freeing up the in-house team to deal with other more important matters, isn't always feasible, the legal team's annual budget often won't stretch far enough to pay the fees which firms typically charge (either on an hourly rate basis or on a fixed price).
- Aggregate risk: although individually each contract might not be significant, the collective effect of these contracts not being reviewed can mount up to represent a significant risk to the business.

The authors' firm works with many in-house legal teams (many of the firms' lawyers having worked in-house, including some at general counsel level). The firm was only too aware of the pressing need for a solution to these problems.

In 2014, the firm started to look for a solution. It started with a blank sheet of paper to design a new solution that would meet the need on an effective and affordable basis. The main component parts of the solution would focus on:

- Scope: business-as-usual contracts didn't need to be reviewed in great detail, but rather there were specific aspects (around main risks and business policies) that could form the basis of a review. This would pick up the vast majority of what the business needed to know about these contracts.
- Process: the types of risks to be reviewed within that focused scope are so typical in contracts of this type that the firm was confident that it could create an algorithm (or, as we lawyers are more accustomed to say, a 'playbook') that would act as a checklist and decision tree to guide the review of the contract. This could be done in a way that ensured that:
  - all the key risks within scope would be picked up;
  - the methodology and output would be consistent across all contracts reviewed;
  - the time taken to review a contract would be significantly reduced; and
  - the level of experience and legal knowledge required by the reviewer would be vastly reduced.
- Labour arbitrage: the playbook reduced the level of experience and legal knowledge required of the reviewer. The firm engaged a number of paralegals to undertake those reviews.
  - Many law graduates struggle to secure training contracts so there's lots of highly talented people who are keen to gain experience in a law firm as a paralegal. Indeed, they were

so good that many of the paralegals the firm employed subsequently went on to secure training contracts at the firm, making way for new paralegals to be brought in and given the same opportunity.

· To ensure the quality of the reviews (notwithstanding the confidence in the playbook that formed the backbone of the process), a senior associate experienced in commercial contracts checked the output before delivering the results to the client. Both the total time spent and the total cost of labour were dramatically lower than when the contracts were previously being reviewed on a traditional basis.

· Pricing: the certainty in the process and cost of labour meant the firm could offer not only fixed prices for each review, but also subscription-fee models based on commitments to certain volumes of reviews being ordered. This made the reviews far more cost-effective than previously, but it also gave the general counsel the certainty they needed that the solution would be affordable within their annual budget.

· KPIs: the firm's confidence in the resourcing structure and process also meant that it could now also guarantee to turn around a contract review by the next day.

Many characteristics of the NewLaw model were applied in developing this solution – Spotlight – which was launched in 2015. It proved to be successful – within just a few weeks the firm had household-name clients subscribing to the service and it took on even more paralegals to meet the demand.

Fast forward to 2018: Spotlight remained popular with clients. But the firm was conscious of Chin's seven most dangerous words in business (see above). It asked: is there a smarter, faster and better way to do this now? It was clear that *what* the firm was producing for clients was what they needed and wanted. The question was therefore refined: "can we be smarter, faster and better in *how* we produce that output?".

It didn't take long to work out that technology could be the answer. Around this time, several new AI-powered tools were becoming available in the market:

· developments in natural language processing (NLP) had made these products readily applicable to document-based use cases in a legal context; and

· platforms such as Luminance and Kira were gaining traction in the market, performing comparative reviews of large numbers of documents in a portfolio, such as is required in a typical due diligence exercise in a corporate transaction, when large numbers of contracts or leases need to be assimilated.

However, what the firm needed was AI that was designed, not to compare large numbers of documents, but rather to look at a single contract in detail, applying the playbook that it had developed for Spotlight.

The firm identified an AI platform – ThoughtRiver – which appeared to have all the credentials that the firm needed. After ThoughtRiver demonstrated its platform, the firm was confident that it could use ThoughtRiver's AI brain and train it to apply its playbook. It began working with the tech company to train the AI brain, feeding contracts into the system and 'marking the AI's homework' whenever it got anything wrong. When the firm started this process, the level of accuracy of the AI in applying its playbook was around 50%. After two years of training, it had got the accuracy up to 94%. The updated product was ready to launch.

With a new name – Cia (*Contract Intelligent Analysis*) – the firm launched the new product in March 2021. The timing was ideal, as businesses were looking to 'build back better' following lockdown and hungry to hear how innovation could help. Offering lower fixed prices than its Spotlight predecessor, as well as faster, guaranteed turnaround times, Cia was a success. More household-name businesses signed up for the service, appreciative at how quick, effective and affordable it was. (The firm ran a campaign to demonstrate to its clients that Cia could review one of their commercial contracts faster than the general counsel could make a hot drink – "go make a brew, we'll do the review".) The firm now offers Cia as a product to clients in three different forms, namely:

- as a purely self-serve product, allowing the client to use the AI tool themselves with no human input from the firm whatsoever (ie, a purely legaltech model);
- as a managed service, through which the client sends the firm their contracts and it runs them through the AI tool and also applies a human overlay to the AI review to decide which of the recommendations made by the AI should be incorporated into the drafting of the contract, before it delivers the duly amended contract back to the client (ie, a hybrid legaltech/NewLaw model); and
- as a managed service, but with additional human support being offered to not only amend the contract but then to undertake and manage the subsequent negotiation of the contract to its conclusion (ie, a hybrid legaltech/NewLaw/'traditional' model).

As this case study shows, no one business model necessarily has all the answers. In the 'hybrid era', many solutions will be hybrid too. The most important guiding principal is to concentrate on a client need and then to continually focus on the best way to meet that need.

8. Practical tips on new law models

We set out below some practical tips on new law models.

- Don't get hung up on terminology (ABS, ALSP, NewLaw, tech arbitrage etc): the important thing is to consider new things that you can offer clients or new ways you can deliver existing services.
- Be client-centric: if you are only improving internal efficiency without that resulting in some benefit to your clients (reduced cost, faster turnaround, improved accuracy – preferably all three) then your short-term profitability may increase, but your long-term relevance will reduce in the face of competition from new market entrants and existing firms that are evolving. Investing in improvements that directly feed through to your clients is the key.
- Think about the structure: if you do establish one or more business streams offering services or products to clients in new ways, think about how best to structure this:
  - there may be advantages to delivering them from within existing 'traditional' divisions in your firm (eg, the people in the traditional divisions are then motivated to promote the new offering because it grows the success of their division); or
  - there may be advantages in a completely separate management (and even a separate corporate) structure – for example, one that has more separation between the management and the ownership, such that investment decisions can be made more along corporate lines and less constrained by the traditional partnership model.

There are pros and cons to each. At the end of the day, the decision may be swayed by the extent to which the new business stream can help to grow the traditional business or whether it's effectively a parallel business having little synergy with the mainstream firm. But many other factors come into play including, fundamentally, whether there will be external ownership and investment.

- Consult the CQR team: this should be done early in the process when considering the best structure through which to deliver your new offering. There'll often be regulatory and insurance aspects to consider, along with processes to maintain quality assurance.
- Invest when business is going well: there can be a reflexive resistance from some partners within law firms to seek to develop new offerings

when the firm is doing well and there seems to be no burning platform to impel the firm to evolve. However, it is precisely when times are good that investment decisions (in terms of both time and financial investment) should be made. Not only may the decision be harder later on when times are leaner, but it may also be too late then to make an impact with what you propose to deliver, particularly given the speed at which some other firms and legal services providers are already developing new offerings.

- Focus on client needs: whatever you propose to do, base it on meeting client needs that aren't currently being met or which can be met in a better way. Always ensure your proposal is a clever solution to a genuine need and not just something clever that has no underlying demand.
- Be clear on your objectives in creating a new offering:
  - Is it to be, say, more efficient, faster, less costly or accurate for your clients?
  - Is it to generate a new income stream or make an existing income stream more profitable?
  - Is it to create a new touchpoint that allows you to develop your existing client relationships so as to be better placed to offer more of your existing services or products?
  - Do you propose a complete suite of complementary new services and products?
  - Is it to raise your profile for innovation externally and internally?
  - Is it to motivate ideas for innovation among your people?

Each of these can be a justification in itself for doing what you propose. But be clear from the outset what objectives you seek to meet so that you can subsequently gauge success by reference to those objectives.

- Always talk your ideas through with clients in order to gauge their appetite and views:
  - is it something they'd find useful?
  - would they buy the product or service from you if you were to develop it and offer it?
- Don't be put off attempting to innovate merely because of the fear of failure: remember, the seven most dangerous words in business mean that it's better to try and fail than to not try at all. The former has a chance of success; the latter is doomed to failure.

Don't be afraid to cannibalise existing work streams through innovation: if you don't do it then someone else will. And your clients will ask you why you didn't do it in the first place. Rather than losing traditional work, you might be surprised at how much additional market share you gain by being the most innovative in the market at what you do.

Notes

1   *Digital vs Traditional Media Consumption* (Globe Web Index, 2019),
    www.amic.media/media/files/file_352_2142.pdf.
2   Tim Ingham and Amy X Wang, "Why Superstar Artists Are Clamoring to Sell Their Music Rights"
    (*Rolling Stone*, 15 January 2021), www.rollingstone.com/pro/features/famous-musicians-selling-
    catalog-music-rights-1114580/.
3   *Mapping unregulated legal services* (Legal Services Board, June 2022),
    https://legalservicesboard.org.uk/wp-content/uploads/2022/06/20220616-Mapping-unregulated-
    legal-services-FINAL.pdf.
4   Nick Hilborne, "Philip: If it's a new law firm, it should be an ABS" (*Legal Futures*, 15 October 2015),
    www.legalfutures.co.uk/latest-news/philip-if-its-a-new-law-firm-it-should-be-an-abs.
5   Department for Constitutional Affairs, *The Future of Legal Services: Putting Consumers First*
    (October 2003),
    https://assets.publishing.service.gov.uk/government/uploads/system/uploads/attachment_data/fil
    e/272192/6679.pdf.
6   Legal Services Board, *The State of Legal Services 2020*, https://legalservicesboard.org.uk/wp-
    content/uploads/2020/11/The-State-of-Legal-Services-Narrative-Volume_Final.pdf.
7   Centre for Strategy & Evaluation Services, *Impact Evaluation of SRA's Regulatory Reform
    Programme*, www.sra.org.uk/globalassets/documents/sra/research/abs-
    evaluation.pdf?version=4a1ac2.
8   "Market structure dashboard" (Legal Services Board), https://legalservicesboard.org.uk/market-
    structure-dashboard.
9   Neil Rose, "ABSs making their mark in £22bn legal market, report finds" (*Legal Futures*, 6 June
    2017), https://www.legalfutures.co.uk/latest-news/abss-making-mark-22bn-legal-market-report-
    finds.
10 Neil Rose, "Pioneering ABS wants to be 'national local government leader'" (*Legal Futures*, 7
    September 2021), www.legalfutures.co.uk/latest-news/pioneering-abs-wants-to-be-national-local-
    government-leader.
11 Legal Services Board, *The State of Legal Services 2020*, https://legalservicesboard.org.uk/wp-
    content/uploads/2020/11/The-State-of-Legal-Services-Narrative-Volume_Final.pdf.
12 *Ibid.*
13 Jon Molot, "Guest comment: An argument for outside investment in law firms for the post-Covid
    era" (Legal Business, 1 July 2020), www.legalbusiness.co.uk/blogs/guest-comment-an-argument-
    for-outside-investment-in-law-firms-for-the-post-covid-era/.
14 Fox Williams, *ABSolutely fabulous? (A study of Alternative Business Structures and their role in a
    changing legal market)* (June 2012), https://byfieldconsultancy.com/wp-
    content/uploads/2021/03/ABS-Report_A4.pdf.
15 Matt Byrne and Richard Simmons, "Six scenarios for disruption in the legal profession"
    (*The Lawyer*, 11 March 2019), www.thelawyer.com/law-firm-pyramid-cover-feature/.
16 Madison Darbyshire, "Law firms act as beacons to show the way" (*Financial Times*, 4 October
    2018), www.ft.com/content/749982dc-90c7-11e8-b639-7680cedcc421.
17 Neil Rose, "EY makes big move with Riverview Law acquisition" (*Legal Futures*, 7 August 2018),
    www.legalfutures.co.uk/latest-news/ey-makes-big-move-with-riverview-law-acquisition.
18 Mark Taylor, "EY's plan to split audit and advisory divides opinion" (AccountingWEB, 31 May
    2022), www.accountingweb.co.uk/business/financial-reporting/eys-plan-to-split-audit-and-
    advisory-divides-opinion.
19 Louis Goss, "Big Four accountancy firms capture larger share of UK legal market" (*City A.M.*,
    15 August 2022), www.cityam.com/big-four-accountancy-firms-capture-larger-share-of-uk-
    legal-market/.
20 Legal Services Board, The State of Legal Services 2020, https://legalservicesboard.org.uk/wp-
    content/uploads/2020/11/The-State-of-Legal-Services-Narrative-Volume_Final.pdf.
21 "Interview with Eric Chin, the man who coined the phrase 'NewLaw'" (*Josef*, 9 April 2019),
    https://joseflegal.com/blog/interview-with-eric-chin-the-man-who-coined-the-phrase-newlaw/
22 *Ibid.*
23 *Law firm strategy and investment survey* (HSBC UK, October 2021), www.briefing.co.uk/wp-
    content/uploads/2021/09/Briefing21_HSBC_FINAL.pdf.
24 David B Wilkins and Maria José Esteban Ferrer, "Taking the 'Alternative' out of Alternative Legal
    Service Providers" (*The Practice*, volume 5, issue 3, July/August 2019),
    https://thepractice.law.harvard.edu/article/taking-the-alternative-out-of-alternative-legal-service-
    providers/.
25 "Stop Calling Elevate 'Alternative' – We Are a Law Company" (*Artificial Lawyer*, 15 November 2018),
    www.artificiallawyer.com/2018/11/15/stop-calling-elevate-alternative-we-are-a-law-company/.
26 David B Wilkins and Maria José Esteban Ferrer, "Taking the 'Alternative' out of Alternative Legal
    Service Providers" (*The Practice*, volume 5, issue 3, July/August 2019),
    https://thepractice.law.harvard.edu/article/taking-the-alternative-out-of-alternative-legal-service-
    providers/.

27 Paul Rogerson, "Get Happy" (*Law Society Gazette*, 2 January 2022),
    www.lawgazette.co.uk/commentary-and-opinion/get-happy/5111332.article.
28 Centre for Strategy & Evaluation Services, *Impact Evaluation of SRA's Regulatory Reform
    Programme*, www.sra.org.uk/globalassets/documents/sra/research/abs-
    evaluation.pdf?version=4a1ac2.
29 John Hyde, "Cocky Co-op has to lick its wounds" (*Law Society Gazette*, 5 September 2014),
    www.lawgazette.co.uk/commentary-and-opinion/cocky-co-op-has-to-lick-its-
    wounds/5042892.article.
30 *Ibid.*
31 Centre for Strategy & Evaluation Services, *Impact Evaluation of SRA's Regulatory Reform
    Programme*, www.sra.org.uk/globalassets/documents/sra/research/abs-
    evaluation.pdf?version=4a1ac2.
32 *Ibid.*
33 "These are the 3 major impacts Amazon has when it enters new markets" (*Business Insider
    Australia*, 7 August 2017), www.businessinsider.com/these-are-the-3-major-impacts-amazon-has-
    when-it-enters-new-markets-2017-8?r=US&IR=T.
34 "Build digital legal services" (Legal OS), www.legalos.io/.
35 "COVID-19: Implications for law firms" (McKinsey & Company, 4 May 2020),
    www.mckinsey.com/industries/financial-services/our-insights/covid-19-implications-for-law-
    firms.
36 John Hyde, "SRA intervenes to shut down Metamorph firms" (*Law Society Gazette*, 14 December
    2022), www.lawgazette.co.uk/news/sra-intervenes-to-shut-down-metamorph-firms/5114593.article.
37 Nick Hilborne, "Tech firm buys conveyancers to test products in 'live environment'" (*Legal
    Futures*, 12 October 2021), www.legalfutures.co.uk/latest-news/tech-firm-buys-conveyancers-to-
    test-products-in-live-environment.
38 *Mapping unregulated legal services* (Legal Services Board, June 2022),
    https://legalservicesboard.org.uk/wp-content/uploads/2022/06/20220616-Mapping-unregulated-
    legal-services-FINAL.pdf.
39 Nick Hilborne, "Philip: If it's a new law firm, it should be an ABS" (*Legal Futures*, 15 October 2015),
    www.legalfutures.co.uk/latest-news/philip-if-its-a-new-law-firm-it-should-be-an-abs.
40 Neil Rose, "Keen: 'Room to review' legal regulation regime" (*Legal Futures*, 28 February 2019),
    www.legalfutures.co.uk/latest-news/keen-room-to-review-legal-regulation-regime.
41 Stephen Mayson, *Reforming Legal Services: Regulation Beyond the Echo Chambers* (Centre for
    Ethics & Law, University College, June 2020), https://www.ucl.ac.uk/ethics-law/sites/ethics-
    law/files/irlsr_final_report_final_0.pdf.
42 Competition & Markets Authority, *Review of the legal services market study in England and Wales*
    (2020),
    https://assets.publishing.service.gov.uk/media/5fd9e53cd3bf7f40ccb335e1/Legal_Services_Review_
    -_Final_report.pdf.
43 "Atrium" (Y Combinator), www.ycombinator.com/companies/atrium.
44 Justin Kan, "I Messed Up and I'm Sorry – Storytime with Justin Kan" (13 May 2021),
    https://youtu.be/3dANQmtlkEo.
45 Josh Constine, "$75M legal startup Atrium shuts down, lays off 100" (*TechCrunch*, 3 March 2020),
    https://techcrunch.com/2020/03/03/atrium-shuts-down/.
46 Justin Kan (@justinkan), "10 months ago we shut down Atrium after raising $75m in venture
    capital. Anyone hearing that knows I made tons of mistakes along the way. Someone asked me
    today what my biggest lessons learned were. Here they are", Twitter, 6 January 2021,
    https://twitter.com/justinkan/status/1346677733921705984.
47 *Ibid.*
48 Justin Kan, "I Messed Up and I'm Sorry – Storytime with Justin Kan" (13 May 2021),
    https://youtu.be/3dANQmtlkEo.
49 *Ibid.*
50 Marc Andreesen, "Product / Market Fit" (Stanford University, 25 June 2007),
    https://web.stanford.edu/class/ee204/ProductMarketFit.html.
51 "Atrium" (Failory), www.failory.com/cemetery/atrium.
52 John Armour and Mari Sako, "Lawtech: Levelling the Playing Field in Legal Services" (University of
    Oxford, 5 February 2021), https://conferences.law.stanford.edu/legal-tech-and-the-future-of-civil-
    justice/wp-content/uploads/sites/101/2021/02/Stanford-Armour-Sako-paper-5Feb2021-v4.pdf.
53 "Atrium" (Failory), www.failory.com/cemetery/atrium.
54 "The Legal Sector R&D Gap: 1% vs 5% Average" (*Artificial Lawyer*, 26 July 2021),
    www.artificiallawyer.com/2021/07/26/the-legal-sector-rd-gap-1-vs-5-average/.
55 Justin Kan, "I Messed Up and I'm Sorry – Storytime with Justin Kan" (13 May 2021),
    https://youtu.be/3dANQmtlkEo.

Chapter 8:
In-house lawyer

Companies dominate our world. They govern almost every aspect of our lives.

If we look, for example, at Maslow's hierarchy of needs – the pyramid of human needs in which needs lower down the hierarchy need to be satisfied before those higher up can be attended to – companies feature throughout. They feed us, clothe us and give us shelter. They help us connect with each other and sometimes even fall in love. They nurture us as new-borns and bury us when we die. They are everywhere and (almost) everything.

And yet they're a relatively new phenomenon in the history of humankind. Only 300 years ago, under the Bubble Act 1720, all bodies which "presumed to act as a corporation" or which issued transferable shares were banned unless incorporated by Royal Charter or a special Act of Parliament. Sanctions for contravening the Act included the seizure of the offender's entire estate. Half-a-century later economist Adam Smith in *The Wealth of Nations* said that when business is organised through a company "negligence and profusion ... must always prevail, more or less".[1] Smith clearly wasn't a fan.

But times have changed. Nowadays, according to Companies House, there are over four million limited companies registered in the United Kingdom and, every year, over half-a-million new companies are set up.[2]

Each of these companies, from an incorporated micro-enterprise to the largest multinational, is a gift from the state. The state imbues it with legal personality (as it might well do in the future for, say, robots. It might tax them too). In effect, the non-human has life breathed into it. Like that classic scene in the 1931 film *Frankenstein* – "It's alive! It's alive!" – humans have created an entity that has taken on a life of its own. We sometimes forget what a radical fiction this is: all these companies, new and old, able to enter into their own contracts, own property, sue and be sued.

The lifeblood of 21st-century business is the ubiquitous company, in all its varied legal forms. But where does the legal profession fit into all of this? Lawyers help to craft the laws that create these entities. Other lawyers go on to create countless companies every day. Different lawyers counsel these companies on what they can and can't do. In time, many of these companies don't make it but others become so big they enter our language (Google it) and become bigger than many nation states.

If all this sounds a bit profound, that's because it is. On a collective and individual level, our prosperity and wellbeing – and overcoming many of the challenges we face in the years to come – are inextricably tied to this ubiquitous legal institution.

Lawyers, having been so involved in their creation and operation, are in a privileged position to nurture and guide the companies that hold sway over so much of our lives.

And now legaltech is knocking at the door too. The *Financial Times* calls it the "reinvention of the in-house lawyer".[3] And this tech's not going to go away. As a survey in *The Lawyer* in April 2021 noted, in-house lawyers know that legaltech is about to change how they work – many just aren't sure by how much yet.[4] As this chapter shows, for the most progressive in-house teams, it will be a lot.

In this chapter, we bring this all together. We explore, among other things:
- how in-house lawyers need to be the 'Department of Let's See What We Can Do';
- how they can support their businesses (and how to break down barriers);
- using data to drive their teams forward;
- developing the in-house team's 'front door';
- using external firms and other legal services providers; and
- attracting and retaining talent.

We then look at two case studies and finish with some practical tips for in-house lawyers.

While a lot of the focus in this chapter is on the private sector – where most in-house lawyers work – there's also a lot in this chapter that will interest in-house lawyers in the public sector too, particularly on tech.

1. Understanding the background

In recent years, the number of in-house lawyers has grown steadily. According to the Law Society's *Annual Statistics Report 2021*, 25% of the 153,282 solicitors with practising certificates (at the time of the report) have torn up their time sheets and moved to work in-house.[5] The majority work in commerce and industry, with a significant minority working in the public sector.

But the figures may be even larger still. As the Law Society notes, the statistics are probably an underestimate as not all holders of practising certificates who work in-house are officially recorded as such.

Why has there been such an increase in in-house lawyers?
- Faced with rising legal bills, many businesses have looked to cut costs by bringing legal work in-house.
- The role has become more varied. Research commissioned by the SRA noted in 2014 that the in-house lawyer's role had "grown into one that is multi-layered, replete with demands from a range of constituents, more business-oriented and generally more complex and demanding than that of 20 years ago".[6] Challenging, yes, and certainly more stimulating.
- There's more prestige working in-house than there was in the past.
- Some lawyers want to get away from time recording. They want to get away from the tyranny of the timesheet.
- Winning work is not for everyone. In-house lawyers do not have to go out and win work – they have enough (often more than enough) work thrown at them.

But the pressures on in-house lawyers have also risen.
- In-house lawyers continue to operate against significant budget and headcount pressures. In June 2021, a survey by OMC Partners, in association with Ashurst Advance, found that 75% of law department leaders expect no growth in headcount, with about 5% expecting headcount to slump by 20% or more.[7] As for budgets, the same survey found that budgets will stay the same or, worse, be slashed – with over 40% of leaders looking at reduced legal spend, typically between 5% and 30%.[8]
- As a result, in-house teams are having to deliver more for less and, at the same time, the burden of regulation has increased their workloads.

> Almost two-thirds (64%) of leaders expect an increase in what lands on their (virtual) desks with regulatory, data protection and employment issues leading the pack.[9] And that's before they need to also look at CSR agendas and ESG programmes.
> - In-house lawyers are also expected to play a more strategic role. As the SRA noted in its 2014 report, the role has moved "from one focused on compliance, to a more complex and demanding 'counsel' or even 'entrepreneurial' role".[10]

Finally, as the worst of the pandemic retreats further away in our rear-view mirrors, there's the cry to 'build back better': a rallying call that has been picked up by politicians and businesses alike to start afresh: to refocus, reorganise and rebuild. It's both an opportunity and an imperative.

The problem is that in-house legal terms have often lagged behind other in-house functions on being innovative and progressive: witness the finance team's impressive systems and presentation tools versus those often used by the lawyers. Building back smarter, faster and better demands a change of mindset and approach.

However, the authors' experience is that things are now changing and it's happening quickly. The whole legal sector is waking up to tech and more and more general counsels and heads of legal are keen to add even more value and, as importantly, be seen to be doing so.

Of course, it's always better for in-house lawyers to shine a spotlight on themselves and their teams in a proactive way before someone else does it for them, perhaps in a way that might not be to their liking.

2. Engaging with nuance

What's more, in-house lawyers work in a richly nuanced environment.

The need to act legally and ethically, while also acting 'commercially', are the hallmarks of their day-to-day practice. Tipping the scales and getting the balance right between these requirements, with finesse and integrity, is a skill that all in-house lawyers work on every day. And as legaltech enters the in-house scene, this applies as much to any work done with technological help too: using tech is not a get-out-of-jail-free card to circumvent compliance.

As Table 1 shows, there's no realism at either extreme of the in-house legal team stereotype spectrum.

Table 1. The 'Department of No' and 'Department of Yes'

'Department of No'	
The stereotype of a dysfunctional in-house legal department. A "no" to every query hinders business, blocks progress and means staff contrive messy or unlawful work-arounds to the legal issues they face. It's also sometimes known as the 'Business Prevention Department'.	The reality? If in-house lawyers were to say "no" to everything they'd have nothing to do. Every answer to a question would be preordained. Their jobs would be replaced with a bit of tech, the sole job of which would be to exclaim a robotic "no" to every incoming request.
'Department of Yes'	
The stereotype: saying "yes" to everything, in the spirit of 'being commercial'.	The reality? There are far too many 'shall nots' set out in the law to ever make this a reality. Can we say "yes" to everything our clients want to do? Not if the law has anything to do with it.

When we reduce the position of in-house lawyers to such absurd extremes, we can see that neither of these unfair stereotypes represents the truth on the ground.

The truth is that, more than ever, most in-house lawyers need to be the 'Department of Let's See What We Can Do' – and to be seen as such.

Put simply, in order to thrive in-house lawyers need to engage positively and effectively with the business, and engage right across their businesses. Getting this right helps in-house lawyers to, among other things, foster innovation; collaborate with the business to work through complex problems better; reduce risk; retain talent; and strengthen their networks. Technology can play a huge part in helping with this engagement.

3. Sporting many hats

Not only do lawyers have to be authoritative in the art of nuance, but they also have to be experts in the art of millinery. When needs must, in-house lawyers have to raid the corporate dressing-up box and don all manner of head gear.

In general, in-house lawyers provide legal services to their businesses, but that's not the only hat they wear. In-house lawyers are tacticians and strategists; administrators and go-getting entrepreneurs. (This list can probably extend to be as long as the types of hat in existence.)

Reducing risk for the business may be the most obvious perceived value that the legal team brings, but there are plenty of other ways in which a modern in-house team adds value to the business, way beyond just keeping the directors out of jail (what some commentators call the 'cops' function), such as:

- contributing beyond just the purely legal aspects (acting as "'diagnosticians' of their company's legal needs")[11] by offering innovative solutions and giving a different perspective to a problem;
- offering objectivity and a clarity of thought, acting as a valuable sounding board or devil's advocate for business ideas; and
- using a 'helicopter view' to act as a facilitator to join together people in the business who might not otherwise appreciate how they can help each other: the in-house legal team tends to be a common denominator in most of what is happening in the business.

'To protect and partner' is how one general counsel aptly described their value proposition to the authors.

It's often the in-house lawyers, as "the primary 'purchasing agents",[12] who are the ones that procure legal services for the business from external legal providers. They therefore have a lot to say about the innovation they want to see from those external firms.

4. Evolving to support their businesses better

Although they don't need to win clients or work in the same way as law firms, and therefore don't need to generate profits from the provision of their services, in-house lawyers face many of the same factors and challenges that will drive firms to adapt going forward.

At the same time, however, there are fundamental differences affecting the practice of law in-house that call for a different approach and different solutions.

Before we look at some of the most important of these, in-house teams shouldn't forget that the answer to the problems they're dealing with may well be found in-house. Unlike law firms, which use tech for delivering legal services, other businesses typically use a wealth of tech for many other purposes. This means that they often have large IT teams who can help:

- general counsels and heads of legal can speak to the heads of other departments to swap notes on their tech journeys and the extent to which they were able to get support internally or whether they had to seek help from outside;

- some of the tech that those other departments use could be used in the legal team too (possibly with modification). The authors know one head of legal who built a worthwhile tool specifically for the legal team based on the existing 'tech stack', which was available in the business.

4.1 Basing decisions in fact not folklore

In 2021, Kenny Robertson, Head of Outsourcing, Technology and IP at NatWest, attended a webinar with two of the authors. Robertson reiterated the need to base business decisions on fact and not folklore: the traditional stories, narratives, myths and beliefs of how things are always done. We all like good stories – our brains are hardwired to process them – and particularly ones that are anchored in the weight of tradition, but these sorts of traditional stories and beliefs in a business are risky.

And there are two main reasons why:
- traditions aren't always based on fact; and
- traditions never stay the same for long. For a start: memories fade. And stories can change, bit by bit, when passed from person to person.

In essence, folklore is pretty vague and messy. And yet a lot of business is based on 'corporate folklore': the perceived 'just-ares' of corporate life which are based on something that may have been decided or happened five, 10 or even 50 years ago (or possibly never at all).

But folklore is often all that in-house lawyers have. Traditionally, unlike law firms which have tech-based systems to capture the instructions that their lawyers are working on (and the time they are spending on them), most in-house legal teams don't. What's more, although some in-house teams record their time, the majority don't as they're not funded by selling time to their internal clients. They're a cost centre – as many are unhelpfully reminded on a regular basis.

Whereas most firms can, at the press of a button, see a multitude of data on what their lawyers are up to, general counsels and heads of legal can't. Often manually compiled and unwieldy Excel spreadsheets are the only tool that in-house lawyers have to hand to keep track of the thousands of matters they handle each year. Even then, these spreadsheets don't usually capture all of the *ad hoc* queries, phone calls, and – most typically of all – people arriving at their doorway unexpected or waiting next to the kitchen kettle: "Oh, as you're here, can I just have five minutes ..."

As a result, most in-house teams don't have:

Just as technology is changing how we consume and tell our stories generally, from the oft-reported death of the novel to the rise of the Twitter thread, so technology now allows in-house teams to do things differently too and, in particular, to embrace more evidence-based decision making.

- all of the data they'd like on, for example:
  - the time taken to complete matters so that they can better plan resources and manage the business' expectations;
  - pinpointing peaks and troughs of demand to better anticipate when extra resource may be needed;
  - working out the costs of doing work internally versus engaging external lawyers, which includes working out the optimum head-count versus external resources (such as contract lawyers or external firms); and
  - identifying where internal clients could benefit from self-help;
- the means to produce reports at the press of a button. One general counsel we know used to spend an entire weekend every quarter manually compiling reports for the board.

The upshot is that in-house lawyers are missing a trick in terms of:
- objectively demonstrating just how much they do for their businesses; and
- potentially getting increased budget or making internal re-charges based on full, objective data.

But just as technology is changing how we consume and tell our stories generally, from the oft-reported death of the novel to the rise of the Twitter thread, so technology now allows in-house teams to do things differently too and, in particular, to embrace more evidence-based decision making. Matter tracking systems, for example:
- make in-house teams more efficient and consistent on:
  - work allocation;
  - risk management; and
  - turning matters around;
- show in real time the progress of matters by using functionality like 'chess clocks', where in-house legal teams can tell their businesses immediately how long they've been waiting for various responses from them: "they've been on your desk for a week" (of course, various matters could well have been on the in-house lawyer's desk for the same amount of time, and the system will show this too, but it will have given the in-house lawyer lots of automatic reminders in the meantime);
- give data insights so in-house teams can, for example, work out quickly which low-value, high-volume enquiries are taking up a disproportionate amount of time:
  - Could such enquiries be processed in a different way?
  - Might technology (such as an AI-powered contract review tool) be used to take the strain?

- Would it help to make templates (or even automated templates) available directly to the business?
- What about training the relevant teams to process basic matters themselves using playbooks?

- help general counsels get the most from their in-house teams and show their value. They can see who is doing what and when; and they also have the facts to back up, for example, any well-deserved promotions. The general counsel of Weetabix, Helen Wilson, told the authors that she can justify her team's existence (as a support function and cost centre) and generate a business case for headcount based on objective data from her matter tracking system); and

- help general counsels manage new and unexpected developments. Most recently, capturing data on their in-house teams has meant that such teams have been able to demonstrate, in an objective way, that their productivity remained high during lockdowns. Such systems also help to form better views on the impact of hybrid working going forward.

As Wilson told the authors, "access to better data means better decisions to drive our strategy".

4.2 Developing the in-house lawyer 'front door'

As stressed above, in-house lawyers and their businesses need to engage, otherwise the lawyers aren't doing their job. Whereas law firms have to go out and win work, in-house lawyers don't have to win work in the same way, but they do still need to build strong relationships and understand their businesses. As Sarah Holford, Head of Legal and Compliance at Scania says: "You could be the most experienced technical lawyer in the world, but if the business is not engaging with you, you are not reducing risk."[13]

Just as how law firms' virtual front doors (ie, their websites and, increasingly, web-based platforms to engage with clients) are evolving, the visibility and, more importantly, accessibility of the in-house legal team needs to be increased too, particularly in a time of hybrid working. Out of sight can still mean out of mind: digitisation hasn't changed this long-standing principle. The good news is that in-house legal teams *can* design virtual front doors specifically to be super-accessible to their internal clients. (On the other hand, law firms have a much tougher time of it, having to attract and cater for a much wider-ranging client base on their websites.)

There are many tech solutions that are already being used by in-house legal teams to improve engagement with the business and make the legal team more accessible. These include:

- a central legal team email address to which all business enquiries can be sent for triage;
- an intranet site maintained by the in-house legal team for the business to access which might include:
  - instruction forms designed to be quick and easy for the business to use, while ensuring that the legal team gets all the information it needs to get a matter moving, without asking for further details that otherwise are so often omitted;
  - self-help advice sheets, FAQs and playbooks: to reduce the volume of low-complexity requests hitting the in-house legal team's desks;
  - access to templates and possibly even access to document automation: the user in the business is presented with a simple questionnaire and, on completion, a perfectly formed draft contract is produced, ready for the user to send out. This process can even have failsafe mechanisms built in, for example:
    - to alert the legal team where authorisation is needed or advice should be sought by the user before they can proceed with the questionnaire;
    - to prevent the user from inputting data outside of prescribed limits (for example, by accepting only a limit of liability within a prescribed range).
  In these ways, not only can the process of document production by the business be made quicker and easier, and the demands made on the in-house lawyers reduced, but the risk profile in contracts can be far more consistent and controlled. In-house lawyers can also be sure that the business is always using the latest version of a template;
  - chat functions to allow *ad hoc* questions to be submitted which the in-house legal team can deal with when they have capacity to avoid *ad hoc* phone calls interrupting more urgent work; and
  - automated email responses to internal clients which acknowledge new instructions; confirming who will be handling their matter; informing them of any temporary change in personnel, such as during annual leave; and seeking feedback on closing matters.

As well as being more efficient than traditional methods, all the above features have a strong impact on the business' perception of the in-house legal team. As Sarah Holford at Scania told the authors, it means that her team is, and is seen by the business to be, "on it".

4.3 Creating the 'wow factor'
Beyond being accessible and much more organised, some in-house legal

teams have already started to explore what technology can offer that not only increases their efficiency, but also makes the business sit up and take notice of them – the wow factor.

There's probably never before been a moment in the history of in-house legal teams when something they pull out of the bag makes other in-house functions look positively Stone Age. But in-house teams now have numerous new powerful tools at their disposal. Take, for example, the possibilities of AI. In the past, someone in the procurement team wanting a 60-page supply agreement to be reviewed might not come top of the to-do list. Indeed, in some organisations, many business-as-usual procurement contracts weren't even getting a legal review at all, given the countless other priorities on the in-house legal team's time.

Therefore, imagine the reaction when the response from the in-house legal team to that contract review request is no longer "well, leave it with me and I'll try to get round to it" but rather "of course, no problem, and we'll let you have the report and mark-up in the next two hours". Science fiction? No, science reality. Already a number of in-house lawyers are using AI contract-review tools to do just that. And as well as getting reactions of genuine disbelief from the business, these in-house lawyers are also:

- turning those contracts around at a fraction of the historic cost;
- achieving a greater degree of consistency in risk profile: the AI solution is almost 100% consistent, whereas any two lawyers will typically never come up with exactly the same mark-up. (In fact, if you gave the same contract to the same lawyer a month later, it's unlikely they'd produce exactly the same mark up as they did the first time); and
- freeing up hours – typically, in fact, three to five hours per contract – of their time to devote to other work that's more demanding of their personal expertise and knowledge of the business, not to mention more satisfying to the lawyers to be doing and thus more likely to lead to their own career progression.

Technology also helps to:
- raise the profile and brand of the in-house team;
- give the in-house team some well-deserved recognition;
- increase the in-house team's engagement with the business – they're really 'on it' – and, in turn, develop deeper relationships;
- shake off the fusty 'Department of No' or 'Business Prevention Department' image and turn it around to the 'Department That Makes The Business' Life Easier'; and
- get the in-house team's next big idea supported if the business knows that the last one was a success (and there's the data to prove it).

4.4 Answering the million-dollar question ... how much?

A July 2021 report from LawtechUK[14] notes that the average investment in R&D across all business sectors in the United Kingdom is 5% or more of revenue. As for the legal sector – according to the report, "few legal businesses target as much as 1%", although the LawtechUK report notes that investment in R&D is increasing in legal businesses and in house.

It doesn't need to cost a fortune to achieve transformational change within an in-house legal team. For example, one Head of Legal told the authors that her total spend on new systems was equivalent to what one paralegal in her team would cost, and those systems had had a transformational impact.

There are also ways that in-house teams can piggyback on much of the work done by law firms and other providers. As the LawtechUK report notes:

> *Greater focus on process optimisation and leveraging the opportunities of technology and R&D can enable legal teams to be run to the level of capability now expected across business operations and in the face of ever tightening budgets. One way of achieving this without increasing their expenditure is leveraging the capabilities of their legal service providers, particularly those who highlight their innovation and technology programmes.*[15]

5. Using external firms and other legal services providers

Law firms can certainly help in-house legal teams get to where they need to be by collaborating more closely with them. Put simply, in-house teams that aren't being supported by their external law firms on the subject of legaltech are not getting the service that they deserve in this digital age. Put another way, any external firm that isn't *able* to support their in-house clients on the subject of legaltech are probably not themselves sufficiently 'on it' and risk becoming obsolete to their clients in the not-too-distant future. Law firms that are on the ball will positively want to help their clients in their legaltech journeys. And the more that external lawyers get to the know the business, the more the in-house teams are going to want to use them. It's a virtuous circle.

Law firms can help their in-house lawyer clients in many areas relating to legaltech.
- Tech procurement: many firms possess a wealth of experience to guide in-house lawyers through the maze of available tech (but in-house teams need to be mindful to only listen to firms which truly

understand the in-house world and the important distinctions involved). Firms have also been through the learning process of what works and what doesn't. For example:

- some firms have, on the recommendation of their IT teams, con-solidated and reduced the number of different systems that they use, only to find that a more fragmented best-in-breed approach would've been far better. Take document automation platforms, for example: one system may be better-suited to a firm's internal use, but another may be more suitable to be made available for use directly by clients; and
- the experience of firms in having investigated many different types of legaltech (and different options within one type) can be invaluable to in-house lawyers to help point them in the right direction, save huge amounts of procurement time and avoid making costly mistakes.

- Legal ops: most large firms have someone (often more than one person) who's wholly or partly dedicated to improving the firm's internal efficiency. However, only the larger in-house legal teams typically benefit from a dedicated legal ops function. Firms are therefore in a position to offer in-house teams the experience and support of their own internal resources. At least one general counsel told the authors, for example, that they'd value a legal ops secondee right now more than a lawyer secondee with four-years' PQE (and that's saying something!).
- Data analytics: large firms are increasingly starting to analyse data. Some have already engaged full-time data analysts into their ranks. The tools and techniques they're developing in data mining and analysis can be incredibly useful to an in-house legal team. For example, the firm could put a client's portfolio of contracts or leases through their data analytics tools to establish the risk profile in the client's portfolio and to compare that against the market norm. This support can also offer further insight over time, for example, how has the client's contract risk profile changed over the last year? Is it moving in the right direction? Specifically, what aspects of risk should the client be concentrating their attention on improving (see Chapter 6).
- Document automation: many law firms have invested in software to automate the production of documents in the course of their work for clients. But how many law firms have gone on to consider how they can give their in-house clients direct access to that document automation? Historically, the terms of doc auto software licences have precluded firms from being able to do this. However, there are many new doc auto suppliers now emerging in the market who are more commercial in their terms.

Law firms that offer this type of support to in-house teams can give them a useful boost to get one or two rungs up the legaltech ladder without going through the same time, effort (and often frustration) that the firm has experienced in the process. It's all part of how a truly future-facing law firm adds value in a digital age.

6. Breaking through the barriers

The question is, what's holding in-house legal teams back?

Table 2 sets out some of the most common hurdles the authors hear.

Table 2. Common hurdles

Hurdle	Steps to overcome it
Lack of reliable data on which to base decisions on where improvements can be made through investment in tech.	As this chapter shows, matter tracking systems offer such data. Sensible providers will typically offer a 'try before you buy' so in-house teams can determine whether it works for them.
Lack of budget.	As mentioned above, it doesn't need to cost a fortune. The key is to achieve a success that the business can see has worked, so that the next request for budget/support will be approved. Also, in-house teams should ask proposed tech suppliers for case studies from other in-house teams who have gone before and achieved improvements as a result.
Lack of time to think about change, like the woodcutter too busy to stop to sharpen their axe.	Get someone in the team who wants to take this on as a project and who (a) has the respect of the rest of the team and can get them to follow, and (b) has the headspace not only to explore what needs to be done but then to implement and embed those changes.
Ever-increasing choice of tech on offer, and it's often obscure what each actually does.	Solution: in-house teams should: • get their external firms to help guide them; • speak to contacts in other in-house teams who are using tech to see what did (or didn't) work for them.

Something is better than nothing; 80% is better than 0%. In-house teams should thus not let perfection be the enemy of good. No technological solution is perfect, so if the in-house team is most of the way there with a solution, then it's time to crack on.

Like law firms, in-house teams need to offer flexible working, while still ensuring that the team is accessible and developing strong relationships within their businesses.

7. Attracting and retaining talent

Will in-house legal teams face the same challenges as private practice in attracting and retaining talent in the 'hybrid era'?

Yes, but with some nuances in certain respects:

- Like law firms, in-house teams need to offer flexible working, while still ensuring that the team is accessible and developing strong relationships within their businesses.
- Like law firms, in-house teams also need to demonstrate to future talent that the leadership of the team is forward-thinking, and that the leaders will shape the future they want to see rather than wait for the spotlight to be shone on them by the board or C-suite.
- Whereas law firms need to draw on a wider range of skill sets than they currently do, such as employing and engaging more data analysts, project managers (etc), these skill sets are more likely to be found already in other departments within the in-house team's business. (In any event, in-house lawyers are less likely to need to extend these skills within the in-house team.)
- The prospects for in-house career progression are likely to grow as in-house legal teams become increasingly engaged in partnering with the business and positively contributing to strategy and achieving business objectives, rather than merely being protectors of the business and keeping the directors out of jail. More in-house lawyers may find their way to the C-suite and the status of them in the business is likely to be raised. While only about a fifth of general counsels are on the board, according to a survey the authors' firm ran with *The Lawyer* in 2019,[16] almost half "help the board make informed decisions around strategic direction". In the accompanying report, C-suite contributors to the survey suggested that opportunities for general counsel were there for the taking, particularly if in-house teams aren't just seen through the prism of the 'risk agenda'. This agenda can be "a bunker for the GC" and "prevents the wider spectrum of their contribution being properly perceived or capitalised on by the board". The risk for in-house legal teams is concentrating too much on risk. There's so much more that they can offer.

What do in-house lawyers need to take away from all this?

Tech won't replace in-house lawyers, but in-house lawyers who use tech will replace those that don't. Why?

- The great value that in-house lawyers bring to their businesses is their deep understanding of those businesses. Robots will never replace this.

- But in-house lawyers who shun new technology won't be seen as forward-thinking. Over time, they'll lose the confidence and engagement of the business.
- New technology will also help in-house lawyers handle business-as-usual work more efficiently and so create more time to provide their experience and skills to their businesses.
- Tech will also help in-house lawyers demonstrate their value to the business in objective terms.

In-house lawyers who behave like robots will be replaced by them:

- The real value of in-house lawyers is in their relationships with, and detailed understanding of, the business. If an in-house lawyer is not prioritising both of those things, then they are not adding the value that they could.
- This is even more acute now that tech solutions are becoming available for more routine legal tasks that don't involve such relationships or understanding. Whereas an in-house lawyer who behaves like a robot may have been a necessary functionary in the past, they will eventually become redundant as technology advances.

In-house legal teams that combine tech and EQ will prevail above all. By using tech, in-house lawyers will not only serve the business more quickly, cheaply and consistently than before, but they'll also create the headspace they need to invest in building relationships, empathy, support and understanding that will truly add value to the business.

8. Case studies

8.1 Case study 1: Delivering technological and innovative change in house

In Scania's annual report in 2020, the then-President and CEO, Henrik Henriksson, said the vehicle industry "will experience some of the greatest shifts in its history",[17] adding: "ahead of us we are looking at huge, transformative leaps. To navigate this new world, we need to be ready to explore new ways of working".[18]

As a result, Scania is changing. It has to. It already uses technology like AI in its workshops to solve vehicle issues quicker. But, to remain relevant, all teams in the business need to change. The in-house legal team is no exception to this rule. Why would it be? After all, the legal 'workshop' can't act like a stubborn mechanic who refuses to use the latest advanced diagnostic techniques, thinking they can just rely on a wrench and a wry smile to fix any fault. Things have moved on. And, to remain relevant, so must lawyers in the in-house legal world.

Geldards-trained Sarah Holford was Head of Legal and Compliance at Scania UK. When she started at the heavy goods vehicle maker, she was handed a blank slate by the business. As she told *The Lawyer*: "the only remit I was given was to deliver change"[19] – an impressive vote of confidence in Holford who'd only qualified two years earlier ("ahead of her years" as *The Lawyer* noted when she was listed among their 'Hot 100' in 2021).[20] Put simply, the legal function had to become, in the words of Holford, "more commercial and approachable".[21]

Holford's initial strategy was to capture data and be smarter in tracking what her team did. Not being a fan of spreadsheets – a technology designed as an accounting tool and not for managing files – she prioritised matter tracking software. In a seminar on legaltech and new ways of working (involving the authors' firm), Holford told attendees that such systems are an "easy win" with the result that she can demonstrate "objectively the value of the team" to the business. With this sort of software, she can share transaction timeframes and matter information; manage budgets; organise documents; schedule reminders; allocate tasks; and auto-generate client notifications. Importantly, she also has metrics to hand to show her business how busy her team is, enabling her to manage her time and resources much better.

As Holford told us:

> The value of my team has been transformed – Scania now sees us as a true ally. By refreshing our processes and using legaltech solutions smartly, we are now seen as aligned with business needs, forward-looking and super-responsive.

Better data has meant better decisions. The virtual 'front door' for the business has fostered quick and direct engagement with the business.

This all proved to be vital when COVID meant the team, with very little notice, had to abandon their desks and work remotely. In effect, Holford's attitude to tech before the pandemic meant her team could hit the ground running and work as efficiently as when they were all in the office together. The virtual 'front door' meant the team's internal clients could access them with no disruption. Furthermore, through the analytics that her matters management system automatically generates, Holford was able to see that her team were still efficient while working from home and that they were continuing to deliver for the business: on time, on budget and with strong levels of satisfaction.

Holford stresses the importance of external law firms in delivering innovation to their in-house clients in what she calls a 'do-more-with-less world'. She wants quicker solutions which allow her time to be freed up to deal with more strategic matters. A partnered approach from external firms is key – and also to work with firms which genuinely want to hear her views.

Holford's open-mindedness to new tech and processes, including using AI-powered contract review software, helped her team be recognised and named as *Legal Business*' "Most Transformative In-House Team of the Year" in 2021. Her achievements haven't gone unnoticed internally either: Holford now works for the Scania Group Executive Board in Stockholm dealing with Venture Capital and M&A.

8.2 Case study 2: Delivering technological and innovative change in house

The retail sector includes many brands which people have loved for generations. The Co-op (1844) and Marks and Spencer (1884) are two examples of stores which have weathered numerous economic storms and overcome significant social change to become household names. They've weaved their way into the national psyche.

These high street stalwarts might look like unchanging retailing behemoths, but they've succeeded over the years by reinventing themselves and never standing still. And, to the surprise of many, both in and out of these businesses, technology is at the forefront of much of their success. Some retailers, for example, employ as many people in their technology teams as they do in other key teams, such as their buying and merchandising teams. But out of sight is out of mind. We tend not to think about all the technology behind the scenes when we're buying a tin of beans.

And there's no doubt that the world of retailing, like the law, is also seeing transformative change. The pandemic accelerated the transformation of the sector, delivering, in a couple of years, changes it had expected to see in half-a-decade or more. Things are moving quicker than ever and in-house teams can't afford to fall behind in the businesses that they serve, with outdated working methods and old technology.

The authors worked with an in-house lawyer in a large retailer. Like many in-house teams, this general counsel's team (of only a handful of lawyers) dealt with a wide variety of matters: from low-value, run-of-the-mill commercial agreements to high-value, bespoke software contracts (among others). Given the sheer volume of commercial contracts in the business, the general counsel was keen to find legaltech which could help the team with its capacity issues. There was a significant demand on the team's time and, even with the best will in the world, only so much that it could do. For many of the business' contracts, the team was often doing the same thing over and over again. Common sense said these should be automated in some way.

The general counsel went on the search for something – anything! – which would allow the team to process day-to-day contracts more effectively. The key was to concentrate on just the most important parts of business-as-usual contracts and not on the minutiae. The GC was willing to consider AI; after all, in-house lawyers have been using this technology for many years. For example, in 2017, JP Morgan announced that it had developed COIN (for *Contract Intelligence*) to power through commercial loan agreements, saving a reported 360,000 hours of work in the process.[22]

Unlike JPMorgan, however, it wasn't feasible for the business to develop its own AI tool in house, so the GC opted to use one of their external law firms' AI-powered contract review tool. The team now uses this technology to help it prioritise how it applies its limited resources. In particular, it:

- allows the in-house team to focus on more important and interesting work. AI deals with many of the team's run-of-the-mill contracts much more quickly;
- helps the team to spot 'bear traps' (ie, key risks for the business); and
- is cheaper, the AI does much of the work. Although it doesn't understand everything the business wants or needs or indeed the nuances of a particular deal, it does allow the in-house team to take the initial grind out of each job.

Of course, any AI-powered contract review tool can't do everything. And by no stretch of the imagination are they perfect (but neither, alas, are lawyers). AI tools always need to have some level of human oversight. But technology is, as the authors mention elsewhere in this book, about people *and* tech; not people or tech.

The business has done well over the years through its customer-centric approach and its use of technology. Retailers generally are using AI more and more to manage inventory and customise promotions. As retailers embrace the latest technologies, it's not *if* they'll expect their in-house teams to do the same, but *when*.

9. Practical tips on in-house lawyering

We set out below some practical tips on in-house lawyering.

These tips are split as follows:
- adding value to the business;
- getting support on your tech journey;
- being strategic in using legaltech; and
- attracting and retaining talent.

9.1 Adding value to the business
- Create a clear in-house team mission statement to consistently rally behind to ensure that you're valued. The authors know of one general counsel who enlisted the business' brand department to develop a strong brand for the in-house team within the business.
- Align the in-house team ethos and brand to the business' strategy (eg, if customer experience is important to the business, ensure your internal clients receive the same customer experience).
- Contribute beyond just the purely legal aspects of your job by offering innovative solutions and giving a different perspective to problems.
- Offer clarity of thought and objectivity by acting, where you can, as a valuable sounding board for business ideas.
- Connect with the business at all levels in the team, both to build relationships and to better understand the business:
  - as one general counsel once told the authors: "know the business and build relationships. Without this, the in-house team simply can't achieve its goals or expect to be valued";
  - act as a facilitator to join together people in the business who might not otherwise appreciate how they can help each other. Because the in-house team tends to be a common denominator in a lot of what is going on in the business, they can use a 'helicopter view' of what's going on; and
  - create modern platform-based 'front doors' for the business to access the in-house legal team, not only to make the team more accessible in an agile working environment, but also to process instructions more efficiently – to show that the team is open for business and 'on it'.

9.2 Getting support on your tech journey
- Expect more innovation from your panel firms. If they purport to understand your needs, they should be offering clever solutions to enable you to work smarter, faster and better (particularly on business-as-usual matters) and to free up your time to concentrate on

adding value to your business where it really matters. Also, they'll be spending a lot of time and investment in adopting technology to make themselves more efficient, so ensure that this benefit is passed on to you.

- Ask whether any solutions are designed specifically for lawyers (ideally for in-house lawyers), rather than generic solutions that are shoehorned into an in-house legal context. (And if they're also designed by lawyers for lawyers, then all the better!)

- Consider asking your external firms for added value support in your legaltech journey. Many law firms will be more experienced than in-house legal teams at procuring legaltech. Swapping notes on what's in the market, and law firms' experience of those solutions in practice, can be hugely helpful to an in-house team. Most large panel firms also have extensive legal operations, IT and innovation teams that work full-time on improving legal process efficiency. They'll have great experience to share with you on your legaltech journey.

- Remember to speak to your colleagues in other business functions for ideas and inspiration. And consider exploiting your business' existing tech stack. If you can make improvements within existing business software licence arrangements, you could save your valuable budget for buying in the tech that just can't be found in-house.

- Speak to your internal clients and ask what they'd like to see. Much of the change that's being seen within private practice is driven by client demand and expectation. Therefore, ensure that your plans for change put your internal clients at the centre of everything you do.

- Consider reverse or mutual secondments with law firms so your team can get experience of what innovation is going on within firms. Also consider asking your firms if your people could spend some time in the legal operations team (rather than at the lawyering 'coal face'). The experience that your team can glean from a highly active and experienced innovation support function within a firm can be invaluable.

- The authors often speak to general counsels and heads of legal who are keen to implement change but who simply don't feel that they have the bandwidth to carry it through, after identifying what needs to be done. Identifying a keen right-hand person within your team who's interested and motivated to ensure that actions are followed through is a crucial asset. (This is also a great opportunity for someone to really make their mark. Just as in private practice, there's a huge opportunity for junior in-house lawyers to help the more senior lawyers to navigate, assess and implement legaltech. They can be highly supportive and effective agents for change within your team.)

- Encourage everyone in your team to talk about tech with their network of peers at law firms and other organisations. Encourage them to be interested in finding out what new processes and technology are being developed and to think about how this might be relevant to your team and the wider business.
- Remember, 80% better is better than 0% better: do something!

9.3 Being strategic in using legaltech

- Remember that what you do has got to lead to a better outcome for the business. Giving your team more time (through innovation) to focus on achieving the business' goals (and show more EQ and demonstrate more business acumen) will help the business and make you and your team look great.
- Lead the change. Just as law firm leaders who fail to prioritise modernisation are dooming their firms to eventual failure, so are in-house legal leaders. Although you might think that the dynamic of having a captive internal client makes a fundamental difference, the fact is that no business can afford to allow any function within an organisation to operate otherwise than with optimal efficiency. (Remember, as firms get more efficient the cost of outsourcing will inevitably reduce.)
- Prioritise the capture and analysis of data: in an in-house context, the value of data is massive; and yet it's seldom captured by systems or subjected to detailed analysis. Many general counsels or heads of legal, for example, don't have enough visibility of exactly what their teams are doing day to day for the business (apart from those who currently use matter-tracking and analytics systems). Just some of the uses that the authors have discussed on data with in-house lawyers include:
  - managing resources and anticipating peaks and troughs in demand;
  - demonstrating just how much work the legal team is doing for the business, including all those *ad hoc* queries that come in and take up time, but are seldom recorded;
  - identifying for which internal clients the most resource is being applied;
  - spotting where self-help can be given to an internal client to reduce demand on the legal team;
  - knowing reliably how long different matters typically take to complete so that you can plan resources better and also manage your internal clients' expectations and help them to plan more realistically;
  - comparing the value of work done by your team against the cost of comparable work from external firms. This might make the

case for bringing some work back in-house and support a case for internal recruitment;
- managing external law firms by keeping track of whether they are completing instructions on time, on budget and to your satisfaction;
- identifying repeat queries from the business, which might justify FAQs and help sheets to be created to answer them in future; and
- identifying when someone in the business is contacting someone in the legal team and, when they don't get the answer they want, they contact someone else in the hope they will get the answer they want. (This seems to happen with alarming consistency across many businesses!)

The list could go on.
- Be gradual in the changes in behaviour that you hope to engender among your business users. Consider trialling new tech with your closest contact before wider roll-out. Whatever you do, ensure the tech works before exposing it to the business. Over time, when you're confident that the tech can make a significant positive impact on the business, then think about introducing incentives on the business to use it. (One head of legal the authors know told the business that they'd get their matters dealt with more quickly if they used newly prescribed instruction forms through a virtual 'front door', than if they just insisted on emailing members of the legal team for help. She had a positive response from the business, who found the new forms easy and quick, and they loved knowing they were getting faster turnaround as a result.)

9.4 Attracting and retaining talent
- When recruiting, ensure that the candidate doesn't assume that the rate of change in an in-house role will be any less than that in private practice. Nor should they think that an in-house role offers less opportunity to achieve positive change for the business. More than ever, in-house lawyers have the opportunity to make changes that will enable the legal team to be more visible, and to add more value, than ever before.
- Equally, a candidate mustn't think that an in-house role is immune from the pressures of change at least equal to those that exist in private practice. Therefore, be sure to demonstrate that the in-house legal team has forward-thinking leaders who'll shape the future that they (and the candidate) want to see, rather than being reactive and hoping for the best.
- The 'hybrid era' affects in-house teams just as much as law firms. Current and new in-house talent want and expect more flexibility in

the balance between office and home working. But whereas almost all law firms have systems to track how busy their people are (wherever they are working) and help to keep them connected to all the information they need to work remotely, relatively few in-house legal teams have yet adopted matter tracking systems to help with these important things. Those that have adopted such systems have seen tremendous benefits for both individual team members as well as for the team as a whole. The natural reaction of a junior in-house lawyer might be this is exactly the sort of scrutiny that they expect to avoid compared to working in private practice. However, in reality, nothing could be further from the truth. If the general counsel or head of legal is seen to be looking for systems to capture data, that can only be a great thing for each individual lawyer and for the team, to show the value they are adding and to capture the data needed to make the right investments (and to assist with obtaining budget for those investments) going forward.

Notes

1   Adam Smith, *An Inquiry into the Nature and Causes of the Wealth of Nations* (T Nelson, 1852), p311.
2   "About Companies House" (Companies House), https://companieshouse.blog.gov.uk/about-companies-house/.
3   Bruce Love, "Reinvention of the in-house lawyer" (*Financial Times*, 4 March 2021), www.ft.com/content/371149d0-3730-48a3-80b3-e22dd3cc6538.
4   Jesse Middleton, "Download: How GCs are using legal tech" (*The Lawyer*, 30 April 2021), www.thelawyer.com/download-how-gcs-are-using-legal-tech/.
5   "Annual statistics report 2021" (Law Society, 21 September 2022), www.lawsociety.org.uk/topics/research/annual-statistics-report-2021. As Chapter 10 shows, there are, at the time or writing, almost 160,000 practising solicitors.
6   *Ibid.*
7   *Legal operations: the shape of things to come* (OMC Partners, 2021), https://ashurstcd.azureedge.net/-/media/ashurst/documents/innovation/legal-operations—-the-shape-of-things-to-come.pdf?rev=50a5b48738924582bea62c4f154f1149&sc_lang=en&hash=B65615 8C2A5162C8E46DE7598BC5494F.
8   *Ibid.*
9   *Ibid.*
10 *The role of in-house solicitors*, www.sra.org.uk/globalassets/documents/sra/research/role-in-house-solicitors.pdf?version=4a1ac6.
11 David B Wilkins, "The In-House Counsel Movement" (*The Practice*, volume 2, issue 4, May/June 2016), https://thepractice.law.harvard.edu/article/in-house-counsel-movement/.
12 *Ibid.*
13 "Hot 100 career quiz: Scania's Sarah Holford" (*The Lawyer*, 2 August 2021), www.thelawyer.com/hot-100-career-quiz-scanias-sarah-holford/.
14 LawtechUK, *Shaping the Future of Law – The LawtechUK Report 2021* (July 2021), https://technation.io/wp-content/uploads/2021/07/LawtechUK-Report-2021-Final.pdf.
15 *Ibid.*
16 "Building GC influence in the boardroom" (*The Lawyer*), www.shoosmiths.co.uk/-/media/download-documents/reports/shoosmiths_building-gc-influence-in-the-boardroom.pdf.
17 *The Scania Report 2020*, www.volkswagenag.com/presence/investorrelation/publications/annual-reports/2021/scania/scania-annual-and-sustainability-report-2020.pdf.
18 *Ibid.*
19 "Case study: Sarah Holford on improving business engagement through tech" (*The Lawyer*, 29 March 2021), www.thelawyer.com/case-study-sarah-holford-on-improving-business-engagement-through-tech/.
20 *The Lawyer* (@TheLawyermag), "'Ahead of her years' is an understatement for @ScaniaUK head of legal Sarah Holford, one the youngest lawyers in #TheLawyerHot100 2021, www.thelawyer.com/event/lawyer-hot-100/" Twitter, 25 January 2021, https://twitter.com/thelawyermag/status/1353682121378902016?s=11.
21 "Case study: Sarah Holford on improving business engagement through tech" (*The Lawyer*, 29

March 2021), www.thelawyer.com/case-study-sarah-holford-on-improving-business-engagement-through-tech/.

22   Hugh Son, "JPMorgan software does in seconds what took lawyers 360,000 hours" (*Independent*, 28 February 2017), www.independent.co.uk/news/business/news/jp-morgan-software-lawyers-coin-contract-intelligence-parsing-financial-deals-seconds-legal-working-hours-360000-a760325 6.html.

Part 4:
People

Our time on this planet is short. The King James Bible famously refers to three score years and ten. A few centuries on from when it was written, most people can now expect to make it into their eighties.

But what's this figure in weeks? (After all, the drumbeat of our professional lives is measured more in working weeks than years.) It's roughly about 4,000 weeks. Therefore, each of us has about half that time, about 2,000 weeks, in the bank for the stereotypical legal career – and a pretty long career at that.

In reality, 2,000-odd weeks isn't a great deal of time when you consider how quickly each working week seems to flash by. Think of how many weeks are spent cumulatively in meetings, on trains, popping out for a coffee or fighting with uncooperative IT systems. (More than we'd care to imagine.)

The relentless waves of technology and innovation also mean that in just one-quarter of this 2,000-week period – if not sooner – the profession is likely to see radical changes. If the last 2,000 weeks (from the early 1980s) have seen remarkable changes, the next 2,000 weeks (to the early 2060s) will see things that even the best futurologists can scarcely conceive of now.

In this part, we look at the importance of EQ (emotional intelligence): our trump card in a time of accelerated technological and innovative change. We also look at what advanced lawyers need to know to ready their firms and the aspiring and associate lawyers in them for the change ahead of us. It looks at what law firms also need to be thinking about for these cohorts and, to a limited degree, the non-lawyers who will also help build the law firms of tomorrow.

We don't have as much time as we think. Time is one of our greatest gifts. Unlike most other humans, we've chosen to convert it into six-minute increments. Let's use it well.

Chapter 9:
EQ ≥ IQ

On 24 June 1982, a British Airways Boeing 747 flew into a cloud of volcanic ash near Mount Galunggung in Indonesia. Sulphurous-smelling smoke drifted into the cabin. One by one each of the aircraft's engines 'flamed out'. The engines became choked with tiny fragments of rock, minerals and volcanic glass.

At about 8.45pm local time Captain Eric Moody announced over the PA system:

> *Ladies and gentlemen, this is your captain speaking. We have a small problem. All four engines have stopped. We are doing our damnedest to get them going again. I trust you are not in too much distress.*[1]

Captain Moody's clipped pronouncement was a masterclass in understatement and strategic cushioning. Plunging engineless towards the Indian Ocean was, in the captain's words "a small problem". Despite Moody's statement not technically being true – the problem was quite big (there's a bit more understatement again), it seemed to have the desired effect. Reports from passengers were that the cabin was eerily quiet.

This form of speech is used a lot in England. It's a trait many foreigners find "utterly bewildering and infuriating" – or "a bit confusing", as many in England might well put it.[2]

In essence, what people say isn't always what they mean.

The hidden rules that govern our behaviour are something that anyone new to the game, say someone moving to England for the first time, will struggle to understand.

Therefore, if humans struggle to understand why other humans are acting in a certain way, how can we expect technology to cope? Humans are much more nuanced that we think.

As lawyers, we have a similar role of helping to interpret human meaning and behaviour. And we shouldn't underestimate what a skill this is and its importance in the practice of law.

Lawyering is a people business. It requires not only a high IQ, but also a high EQ. Lawyers are often engaged by people when they are going through tough times: a loved one has passed away; a cherished business is being sold; a marriage is ending in divorce. Kevin Roose, technology columnist in the *New York Times*, suggests lawyers will morph into what he calls "legal therapists", "creating trust with clients and helping to solve their problems, rather than simply writing briefs and doing research".[3]

The ability to read people and to 'get' them, individually and collectively, is a vital skill for lawyers.

While technology is going to help us in many ways in the future, the need for us to understand and deal with the quirks and subtleties – the "strategic misrepresentations"[4] – of our colleagues and clients isn't going to go away. And it will remain key to being trusted advisers to our clients.

In this chapter we look at:
- how EQ is equal to or greater than technical intelligence;
- understanding EQ generally;
- embracing imagination and the serendipity that can follow when doing so;
- our EQ trump cards and understanding; and
- the importance of EQ, including:
  - reading the situation;
  - showing compassion;
  - explaining;
  - fostering trust;
  - spotting links;
  - giving structure to things;
  - negotiating;

- persuading;
- enjoying ourselves; and
- giving prestige.

We then look at two case studies and finish with some practical tips.

1. Understanding that EQ is equal to or greater than technical intelligence

In this chapter, perhaps one of the most important in this book, the authors assert that EQ is equal to or greater than IQ.

We examine just how much lawyers do that:
- can't be done by machines; and
- positively adds value to the client experience and outcomes.

These are not 'soft' issues – there's more to providing legal services than just cost, speed, efficiency and accuracy.

This seems to have been largely overlooked in the dystopian predictions that conclude only lawyers operating in highly niche areas will survive the legaltech shockwave.

We see the future differently: it's all about people *and* tech, not people *or* tech. We know that a home only becomes a home when people are involved; otherwise, it's just a house. If only the English language could make the same distinction with technology – to reiterate how much technology depends on a human framework to apply it effectively in a professional context.

That's not to say that we lawyers can be complacent, that we will never be replaced by machines. Lawyers who behave just like robots can expect to be replaced by robots (see the second law of legal practice in Chapter 12). This chapter lists those attributes that will allow lawyers not only to survive but also to thrive in the digital age, including the ability to imagine the future we want to see. These intensely human skills are what will put lawyers in the best place to continue to be the predominant providers of legal services.

To a greater or lesser extent, these form part of our daily jobs. Some may come naturally and effortlessly. Some may be harder to do. But, one way or another, we all do these things and will continue to do these things – a lot!

Although there's been almost immeasurable advancement in the technology applied in delivering legal services over the last 40 years, there's been hardly any discernible advancement in most of the very human attributes listed below. It's as if everyone has seen the obvious advantages that come with new technology, but that the human side of lawyering has always been beyond improvement. The authors contend that not only is there considerable room for improvement, but that improving these human skills will be far more achievable in a world where tech does more of the heavy lifting, and where the human touch will become the factor that distinguishes legal service providers from each other.

2. Understanding EQ

Emotional quotient (EQ) or emotional intelligence (EI), whatever you prefer to call it, there are plenty of terms and initialisms to describe a trait which is core to being a successful lawyer in a digital age.

In Daniel Goleman's seminal book *Emotional Intelligence*, published in 1995, the science journalist outlined what he believed are the five main elements of EQ:[5]

- self-awareness;
- self-regulation;
- internal motivation;
- empathy; and
- social or interpersonal skills.

Despite the importance of the above in the day-to-day work we do as lawyers, Goleman noted that people are still unwilling to embrace EQ. People think it can't be defined. They think that they can't get better at it; that it's something that they either have or don't have. Even so, Goleman said that you can get better at it.

Sometimes many of these EQ elements are also called 'soft skills', a term which downgrades their vital role and means they may not be taken as seriously as they need to be. Culturally, for example, 'soft' drinks are regarded as a lesser class of drink compared to, say, a 1961 Château Mouton Rothschild. A 'soft' launch, while it has its place, isn't typically as game-changing as a 'hard' launch of a product.

It seems that the same attitude pervades how we perceive soft skills. Hard technical skills are a must-have in what we do, whereas soft skills too often fall under the nice-to-have category. This dichotomy will no longer hold. As Dan Kayne, founder of The O Shaped Lawyer pointed out to the authors, these interpersonal skills are "some of the hardest skills you'll ever have to practise".

And we mustn't think for a moment that EQ is the sole preserve of extraverts. Although extraversion often correlates in people's minds with EQ, and there is a cultural bias which tends to favour extraversion (think of all of those reality TV programmes in the TV schedules), introverts and ambiverts need EQ too. Research in 2013, for example, showed that ambiverts can be some of the best salespeople as they are good at listening to their clients – as introverts are apt to do – but they can then summon up the enthusiasm which is typical of extraverts to seal the deal.[6]

As technology is used more and more in the working life of lawyers and such tech represents more of the 'IQ' in the work that we do, EQ is a trait that will, year on year, come more to the fore. As lawyers – introverts, extraverts or ambiverts – we need to recognise its role, celebrate it and, where we can, get better at it. Soft skills? Hardly!

3. Embracing imagination

A vital part of EQ is the ability to use our imagination. But, too often, we dismiss it out of hand. And we're not alone: there's a long tradition of downplaying this key skill. Eighteenth-century man of letters, Samuel Johnson, called imagination a "licentious and vagrant faculty" designed to "baffle the logician, to perplex the confines of distinction, and burst the enclosures of regularity".[7]

Perhaps that's why we lawyers often struggle with the whole 'imagination thing'? "Use your imagination", they say. But we can't quite pin the concept down. It's all a bit vague and fluffy. As life's natural cynics, perhaps we find it all a bit naïve. We don't have the time to waste on wishful thinking.

It especially jars our legal sensibilities. Our legal tradition is committed to the clear, the consistent and the predictable and yet imaginations are often, in their very nature, obscure, fickle and unpredictable.

To understand why we should make the effort and not just exile our imagination to the fringes of what we do as lawyers, it's worth reminding ourselves why this most remarkable of human traits has such an important role to play.

At its simplest, imagination is what drives humans to do and be better.
- It's little-known people like mechanical engineer Nils Bohlin, who had a vision of a safer and more simple-to-use seatbelt. Over half-a-century on and there's "a little bit of Nils Bohlin in every car".[8] Countless lives have been saved.
- It's the (now famous) married couple, Dr Özlem Türeci and Professor

We're all capable of imagining big things. But, equally, there's nothing to stop us taking a few nervous baby steps and starting small, like dieters making their first tentative efforts on a new diet and exercise regime on New Year's Day. Any start is a good start.

Uğur Şahin, founders of biotechnology company BioNTech, who imagined that they could vaccinate against COVID and resolved to do something about it – at lightning-fast speed.[9] After reading about the rapid spread of a new coronavirus called SARS-CoV-2 in *The Lancet*,[10] Şahin committed 400 staff to develop a vaccine.[11] Ten months later, on 2 December 2020, the UK Medicines and Healthcare products Regulatory Agency gave its approval for the Pfizer/BioNTech vaccine.[12] The seemingly impossible became possible.

- It's lawyers too: take Dr Tunde Okewale MBE, criminal barrister at Doughty Street Chambers, who grew up on a council estate in Hackney and was the first person in his family to go to university. His vision? Society has to move beyond the "soft bigotry" of low expectations that working-class kids face.[13] He foresees a world where those from both Eton and Edmonton have the same aspirations and where everyone can think big and do "something that's important and change[s] the world".[14] The charity he founded in 2010, Urban Lawyers, has helped thousands of young students achieve their career goals. His imagination has tangibly transformed many lives.

We're all capable of imagining big things. But, equally, there's nothing to stop us taking a few nervous baby steps and starting small, like dieters making their first tentative efforts on a new diet and exercise regime on New Year's Day. Any start is a good start.

What's more, this isn't a self-righteous self-help book with the message 'go big or go home'. The authors aren't whooping and clapping in encouragement as we write this. But it is a book which is keen to give you a gentle nudge to develop your 'muscle memory' for imagination and to encourage others to do so too. Ultimately, the key is to give it a go and keep going: to be a bit less like Johnson and a bit more like Bohlin, Türeci, Şahin and Okewale.

There's no doubt the legal profession can't afford to wallow in an unimaginative, no-one-else-has-mentioned-this-issue-before mindset, no matter how busy we are. We need to be that awkward first person to challenge the *status quo* and say something ("well, I'm mentioning it now") and help to create solutions to the problems we face now, and in the years to come.

Our frustrated minds wandering can be the catalyst for so much needed change, provided that we allow ourselves the time to listen to our internal thoughts and then, most importantly, to give them priority and do something about them: "is it just me, or is our billing system not really up to scratch? Have we thought about doing x, y or z?" The solutions don't need to be perfect. Nothing in life ever is. And, of course, there are some battles that aren't worth fighting. But we can't let perfection be the enemy of good (or even survival). With a crash course in office politics and a dash of realpolitik, our splendidly capricious and unconstrained imaginations can, collectively and individually, take us to places that we've never imagined.

Perhaps it'll be new and lucrative income streams for new legal problems or it might be new ways of delivering existing legal services. After all, who knows what extraordinary technology will exist 10 years from now? In fact, it could even be to boldly go where no firm has gone before.

Ultimately, if we don't imagine the change we want and need to see, then who will? The Big Tech companies? New tech start-ups? Other NewLaw arrivals? Legaltech from China? (A shortage of lawyers and leadership in AI means China has been filing legaltech patents at a fair clip.)

Samuel Johnson may well have castigated the faculty of imagination for being illogical, indistinct and inconsistent; but it's this fuzzy, messy and oh-so human trait that will power so much of the profession in the future, no matter how powerful and ubiquitous computers may become.

The good news is that it comes fitted as standard in the human brain. But it's only available if we switch it on and use it.

4. Understanding the importance of day-to-day EQ

If imagination is part of the EQ bigger picture, there are numerous other traits which will be key to being successful in the profession in the 2020s and beyond.

These are characteristics that technology can't replicate easily or indeed at all. They're our EQ trump cards.

4.1 Reading the situation
When little or no progress is being made in a deal there often comes a point when somebody has to have the guts to bang the table and make the tea-spoons jump. This may lead to an ultimatum and being prepared to walk away from a deal. Of course, it may end up with a deal being agreed.

There's no machine on Earth that can yet tell a client when that point has come. Even the popular 'dad-dancing' humanoid, Atlas, developed by robotics company Boston Dynamics, has probably got better things to do than to bang its claws on expensive boardroom tables.

Moreover, although mind-reading technology – known as brain wave or brain-computer interface (BCI) technology – does exist, and is developing all the while, a lot of current 'brain tech' is still focused on invasive technology such as implantable brain–machine interfaces. That's not to say that in the future non-invasive technology won't be able to read our opponents' minds or interpret their behaviour – or indeed read a room – but future human rights law might well prohibit such privacy-invasive technology in most circumstances. We don't have to worry just yet.

So, for the foreseeable future, lawyers will continue to use all of their soft skills, all hewn from their very human experience, in meeting rooms and courtrooms the length and breadth of the country. And many of these skills will be non-verbal.

One often-quoted statistic on the internet is that human-to-human communication consists of:
- 55% body language;
- 38% the voice (used as an instrument: its rate, pitch and loudness etc); and
- 7% actual words spoken.

These disputed (and often misunderstood) figures – the 7-38-55 formula – derive from two research studies in the 1960s[15] and have almost become a cliché. As associate professor David Lapakko asks: "If the meaning in communication is in fact 93% non-verbal, what would be the point of learning a language?"[16] Indeed.

However, even if the exact figures are disputed, there's no doubt that understanding and using non-verbal communication is vital in what we do:
- We see the 'hidden', often subconscious, messages through posture and body language; touch; and eye contact. All of these 'tells' can betray what people are truly thinking. This is where face-to-face meetings or being in a courtroom can be essential to further a matter.
- We build trust: studies show that handshaking can make us cooperate and help us negotiate better outcomes. Handshakes release the hormone oxytocin – the "moral molecule"[17] – in the brain, which helps us to build trust in strangers.
- When we're physically together, we tend to pay more attention. If a meeting attendee sits fiddling with their phone, updating their Instagram or Twitter feed, it's more likely than not they'll be noticed doing so. Getting together in person says, 'this meeting is important'. (The pandemic has shown many of us that we may have undervalued the importance of meeting in person.)

Remember Clippy, the anthropomorphic paperclip in Microsoft Office? This feature seemed to be programmed to pop up at the worst moment, with its Groucho Marx-style eyebrows flexing every few seconds so that it was impossible to ignore: "It looks like you are trying to write a letter. Would you like help?" (The answer was invariably "no".)

- We can use the mirror neurones in our brains. Associate professor Marcus Holmes notes: "The brain has discrete architecture and processes devoted to parsing others' intentions via cues in face-to-face interaction."[18] When we smile, your counterparty may well feel compelled to do the same. They mirror your emotions which can often change the whole tenor of a conversation.

4.2 Showing compassion

We are sorry to announce that the 07.55 Avanti West Coast train service to London Euston is delayed by approximately 23 minutes. We apologise for this late running and the inconvenience caused.

For anyone who hops on a train regularly, staccato messages such as this are the traveller's curse. But who's the 'we' in this apology? The computer? Can an automated announcement truly feel remorse for a delayed train? It's doubtful that many travellers are left thinking "well that's a real pain, but at least I got a lovely apology from them".

Contrast this sort of disembodied apology with, for example, one given by a member of staff on the train platform. Eye contact, a remorseful look of concern and open body language mean so much more. It's the difference between an 'unexpected-item-in-the-bagging-area' sort of apology and one where you feel your frustration has been acknowledged and, all being well, acted upon.

And even where technology tries to be less robotic and all chatty and human-like, it can still fail miserably. Remember Clippy, the anthropomorphic paperclip in Microsoft Office? This feature seemed to be programmed to pop up at the worst moment, with its Groucho Marx-style eyebrows flexing every few seconds so that it was impossible to ignore: "It looks like you are trying to write a letter. Would you like help?" (The answer was invariably "no".) Of course, you'd be five minutes away from an immovable court deadline at this point. Clippy empathetic? Not so much.

We humans are social animals. Unlike the clunky Clippy, we're designed to be empathetic. It's in our nature. It's the spark that ignites compassion. Professor Edwin Gale in the *Species that Changed Itself* believes modern humans are more empathetic than our ancestors.[19] The result is that, year on year, we're getting better at it (although perhaps not so much on social media) and with more people in the world and human networks increasing in size and scope – both on and offline – it's a skill that continues to grow in importance.

For lawyers, empathy and compassion aren't optional extras; for a lot of what we do they're essential.

But it's vital to recognise that there *is* a difference between the two. In the long term, we mustn't fall into the trap of feeling *with* our clients (empathy) rather we should feel for them (compassion). Empathy is a natural starting point, but unless it's turned into something constructive it can be draining. It saps our energy. And it's not always useful or constructive. Empathy is about sharing someone's emotions; compassion is acting on them. If a friend were to receive an email from their firm saying their files had been hacked, empathy would be to feel as distressed and angry as your friend, whereas compassion would be to help them do something about it. Truly empathetic lawyers don't last long. Like vicarious liability, you feel the pain. You're on the hook.

And science backs this up. Research shows that compassion activates different neural networks in the brain. And all these networks come to the fore when supporting our clients during their most challenging of times, such as:

- in specific personal contexts, such as death, personal injury, family breakdowns or selling a long-established family business, which are often more emotionally draining than you'd think;
- in the context of many business transactions. Deals are often complex and challenging, even fraught and occasionally aggressive. An emotionally intelligent lawyer can transform how even the most seasoned corporate client feels during that deal – we can truly have the client's back; and
- in other less personal contexts where we might least expect it, such as in the development of legaltech. We need to design tech that engages with users and deals with their needs.

Of course, there are exceptions to this rule and compassion is by no means always needed when giving legal advice. As with most things, there's a time and a place. However, we believe that it'll continue to be needed in some form in much of what we do, and increasingly so if we as a profession are to give our clients the best possible experience when using lawyers, so that they continue to prefer us over purely tech-leveraged legal service providers.

A couple of last thoughts on empathy and compassion before moving on. Some may suggest that, insofar as empathy and compassion are required in the profession, this requirement is often exaggerated. The authors have, in aggregate, amassed decades of day-to-day practical experience of lawyering; met with wave after wave of transformative technology; and have achieved some success in the profession. Our conviction is that the role and value of empathy and compassion in lawyering is, if anything, underplayed and that there's great potential to deliver better outcomes for clients, and better workplaces for our colleagues, if these attributes are developed and applied more assiduously in the work that we do.

It's also been suggested, if these attributes really are worth featuring in the provision of legal services in the future, that they could perhaps be dispensed by individuals specifically engaged purely for this purpose. Again, our view is that empathy has to be authentic to be effective (remember the delayed train apology). And authenticity is also the bedrock on which trust is built for our clients. We're not convinced, for example, that an individual popping up somewhere in an otherwise completely automated process saying "Hi, I'm Andy, and I'll be your personal empathiser for this transaction" will cut it.

4.3 Explaining
The interface between technology and users has been improving considerably and will, no doubt, continue to do so. However, in providing legal advice, several factors come into play that put machines in the shade compared to lawyers.
- We lawyers can gauge what information the client is mostly concerned about, sorting the wheat from the chaff.
- We can assimilate an infinite range of variables and decide what is going to be most relevant to the client.
- We can, of course, deliver information with sensitivity where the circumstances require it using appropriate body language.
- We can explain complex situations by telling narratives and keeping things simple.

Above all, we can tell when our clients eyes start to glaze over and it's time to change tack. As legal commentator David Allen Green says: "Black letter law is dull – it is akin to reading sheet music and attempting to create the tune in your head. Law, like music, comes alive in its performance."[20]

4.4 Fostering trust
Despite the many jokes about our lack of honesty (which might be hurtful were they not so funny), we are a trustworthy bunch. We are trustworthy by design. For solicitors, the SRA's Assessment of Character and Suitability Rules mean all individuals applying for admission or restoration to the roll of solicitors must be of satisfactory character and suitability.

In 1994 Lord Bingham, then-Master of the Rolls, also spoke of the need to maintain high public trust in the solicitors' profession in *Bolton v Law Society*,[21] which he said required a confidence that solicitors are people of "unquestionable integrity, probity and trustworthiness". This remains "good regulatory law" under SRA Principle 2 ("public trust and confidence").[22]

The increased intensity with which regulators such as the SRA shine their spotlights on our business activities and personal behaviour has never been higher. Nor has it ever been more appropriate.

Trust and regulation ought to distinguish us from our less-regulated NewLaw competitors. In an ever-complex world, trust allows us to help our clients to simplify how they deal with life's complexities that, without trust, would require unrealistic efforts from them to untangle.

And it's unlikely that AI will make any inroads into this inherently human trait anytime soon. AI-powered chatbots, for example, can't truly sympathise with client problems. Law is an intensely human business: engagements with clients are built on trust, not algorithms. (Although there are times, of course, where anonymity plays a role too: some people may prefer to 'discuss' personal details with machines rather than with humans as it avoids any fear of embarrassment or being judged.)

We should therefore embrace the work regulators are doing to ensure that our profession is beyond reproach.

4.5 Spotting links
In all but the most basic legal processes, the propensity for a change or occurrence in one parameter to affect one or more other parameters is high. This is often the case where you're dealing with a single document. This is increased massively where you're dealing with a suite of related documents or parallel transactions.

Whereas document automation can be tremendously helpful in ensuring that a change of detail (eg, the registered office of a party) is reflected in all relevant documents, that is pretty much where it ends.

Some may argue that, as soon as a computer was able to beat a human at chess, the ability to make a machine that can spot these types of linkages in legal processes can be made. However, chess is just one game. Imagine creating a machine for every game on the planet. Then imagine that there are an infinite number of new games that could arise at any time to be covered as well. That machine is akin to what an experienced lawyer is carrying in their head all the time.

As futurist Antoine Buéno notes, the plasticity of the human brain means that it can make almost limitless connections for an almost limitless number of connections.[23] On a practical legal level, this means that lawyers will be needed where yes or no answers aren't available. As former Clifford Chance partner, Laura King, noted in the Law Society's future-gazing report published in June 2021: "There will always be a place ... knowing your client, knowing the history of your client, knowing what your client's potential strategy is. There are so many variables at play."[24]

4.6 Giving structure to things

Given many variables, experienced lawyers are great at proposing the best structures for deals. However, that same ability to structure transactions and legal actions may one day be possible through the use of complicated and very thorough decision trees.

That said, anyone who has ever dialled an automated switchboard will have experienced the frustration of going through five decisions before being put through to the relevant human (if you're lucky). Often, it would take much less time if you could speak to a human in the first place.

Imagine that frustration multiplied exponentially in an AI deal-structuring platform.

4.7 Negotiating

Is this the end of the art of negotiation? It doesn't seem so; certainly not for larger and bespoke contracts.

There are still many reasons why standard-form contracts and risk profiles don't exist and, therefore, negotiation is still needed, for example, in relation to:
- the relative bargaining power of the parties;
- the need or appetite to enter into the deal;
- the trade-off between price and risk;
- the specifics of the deal;
- different corporate policies on risk profile; and
- changing market-norms.

That said, while negotiation is likely to be important for complex, large-scale contracts, we may nonetheless see less negotiation and ongoing involvement of lawyers for many run-of-the-mill transactions, particularly where, as barrister and author Jamie Susskind notes "the relevant rules are embedded in the technology we encounter".[25] Using technology means we submit to its code. It's not something that we can ignore or get around, it's as pointless as trying to negotiate terms and conditions with Google.

For those contracts where negotiation is needed, there are countless books and podcasts on the art of negotiation from Donald Trump's *The Art of the Deal* to Sun Tzu's *The Art of War*. It is pointless to deal with them in this work. What's clear is that a valuable lawyer is trained to see the wood for the trees and to be commercial in their approach.

A valuable lawyer looks to speed up the deal, not slow it down.

A valuable lawyer can read when to stick and when to move on.

And a valuable lawyer realises that often the deal will be the start of a journey between the parties, not the end, and so getting that journey off to a great start – not soured by the battle of negotiation – is such an important job.

4.8 Persuading

Persuasion plays a part in negotiation, but persuasion is a skill in its own right, such as impressing upon a client that the best course of action is not to let emotion take over, but to take your advice. Or galvanising a client not to give in when it isn't in their best interests to do so.

While persuasive design and strategies have been used for decades – such as in advertising generally or even in more niche operations such as those advocated by the Behavioural Insights Team (or Nudge Unit) – the art and science of persuasion is something that we lawyers can use to get the best for our clients.

In a human business such as the law, the use of:
- voice and timbre;
- timing; and
- silence (one of the most powerful tools in negotiation. It can convey confidence, shows that you are listening and demands a response: humans typically just want to fill in the awkward void);

remain key to helping our clients reach the decisions that work best for them. No robot can yet do these things.

4.9 Enjoying ourselves

Marcel Proust, who studied law at the Sorbonne before he became one of the 20th-century's greatest novelists, once said, after just two weeks of work experience in a firm: "In my most desperate moments, I have never conceived of anything more horrible than a law office."[26]

Exactly what went on during Proust's brief internship is – to borrow from his most famous work – lost in time, but it's safe to say that a deskbound fortnight among learned legal tomes was probably enough for the literary Frenchman.

While most people don't have such a visceral aversion to law firms, 'fun' isn't typically the first term that springs to mind when they consider the work that lawyers do. Articles for those starting in the profession[27] are often gloomy, referring to the perception of "punishing workloads and crippling stress". There's talk of all-nighters, getting the big deals "'over the line' at any cost" and legal practice being incredibly boring.

In fairness, these types of tell-it-like-it-is articles usually end up, after some playful toing and froing, on the optimistic side of the scale. They remind the reader, for example, that "there will always be people trying to scare you about what a future in law might hold".[28] Yes, aspects of a lawyer's work can be a tad humdrum at times. But the same could be said for doctors (think of all of those NHS forms to fill in), accountants (replace 'NHS' with 'HMRC') or pilots (even flying to the Seychelles becomes tedious after a while – well, that's what the authors are choosing to tell ourselves anyway).

What's more, if any job was fun for every hour of every day, it'd be ridiculous – as unconvincing as when people move to a large house in the mountains or next to the sea and exclaim: "It's great. It's like we're on holiday all of the time!", as if suddenly they've somehow become immune to the vicissitudes of life.

For some jobs we do, being a lawyer is hard because what our clients are going through is hard. There are ups and downs. However, having the EQ to know when a bit of humour or light-hearted small talk is required to defuse a situation is a vital skill that no robot or computer can replicate. This innate human skill can make all the difference to the day-to-day work we do and, ultimately, how our clients feel about us and the advice we give.

But, of course, we need to tread carefully. The considerate use of humour can be useful to put a nervous and vulnerable client at ease. It can help a client warm to us during a tough deal or intractable court case – "the rumours are true: my lawyer is human after all" – but its use demands a savvy lightness of touch. Nobody wants to be a heavy-handed office jester like the tragic David Brent character in *The Office*, where he's constantly having to row back from a cringeworthy comment here or crass foot-in-mouth joke there.

There's a fine line between funny and facetious. And if, like the fictional Brent, you have to explain what's going on, you've probably gone wrong somewhere. But get it right and a sense of humour could well be another bit of 'job security for humans': a very human trait for the very human business of practising law.

And it's not just clients who appreciate the less serious side of things. The best people don't want to work, and don't deliver their best, in a sterile, lifeless environment. In the search for the best talent, firms will be in competition with many other professions in the years to come, many of which don't even exist yet. The more we come across as pompous, arrogant and self-important, the more we are likely to drive that talent away.

4.10 Giving prestige

In the main, our status in society is high (see Chapter 11), which explains why parents and grandparents are so proud when a child or grandchild graduates in law and gets a coveted LLB (Hons).

Within the profession itself, status also plays a role. There are numerous accolades for the best law firms and lawyers, from being ranked highly in the legal directories to winning awards at annual events like the Legal Business Awards. Some law firms and lawyers have cultivated a strong media presence too.

Lawyers who are recognised for their profile and expertise are sought after by clients. Type in "by your side" into *Legal 500* or *Chambers and Partners* (or something similar) and numerous client quotes will appear along the lines of "you'll want x by your side if you are doing y". Engaging a well-known firm or lawyer (or both) means that their reputation precedes them. Clients value this and are aware of the potential leverage this may give them.

5. Embracing the EQ continuum

Like many matters in this book, EQ sits on a continuum. In a diverse and inclusive workforce, there is no right or wrong amount that we can point to as being optimum. We're all different and have different skills to bring to the table.

- This means that we need to embrace those who are neurodivergent too. That is, people who think differently from the norm (whatever normal is!). This includes people who, for example, have attention-deficit/hyperactivity disorder (ADHD) or who are on the autism spectrum. Those in the profession who think differently should expect to be treated with as much respect and given as much opportunity to those who are considered to be neurotypical. We need to recognise and celebrate the different EQs of others and adapt accordingly. The Exceptional Individuals Agency notes, for example, that neurodivergent people make great innovators: "The fearless and sometimes irrational approach that those with ADHD can often exhibit leads to bold, innovative ideas."[29]
- This also means thinking how we configure our office spaces to take into account neurodiversity, so people can work to their best

advantage. There's no one-size-fits-all: not everyone is comfortable, for example, sitting in large groups.

If we're as good as we think we are at EQ, then we should be experts in being respectful, understanding and kind to those in the profession who might, say, struggle with EQ or need a bit more help.

All of these attributes are why AI will never replace lawyers in anything other than the basic and most labour-intensive aspects of our jobs.

That's not to say that AI will not be essential to all of us continuing to be competitive in the way we work and service our clients: it absolutely will be.

The reality is we can amass all of the AI tools we need to serve and support our lawyers. But it's far harder for purely process-driven, AI-powered NewLaw or tech-leveraged practices to conjure up the excellence in the human elements necessary to deliver the best legal service.

And for us lawyers, the replacement of more of our routine and time-consuming tasks – or legal grunt work, if you prefer – with AI is a great opportunity for us to hone our human skills even further. (Although the extent to which we'll need to take performance-enhancing drugs to optimise these EQ skills, as one report from the Law Society suggests,[30] remains to be seen.) In the meantime, it's time to invest in developing those skills to a higher level in more of our people. That is the future that we want our profession to shape for itself.

In 2018, Garry Kasparov (the former World Chess Champion who bravely took on an IBM supercomputer in 1996 – and lost in 1997) noted in an interview how humans and computers can work together and how "we have to find a refuge in our humanity".[31] Machines lack things like creativity and intuition. Kasparov said we need to work out where machines can focus their efforts.

And speaking of other world champions who've pitted their wits against the steely demeanour of supercomputers, the authors recommend watching the 2017 documentary film *AlphaGo*. The film charts the development by Google's DeepMind development team of an AI-powered computer program, AlphaGo, that became expert in the game of Go. (Invented 3,000 years ago in China, and thought to be the oldest board game, Go is considered far more complicated than chess, having many more possible board configurations than there are atoms in the universe.) The battle with the eponymous program in the film is tense, particularly as the players gradu-

As humans, we are experts in translating the art of the possible so that it becomes the art of the probable. Our collective IQs and EQs as lawyers are much more than what computers can do alone. Provided we act on them.

ally come to understand what they're up against. But (spoiler alert!) here's the inevitable outcome: DeepMind's program beat 18-time Go world champion, Lee Sedol, four games to one in a tournament in Seoul. The documentary leaves anyone who watches it in no doubt of the awesome potential of AI. And although the AI wins the game and leaves us openmouthed at its superhuman show of power, it's Sedol, gracious in defeat, who wins our hearts – something AI simply can't do.

As humans, we are experts in translating the art of the possible so that it becomes the art of the probable. Our collective IQs and EQs as lawyers are much more than what computers can do alone. Provided we act on them.

6. Case studies

6.1 Case study 1: The O Shaped Lawyer

Whilst the legal profession has always been known for its technical excellence, it is seldom seen as a profession that places the same level of importance on the engagement and development of its people. That is why the 'O' came about – to recognise that success requires a holistic approach. More rounded and engaged lawyers make for better lawyers and ultimately a profession which better serves its customers. I want the 'O' to be the driving force to making this happen.
Dan Kayne

In 2019, Dan Kayne, ex-general counsel at Network Rail and *alumna* of Dechert, founded the O Shaped Lawyer. Supported by general counsel from businesses like BT, easyJet, Lloyd's Bank, Ocado and Sky, the programme is driven by a framework of five behaviours and mindsets. In May 2022, Browne Jacobson became the first law firm to join the initiative, becoming an official partner. The firm will embed O Shaped's purpose and vision into its own culture.

These are the skills that the O Shaped Lawyer believes lawyers of the future will need to be:
- Optimistic. As Kayne told the authors: "Lawyers are traditionally trained to find fault in everything, which means we're often labelled as business blockers." It's time to move away from unhelpful nit-picking. Kayne adds: "Creating a positive mindset will allow lawyers to be seen as business partners, not business blockers."
- Accountable. Our training is still of a mostly technical nature. As a result we can, if we're not careful, be remarkable fence-sitters. We too often step back from difficult business decisions, afraid of being accountable for our actions. This makes it much tougher to be true business partners.

- Open-minded. Our mindsets need to be prised open and liberated. Commercial lawyers, for example, need to think more about framing their work as solving business issues and not just legal issues. After all, the law doesn't exist in a vacuum.
- Opportunistic. That old chestnut of risk avoidance means opportunities can be rejected without a second thought. The upshot is that we need to understand and manage risk much better to ensure our first thought focuses on what could be done, as opposed to why something shouldn't be done. As one general counsel of a FTSE 350 company told Kayne: "I want someone who will come to me with opportunities – a true business partner."
- Original. Precedents do have an important role to play, but they can constrain us and be backward-looking too. Kayne says we also need to be more innovative and creative in our problem solving. Less thinking outside of the box and more, where required, thinking outside of the precedent.

But this change needs to be authentic. This 'people first; then lawyers' movement is not designed to be the latest fad. It's designed to effect real change in the profession so lawyers are not left behind as 'change3' powers through our professional lives.

As Kayne told the authors: "The lawyer of the future will practise in a more human-centric and emotionally intelligent way and we want to lead that change." The 12 O Shaped attributes, created after interviewing 18 leading general counsel from a range of FT350 companies, fall under three headings.
- Being adaptable
  - having courage;
  - being resilient;
  - seeking feedback; and
  - continuously learning.
- Building relationships
  - having empathy;
  - influencing;
  - communicating; and
  - collaborating.
- Creating value through legal initiatives
  - identifying opportunities;
  - solving problems;
  - synthesising; and
  - simplifying complexities.

If all goes to plan, this will mean more rounded lawyers. They'll be 'more O'.

6.2 Case study 2: Negotiating a challenging contract

Retail is a tough business. In the United Kingdom, retailers' profit margins have slumped in recent years. In 2019, a report by Alvarez & Marsal, in partnership with Retail Economics, noted that pre-tax profit margins at the United Kingdom's top 150 retailers plunged from 8.8% in 2009/10 to 4.1% in 2017/18.[32] Since then, times have not got any easier.

Lots of retailers are struggling to maintain profitability. And this often shows in the negotiating strategies and tactics used by them. Margins are tight, stances are often set in stone and there's little room for manoeuvre. A strong EQ is vital to oiling negotiations, budging seemingly unbudgeable positions and unlocking deals.

Let's look at the time when the authors' firm acted for a supplier in its tricky negotiations with a retailer.

The retailer was experiencing unacceptable performance failures from its incumbent supplier for a particularly important product, one that the retailer needed large volumes of. Any loss of continuity of supply would have impacted the retailer badly: no retailer ever wants to see gaps in their shelves.

What's more, it needed to conclude the new contract in just one week. The new supplier, our client, was keen to become the replacement supplier, but not on any terms, as the margins for the product were so tight.

The retailer's lawyers were acting for a business that had a lot of commercial muscle. Like a powerful monarch at the top of the pyramid, they were used to dictating terms. However, the supplier was also a very large business and was itself not used to acceding to retailers' standard terms of purchase. What's more, as the margins in the product's pricing were so small, even just a few adverse contractual provisions could erode any profit that the supplier stood to gain from the contract.

Being used to a take-it-or-leave-it approach, from the outset the retailer's lawyers took an aggressive stance. As well as taking a hard line on major contractual risks, they also went into unnecessary levels of detail on unimportant points. Both of these things made it look like reaching agreement in the timescale available was going to be unlikely.

From the outset, tempers frayed. At one point the retailer suggested that the commercial representatives of the supplier didn't know what they were doing; an inappropriate comment that was immediately called out by us, as the supplier's lawyers. The supplier was absolutely assured that we had their backs. This in turn gave them confidence to listen to us and agree the tactic that we were proposing.

Within just a few hours of the negotiation of the contract starting, we could see that the retailer's lawyers were not appreciating that:
- their attitude to major contractual positions was not appropriate given the low margins;
- their treatment of the supplier as if it were a small business, rather than a multinational of at least equal bargaining strength, was a fundamental mistake;
- their client needed the new contract more than our client; and
- their pedantic approach to trivial points was exacerbating an already tense situation.

The result? We halted the negotiations after just two hours and, having the full backing of our client, said there was no point in continuing with the discussion. Instead, we'd simply mark-up the contract on a basis that should be acceptable to both sides and, if that wasn't accepted, then the supplier would walk away from the deal.

The retailer's lawyers were put on the back foot. From a negotiating perspective, they had nowhere to turn. We marked up the contract on a reasonable mid-ground basis, the retailer accepted it and the contract was completed within the one-week timescale.

Had the retailer's lawyers had the EQ to gauge just how objectionable their initial stance was to the supplier, it's entirely possible that they could have achieved a better end position for their client and not lost face in the process.

On the other hand, by appreciating the relative commercial positions and gauging exactly the right moment to call the retailer's lawyers out, the supplier's lawyers achieved a solid position for our client (which, in fact, that client is now using as a template for future supply contracts).

Of course, EQ is also not about gloating. Upending the boardroom table as you 'win' a series of points and then celebrating with fist pumps and high fives would show an egregious lack of EQ. EQ is as much about knowing when not to do something so both respective clients can shake hands with a smile on their faces and take their relationship to the next level.

7. Practical tips on EQ

We set out below some practical tips on EQ.

These tips are split as follows:
- capturing imaginations;
- understanding EQ;
- improving EQ;
- working with tech; and
- recognising and nurturing your people.

7.1 Capturing imaginations
- Capture the imagination of the profession: inspire your people with a proposition that delivers on the things that are important to them. Support them to think differently and creatively. Provide them with the tools and support they need to succeed and a platform to do all that.
- Capture the imagination of others in your firm: this may mean changing the narrative and taking back control of your firm's story in the market.
- Harness and nurture your capacity to imagine: Reimagining how you do things in the current world is critical. We saw evidence of this during the pandemic in the way in which we all now work and live. Who would have imagined this was possible on New Year's Eve 2019? Imagine a different way of doing things so you can spot where the world is moving and so you can adapt and develop new ways of doing things.
- Capture the imagination of your clients and prospective clients. People don't just buy what you do, they buy why you do it. Articulate to your market what your purpose is – why you do what you do. Because in having a clear purpose, you'll be able to attract people who believe what you believe.

7.2 Understanding EQ
- Learn about EQ: read this book and articles on finetuning your EQ. See what 'soft skills' courses you can take.
- Expect to use EQ a lot: the future of the profession will increasingly be founded on EQ and lawyers' ability to engage well with their clients. Don't underestimate the value of EQ.
- Train well: ensure that high emphasis is placed on training in these human attributes. But such training will mainly be on the job by experienced lawyers, not just by learning and development teams.

7.3 Improving EQ
- Work on improving your human skills: even the most experienced

lawyers can work on improving their human skills (and many should!). Most who are currently lacking will probably make it through to retirement given their seniority, but anyone who wants to remain relevant in the profession needs to have these human skills in spades.

- Work on your virtual EQ: bear in mind that, in the past, many of these skills will have been put into practice face to face in meeting rooms. Given that more remote working is inevitable in the future, we need to be as effective on a computer screen as we are in person in a room. That's not an easy task and must not be taken for granted. (For example, witness all those senior partners who have been wheeled out on countless webinars while on lockdowns, who may be highly charismatic and persuasive in person but can often come across somewhat lacking on our laptop screens.) Conversely, some lawyers who may not perform as well in a room of people may find themselves in their element negotiating by Zoom. Everyone is an individual and we should play to each person's strengths.

- Play to your strengths: ironically, given the skill sets required to thrive as a lawyer in the future, we may find that the most long-in-the-tooth lawyers need to remain in fee-earning roles for as long as possible, rather than moving up the management ranks, as their skills as trainers of the requisite technical skills remain highly relevant. Conversely, those to be put in the ranks of management should perhaps be those who understand more clearly what the future holds and particularly how technology will play a huge part of any firm going forward. Heretical as this may sound, it is just an example of playing to individual strengths in the digital age.

- Join the O Shaped Lawyer!

7.4 Working with tech

- Don't forget tech: it is likely that every field of legal advice going forward will incorporate tech as part of the process. Review your processes now and identify which aspects can be made smarter, faster and better. There's a dangerous myth in some quarters of the profession that 'quality law' is above the reaches of technology and, indeed, that talent may be put off joining a firm that pollutes its purist approach to such lofty pursuits with technology. How wrong they are! Tech-enabled IQ ('know-it') and EQ ('know-how') will work hand-in-glove together.

7.5 Recognise and nurture your people

- Recognise the true value of your people. Create a culture that values, promotes and rewards those human skills.

- Encourage individualism, creativity and a sense of humour. These attributes will never compromise the quality of professional service provision if wielded well, and yet they will be key distinguishing factors in the future. Also, unless we continue to attract the best talent into our profession by offering a vibrant and dynamic working environment, they will prefer to join other professions that offer this.

- Recruit well. Consider the basis upon which you recruit (both trainees and lateral hires). Academic results may not be a good measure of all the required human skills. Consider whether your interview process is currently attuned to pick up on all the requisite skills. Also, consider making an understanding of the importance of both tech and EQ in legal practice as one the criteria for passing an interview. Weed out those who wear the badge of Luddite with honour, along with those who would not be out of place in a ware-house of robots.

Notes

1   Henry Blodget, "The Best Airline Captain Announcement Ever Came On A British Airways 747 After All Four Engines Failed …" (*Insider*, 24 February 2013), www.businessinsider.com/captain-announcement-after-all-four-engines-failed-2013-2.
2   Kate Fox, *Watching the English* (Hodder & Stoughton, 2004), p67.
3   Kevin Roose, *9 Rules for Humans in the Age of Automation* (John Murray, 2021), p70.
4   Henry Hitchings, *Sorry!* (John Murray, 2013), p137.
5   Daniel Goleman, *Emotional intelligence* (Bantam Books, 1995).
6   Adam M Grant, "Rethinking the Extraverted Sales Ideal: The Ambivert Advantage" (2013) *Psychological Science* 24(6) 1024–1030, https://faculty.wharton.upenn.edu/wp-content/uploads/2013/06/Grant_PsychScience2013.pdf.
7   *The Rambler*, no 125, 28 May 1751.
8   "Nils Bohlin, 82, Inventor of a Better Seat Belt" (*The New York Times*, 26 September 2002), www.nytimes.com/2002/09/26/business/nils-bohlin-82-inventor-of-a-better-seat-belt.html.
9   "A conversation with BioNTech co-founders Uğur Şahin and Özlem Türeci" (Atlantic Council, 8 November 2021), www.atlanticcouncil.org/event/a-conversation-with-ugur-sahin-and-ozlem-tureci/.
10 David Gelles, "The Husband-and-Wife Team Behind the Leading Vaccine to Solve Covid-19" (*The New York Times*, 10 November 2020), www.nytimes.com/2020/11/10/business/biontech-covid-vaccine.html.
11 "Coronavirus: Turkish Germans raise new Covid vaccine hopes" (BBC News, 10 November 2020), www.bbc.co.uk/news/world-europe-54886883.
12 "UK medicines regulator gives approval for first UK COVID-19 vaccine" (Medicines and Healthcare products Regulatory Agency, 2 December 2020), www.gov.uk/government/news/uk-medicines-regulator-gives-approval-for-first-uk-covid-19-vaccine.
13 Mary O'Hara, "Tunde Okewale: 'I still think there are many more things for me to do'" (*The Guardian*, 27 July 2016), www.theguardian.com/society/2016/jul/27/tunde-okewale-barrister-campaigner-young-people-legal-profession.
14 *Ibid*.
15 A Mehrabian and M Weiner, "Decoding of inconsistent communications" (1967) 6 *Journal of Personality and Social Psychology* 109–114; A Mehrabian and S Ferris, "Inference of attitudes from nonverbal communication in two channels" (1967) 31 *Journal of Consulting Psychology* 248–252.
16 David Lapakko, "Communication is 93% Nonverbal: An Urban Legend Proliferates" (CTAMJ Summer 2007, p7), https://cornerstone.lib.mnsu.edu/cgi/viewcontent.cgi?article=1000&context=ctamj.
17 Robin Hough, "The Moral Molecule: How oxytocin can revolutionise your organisation" (*The Guardian*, 4 June 2013), www.theguardian.com/media-network/media-network-blog/2013/jun/04/moral-molecule-oxytocin-revolutionise-organisation.
18 Marcus Holmes, "The Force of Face-to-Face Diplomacy: Mirror Neurons and the Problem of Intentions" (2013) 67 *International Organization* 829.
19 James Marriott, "The Species that Changed Itself by Edwin Gale review – how the age of abundance has made a new type of human" (*The Times*, 17 December 2020), www.thetimes.co.uk/article/the-species-that-changed-itself-by-edwin-gale-review-how-the-age-of-abundance-has-made-a-new-type-of-human-wqchqk0m6.

20   David Allen Green, "Why blog about law and policy?" (*The Law and Policy Blog*, 22 December 2021), https://davidallengreen.com/2021/12/why-blog-about-law-and-policy/.

21   *Bolton v Law Society* [1984] 1 WLR 512.

22   "SRA Principle 2 – public trust and confidence" (Solicitors Regulation Authority, 25 November 2019), www.sra.org.uk/solicitors/guidance/sra-principle-2/.

23   Antoine Buéno, *Futur* (Flammarion, 2020), p181 (authors' translation).

24   "Images of the Future Worlds Facing the Legal Profession 2020–2030" (Law Society, June 2021), https://prdsitecore93.azureedge.net/-/media/files/topics/research/fw2050-images-facing-legal-profession-report-june-2021.pdf?rev=993d9779e72f4fa9989de0e158978588&hash=02273EC818F251A5E3A7B67696CA9C1B.

25   Jamie Susskind, *Future Politics* (Oxford University Press, 2020), p73.

26   Quoted by Michael Foley, *Embracing the Ordinary* (Simon & Schuster, 2012), p25.

27   "Fact or fiction the truth behind life in a city law firm" (*Legal Cheek*, 19 April 2017), www.legalcheek.com/2017/04/fact-or-fiction-the-truth-behind-life-in-a-city-law-firm/.

28   *Ibid.*

29   "Jobs for ADHD" (Exceptional Individuals), https://exceptionalindividuals.com/jobs-for-people-with-adhd/.

30   Nick Holborne, "Lawyers fed performance-enhancing drugs in Law Society dystopia" (*Legal Futures*, 9 June 2021), www.legalfutures.co.uk/latest-news/lawyers-fed-performance-enhancing-drugs-in-law-society-dystopia.

31   Jordan Teicher, "Garry Kasparov: it's time for humans and machines to work together" (IBM, 20 February 2018), www.ibm.com/blogs/industries/garry-kasparov-its-time-for-humans-and-machines-to-work-together/.

32   "Major U.K. retailers operate at 20 percent over-capacity" (Alvarez & Marsal, 23 October 2019), www.alvarezandmarsal.com/insights/major-uk-retailers-operate-20-percent-over-capacity.

Chapter 10:
The aspiring and associate lawyer

Surfers: they crop up in almost every type of advert – often when we least expect it – from luxury watches to top-of-the range cars (the irony being that these are things that most surfers can't actually afford). Including a surfer promises an exciting future ahead, provided 'you've got the guts to get out there and attack it'. They speak of freedom and peril; living life to the full; and ultimately triumphing over the odds.

Surfer Laird Hamilton, who knew a thing or two about perilous endeavours, having surfed some of the biggest waves on the planet, has appeared in a fair few ads himself. He told one magazine that the only thing which is "crazier than riding big waves is living in the city and working in an office".[1] (And he probably didn't mean it in a good way.)

Even so, in the fluid world of 'change3', the surfing metaphor is more apt than ever – even for us poor office workers.

Like surfers, we lawyers need to be experts at reading the waves of what's heading our way in the months and years to come. Surfers are famously methodical about the tides, winds, currents and swells of their ocean environment: they need an acute sense of where they are at all times.

More than ever, we need to understand the trends and patterns that ebb and flow and underpin what we do too. We need to understand that, yes, like the best surfers we'll catch some waves – perhaps most of them; but, no, we won't be able to catch them all. As each wave crests and falls, we'll need to look ahead to the next one. We'll need to learn about the importance of timing and also when to sit some waves out. Sometimes, for a bit, there'll be no waves at all. And, of course, mistakes and wipe outs will happen to the best of us.

When the internet first arrived in law firms, most lawyers had to learn how to 'surf the net'. The person who reportedly popularised the use of this surfing-inspired term wanted to "evoke a sense of randomness, chaos, and even danger".[2] (No wonder it felt so exciting at the time.) Today, like we did a generation ago, we need to learn how to 'surf the tech': the roiling, unfurling waves of technology and innovation which are barrelling towards us, whether we like it or not.

We can either try to surf it as best we can – and embrace it, enjoy it and thrive on it – or we can resign ourselves to bobbing up and down in the cruel sea, at the mercy of waves crashing down on us, and find ourselves dazed and confused about what just hit us.

What does this mean for law firms?
- Firms, and the people within them, need to be ready: we not only have to prepare our businesses for this world (with the help of this book, of course), but we also have to ensure that our aspiring and associate lawyers (and non-lawyers) are ready to 'hit the waves' too. The future of our firms ultimately rests with all the people in them being able to cope with this uncertain, dynamic environment, week in and week out, and come back wanting more.
- Firms need to prove to the outside world that we're getting ready: we have a duty to show people that we get it; that we understand the world is no longer as linear as it used to be (see the 'seven ages of lawyering' in Chapter 11); and that we're doing something about it. We're changing from a stereotypically staid profession to one in which the future is embraced – a 'wigs to waves' strategy, if you will.
- Firms need to make this all as fulfilling as possible: aspiring and associate lawyers shouldn't be left shivering on the beach, worried about what lies ahead. The authors aren't convinced that working in an office is 'crazier' than surfing (although some stories from *RollOnFriday* might suggest otherwise)[3], or that there won't be difficult days at work, but this doesn't mean that we can't make the jobs of the future as rewarding as possible and support our lawyers to bring this about. We owe our future talent this much at least.

And this takes us on to the final ingredient which law firms need to think about: passion.

The problem? People are passionate about almost *everything* nowadays. As a currency, it's become devalued. In a work context, it's not a characteristic that many of us have in any event – at least that we're happy to admit to in public (stiff upper lip and all that). Anthropologist Kate Fox has spent years studying workplaces in England.[4] She says, for example, that typically staff take work seriously, but not too seriously; have a sense of duty, but are "grudging" with it; like a good moan, but do so with good humour and have a "stoical pride in 'getting on with it'".[5] This is quite a charge sheet. But there's nothing within it which particularly screams 'passion'.

And yet aspiring and associate lawyers are bombarded with calls on social media and elsewhere to "live their best life" and "follow their passions". "Find a job that you love and you'll never work another day in your life", say countless influencers on Instagram, perhaps accompanied with hashtags like #MondayMotivation or #DoWhatYouLove. At first sight, it's a tempting proposition. It feels quite motivating. (Who wouldn't want to do what they love?)

As this book shows, we've a lot to be positive and motivated about. And we need to convey this to aspiring and associate lawyers. But we also need to dial down this 'passion' rhetoric a bit: all jobs have their ups and downs; there are good days and bad days. The fact is that working hard and enduring a degree of hardship is baked into our profession as much as the satisfaction of a job well done – if anything, this makes this satisfaction taste that much sweeter.

Don't get the authors wrong: we still need 'fire in our bellies'. Passion, drive, get-up-and-go – whatever we want to call it – is something which no robot can replicate or replace. It's the uniquely human 'right stuff' that law firms need to move forward in this time of 'change3'.

If we choose the right path, the authors believe that the legal profession is going to offer aspiring and associate lawyers a greater variety of opportunities than today, many of which won't necessarily involve them being a 'typical lawyer'. We think that being a future lawyer will be rewarding because of the challenges that we face, not despite them. Passion might well get us started; it could be the initial spark that brings about change; but EQ skills, such as patience, resilience, tenacity and compassion will be the traits that will take aspiring and associate lawyers to the next level of lawyering. And these EQ skills bear little resemblance to the superficial veneer – the high-fiving 'passionfest' – that many influencers sell with a forest of hashtags online.

In this chapter we look at some of the key aspects of being aspiring lawyers (which includes law students and trainees) and associate lawyers (junior qualified lawyers) and managing this talent in the unpredictable years ahead, including:

- working with non-lawyer colleagues;
- creating a profession for all;
- getting the talent in – and keeping it in!;
- making business happen;
- being enablers for change outside of the profession too (after all, we sit at the crossroads of many disciplines, sectors and industries); and
- having a culture of life-long learning.

We then look at two case studies and finish with some practical tips on aspiring and associate lawyers.

1. Reminding our people that the profession does have a future, albeit a different one from now

Despite the challenges set out in this book, it's clear that the future for lawyers is far from over. The reports of its death are greatly exaggerated: there's still 'life in the old legal dog yet'!

However, 'change3', the 'data boost' and more hybrid ways of offering legal services and working (including through automation) does mean that jobs of aspiring and associate lawyers won't be the same as they are now. New roles will appear too:

- The risk of automation for most legal jobs in the legal sector seems to be relativity low, although some jobs are at greater risk. One 2013 report noted that the sector could grow through becoming more agile, which would be "enough to offset some of the aggregate employment losses".[6] The story on automation is certainly mixed:
  - Christina Blacklaws, chair of LawtechUK, said in July 2022 that the "hype" of robots taking over almost all lawyers' jobs has shifted to something "much more realistic".[7] The Office for National Statistics has estimated that there's a 23% risk of "some or all"[8] of the duties and tasks of a solicitor being automated, putting the occupation in the 'low risk' category (although it's worth bearing in mind that there's a fair difference between 'some' and 'all' in the ONS prediction above);
  - a report in 2013, however, put "paralegals and legal assistants" in the "high risk" category[9] although continued cost pressures

mean that they'll remain an attractive proposition for many firms for the foreseeable future.[10]

- Career paths won't be as linear as in the past: a job for life is increasingly an anachronism for many.
- Some tasks within the profession, through technology and innovation, will be de-professionalised (ie, deskilled), unbundled and commoditised. Some tasks will be outsourced too through, for example, legal process outsourcing (LPO).

As the waves of technology and innovation roll in and continue to crash around us we need to help our aspiring and associate lawyers adapt to this changing profession. The authors have certainly noticed the following in recent years:

- Aspiring and associate lawyers expect and want to see technology and innovation in law firms. If a firm falls behind the tech curve, they start to ask themselves: "Why should I waste hours doing a dull, repetitive task, when tech could be doing it for me?" Lawyers want to spend time doing better work, not boring work. They also want to feel that the firm they're with is going places and has a future; they want to see tech being prioritised and invested in.
- Automation is happening now. From the authors' experience of developing contract review tools (see Chapter 5), aspiring and associate lawyers have much to contribute to the innovation process, bringing a valuable perspective on how they use tech in their daily lives and how that might influence the legal tools of tomorrow.
- Change is coming. It's unsettling and needs to be managed. As Kate Fox also notes, persuading office workers in England to change needs to take into account that they aren't always keen on it. She suggests that a typical rallying cry would be: "'What do we want?' GRADUAL CHANGE! When do we want it? IN DUE COURSE!".[11] But change is likely to come quicker than this at times. Good and constant communication is therefore vital.
- We're seeing more of a blurring of the lines between lawyers and 'techies'. For a while now, to get a more rounded perspective, many firms have had aspiring and associate lawyers doing six-month seats in IT-related functions or secondments in tech businesses. These firms want to have an input into how technology works and meets their needs and those of their clients. They're rolling up their sleeves and getting more involved.
- The extinction of a traditional job for life means that progressive firms think of lawyers as being 'lawyers+'. We are no longer pinstriped one-trick ponies. From summer placements to searching the market for senior associate talent, the message is "you might be joining a law firm, but you can be more than a lawyer if you want". In

practice, this could mean lawyers 'moving sideways' and doing less fee-earning, perhaps because a part of their job has changed. Or it might just be they simply fancy shaking things up a bit:

- an experienced associate spends half their time working on major internal IT projects, including developing new legaltech and giving the IT team the legal perspective on these projects;
- a paralegal reskills to become an expert in training AI systems, such as document-review tools;
- an associate spends a day a week working on legal design projects for an internal team, fixing the UX of legal documents using the latest design techniques; or
- an in-house barrister becomes a metaverse compliance officer and expert in the legal aspects of AR, MR or VR (augmented reality, mixed reality and virtual reality).

- Once associate lawyers have settled into their careers, the identity of being a fee-earning lawyer can feel like it's the be all and end all. Innovative firms reiterate that while fee-earning work is important, non-fee-earning work is of value too.
- Deskilling aspects of legal work doesn't have to mean de-humanising it. Unbundling, commoditising and outsourcing work can be done with respect and dignity too. These firms:
  - treat their lawyers with respect. In Singapore, a world leader in digital transformation, government agencies are already producing guidance on 'redesigning work'. One key element is the need to prioritise "the dignity of their employees"[12] when, say, AI is adopted;
  - help those who are most affected. Sometimes the change will arrive without warning. Aspiring and associate lawyers need to know that firms will have their backs and, if needs be, will retrain them and try to offer them alternative stimulating work:
    - in another legal field; or
    - in another area altogether.
    - Lifelong learning is valued. Norton Rose Fulbright's change and innovation programme, NRT Transform, for example, has seen its employees upskill and become process engineers, legal designers and legal technologists.[13] Lawyers are learning new skills.

Of course, no career can be future-proofed entirely. But law firms can help aspiring and associate lawyers find their purpose and help them nurture it.

2. Welcoming the new entrants to the job market

This often falls under the radar, but there's a lot of potential human talent coming our way. In a tight labour market, this is welcome news for many firms.

2.1 In the United Kingdom: a mini baby boom

By 2025, the number of 16- to 18-year-olds is expected to increase. According to the Association of Colleges, this means that an extra 90,000 more young people will be in education by 2024–2025.[14]

This type of opportunity doesn't come around often. The 2020s – the United Kingdom's "digital decade"[15] in the words of the Master of the Rolls, Sir Geoffrey Vos, is the time to put this cohort to work. This group of students could well include the lawyers, data experts and other roles that firms desperately need. Instead of seeing this young talent end up in run-of-the-mill, low-paid jobs, we could offer them a great opportunity to help us to modernise our firms while also preparing them for the digital future.

Demand for talent in areas like technology continues to increase, but the birth rate is going down. This might be the last UK baby boom for a while. The time to act is now.

2.2 Overseas talent

The talent in our firms, both legal and non-legal, may also come from further afield:

- Through trade deals, such as the UK-New Zealand agreement. The agreement with New Zealand contains provisions in it to work towards liberalising both countries' professional services markets. Even before this happens, officials have estimated that tens of thousands of New Zealanders may emigrate in the next year or so. Many of these could well be lawyers, particularly in the coveted NQ-to-a-few-years-PQE market. Similar trade deals might have similar effects.
- Through the United Kingdom's new immigration system. The UK Global Talent Visa scheme allows those with, say, digital technology expertise to move to the United Kingdom for up to five years, without a sponsor or job offer. The *Tech Nation Visa Report 2021* noted that a third of applicants for this scheme are from India and just over 11% from Nigeria.

And having a newcomer's point of view could just give us the edge that our firms need. One venture capital investor noted that over half of the top tech companies in the United States were founded by people born outside of the United States or children of them.[16] As tech entrepreneur Catherine Wines said in 2018: "To become a visionary, you have to take the perspective of an outsider in order to see the things that are taken for granted by insiders."[17]

A diverse workforce needs to be inclusive too. Inclusion is the vital 'how' which must come with diversity: "how do we build a work environment in which everyone's contributions are heard and valued?"

3. Creating a profession for all

Closer to home, the makeup of our profession is changing too. The public still seems to think that the profession is stuck in the past (the wigs probably don't help) but the reality is different. Women, for example, have made up most entrants to the profession since the 1990s and, in 2018, they overtook men in the profession as a whole. We've come a long way from the Sex Disqualification (Removal) Act 1919, which removed the legal barrier to women becoming solicitors. We see the consequences of this change today. In 2020, for example, Georgina Dawson was appointed as senior partner at Freshfields Bruckhaus Deringer. A year later, Rebecca Maslen-Stannage was appointed as chair and senior partner at Herbert Smith Freehills.

But there is still much to do. Dawson and Maslen-Stannage are notable because there are still so few women at the top of the profession as CEOs and managing partners and even fewer when we look at representation of Black and minority ethnic leaders. Aspiring and associate lawyers have seen opportunities open up for them as they enter the profession. They'll expect (and rightly so) that this continues. "Welcome to the profession. Sorry about the glass ceiling; we've not had a chance to fix it" might not be quite the message they want to hear.

In this section we look at creating a profession for all. But we also need to remember that diversity is only ever the first step. A diverse workforce needs to be inclusive too. Inclusion is the vital 'how' which must come with diversity: "how do we build a work environment in which everyone's contributions are heard and valued?" As Vernā Myers, lawyer and VP of Inclusion Strategy at Netflix, says: "Diversity is being invited to the party; inclusion is being asked to dance."[18]

3.1 The case for diversity and inclusion
There are two main cases for diversity and inclusion (D&I): the business case and the ethical case. D&I also helps firms comply with their legal and regulatory obligations, such as under the Equality Act 2010 and the rules and regulations of the SRA.

The business case is well known:
- Internally, there's strength in diversity and inclusion: the more viewpoints we can get around the table, the better. Put simply, this cognitive diversity can help businesses avoid group think. A McKinsey study in 2020 on D&I programmes found that "the greater the representation, the higher the likelihood of outperformance".[19]
- Externally:
  - with our clients: they're demanding change and want to work with

law firms which reflect the diversity that they see in their own businesses and senior teams. Clients have told the authors: "we want diverse teams". And they are using data to help them do this:

- in the United Kingdom, the InterLaw Diversity Forum UK Model Diversity Survey is a new standard for the reporting by many top law firms of their D&I metrics. As the Forum notes, in-house legal teams can compare firms over time "if they wish to consider performance around diversity, inclusion, and culture when handing out work".[20] The General Counsel for Diversity and Inclusion is also creating standards and metrics templates. In 2021, Microsoft offered a 3% bonus to panel firms hitting its D&I targets;[21]
- US and Australian companies can now use data-driven tech, such as PERSUIT, to help them ensure D&I goals are met. In the United Kingdom, companies like Pirical offer on-demand analytics on D&I;
- with prospective aspiring and associate lawyers:
    - they're demanding change too. Aspiring and associate lawyers want to work in firms in which dignity, respect and opportunities are given to all, not just a select few;
    - a more diverse pool of talent is a bigger pool of talent;
- legaltech needs it: diverse teams developing a new piece of legaltech have fewer echo chambers and are more likely to spot biases. Wrong data can mean the wrong insights and thus the wrong solutions for our teams and clients. AI, in particular, has the power to turbocharge biases and inequalities if we're not alive to the dangers.

But the authors would rather focus on the ethical case; namely: it's the right thing to do. Embracing D&I is a people cause. It means that all of our people are treated with respect and dignity. As lawyers, it speaks to our sense of justice and fair play. It helps to make what we do as fulfilling as possible. It's in all of our interests.

3.2 The political dimension

Despite the clear business and ethical case, D&I has become a bit of a political football in recent years. But all life is politics, in some way or another. When the England squad won the 2022 UEFA European Women's Football Championship, for example, the team wrote to the two candidates for the Conservative Party leadership at that time (both of whom subsequently became Prime Minister) to ask that they prioritise investment into girls' football, saying that they were "often stopped from playing" when they were younger. Some say: "keep politics out of football". But why shouldn't the England squad fight for a better future? Why should they accept the *status quo* in which, compared to the men's team, they were marginalised? How else does change happen?

D&I faces similar calls: why politicise diversity? Like football, D&I *is* political. Politics is all about ends and means: changing the *status quo* to achieve desired ends, albeit doing it in a way and at a speed (ie, the means) which are open to debate. It would seem people agree on the principle of a more diverse, inclusive and fair profession, but less so on the politics of how we get there:

- The ends: there's more we agree on than many in the press would have us believe. For example, the More in Common initiative, in a major 2020 report, found "common ground in Britain on many issues", adding that there were "large majorities ... committed to gender equality and racial equity"[22] (even though there is still much progress that needs to be made in these areas).
- The means: but how we achieve a fairer society and profession is often where much of the heat of the debate is generated. Take ex-Attorney General Suella Braverman KC, who launched a broadside against D&I in August 2022. She said that D&I is a "dangerous new religion" and "the new orthodoxy to settle old scores". On the other hand, she went on to say that she's "all for building an inclusive workplace which is meritocratic and welcoming".[23] There's a lot to unpack and debate here, and there certainly isn't the space in this book to do so, but it's often the case that a lot of political grandstanding doesn't survive the first touch with the reality on the ground. If firms follow the route of stopping or paring down D&I programmes they will put themselves on the back foot if, for example, any discrimination claims are brought against them or risk devaluing their employee value proposition as an employer of choice.

The technology and trends we explore in this book aren't just changing the playing field for lawyers, but for politics too. Algorithms on social media don't tend to favour nuance or the exploration of different aspects of a debate. Rapidly evolving news cycles mean people might 'throw red meat' at their followers for short-term tactical gain, with little thought for long-term strategy. They may use more intemperate language to be heard above all the noise. In turn, this can further polarise and entrench points of view. Law firms need to remind themselves now and again about these dynamics and keep their focus on the long-term benefits of treating their staff fairly through D&I programmes and initiatives.

3.3 The rules of the race

A helpful way of conceptualising how privilege, or the lack of it, can have a real impact on the lives of aspiring and associate lawyers is to think of a legal career as a race. Given how competitive lawyers are, this shouldn't be too tricky. For simplicity, let's say the finishing line is becoming a partner.

In this scenario, the finishing line always stays the same, but the starting line doesn't. We start to ask questions like:
- What is the highest level of qualifications achieved by either of your parent(s) or guardian(s) by the time you were 18?
- What type of school did you mainly attend between the ages of 11 and 16?
- Thinking back to when you were aged 14, what best describes the sort of work the main/highest income earner in your household did as their main job?

The questions relate to things which show advantage or disadvantage in some way. Not having a parent who went to university can mean, for example, that the aspiring lawyer doesn't receive the same level of support as university-educated parents can offer.

We now draw the starting lines for the race. If the answer:
- demonstrates an advantage, the lawyer can stay where they are; and
- demonstrates a disadvantage, the lawyer is asked to take one or more steps back, depending on the level of the disadvantage in question.

Already some aspiring lawyers find themselves a fair (or, rather, unfair) distance from the starting line. And, of course, the disadvantages aren't just socio-economic, they relate to all types of unlawful discrimination (race, sex, disability, gender reassignment, sexual orientation etc) and other types of prejudice too, such as having the 'wrong' accent or even things like having a visible tattoo.

The starting pistol goes. From the very start, marginalised or underrepresented lawyers are playing catch up. And just as we start playing the game, there's a further twist. Somebody runs onto the track and puts hurdles in front of some of the lawyers. In the end, those who don't have hurdles in front of them are in the minority. As the LSB reminds us: "It is still harder to progress to senior levels ... if you are, for example, a woman, from a minority ethnic background, a disabled person, LGBTQ+, or are from a lower socio-economic background."[24] The result? Some lawyers end up with quite a few hurdles in front of them.

Of course, everyone's lived experience is different. There's not an exact number of steps or hurdles. Some do well, despite the lack of a level playing field. Many others struggle to reach their true potential. Some end up leaving the profession altogether.

Figure 1. The starting line and racetrack

So where do law firms go from here? In the simplest of terms, our aim must be that we do all we can to ensure that everyone starts from the same place and that as many hurdles as possible are removed from the track.

There are many books which set out how to make D&I part of a firm's DNA, from undertaking reverse-mentoring schemes to developing outreach programmes. It might mean setting up a shadow board and staff networks; or removing applicants' names and universities from application forms. Whatever approaches are taken, associate and aspiring lawyers want authenticity and will see through any programmes which just pay lip service to D&I. They want to see real progress. They want to see change.

We're well aware, however, that the thoughts of three white, middle-class men on this subject might be jarring for some – but we're equally aware that our privilege comes with a duty to help those who are less fortunate than ourselves. Particularly as it wasn't always the case that the authors were middle-class. Circumstance, chance, luck (and hard work) has made it so, but this fact provides even more responsibility and motivation to ensure that the next generation face far fewer and ideally no hurdles in their careers. So, we finish this section with three overriding things that those of us who are in senior positions can do.

We can:

- be allies to those who are marginalised and underrepresented: as one Law Society report noted in 2019, for example, "engagement and support from men is critical to achieving true diversity and inclusion in the profession";[25]

- speak up: there's always the risk, of course, that in trying to work out what the best or right thing to say is, we end up saying nothing at all (although note that useful guidance on appropriate language can be found on the Law Society's website). We're afraid of getting it wrong, so, we don't engage. The outcome? Nothing changes. We're back at square one and nothing has been achieved. In this 'hybrid era', we need, perhaps, more conversations in person and fewer online so we can gauge each other's better natures. Life is about learning and growing and developing and this isn't easy to do if we're shouting at each other online. President Barack Obama, in his first volume of presidential memoirs, reminds us that we sometimes need to rely on "the forbearance and goodwill" of those around us "to fill in the blanks" and "catch our drift" if we inadvertently put our foot in it;[26] and
- push for real change: we need to do more than just empathise with the difficulties that those who are marginalised or underrepresented face in our firms; we need to be compassionate and do something about them. This isn't an area where there are lots of easy fixes, nor is it all about ticking boxes (which can lead to D&I programmes failing).

Finally, before we move on, the authors would also like to ask a small favour from those who've fought tooth and nail to get where they are today: tell the profession about it! At times, this might be a brave thing to do. There's certainly no obligation to do so, but stories stick in people's memories; they build connections and sometimes give people cause to ask difficult questions of themselves. They are one of the most powerful weapons we have at our disposal.

4. Working with the talent in our firms

In the years to come, we'll be working in a more diverse and inclusive profession. And it's also a profession that will be more reliant on non-lawyers than ever before too.

According to *The Lawyer* in September 2021, lawyers will become a minority in firms (in a minority of firms this is already likely to be the case; and, in NewLaw and highly tech-leveraged legal businesses, this is almost certainly the case).[27] The result? Aspiring and associate lawyers need to get used to working with non-lawyers more, including in multi-disciplinary teams (MDTs). We need to build a culture where non-lawyers are nurtured, respected and given the status they deserve.

While this chapter considers the role of aspiring and associate lawyers, we need to instil in them the need for them to be able to work with all manner of other people, in particular:

- lawyers who have other non-legal skills which a firm is keen to use. Why look for talent externally when sometimes internal legal talent is staring us in the face? (ie, 'lawyers+');
- other lawyers with key roles to play, such as paralegals and in-house barristers;
- non-lawyers with expertise in technology and innovation; and
- non-lawyers with expertise in other areas: these are the people that lawyers have been working with for years, often referred to as 'support staff'. Year on year new areas of expertise are being added, from social media experts to multimedia creatives.

Collectively, the growing group of non-lawyers are the hands that hold lawyers up. We need to nurture what they do more. What career paths are open to them? Can non-lawyers become partners? The firms which tackle and resolve these questions will reap the rewards.

5. Getting the talent in

Getting the people into our firms is something that we can't take for granted. Will the amount of people wanting to become lawyers continue as now?

Yvon Chouinard, founder of the outdoor clothing and gear company Patagonia, wrote in the manual for his staff, *Let My People Go Surfing*, on how he's "been a businessman for almost sixty years".[28] Chouinard has gone from making climbing gear out of a chicken coop in the 1950s to having stores spanning five continents. Despite all of his successes, he said that it was as tricky for him to admit to being a businessman, "as it is for someone to admit to being an alcoholic or lawyer".[29] Ouch.

In spite of the dim view that some have of us, we lawyers are aware of the value of what we do, even though we don't always give it much thought. As the LSB states simply: "The law matters. It keeps us safe. It provides ways to resolve disputes without violence, and gives the weak a voice in the face of the strong."[30] Or, in the words of Lord Goff of Chieveley: "We are there to oil the wheels of commerce, not to put a spanner in the works, or even grit in the oil."[31] In a time of 'change3' and rapid technological change, lawyers are called upon more than ever to protect people and businesses; to have their backs and move society forward. These lofty ambitions change lives.

So how do we persuade the young Chouinards of this world that being a

Attracting aspiring lawyers into the profession means looking at the three typical stages of education and training and seeing what we can do as a profession to nurture the talent that our firms need now and in the future.

lawyer is a good and noble cause? Equally, how do we convince those who don't want to be lawyers that they have a crucial contribution to make in our firms, so that lawyers can do all the things above? This section explores how.

5.1 Attracting aspiring lawyers

At present, the pipeline of aspiring lawyers looking to join the profession remains at a healthy level, with the number of law students having increased in recent years. The number of practising solicitors also continues to increase: it's up almost 30,000 in a decade to a grand total, at the time of writing, of just over 160,000.[32] But we can't take it for granted that the profession, or all parts of it, will always flourish. Only 4% of criminal duty solicitors are under 35 years of age.[33] Attracting talent into our firms, particularly in a tight labour market, is likely to get tougher.

The number of training contracts, however, has remained relatively stable in England and Wales: 5,495 in 2020–2021.[34] As has been the case for many years, there are more graduates than training contracts available.

But change is afoot. How the once-in-a-generation change to the Solicitors Qualifying Examination (SQE) will affect the pipeline of those wanting to join the profession is unknown, as the first SQE assessment results only came out in January 2022. But as the SQE beds in:
- the profession needs to move away from the mindset of there being one 'ideal' way into the profession (ie, previously a law degree and LPC). There are now a multitude of pathways to becoming a solicitor; and
- we need to help other would-be lawyers, who may not want to sit the SQE, find other equally valuable niches in our firms too.

Attracting aspiring lawyers into the profession means looking at the three typical stages of education and training and seeing what we can do as a profession to nurture the talent that our firms need now and in the future.

(a) First-degree level

Universities will continue to play a role in the training of most lawyers. However, there are a number of important dynamics we need to bear in mind when we consider how this sector can contribute towards creating the lawyers of the future.
- Universities are academic institutions: their focus is more on making the intellectual life of their institutions flourish and less on vocational matters, although the marketisation of higher education

and increasing cost of undergraduate degrees has cut across this approach somewhat.[35]

- Law schools' first duty is to their university and then perhaps to the profession. This means that we shouldn't necessarily expect this sector to provide all of the solutions that we need and want to see.

Under the new SQE regime, qualifying law degree (QLD) status will also cease to exist. This means that law schools can now design less traditional law degrees, perhaps in new areas of law or in areas which are more vocational such as commercial awareness, understanding technology and developing EQ. Some have already started to do so.

- Will universities take advantage of the removal of this status to innovate? As long ago as 2008, Professors Andrew Boon and Julian Webb noted that specialisation means large chunks of the law degree were "*de facto* redundant".[36] Professor Webb, among others, calls for a profound rethink on what is taught. Some universities are keen to hear from law firms for real-life practical experience of what life is like for a modern lawyer, so that they can ensure they are preparing law undergraduates in the best way.
- Will SQE providers do more? Recent developments are encouraging. In April 2022, the O Shaped Lawyer (see the case study in Chapter 9) partnered with BARBRI to help shape its 'Prep for Practice' programme.
- Will more firms work with universities to help them develop innovative courses? The Legal Innovation Centre at Ulster University works with other stakeholders, such as investment bank Citi, on its MSc/LLM in Corporate Law, Computing and Innovation.
- Will the removal of QLD status impact on the number of students choosing to study law as a first degree? If so, how?
- Will students choose to study other subjects to get a broader education and then return to the law via the SQE? Will some of them love their subjects so much they end up being lost to the law for all time?
- How will the post-18 review of education and funding (the 'Augar review') affect the numbers of those who want to join the profession?[37] Will the prospect of paying thousands of pounds more for their undergraduate degrees over their lifetimes put some students off?

(b) Vocational training

In the 12 months to the end of July 2022, 77.6% of new solicitors took the LPC.[38] As the profession transitions to the SQE regime, this figure will eventually drop to zero. But is the SQE going to be enough? A survey done of 43 leading firms by *Legal Cheek* in January 2021, in association with the University of Law, found that 70% of firms say it falls short and that further top-up courses will be needed.[39] To attract aspiring lawyers, firms are having to think much more about their internal training and how the lawyers of tomorrow are created. These questions include the following.

- How are we transitioning to the SQE generally?
- What bespoke courses do we need to create (if any)? (While larger firms have the resources to create top-up courses, smaller firms may need to pool their resources. Wills and probate specialists, Right Legal Group, for example, run a training academy. A similar system, franchised out to others, might be a solution for top-up courses in other sectors of the profession.)
- How can we build in more training on technology and innovation? Should we wait to see what works? Or should we strike now?
- What are the costs of creating top-up courses if they're provided by third-party providers like law schools?
- How will transitioning to the SQE affect diversity, equity and inclusion? Early indications are not encouraging.
- Do we need to look more at solicitor apprentices?
- What about the training for mature students and career changers whose needs are different?

One of the biggest challenges is for prospective lawyers and those interested in technology and innovation in firms to compare what's on offer. Here are some examples of what firms or groups of firms offer now (or will offer):

- Addleshaw Goddard offers a six-month seat in its Innovation and Legal Technology (ILT) team (it also runs the Innovation and Legal Technology Graduate Scheme where, at the end of the scheme, graduates are awarded with the job title 'Legal Technologist').
- Allen & Overy offers solicitor apprenticeships and a LawTech Graduate Programme where graduates can work in teams in its Advanced Delivery & Solutions team (Markets Innovation Group, Project Management, Legal Tech and Fuse – its tech innovation hub – or eDiscovery).
- Ashurst has partnered with the University of Law which all trainees attend. The firm will run an "LLM Legal Practice Course (SQE 1&2)" designed specifically for the firm. It also runs its Ashurst Advance Pathway Programme where graduates can work in numerous areas such as legal operations, legal process improvement, legal project management and legal technology.
- The City Consortium: Freshfields Bruckhaus Deringer, Herbert Smith Freehills, Hogan Lovells, Linklaters, Norton Rose Fulbright and Slaughter and May, partnering with BPP University Law School, have created a SQE programme.
- Clifford Chance: the firm already operates IGNITE, its lawtech training contract. The University of Law has partnered with the firm to deliver the SQE.

There is no settled route now into qualification. Aspiring lawyers have a lot to work through. Firms have plenty to think about too.

(c) The job itself

Attracting talent into our firms involves looking both at the supply side (students) and the demand side (firms). The latter is too often overlooked when the potential supply remains so strong, particularly for BigLaw:

- Supply side:
  - Firms need to be aware of what drives students to become lawyers and any gradual changes in these drivers, so they aren't caught off-guard. Advance HE published a report in April 2012, *Career Expectations of Students on Qualifying Law Degrees in England and Wales,* in which students said the most important reasons for choosing to become a solicitor:[40]
    - were career satisfaction and security (first and second in the ranking of importance), with the potential to earn well coming in at third; and
    - matters like professional status and career progression came in at fourth and sixth respectively.
  - The approach of smaller firms is likely to differ from larger firms. While the above still apply, smaller firms often have a bit more work to do to attract talent. Focusing on culture helps.
- Demand side:
  - Firms are still narrowing the pipeline of potential lawyers into their firms too much: according to UCAS, AAA to BCC at A-level are the typical entry requirements for a law degree. The most common request is for ABB.[41] Many firms are similarly strict with the A-levels that they require. Putting aside for the moment how these sorts of requirements can impact diversity and inclusion, we need to question the importance we place on A-level results, which tend to test IQ over EQ. It's easy to go for AAA by default or rely on universities to set up a high hurdle to entry. As a result:
    - there's a lot of potential talent that firms are missing out on.[42] Check out the hashtag #LawyersWithRubbishAlevels on Twitter for plenty of stories of 'failure' at A-level, but success at the law. How sustainable is this?
    - the authors can also think of several examples of academically brilliant students who struggled with people skills and never achieved their potential. A mixture of talents is needed. After all, if a football team is comprised only of strikers they'd lose most matches.
  - Firms often ignore those who don't choose to become lawyers after doing a law degree: there's a rich seam of graduates who've read law, but who are lost to law firms. Law graduates tend to

favour roles that align with their degree, but we're not always great at mining this seam of talent. There is also a slightly higher unemployment rate for law graduates compared to graduates generally. The question is: how can we retain and use this talent more? Before someone else does?

5.2 Attracting associate lawyers

If attracting aspiring lawyers is difficult, it doesn't get any easier with associate lawyers. In October 2022, the 31st *PwC Law Firms' Survey* found that the "number one concern" for firms in the top 100 was the shortage of talent.[43]

We need to remind ourselves sometimes that we don't hold all the cards. It's a two-way process. Yes, firms invest a lot of time and money in their new lawyers. But new lawyers also 'invest' a lot into their careers and they want to choose right. Working for a firm that pays them an incredible amount of money, but for which they get beasted, is unlikely to generate loyalty and keep associate lawyers on side for the long term.

Pay is, of course, important, as is the prospect of an interesting and engaging career. But finding the sweet spot on pay that works for both parties can be tough. Let's look at these two vital ingredients in turn.

(a) Pay

With pay, the risk is that we pay our aspiring and associate lawyers under the odds. But there's also the risk that we pay over the odds too.

What happens if we pay too little?

- We often think of pay in absolute terms: "we pay our three-year PQE lawyers £x". But we rarely step back and think much about pay in the context of how much it costs to live as a, say, three-year PQE associate. Do those who set pay levels know roughly how much, for example, a three-year PQE associate lawyer is paying on average for major outgoings such as housing costs? Or on student loan repayments? Some advanced lawyers might assume (wrongly) that pay should roughly be the same as when they were a handful of years into their careers, adjusting for inflation.
- The result of paying too little means that our talent becomes unmotivated. They feel that they aren't being treated fairly. In some areas of law, the consequences are even more stark. As we mentioned earlier, there are now areas in England and Wales where there's no one under the age of 35 working in certain fields. In that case the firms in question would like to pay more, they just don't have the money to do so.

Pay sorts out the basics in life; progression and recognition give it meaning. If there's no path to progress and everything is ad hoc, *firms risk losing their associates to other firms and other sectors.*

Conversely, what happens if we pay too much?

- In October 2021, the online *Financial News* noted that large firms in London were taking on "anyone with a pulse"[44] as firms struggle to keep their associates on board. Even the BBC led with talk of £150,000 starting salaries and firms battling to get the best staff. And already, at the time of writing, even this figure has been considerably exceeded by some firms. Supply and demand means that throwing money at the problem is tempting, but ultimately it may create more problems than it solves.

- How sustainable are such salaries? What about economic cycles? Are they a short-term fix for a long-term problem? What happens when to be a 'good lawyer' is all about pay?

- It can create an environment where firms squeeze every penny out of their associates. One US recruiter, based in Los Angeles, blogged about the expectations of certain firms with the title "Why Law Firms Lawyers Must Work Weekends and Holidays: Law Firms Own Your Time and You Do Not".[45] The author referred to them as "inhumane truths". The result of paying *too much* means that these attitudes become widespread. Stress rises and people get hurt. What's more, unlike bonuses, once the bar is set for a salary, scaling it back is all but impossible. And what about those above the cohort of newly qualified lawyers? How do you pay and motivate them? How will they feel about the fact that, when they qualified, they didn't get paid anywhere near the salary of the current year's intake?

(b) Progression

Pay sorts out the basics in life; progression and recognition give it meaning. If there's no path to progress and everything is *ad hoc*, firms risk losing their associates to other firms and other sectors. Their 'workplace journey' starts to feel like a trip to nowhere. As is the case now, firms need to ensure that they have systems in place to nurture their talent.

Firms also need to be aware of the barriers to progression. These are things that take associates' focus off their career paths or even make them leave the profession for a simpler life elsewhere. Here are just three examples:

- Long hours and burn out: in September 2021, a LawCare report noted that younger professionals between the ages of 26 and 35 are at a higher risk of burnout (in contrast to those between the ages of 56 to 65 where the lowest risk lies).[46] According to LawCare this is likely to be due to this age group "experiencing higher work intensity, lower autonomy, and lower psychological safety at work".[47]

- Regulatory fears: there's the fear, not often talked about, of making a mistake and having to appear before the Solicitors Disciplinary Tribunal. Are younger solicitors at a disadvantage? Paul Sharma, then-President of Westminster & Holborn Law Society, told the *Law Society Gazette* in October 2021 that there's an inequality of arms in City firms where younger lawyers often can't afford representation when something goes wrong: "This is the dreadful, anachronistic and ironic reality of our profession, where some are clearly more equal than others."[48] Are we supporting our younger lawyers enough?

- Lockdowns: at a critical time in their careers many younger lawyers have been working from home; usually not from bespoke home offices, but from shared houses or tiny urban apartments – sometimes even from the edge of a bed. Supervision and mentoring have been wanting at times. There's been little or no learning 'by osmosis' or interacting with colleagues in person. How can firms now make up for lost time? How can these things be done best in our new hybrid world?

But let's not forget that exciting opportunities for associate lawyers are also there for the taking. Many current advanced lawyers may be struggling with technology and innovation (look at the archetypes in Chapter 11). Associate lawyers with ambition and nous are well placed to help drive forward how their firms use such technology and innovation. Their paths can be as varied as their firms allow them to be. What about a secondment to other non-legal internal teams, such as legal projects, legal ops, project management, the tech innovation team, IT etc? As we mention throughout this book, the options for a legal career don't have to be 100% legal!

6. Keeping the talent in

Attracting talent into the profession is one thing, but keeping that talent in and ensuring people are happy, motivated and avoiding burn out or 'bore out', is something else entirely.

If the press is to be believed, everyone is abandoning their careers or thinking about it. There's talk of the 'Great Re-evaluation', the 'Great Resignation' and even the 'Great Retirement' (with lawyers leaving private practice either to practise in-house or leave the profession entirely).

The figures do seem to back up the excited reporting in the press. According to Codex Edge, a legal-sector analytics firm, the average attrition rate for associate lawyers in the top 1,000 firms in England and Wales has jumped from 10.44% in 2020 to 14.31% in 2021.[49]

This is not a particularly new phenomenon though. Three City workers created Escape the City in 2010 with an open invitation for lawyers and other professionals to step off the corporate treadmill through *The Escape Manifesto*. The mantra? "Life is short. Quit your corporate job. Do something different!"[50]

It's easy for advanced lawyers to moan or even feel slightly aggrieved by all this. Many advanced lawyers have put up with the worst aspects of the job, so why can't aspiring and associate lawyers just "suck it up" and crack on with it "like we did"? While all the authors come from a background where all-nighters were routine, we don't see why associate lawyers should continue to put up with this sort of thing unless absolutely necessary – at the very least because this type of sleep deprivation is so counter-productive (many sleep experts say the cognitive impairment of sleep deprivation is equivalent to turning up to work drunk).

Of course, we don't advocate turning firms into lifestyle businesses. Law is tough, but it can and should be managed smarter and better. The risk is that it becomes tougher still through lack of talent. People get stretched to breaking point, doing the work of colleagues who don't exist, and so they leave. Then what?

What's more, by inflating salaries, most of the biggest firms are still hungry for human hours, rather than prioritising investment in technology so that fewer human hours will be needed and the client stands to receive a better service at lower cost. It all seems a bit, well, neanderthal.

So ultimately, in keeping the talent in, what matters?

As mentioned above, pay and progression are important, but the authors believe that there are many other things that we can do to see the progress that we need to see (and, in doing this, there needs to be top-level support too).

- Visions, strategies and aims matter: firms need to have a focused vision and strategy for their talent, which align with the other strategies in the firm. This vision and strategy should deal with aspiring and associate lawyers, but will also need to include advanced lawyers and non-lawyers too. In particular:
  - How will technology and innovation impact what goes in the strategies?
  - How will the firm compete with its competitors for talent?
  - How will the firm compete with other sectors for talent (data scientists etc)?
- Employees matter: consider accreditation such as Investors in People (IIP). All the talk of tech in this book doesn't mean that the people in firms are second on the list of priorities. We need a future where employees are treated with respect and dignity.

- Culture matters: Culture takes time. Rushing out to buy a pool table and a dart board for a breakout area won't magic a culture into existence. Building the right culture, through implementing the matters in this list (among others), takes time and determination. From the authors' experience, firms will get the best out of their people if they 'uncage' them and give them the space they need to breathe. They're able to bring their whole self to work. We're reminded of the story of when one educationalist bought some battery-farm chickens and let them out into his garden: "They just stood there for hours, nailed to the spot. It took a week before they found the courage to move."[51] Create a framework and let your people have the freedom they need to work within it (a 'freedom within a framework' approach).
- Balance matters: in 2021, Pew Research Center asked people in 17 advanced economies "what makes life meaningful?" In the United Kingdom, the order was family, friends, hobbies and occupation (followed by health). Recognising that aspiring and associate lawyers have lives outside of work is essential. To outsiders, working in a firm is often seen as being glamorous, but it can be physically and mentally exhausting. In some firms, beasting staff until they seek a less punishing life is all too commonplace. We need to drive change and bring balance to our working lives.
- Training and mentoring matters: people want to be valued and developed. Now more than ever (in a world of 'change3') lifelong learning is vital. Reskilling and upskilling our talent is fundamental to our success (see below). And we need to be aware of changes in how we do this. Less rote-learning and more understanding of EQ is a good start. Are we ready for this? Organisations and businesses are also now offering training in legaltech. Many top UK universities also offer massive open online courses (MOOCs).
- Networking matters: being seen in a crowded marketplace is tough. Aspiring and associate lawyers need to be given the headspace, encouragement and training to develop relationships with clients and others. This is not only good for the business, but is also motivating for them (alas, this type of activity, in some firms, is reserved just for advanced lawyers). Their careers depend on it.
- Career progression matters – in all its forms. We should ask ourselves:
  - How do we help those from non-legal backgrounds progress their careers? How do we make sure that they're motivated and not overlooked? Are they able progress as partners? Or to the board? What about those who want to move on and become a lawyer (full or part time)?
  - How do we deal with our lawyers who want to move on and do less or no lawyering (and do something else in the firm instead)?

- How do we help those who are returning to work? What support are they given to reintegrate and be successful in the workplace?
- Brands matter: all of the above helps to build a firm's reputation and the reputations of lawyers within the firm. Aspiring and association lawyers want to work for firms and advanced lawyers with deserved reputations. They (or their recruitment consultants) will look at directories such as *Legal 500* and *Chambers and Partners*. Firms should never ignore how they're perceived in the market – good, bad or indifferent – and do something about it if it needs to be improved.

Ultimately, the profession can be even more attractive for aspiring and associate lawyers, as firms begin to adopt tech and practices that enable working smarter, faster and better. Legaltech can help to take the strain and do some of the heavy lifting. The result is potentially less stress; enough time to sleep and stay healthy; less mundane work; and more variety than now. Aspiring and associate lawyers, as digital natives, are well-placed to get involved in new tech initiatives. What's not attractive about all that?

7. Sitting at the crossroads

The law sits in a privileged position at the intersection of many disciplines, sectors and industries. Aspiring and associate lawyers are also well placed to bring people and ideas together and to change perspectives. And there has never been a more important time for them to do so. Big Tech, for example, wants more of a steer and is asking for help.

Palantir Technologies, the American company which specialises in data analytics, filed documents at the US Securities and Exchange Commission (SEC) in August 2020 to go public. Its CEO, Alex Karp, said: "The engineering elite of Silicon Valley may know more than most about building software. But they do not know more about how society should be organized or what justice requires."[52] This is a remarkable statement from a Silicon Valley veteran.

Lawyers are well placed to be at the heart of these types of discussions about how we live with technology and the innovations all around us. (If not us, then who?)

More and more firms are sector-driven too, such as Fieldfisher, HFW, Osborne Clarke and the authors' firm. Sector-focused firms – whether nascent or otherwise – are in a strong position to forge connections between stakeholders across society, particularly if they are seconded to their clients (see the section below).

If any of us were to ask our clients what more they want from their lawyers, a common answer is: "get to know our business better". And one of the best ways to do so is through secondments.

8. Making business happen

There was a time when advertising by solicitors was banned. The feeling, not only in this country but others too, was that our noble profession shouldn't be sullied by such activities. Justice Krishna Iyer in *Bar Council of Maharashtra v MV Dadholkar*,[53] for example, referred to "soliciting, advertising, scrambling and other obnoxious practices", adding that "commercial competition or procurement should not vulgarise the legal profession". It's safe to say that business development (BD) has moved on a bit since then.

In the future, the amount of BD that aspiring and associate lawyers do is likely to increase, but the authors think that there are two areas, in particular, where aspiring and associate lawyers ought to focus their energies to build on what we've explored above. These are where the long-term payoffs are well worth the short-term investment in time and effort.

8.1 Secondments

If any of us were to ask our clients what more they want from their lawyers, a common answer is: "get to know our business better". And one of the best ways to do so is through secondments. The authors think, as a profession, we should be doing this much more than we do now.

From our experience, secondments:

- are highly valued by clients;
- are an ideal way to strengthen the relationship with them;
- can also help firms establish contacts in a sector and develop expertise there. A lot of new technology or innovation makes little sense on paper. We often have to be 'at the coalface' to truly understand what's going on; and
- are also highly valued by lawyers. One trainee at the authors' firm said that in addition to expanding a lawyer's legal knowledge, it's "the perfect opportunity to gain confidence, build on client relationship skills and gain an understanding of how clients approach different risks", adding "I couldn't recommend this opportunity enough".

Ultimately, secondments can help aspiring and associate lawyers understand clients on a whole new level by 'living the client life' (perhaps for the first time). What could be more client-centric than this?

8.2 Client listening exercises

A client-centric approach also means getting to know our clients in other ways, such as listening to them more, both formally and informally. Many advanced lawyers look back and regret not building deep relationships with their clients much earlier in their careers. It's rarely as difficult as it first seems and the benefits for aspiring and associate lawyers of doing so are manifest.

It's remarkable how little client listening takes place in the profession, particularly given how much other industries and sectors pump out surveys to their customers. Although surveys can work for many legal solutions, for much of the work that aspiring and associate lawyers do an open-ended chat with a client is a good alternative. It doesn't have to be in connection with a matter and, if done well, can be of great benefit to both lawyer and client alike. These may include questions as simple as:

- What are the challenges you face?
- What concerns do you have about x?
- What difficulty do you have with x?
- What's the risk of x?
- How satisfied are you with x?
- What are going to be your biggest challenges over the next x years?
- Other clients tell me this is a problem, what's your experience?
- If you had a magic wand, what problem would you want taken off your desk overnight?

Feedback, good and bad, from clients on specific matters is important too; and not just praise but answers to questions like 'how could we have done better?'.

Often, just the very act of listening is enough to strengthen the client relationship. As Maya Angelou once said, people may forget what was said or done "but people will never forget how you made them feel".[54] Sometimes picking up the phone or heading out for a coffee to be with a client informally is enough in itself. We lawyers like to think of ourselves as rational creatures, but in a time where EQ is emphasised more and more, we need to get better at doing this. And there's also plenty of software available to help manage this and to ensure regular feedback from clients (another example of people and tech working effectively together).

Being with our clients on secondment and listening to them so that we understand better where they're coming from is vital for aspiring and associate lawyers becoming truly client-centric in the years to come. Looking after our clients also means doing what we can to ensure that the law continues to protect them as it does now.

9. Upholding the rule of law

The rule of law is under threat. Governments can chip away at hard-won freedoms and safeguards. On an individual basis, they seem minor. In aggregate, they can be significant. The US National Intelligence Council (NIC) noted the rule of law, together with open commerce and democratic institutions, are at the highest risk of weakening globally in the next decade.

The rule of law often feels like quite a nebulous concept, particularly in a business context, but it matters. A report by Hogan Lovells and others, *Risk and Return*, found that, for example, the rule of law is among the top three considerations when multinationals make investment decisions overseas, after a stable political environment and ease of doing business.[55]

The impact of this can't be understated: the NIC also notes that democracies and open societies (with the rule of law) find it easier to cultivate the right environment for technology and innovation. Aspiring and associate lawyers need to understand the preeminent role that they can play in upholding this principle. In the years ahead, commercial law firms may need to step up more too. They might be called upon to remind those in power that, in the words of the United Nations, the rule of law "provides the basis for commercial certainty and creates the foundation for long term investment and growth, and sustainable development for all".[56] The future of law needs to be built on the rule of law.

10. Training

Finally, in this section, we look at training aspiring and associate lawyers. 'Change3' means that continuous learning is vital for them to thrive in the years to come. It's also at the heart of a high-performing culture.

The skills which are required can be split into three types:
- hard law: aspiring and associate lawyers still need to learn the things that we've always learnt: the so-called 'hard skills' of the law. The likes of *Donoghue v Stevenson*[57] and *Carlill v Carbolic Smoke Ball Co*[58] aren't going anywhere just yet, although the emphasis needs to be more on how we apply these cases in practice;
- soft skills: these are the EQ-powered skills, on which our collective futures will be based (see Chapter 9). We need to do much more to develop these skills, which can sometimes be harder to learn and master than the 'hard' skills above. Initiatives such as the O Shaped Lawyer also focus more on these types of skills. This initiative reminds us why these skills are crucial: "there remains an

overwhelming emphasis on developing technical legal skills at the expense of a broader, more well-rounded education and continuous development. This limits the potential for professionals across the sector to grow personally and develop professionally"[59] (not to mention giving clients a better experience of the legal profession); and

- other skills: including management, IT skills and other technical skills.

We also need to equip people managers with the right skills to support aspiring and associate lawyers in their career development.

We talk a lot about legaltech in this book, but can its equivalent in the education sector – edtech – help us achieve a high-performing culture? The authors think it can. And so do others in this field. The authors spoke to Sarah Hutchinson, a non-executive director at BARBRI Global. The company, which offers SQE preparation courses in the United Kingdom, has developed ISAAC, the Intuitive Study Assistant and Coach, which uses AI to produce tailored learning programmes (*Personal Study Plans*). The AI engine is constantly learning to help the student build on their strengths and remediate any weaknesses. Hutchinson sees this as the future of learning.

There's no doubt that the future of professional development will involve engines like ISAAC. It may also involve VR (virtual reality) or techniques like gamification where systems are enhanced with gaming elements to make learning more engaging and less of a chore. Visiting the Wellmeadow Café in Paisley, where an unsuspecting May Donoghue found a decomposed snail in her ginger beer, is a possibility with VR. So too is gamification where learners are tested on the law of negligence and the famous 'neighbour test'. A great many possibilities open up for training which truly engage the learner.

A study by PwC found that VR learners were almost four times more emotionally connected to the content than their classroom peers; they were four times more focused; and the training was four times faster too. What's more, "learners trained with VR were up to 275% more confident to act on what they learned after training".[60] In this 'hybrid era', it's unlikely that the classroom will be boarded up anytime soon, but keeping our aspiring and associate lawyers up to date is likely to be a whole lot more interesting. And fun.

Ultimately, if we want the legal and non-legal talent of tomorrow to devote their precious weeks – a finite resource – to the law, whether it be 100, 500 or the jackpot of 2,000 weeks, we'd do well to give those who want to join us and build their careers with us the courtesy of letting them know what's in store and why they can be excited about it.

And while technology and innovation is, at times, 'making the ride go quicker' – matters can be turned around more rapidly and more clients are expecting a 24/7/365 experience – this also means we must also make sure that we look after the mental health of our aspiring and associate lawyers too (see the second case study below).

There's a lot for aspiring and associate lawyers to look forward to.

11. Case studies

11.1 Case study 1: Social Mobility Pledge campaign

A widely reported study in 2013 found that certain Norman surnames still dominate the student rolls at Oxford and Cambridge. When the study was published the *Daily Mail*'s headline harumphed: "So much for social mobility ... 1,000 years after William the Conqueror invaded, you still need a Norman name like Darcy or Percy to get ahead."[61] Gerald Cavendish Grosvenor, the 6th Duke of Westminster and descendant of Norman 'master of the hunt' Gilbert Grosvenor, would have been a fitting case study for this *Daily Mail* article. When asked by a *Financial Times* reporter what advice he had for young entrepreneurs, the Duke, one of the wealthiest men in the United Kingdom on his death in 2016, replied that they needed to have an ancestor "who was a very good friend of William the Conqueror".[62]

Almost 1,000 years on, most people don't have an old Norman contact to fall back on. There are, however, bodies which aim to help people who have talent, purpose and ambition to enjoy successful careers. The Social Mobility Pledge, a cross-party campaign co-founded by Rt Hon Justine Greening and entrepreneur David Harrison, was set up to boost opportunity and advocate for social mobility. At the time of writing, seven million people (five million employees and two million students) are covered by the Pledge. Numerous law firms, including the authors', have also joined up.

It has its work cut out. The statistics on social mobility don't make for easy reading:
- research by the University of Law in 2021 found that only 6% of people surveyed, for example, expect to see lawyers coming from a working-class background;[63]

- disadvantaged pupils are as much as seven months behind in their educational development than their advantaged peers, according to the Social Mobility Commission. Even worse, the attainment gaps between advantaged and disadvantaged children are getting wider; and
- the *Global Social Mobility Index*, published in January 2020, has the Nordic countries as the best performers.[64] Among the G7, Germany ranks 11th with the United Kingdom at 21 (and the United States at 27).

The extent of the problem in law firms is difficult to quantify. And it's a problem which affects almost all businesses: according to IPSOS and DIAL Global in 2020, 89% of businesses don't track the socioeconomic backgrounds of their employees.[65]

The initiative (see www.socialmobilitypledge.org) has three main objectives:
- to engage organisations on social mobility and to increase the number of those who are involved;
- to share best practice and build on successes; and
- to drive action on social mobility.

Organisations make their pledge on social mobility by committing to help "people from disadvantaged backgrounds or circumstances" through:
- outreach, such as working with schools;
- access, such as providing work experience and apprentices; and
- recruitment, such as adopting "open employee recruitment practices which promote a level playing field".

How does this look in practice? For example, the authors' firm:
- partners with schools and colleges in social mobility 'cold spots' to:
  - give careers advice;
  - give mentoring and coaching sessions; and
  - offer apprenticeships and work experience placements;
- takes steps to ensure transparent and accessible recruitment processes for aspiring and associate lawyers;
- fosters an environment so people can be themselves at work. Its approach to this is informed by its:
  - inclusion working group;
  - inclusion networks; and
  - pilot initiatives such as reverse mentoring; and
- collaborates with clients and others in wider community networks, to share ideas and combine resources.

In 2019 the firm worked with the Pledge to develop a tailored Social

Mobility Action Plan. As part of this process, the firm was required to audit its existing efforts. The Pledge team also carried out extensive community-based research, looking at the biggest barriers to social mobility in each of the geographical areas where the firm's offices are based. The firm's action plan was officially launched on 20 October 2020 and proposed 14 recommendations based on the Pledge team's research findings.

Social mobility is something that is falling within the radar of others too, including the Law Society. In August 2022, I Stephanie Boyce, then-President of the Law Society, made social mobility a key priority of her presidency. In the same month the City of London Taskforce launched a report (*Building the Baseline Report*) to baseline socio-economic diversity at senior levels in financial and professional services firms.[66]

This subject is also something the authors have experienced, to varying degrees: none of the authors went to fee-paying schools. Two of them, at times, grew up in council houses and were the first in their families to go to university. All of us have seen a lot of positive change in recent years. We're looking forward to seeing much more.

11.2 Case study 2: Mental wellbeing in the profession

In 2021 LawCare, the mental wellbeing charity for lawyers, published its *Life in the Law* report. It said that there's:

> … *robust evidence that the legal profession is stressed, tired, anxious, at high risk of burnout and that those working practices in the law that undermine mental health need to change.*[67]

LawCare's research found that 69% of participants in their research had experienced poor mental health in the previous year, whether diagnosed or self-diagnosed.[68]

On the other hand, other surveys have placed solicitors relatively high up the happiness league – perhaps to the surprise of lawyers – as the 44th happiest out of 274 professions in 2014.[69] An SRA review in February 2022 (see below), found that "most respondents felt that their firm had a positive workplace culture overall".[70]

So what's going on here?

There's no doubt a whole book could be written on mental wellbeing in law firms. Fictional psychiatrist Niles Crane in the US sitcom *Frasier* once mentioned how good lawyers are as patients: they've got reams of health insurance and they "never get better". An amusing quip certainly, but in reality we can't afford to be this fatalistic. Nor should we think everything is fine and we just carry on as before. Lawyers are *not* emotionless robots. We believe this fact will become even more stark as EQ takes on greater importance in the years to come (see Chapter 9).

The result is that, as a profession, we need to get better at looking after our people. The pandemic showed us all how important mental health is. A good start is to consider the work done by organisations such as the International Bar Association (IBA) and its *Mental Wellbeing Principles for the Legal Profession*.[71] These principles are:

- mental wellbeing matters;
- mental wellbeing is not weakness;
- raising awareness is fundamental;
- a commitment to change, and regular continuing assessment, is needed;
- policies matter;
- maintain an open dialogue and communication;
- address systemic problems;
- recognise intersectionalities;
- share good practices; and
- learn from others.

These principles apply to all lawyers at all stages of their professional life. So what can and should firms do to put these principles into practice?

As set out earlier, throwing money at the problem, in the form of more pay, isn't always feasible, let alone desirable. As the LawCare report shows us, there's perhaps a limit to how long people are willing to live in a miserable gilded cage. The key is to build a culture of compassion.

In 2022, Burges Salmon won the annual RollOnFriday (RoF) *Best Law Firms to Work At*. When interviewed, managing partner, Roger Bull, talked about the firm's culture and having "a genuine courage to care" both in terms of its staff and its clients.[72] To hard-nosed lawyers, having the "courage to care" can sound a bit woolly, but it certainly doesn't mean being unassertive or meek. Doormats need not apply here. It also means having the compassion to do the best for our people and our clients and recognising their humanity. As we mention in Chapter 9, empathy is about sharing someone's emotions, but compassion is about acting on them.

The SRA also published in February 2022, as part of its *Workplace Culture Thematic Review*, information on managing workplace culture and what it expects:

We expect firms to create and maintain the right culture and environ-
ment for the delivery of competent and ethical legal services to clients
with effective systems, supervision arrangements, processes and con-
trols in place.

This includes taking steps to run businesses in a way that supports well-
being by minimising the risk of working practices and workplace
behaviours leading to poor mental health. A failure to put in place
systems that protect employees may lead to an increased risk of breach-
ing our regulatory requirements.[73]

The SRA goes on to highlight that lawyers need to be in good mental
health to deal with the challenges of acting in clients' best interests. If
firms don't support their people, there's the risk that they'll behave uneth-
ically.

The annual RoF *Best Law Firms to Work At* survey is an encouraging
annual read to show what happens with the right culture. TLT, for
example, shows that you can win professional awards and also rank highly
as a caring firm to work for. Having the "courage to care" doesn't have to
come at the expense of professional success.

12. Practical tips on aspiring and associate lawyers

We set out below some practical tips on aspiring and associate lawyers.
- Raise your firm's profile and reputation (both internal and external)
  for forward-thinking, innovation and using tech. The best talent
  would be ill-advised to join or stay with a firm that's stuck in the
  past.
- Encourage and harness your associates' enthusiasm and talent to
  take your firm's use of tech and innovation forward. (In many cases,
  your associates might be more enthusiastic and technically minded
  than many of the partners.)
- If your associates contribute to your firm's tech and innovation
  advancement, then ensure that you reward them for that and ensure
  that they feel valued for it. Otherwise, they (and others) might think
  those efforts are not valued and so they won't bother in future.
- Seek secondment placements for your associates and trainees with
  legaltech businesses.
- Embrace the 'hybrid era'. Give your associates as much flexibility as
  possible (within whatever parameters/framework you need to apply
  in the context of the legal work you do). Having seen the tremendous
  work of our associates during lockdown, we can completely trust them
  to deliver for our firms without mandating their daily attendance in

the office. And ensure you equip them to do their jobs effectively and comfortably on the days they work from home.

- If yours is a firm that visits universities to recruit trainees from law undergraduates, then don't forget also to speak to undergraduates in the other subjects that will be relevant to the future of lawyering (eg, multimedia, social media, data analysis, computer science etc). And don't forget that future lawyers and non-lawyers won't all come from universities.

- Create pathways for your associates to spend time in your internal business support teams (eg, legal ops, IT, projects & innovation, document automation, data projects etc). Not only will they gain useful skills and insight to better equip them to relate to finding solutions for their clients' day-to-day needs, but also those internal teams can learn more about the lawyers' needs and concerns. Remember to reassure the associate that spending time away from front-line fee-earning will only potentially enhance their career prospects with you.

- Think about the skills training that your associates will need in the future:
  - For example, we reckon that enhancing EQ skills is far more relevant than teaching lawyers to code!
  - What wellbeing training is required? What practical tips can you give to aspiring and associate lawyers to avoid some of the more common pitfalls of practice (avoiding catastrophising, managing emails etc);
  - How about creating, say, internal 'TED Talks' (presented by advanced lawyers) on topics such as managing change; developing resilience; using your imagination; being creative, dealing with fear of failure, developing better EQ, being self-motivated, dealing with imposter syndrome etc.

- Reassure your associates that innovation and technology will not put them out of work! There will always be a place for humans in the practice and business of law.

- Ensure your associates appreciate that innovation and technology will make their jobs more satisfying, enable them to achieve more and will:
  - make them better at what they do;
  - reduce many of the more tedious aspects of what they do; and
  - enable them to be even more valued by clients because what they can offer clients will be much enhanced.

- Those who have more privilege need to be allies to those who aren't so lucky; who are marginalised or underprivileged. In particular, given how many advanced lawyers are men, the profession needs to have champions for change who are men.

- We need to ensure that we don't cure an injustice by creating another. This is likely to be counterproductive. We want people of privilege to be allies to the cause, rather than feeling that they are a targeted group.
- We need to be brave. We might fret that one ill-judged remark can torpedo our hard-won reputations, particularly in a world where we've never before been under so much scrutiny.

Notes

1   Jock Serong, "The Short History Of Surfers Doing TV Commercials" (*Surfing World Magazine*), https://surfingworld.com.au/short-history-surfers-tv-ads/.
2   "The women who coined the expression 'Surfing the Internet'" (*Surfer Today*), www.surfertoday.com/surfing/the-woman-who-coined-the-expression-surfing-the-internet.
3   See: www.rollonfriday.com/.
4   Fox refers to 'English' and not 'British', although workplaces in the other countries and regions may recognise some or many of these traits.
5   Kate Fox, *Watching the English* (Hodder & Stoughton, 2004), pp178, 205.
6   Mark Muro, Jacob Whiton and Robert Maxim, "What Jobs Are Affected By AI?" (Metropolitan Policy Program at Brookings, November 2019), www.brookings.edu/wp-content/uploads/2019/11/2019.11.20_BrookingsMetro_What-jobs-are-affected-by-AI_Report_Muro-Whiton-Maxim.pdf.
7   Jane Croft, "Why are investors pouring money into legal technology?" (*Financial Times*, 28 July 2022), www.ft.com/content/b6f0796e-0265-40c6-ad4c-a900cd788c39.
8   "Which occupations are at highest risk of being automated?" (Office for National Statistics, 25 March 2019), www.ons.gov.uk/employmentandlabourmarket/peopleinwork/employmentandemployeetypes/articles/whichoccupationsareathighestriskofbeingautomated/2019-03-25.
9   Carl Benedikt Frey and Michael Osborne, *The Future of Employment* (Oxford Martin Programme on Technology and Employment, 17 September 2013), www.oxfordmartin.ox.ac.uk/downloads/academic/future-of-employment.pdf.
10 As for the role of a paralegal: many paralegals go on to be offered training contracts – this was the case with one of the authors – and this will no doubt continue during the SRA's transitional arrangements to the new Solicitors Qualifying Examination (SQE) regime. The SQE itself should also offer paralegals a more flexible and less expensive route to qualifying. Some paralegals may get more involved with working on the suites of tech products and services that many firms offer, either as paralegals or perhaps in different roles. For every task you take away, you can often add a new one. For example, the authors' firm's contract review tool uses paralegals as the human overlay. There may well be many new opportunities where paralegals can help firms to deal with the challenges of the "Great Unmet Legal Need" too.
11 Kate Fox, *Watching the English* (Hodder & Stoughton, 2004), p205.
12 Infocomm Media Development Authority, Personal Data Protection Commission, *A Guide to Job Design in the Age of AI* (2020), https://file.go.gov.sg/ai-guide-to-jobredesign.pdf.
13 *Ibid.*
14 Association of Colleges, *Forecasting 16-to-18 education growth to 2030* (August 2021), https://feweek.co.uk/wp-content/uploads/2021/08/AoC201620-201920projections20to20203020August2021.pdf.
15 "Smarter Contracts & Digital Assets – Report & Case Studies" (LawTechUK), https://lawtechuk.io/programmes/smarter-contracts.
16 Rani Molla, "More than half of the most valuable US tech companies were founded by first- or second-generation immigrants" (*Vox*, 30 May 2018), www.vox.com/2018/5/30/17385226/kleiner-perkins-mary-meeker-immigration-tech-founders-jobs-slides-code-conference.
17 Catherine Wines, "Why Immigrants Are Natural Entrepreneurs" (Forbes, 7 September 2018), www.forbes.com/sites/catherinewines/2018/09/07/why-immigrants-are-natural-entrepreneurs/?sh=7b0b44df651d.
18 Janet H Cho, "'Diversity is being invited to the party; inclusion is being asked to dance' Verna Myers tells Cleveland Bar" (Cleveland.com, 25 May 2016), www.cleveland.com/business/2016/05/diversity_is_being_invited_to.html.
19 "Diversity wins: How inclusion matters" (McKinsey & Company, 19 May 2020), www.mckinsey.com/featured-insights/diversity-and-inclusion/diversity-wins-how-inclusion-matters.
20 UK Model Diversity Survey (InterLaw Diversity Forum), www.interlawdiversityforum.org/uk-model-diversity-survey.
21 Monidipa Fouzder, "Microsoft offers 3% bonus to panel firms hitting diversity targets" (*Law Society*

Gazette, 20 December 2021), www.lawgazette.co.uk/practice/microsoft-offers-3-bonus-to-panel-firms-hitting-diversity-targets/5110981.article.

22 More in Common (Míriam Juan-Torres, Tim Dixon and Arisa Kimaram), *Britain's Choice Common Ground and Division in 2020s Britain* (2020 version 2), www.moreincommon.org.uk/media/p52fc3q2/0917-mic-uk-britain-s-choice_report_dec01-5.pdf.

23 Suella Braverman, "Diversity zealots have created a dangerous new religion – we must get serious about taking them on" (*Daily Mail*, 3 August 2020), www.mailplus.co.uk/edition/news/news-comment/208578/suella-braverman-diversity-zealots-have-created-a-dangerous-new-religion-we-must-get-serious-about-taking-them-on.

24 "Legal services regulators and tribunals commit to creating a more inclusive profession" (Legal Services Board, 6 June 2022), https://legalservicesboard.org.uk/news/legal-services-regulators-and-tribunals-commit-to-creating-a-more-inclusive-profession.

25 Law Society, *Influencing for impact: the need for gender equality in the legal profession* (March 2019), www.law.ox.ac.uk/sites/files/oxlaw/influencing_for_impact_-_the_need_for_gender_equaluty_in_the_legal_profession_-_women_in_leadership_in_law_report.pdf.

26 Barack Obama, *A Promised Land* (Viking, 2020) p82.

27 Matt Byrne, "Soon lawyers will be a minority group in law firms" (*The Lawyer*, 30 September 2021), www.thelawyer.com/soon-lawyers-will-be-a-minority-group-in-law-firms/.

28 Yvon Chouinard, *Let My People Go Surfing* (2nd edition, Penguin, 2016), p1.

29 *Ibid*.

30 Legal Services Board, *The State of Legal Services 2020*, https://legalservicesboard.org.uk/wp-content/uploads/2020/11/The-State-of-Legal-Services-Narrative-Volume_Final.pdf.

31 Extra-judicial statement by of Lord Goff of Chieveley in *Commercial Contracts and the Commercial Court* (1984) LMCLQ 382, 391.

32 "Population of solicitors in England and Wales" (Solicitors Regulation Authority), www.sra.org.uk/sra/research-publications/regulated-community-statistics/data/population_solicitors/.

33 "Criminal duty solicitors: a looming crisis" (Law Society, 1 September 2022), www.lawsociety.org.uk/campaigns/criminal-justice/criminal-duty-solicitors.

34 "Annual statistics report 2021" (Law Society, 21 September 2022), www.lawsociety.org.uk/topics/research/annual-statistics-report-2021.

35 For law students themselves, the focus is often more on getting value for money and making themselves employable and less on receiving a liberal arts education. Put simply, for many the economics of the qualification have trumped the intellectual adventure.

36 Andrew Boon and Julian Webb, "Legal education and training in England and Wales: Back to the future?" (2008) 58 *Journal of Legal Education* 79.

37 Department for Education, *Independent panel report to the Review of Post-18 Education and Funding* (30 May 2019), www.gov.uk/government/publications/post-18-review-of-education-and-funding-independent-panel-report.

38 "Breakdown of routes to admission" (Solicitors Regulation Authority), www.sra.org.uk/sra/research-publications/regulated-community-statistics/data/routes_admission/.

39 Aishah Hussain, "Exclusive research: Law firms say the SQE alone will not be enough" (*Legal Cheek*, 28 January 2021), www.legalcheek.com/2021/01/exclusive-research-law-firms-say-the-sqe-alone-will-not-be-enough/.

40 *Career Expectations of Students on Qualifying Law Degrees in England and Wales* (The Higher Education Academy, April 2012), https://s3.eu-west-2.amazonaws.com/assets.creode.advancehe-document-manager/documents/hea/private/resources/hardee-report-2012_1568037246.pdf.

41 "Law" (UCAS), www.ucas.com/explore/subjects/law.

42 Equally, are firms taking full advantage of the routes where people have already qualified elsewhere to build the best teams they need? For example: barristers; CILEX practitioners; Registered European Lawyers (RELs); routes for Scottish, Northern Irish and Irish solicitors etc.

43 "Annual Law Firms' Survey 2022: Agility through turbulent times" (PwC), www.pwc.co.uk/industries/legal-professional-business-support-services/law-firms-survey.html.

44 James Booth, "London law firms hire 'anyone with a pulse' as soaring salaries aren't enough for junior lawyers" (*Financial News*, 27 October 2021), www.fnlondon.com/articles/law-firms-struggle-to-retain-junior-staff-despite-soaring-salaries-20211027.

45 Harrison Barnes, "Why Law Firms Lawyers Must Work Weekends and Holidays: Law Firms Own Your Time and You Do Not" (BCG Attorney Search), www.bcgsearch.com/article/60765/Working-weekends-and-holidays/.

46 "New research into lawyer wellbeing makes the case for profession-wide change" (LawCare), www.lawcare.org.uk/latest-news/life-in-the-law-new-research-into-lawyer-wellbeing-makes-the-case-for-profession-wide-change/.

47 *Ibid*.

48 Jemma Slingo, "'Rotten culture': London law society blasts SDT treatment of young solicitors" (*Law Society Gazette*, 4 October 2021), www.lawgazette.co.uk/news/rotten-culture-london-law-society-blasts-sdt-treatment-of-young-solicitors-/5110030.article.

49 William Dougherty, "The Winners in Law's 'Great Resignation' Will Be Firms that Focus on Innovation, Not Compensation" (*Artificial Lawyer*, 29 November 2021),

www.artificiallawyer.com/2021/11/29/the-winners-in-laws-great-resignation-will-be-firms-that-focus-on-innovation-not-compensation/.

50 Rob Symington, *The Escape Manifesto: Quit Your Corporate Job, Do Something Different!* (Wiley, 2013).

51 Rutger Bregman, *Humankind* (Bloomsbury, 2021), p295.

52 Registration Statement on Form S-1 (Palantir Technologies Inc, 25 August 2020), www.sec.gov/Archives/edgar/data/1321655/000119312520230013/d904406ds1.htm#rom904406_9.

53 *Bar Council of Maharashtra v MV Dadholkar* 1976 AIR 242, 1976 SCR (2) 48.

54 Elizabeth Dori Tunstall, "How Maya Angelou made me feel" (*The Conversation*, 29 May 2014), https://theconversation.com/how-maya-angelou-made-me-feel-27328.

55 *Risk and Return – Foreign Direct Investment and the Rule of Law* (Hogan Lovells, 2015), https://f.datasrvr.com/fr1/415/10099/10071_D4_FDI_Main_Report_V4.pdf.

56 United Nations Global Compact, *Business for the Rule of Law Framework*, https://d306pr3pise04h.cloudfront.net/docs/issues_doc%2Frule_of_law%2FB4ROL_Framework.pdf.

57 *Donoghue v Stevenson* [1932] UKHL 100.

58 *Carlill v Carbolic Smoke Ball Co* [1893] 1 QB 256.

59 "Putting people and relationships at the heart of legal services" (O Shaped), www.oshapedlawyer.com/.

60 "What does virtual reality and the metaverse mean for training?" (PwC), www.pwc.com/us/en/tech-effect/emerging-tech/virtual-reality-study.html.

61 Steve Doughty, "So much for social mobility ... 1,000 years after William the Conquerer invaded, you still need a Norman name like Darcy or Percy to get ahead" (*Daily Mail*, 29 October 2013), www.dailymail.co.uk/news/article-2479271/1-000-years-invaded-need-Norman-like-Darcy-Percy-ahead.html.

62 "Duke of Westminster Dies" (*Financial Times*, 10 August 2016), www.ft.com/content/57f2dec2-5e7d-11e6-bb77-a121aa8abd95.

63 Ben Edwards, "Public perception of UK legal profession still seen as male dominated, study finds" (*The Global Legal Post*, 8 March 2021), www.globallegalpost.com/news/public-perception-of-uk-legal-profession-still-seen-as-male-dominated-study-finds-80765350.

64 "Global Social Mobility Index 2020: why economies benefit from fixing inequality" (World Economic Forum, 19 January 2020), www.weforum.org/reports/global-social-mobility-index-2020-why-economies-benefit-from-fixing-inequality/.

65 "New study reveals how far UK firms have progressed in D&I" (Fair Play Talks, 20 November 2020), www.fairplaytalks.com/2020/11/20/groundbreaking-di-study-reveals-just-how-far-uk-firms-have-progressed-across-10-diversity-facets/.

66 *Building the Baseline: Breaking the Class Barrier* (City of London Corporation, August 2022), www.cityoflondon.gov.uk/assets/Business/building-the-baseline.pdf.

67 "New research into lawyer wellbeing makes the case for profession-wide change" (LawCare), www.lawcare.org.uk/latest-news/life-in-the-law-new-research-into-lawyer-wellbeing-makes-the-case-for-profession-wide-change/.

68 *Ibid.*

69 Mark Easton, "Vicar or publican – which jobs make you happy?" (BBC News, 20 March 2014), www.bbc.co.uk/news/magazine-26671221.

70 "Workplace Culture Thematic Review" (Solicitors Regulation Authority, 8 February 2022), www.sra.org.uk/sra/research-report/workplace-culture-thematic-review/.

71 "New IBA report sets out principles for dealing with mental wellbeing crisis in the legal profession" (International Bar Association, 26 October 2021), www.ibanet.org/New-IBA-report-sets-out-principles-for-dealing-with-mental-wellbeing-crisis-in-the-legal-profession.

72 James Dennison, "CHAMPION The Best Law Firm to Work at 2022" (*RollOnFriday*, 21 January 2022), www.rollonfriday.com/news-content/champion-best-law-firm-work-2022.

73 "Workplace Culture Thematic Review" (Solicitors Regulation Authority, 8 February 2022), www.sra.org.uk/sra/research-report/workplace-culture-thematic-review/.

Chapter 11:
The advanced lawyer

Shakespeare declared in *Henry IV* that "the time of life is short!". He wasn't wrong.

Like the authors, most readers of this book will be advanced lawyers. Typically, the reader will be a partner or in some other senior position in their firm. For us – busy as we are – life rattles by at pace. We're aware of time passing. It seems to go quicker with every passing year. We've achieved a lot, but still have a lot more that we'd like to do. (There are certainly plenty of suggestions in this book.)

Most of us will have also followed a rather linear path to get where we are today. These stages – the authors call them the 'seven ages of lawyering' – typically look something like this:
- We learn some law at university.
- Then we get a job in a law firm, or in industry, and apply the law in a real-life context.
- We soon recognise the importance of team-working and building relationships.
- Then – for everyone in private practice anyway – comes the realisation that we need to win clients to survive and thrive. We also learn that the best rainmakers earn more money!
- Then arrives the wonderful zen-like point when we start to know

what it's fine not to know; and that it's okay not to know the answer to everything, as long as we know how to find out the answer. This is a truly beautiful and enlightening moment, which often coincides with being given a trainee or assistant to supervise, who we can get to do some of our research for us.

- As we advance further up the ranks, we start to think more like we're running a business too, rather than just dispensing legal advice. The importance of profitability starts to hit home.
- And finally, the seventh age of lawyering – the pinnacle of our careers – which seems to take one of two forms:
  - for some senior lawyers, this involves them applying their many years' experience to become thought leaders and think strategically about how technology will fundamentally impact their firm in the future. They're genuinely passionate about leaving a lasting legacy through which their staff won't just survive, but will thrive in the future. They ask themselves the question: "where's the puck moving?" and they're intent on guiding their firms to get there in good time; or
  - for other senior lawyers, the seventh age of lawyering simply involves them feeling very comfortable, continuing to do what they've done for decades. They appear to have no concern about the future of their junior lawyers, much less their firms. 'What will be, will be' is their mantra.

The authors admit this doesn't quite have the élan of the Bard's *Seven Ages Of Man* (from which it was shamelessly derived). There's no "mewling and puking" of infants or an undignified end where the protagonist finishes "sans teeth, sans eyes, sans taste, sans everything". No matter.

But what it does have is a crucial split at the end. Unlike Shakespeare's monologue, we have the possibility of a happier ending, provided that we actively choose it. We have agency.

Therefore, the questions that all advanced lawyers need to ask themselves are:

- Do I follow the easier second path in the seventh age of lawyering, one in which the true underlying question is: can I make this last until I retire?; or
- Do I follow the more difficult first path, one in which the future is something to be embraced and not ignored? If I see a future for my firm and the people in it, what can I do to nurture it?

The authors advocate the latter approach.

And we're confident that we're well-placed to create a positive future for our law firms and the people in them.

- We've lived in remarkable times. We continue to do so as the trends at the start of this book transform our working lives. As advanced lawyers, we're the bridge between the relatively comfortable, analogue 'before' and the unknown digital 'after'.
- We also know how to deal with change, after all, we done it often enough. We've decades of experience and wisdom under our belts in many areas.
- We're in a position to help shape the fabric of our society. We make decisions that affect our clients' lives in profound and not-so-profound ways. In aggregate, however, we can bring about more change than we give ourselves credit for.
- We've typically invested significant sums in our firms, which are vital to our legal system as a whole and the rule of law in particular. The investment in our firms means that we must've had some confidence in their futures at some point. There's still plenty of reasons to keep that confidence.
- We're the people within our firms who can make the right change happen. We hold the levers of power or are in positions to influence those who hold the levers (we discuss the types of personalities in law firms in this chapter, and, most importantly, how to deal with them). Now's the time to start pulling and pushing those levers so we create the profession that we want to see.

In this chapter, the focus is on breaking down the barriers to change with advanced lawyers, whether it be dealing with worries about losing status or navigating the day-to-day politics of investing in and implementing technology and innovation. There are numerous books on the market which deal with law firm management generally (including from the publisher of this book). The key in this chapter is to help the reader bring about the changes set out elsewhere in this book.

We then look at two case studies and finish with some practical tips on advanced lawyers.

Before we dive in, there's one final, important point: in any vibrant law firm or legal business there's almost always a tension between the new way and the old way of doing things. This may be obvious or it may be lurking out of sight, unseen, but somehow exerting a force on how the firm operates and the direction it takes.

Just like how any government needs a strong opposition, law firms also need the right alchemy of archetypes to fulfil their aims, visions and strategies, while also ensuring that any risks are minimised and mistakes avoided.

However it manifests itself, we mustn't assume that this is unhealthy: like the tug of war between left and right in politics, a constant and constructive toing and froing between new ideas and the concerns of advanced lawyers in our businesses is a good thing. Any new way of doing things has to be probed and tested, otherwise we risk getting carried away with ourselves. Just like how any government needs a strong opposition, law firms also need the right alchemy of archetypes to fulfil their aims, visions and strategies, while also ensuring that any risks are minimised and mistakes avoided.

Those who succeed in managing these archetypes in the optimal way will give themselves the edge they need to power their firms forward. In the next section, we look at six archetypes we typically see among the senior ranks in a typical law firm.

1. Getting to know the six archetypes

Archetypes are a simple way to pigeonhole and understand personalities. As one expert in the business of law notes, personality traits "have broad implications for the management of lawyers, the cultivation of rainmakers, the retention of associates and a range of other critical issues in the day-to-day practice of law".[1]

Coming up with archetypes is, of course, a reductive exercise; a bit crude perhaps. But they can help us understand how to manage the teams and projects within our firms when adopting and implementing technology and innovation in particular.

What's more, a lawyer may not fit neatly into an archetype. These roles aren't set in stone:
- in time a lawyer may play many parts;
- a lawyer may play some parts at the same time, although some archetypes are mutually exclusive; and
- a lawyer may move from one to another and back again.

The authors have broken down the archetypes as far as possible. In *Top Trumps* fashion, we set out the characteristics and superpowers of each below.

1.1 The heavies
Characteristics:
- Typically in the upper quartile in age.
- Collectively they have the most power and influence in the firm.
- They appreciate the importance of their firm evolving, innovating

and investing, even if they may not personally possess the skills to make it happen.

Superpowers:
- They can make the decisions at senior management level to ensure that the firm has its place among the firms of the future.
- They alone can set the wheels in motion for action to be taken.

However, rarely is there, as one expert in partnerships notes, an "individual heroic leader, as mythologised by the business press".[2] This is why 'the heavies' are in the plural. Each law firm is different. Sometimes leadership is within a small group, in others it's more like "a series of concentric circles".[3]

1.2 The 3 Bs: 'brilliant but busy'
Characteristics:
- Forward-thinking and keen to push the firm forward and to innovate.
- Incredibly busy working on billable hours.
- They can see how innovation can help their work and their clients, but are too busy to make the changes themselves.
- Often keen to get involved in an innovation project, but too busy ever to turn up for the meetings.

Superpowers:
- These lawyers are a delight to work with and an inspiration and roll model to the more junior lawyers in their teams.
- They can strongly influence their team's attitude to innovation and can identify people in their teams who will be ideal to work on innovation projects and to give those people the headspace and encouragement to do so.

1.3 The techies
Characteristics:
- In less polite circles, these lawyers might otherwise be called nerds.
- Likely to build computers in their spare time and to have a bank of Raspberry Pis in their attic that they use as a private server.
- They relish to chance to show off their technical prowess to their peers in a way that is useful to the firm.

Superpowers:
- Sit them alongside the IT department when procuring new software for the firm and they will ask the questions that would never occur to the IT guys to ask.

- They can ensure that the user experience of a new innovation is taken into account right at the outset, so that the roll out and user uptake will be a delight rather than a car crash.

1.4 The strategists
Characteristics:
- Always looking for the direction in which the puck is moving.
- Instinctively good at spotting opportunities.
- Highly commercial.

Superpowers:
- Seeming to occupy helicopters that give a better view than that which is available to everyone else, they bring direction and business justification to propose initiatives and substantiate them to get the green light from the heavies.
- They are essential to ensure that limited resources and time are not wasted on meandering and fruitless quests.

1.5 The agnostics
Characteristics:
- Open minded to the idea of change and innovation and unlikely to actively block it happening.
- But not likely to be putting their hands up to get involved in any meaningful way.
- Often well-established in their own legal practice areas and not facing challenges such that they are personally impelled in any way to explore change or improvement.

Superpowers:
- They are doing a perfectly good job at what they are good at, and not everybody has to be actively involved in pushing innovation forward.

1.6 The sceptics
Characteristics:
- Nay-sayers who think that innovation and technology are really only for commodity work and have no place in 'quality law'.
- Like to wear their scepticism of progress as a badge of honour.
- Usually, but by no means exclusively, of the older generation.

They shouldn't be asked to innovate. Just keep them out of the way of everyone else!

Superpowers:

- None that are particularly useful. The old ones will probably safely make it to retirement. The younger ones will be converted (or otherwise culled for the negativity they engender).

The sceptics are notoriously difficult to handle. In the main, as social psychologist Matthew Hornsey notes, sceptics: don't "[weigh] up evidence in an even-handed way". He adds: "When someone wants to believe something – for whatever reason – then they act more like lawyers trying to prosecute what they already want to be true."[4] In other words, sceptics are prone to manipulate a story to fit their narrative.

Arguably, post-pandemic, there are slightly fewer sceptics in law firms after technology and innovation was able to prove how vital they were in keeping firms afloat. While sceptics do have their place, sometimes as a line of last defence, the authors do wonder whether many of them simply enjoy being grumpily anti-tech (even though most of them have been using tech in their personal and professional lives for years). The best option is to try to convert them to be believers!

2. Understanding how the archetypes interact

These six archetypes build up a mosaic of the variety of people who typically make up the partnership of a 2020s' law firm. In the case studies at the end of this chapter, we examine two projects and how the archetypes can interact well in practice. As these studies show us, every project to bring about change has a different mosaic.

However, we mustn't think of each archetype as being in constant battle with one another, vying for key positions and defending their redoubt at all costs, whether in the firm generally or in projects specifically. This isn't about 'survival of the fittest', an often misunderstood phrase used as shorthand for a dog-eat-dog, cut-throat world view. (It might well be engaging copy for journalists, but it is on dodgy ground from a scientific and business perspective, despite many in the commercial world having taken the phrase to their hearts.)

As it happens, Charles Darwin didn't come up with this memorable phrase anyway. The Victorian biologist's theory of natural selection has never meant that the biggest, strongest, fastest or most aggressive always win like a cackle of aggressive hyenas in a David Attenborough documentary. 'Survival of the fittest' refers to those who are best suited to deal with their environment. In an aggressive environment, the 'fittest' might be those who are constantly at war with one another, but in a non-toxic and progressive firm it's more likely to be those who help each other out the most – what some call 'survival of the friendliest'. It might be those who are the smartest. It all depends on the circumstances.[5] On rare occasions, the odd skirmish might erupt between some of the archetypes on whether a new piece of tech should be introduced or innovative process implemented. But there's usually plenty of quiet, under-the-radar collaboration, and acting like partners in the truest sense of the word.

At the end of Darwin's *On the Origin of the Species* the scientist contemplated a "tangled bank" in which there's a rich ecosystem full of all manner of life. He marvelled at how "these elaborately constructed forms" were so different yet were so dependent on each other "in so complex a manner".[6]

Not unlike a law firm then where complexity is deep within the DNA of the characters in our firms. In our quest to drive our firms forward in a world of 'change3', we must take care not to overlook group dynamics.

Typically, the archetypes interact while working on a project. From the authors' experience good project leaders demonstrate the following (project champions need many of these skills too):

- they are able to work with all of the archetypes in this chapter. They can massage the largest of egos; they can also empower those with imposter syndrome (and who may have valuable contributions to make);
- they are well thought of as experts in what they do, usually with plenty of wins in the bank, or they have the right transferable skills to inspire confidence and gain the legitimacy they need;
- they work collaboratively, but are equally able to lead and act decisively when required. They know when to bash the table, but they equally know not to overplay this sort of tactic;
- they have a nose for office politics but they aren't driven by them;
- they have a vision, backed up by measurable aims and realistic strategies for what they want to achieve. They also know how to communicate this vision to all archetypes. Their main focus isn't on working on a project just for the kudos of doing so (ie, just so they can put it on a partner appraisal form to tick a box);
- they are able to delegate to subordinates. They give subordinates the freedom to decide how to achieve a set of aims, but they also set up a framework to do so (we call this 'freedom within a framework'); they resist the urge to micromanage, but they equally know when they should intervene;
- they are keen to have systems in place to monitor progress, and deploy them wisely. They know that spending too much time monitoring a project, as opposed to actually doing it, is a waste of resources;

There's no doubt that forcing technology and innovation onto unwilling colleagues, without understanding the archetypal dynamics, is a risky strategy. Each archetype has a role to play, even the sceptics from time to time.

- they are resilient. They put the ups and downs in perspective. They have honour in defeat ("sometimes things don't work out; let's try again") and grace in victory ("in fairness, luck came our way a bit");
- they are comfortable processing large volumes of information. They can see the bigger picture when it's more important than attention to detail. Equally, they are able to pivot to the latter where required;
- they are good at spotting where the pressure points are, particularly on the individuals in a team. They don't wait for them to buckle before intervening;
- they are dynamos and know how to keep up momentum and energy. In team meetings, they try to involve all the archetypes and make them as lively as possible;
- they aren't obsessed with hierarchies. They give subordinates the freedom to succeed (and to fail). They are accessible so that relationships can be built;
- they aren't afraid to park a point, record it and come back to it later with fresh eyes. They can say: "we don't know", but they have the drive to find answers and clarity; and
- they foster a safe environment where people don't feel as though they are on the back foot or the defensive all the while. They learn from mistakes ('the past is the past') and invest their energies in the future, not the past.

In successful firms, well-developed soft skills (see Chapter 9) are likely to trump bullying or similar behaviour in bringing successful projects forward. In an increasingly competitive sector, they can make all the difference.

There's no doubt that forcing technology and innovation onto unwilling colleagues, without understanding the archetypal dynamics, is a risky strategy. Each archetype has a role to play, even the sceptics from time to time. For the latter, the strong drink of tech adoption and innovation may need to be sweetened somehow. For others, they may just need a bit more time to adjust. The most keen will be off the starting blocks before the starting pistol has been shot.

The future of law will involve a lot of technology and innovation, but there's a fair amount of people management involved too. Firms need to take care not to overlook this key dynamic.

3. Getting around the status problem

We work in a high-status profession and many of us have achieved high status within it too. 'Survival of the fittest' might certainly feel an apt description for many of us.

And this status can be measured. It turns out that we're almost at the top of the status pedestal. In 1989, the National Opinion Research Center in the US listed over 800 occupations for their occupational prestige.[7] Lawyers came in silver position in the ranking, after physicians who won the gold medal. NORC repeated the survey in 2012 and lawyers were still rated almost at the top.[8] Other surveys over the years might not have been as flattering as this, but, in life generally, we lawyers tend to think quite highly of ourselves, even if we do so in an understated way.

However, status is a strange thing. We like to be recognised and to be validated, although we don't like to admit to it (hence all the 'humble-bragging' on LinkedIn as soon as the latest legal rankings from any directory are published), but the moment we look as though we care about status, the moment our status falls in others' eyes.

The authors suspect that some of us might be quietly fretting about our status in a world of accelerated change and ever-developing tech:

- Doesn't all this technology and innovation put our occupational prestige at risk?
- What if the only way for our status is down? After all, we'll struggle to beat the medical profession – physicians – for the top spot.
- Ultimately, why should we rock the boat and change? Perhaps if we sit here quietly no one will notice and the threat will go away?

Of course, some of us might say to ourselves that we don't care about status one single bit (but would we say that if we didn't have any?).

For the answer, let's quickly go back to the NORC rankings above. The eagle-eyed reader may still be wondering why the authors didn't say who got the bronze medal – just after lawyers. It was computer systems analysts or scientists.

The upshot is that there *is* status, it would seem, in working with technology. Second *and* third place isn't a bad place to be. In the end, we think that lawyers who engage with technology and innovation will see their status *increase*, whereas those that don't will risk a slow deterioration in how they are perceived: they'll be analogue lawyers in a digital world, with none of the retro appeal that has allowed vinyl records to stage a comeback as a viable industry. For analogue lawyers, the only way is down.

4. Understanding the future of advanced lawyers

Let's presume that the status of being a digital lawyer remains high and the talent of tomorrow still wants to progress. But what does this talent look like? What do the future senior leaders, and thus the top of our firms, look like?

Type 'avocado' and 'millennial'[9] into Google – many associate lawyers fall within this definition – and the search engine will usually come up with other questions people ask, such as:

- What is it with millennials and avocados?; or
- Why are avocados associated with millennials?

The green fruit seems to be the go-to symbol for the younger generations. Too much chomping on fancy, la-di-da food today – and not enough getting their hands dirty and grafting seems to be the general, patronising theme. (They should be saving for house deposits instead is another common refrain.) And it isn't just millennials (or 'Generation Y-ers') who are smitten with the fruit. As *City A.M.* reported in 2017, Generation Z reported that this younger generation consumes 226% more avocados than their predecessors.[10]

It all makes for great journalistic copy, but it also makes those in Generations Y and Z look like a bunch of soft-fruit-fixated, live-for-today daydreamers: a classic example where the reductive slapping of labels on people makes it so much easier to dismiss their needs and wants. And yet the Intergenerational Foundation has found that millennials are spending more, not less, on life's essentials than the generations above them. Advanced lawyers need to look beyond the silly stereotypes and facile clichés.

Although there are differences between the generations, and this may impact on how firms structure themselves in the future, they may not be as great as some would lead us to believe:

- In the first known quantitative review of research in this area, an analysis undertaken a decade ago involving almost 20,000 people suggested that, "meaningful differences among generations probably do not exist" (although the word 'meaningful' is doing a lot of heavy lifting there) and that "targeted organisational interventions addressing generational differences may not be effective".[11]
- In 2019, an article in the *Harvard Business Review* declared that generational differences were "quite small"[12] and that the bigger problem isn't any differences *per se*, but a *belief* that there are differences between these cohorts.[13] But even perceived differences have consequences. As this article noted: these sorts of beliefs can "get in

the way"[14] in terms of how we collaborate with each other and thus have "troubling implications" for how people are managed. According to the article, personality differences may matter more than generational differences. Or, put simply, archetypes trump age.

Where does this leave advanced lawyers who are looking to motivate aspiring and associate lawyers to become the leaders of tomorrow?

- Don't forget that the wishes of Generations Y & Z haven't changed that much compared to Generation X or baby boomers, for example, to have an affordable house to call a home and thus be settled to forge ahead in their careers.

- We need to recognise the challenges that Generations Y & Z have gone through, and are going through now, by dint of their coming into the working world at a certain time in history. The Intergenerational Foundation notes, for example, that millennials are "struggling to enjoy the same material standard of living as their parents' and grandparents' generations did at the same stage in life".[15] (This could have unforeseen consequences. As then-OECD secretary-general, Ángel Gurría, said in 2014: "What would be tragic is if the very trait that we count on the young to infuse into our societies – optimism – were to somehow become permanently scarred. We can't afford that.")[16] What can our firms do to help? Do we need to look at what we offer advanced lawyers?

- Question everything in this area. Younger generations are often accused of not being particularly loyal to their employers. We might worry about what this means for the law firms of tomorrow. However, older employees have become more mobile too. According to a report by the Resolution Foundation, millennials are about 30% *less* likely to up sticks and move jobs in their twenties than Generation X before them. Will this continue as they age?

- There *are* differences between the generations. It has always been thus (what generation hasn't tutted and muttered under their breath 'the youth of today!'). But the differences are nowhere near as large as many in the popular press would have us believe. We need to be wary of statements like 'millennials think like this' or 'zoomers will only do that'. This sort of talk tends to widen the perceived schism between the generations, as opposed to bridging the gap. There is no generational war. The pandemic, for example, showed the remarkable solidarity between the old and the young, even though COVID disproportionately affected the former and the measures to protect society disproportionately affected the latter.

In creating the law firms of the future we need to concentrate as much on what we all have in common as opposed to what might divide us from time to time. If we focus on the 'us' as opposed to the 'we' and 'them', then we'll build systems that stand the test of time.

Every day, hour by hour, minute by minute, the old ways of doing things disappear without fanfare and fuss. An everyday item or process has its last day in the office. There are no tears, good-luck cards or farewell drinks. No one notices their passing. It's only when we open a cupboard and see, say, a dusty nest of cables that we're reminded of what once was. And this continues as relentlessly as time passing. Analyst Ming-Chi Kuo, for example, suggests that the Apple iPhone will be obsolete by 2032.[17] It'll be replaced, he believes, by augmented reality.

Our profession, as we know it today, will be unrecognisable in 2030. As advanced lawyers, we've seen remarkable change. There's no doubt that we'll see *a lot* more. Our job now, as senior leaders, isn't to mourn the passing of the world that was, but to lay the groundwork for the world that will be. In bringing a new *status quo* to life, we'll need to summon all of our skills to manage the people with whom we work so we can forge ahead as quickly as we can. We'll need to plan for those who will follow us so that they can embed our legacies. There's a lot to do. But it's an exciting to-do list. And there's no time to waste ...

5. Case studies

5.1 Case study 1: Establishing a connected-services offering
This case study explores the dynamics of creating non-traditional workstreams in the authors' law firm. In recent years, law firms have begun to offer alternative service lines beyond traditional, bread-and-butter legal advice. DWF, for example, launched its connected services division in 2017 and remains an evangelist for offering various legal and other services under one roof. Mishcon de Reya has followed a similar path and set up a corporate structure, the Mishcon de Reya Group, under which it offers various services. Its offerings complement their core areas of work. They range from MDR Brand Management to MDR Cyber, which is the firm's cybersecurity and investigations practice.

This study focuses less on the connected-services solutions themselves and more on how the partners in the firm were able to bring a suite of solutions about and launch them. In a time of 'change3', a surfeit of data and innovative hybrid solutions, it's more important than ever to get the right teams in place, with the right people in them, to drive innovative workstreams forward.

The study uses the archetypes set out earlier in this chapter: the heavies; the 3 Bs (brilliant but busy); the techies; the strategists; the agnostics; and the sceptics. It looks at how the relevant characters in the team were chosen and then managed. It wasn't easy: 'herding cats' is the shop-worn, go-to analogy when lawyers do anything new, but there's an element of truth in this cliché: lawyers can start to wander off in in different directions, particularly if their focus returns to billing targets, as is their wont to do. What's more, like cats, lawyers are independent and don't like being managed. Getting the right mix of archetypes in this project was key.

The project initially involved four out of the six archetypes: one heavy, one strategist, one techie and a handful of brilliant-but-busy partners who completed the line-up:

- A divisional head (a heavy) determined that a suite of connected-services solutions was a priority. The firm's client listening programme revealed client needs, which extended beyond just legal advice. Problems don't come in handy packages marked 'legal only', nor do solutions to them. The firm decided that to add value to the client experience it needed to provide 'more than the law'.
- The heavy picked a partner (a strategist) to deliver the suite of connected services. The heavy recognised that he was best placed to give the project a sense of purpose, champion the project within the firm and set the wheels in motion, but that the commercial acumen, management skills and strong leadership of the strategist would drive the project forward quicker. The strategist was also good at the detail.
- The heavy set the objectives for the strategist and, most important of all, gave him the headspace to deliver it. This meant that fee-earning targets were reduced and that the reduction would be taken into account in his annual performance review.
- The three main objectives of the project were to:
  - offer genuinely clever solutions to meet client needs;
  - increase the firm's reputation and profile for innovation and technology both internally and externally; and
  - spark imitation internally in a 'virtuous circle' of innovation, so that, all being well, even more clever solutions might be developed.
- These three objectives didn't include any financial goals as a primary objective, as it was felt that this would follow the success of the first three.

During the project, the strategist worked with:

- one technology partner (a techie), who spent considerable time on the project – half a day on average for six months;

- several other (brilliant-but-busy) partners, who spent limited time on it (*ad hoc*, as and when required) and who set more junior staff in motion to support all the teams; and
- personnel from the business development, projects and innovation and CQR teams, who were highly engaged, able and a crucial element in propelling the project forward. The IT and finance teams were also involved to a lesser degree.

The result was Shoosmiths8, a suite of 'more-than-just-law' solutions for the firm's clients and prospective clients. These were:
- Innovation Lab: including products like Cia and matters+ (see Chapter 5);
- Contract Lifecycle: a contract management platform;
- The Academy: training on legal and business subjects, including through its eLearning platform;
- Corporate Advisory: a suite of services to help businesses, including a crisis response solution and a solution to help businesses prepare themselves for a sale;
- Privacy & Data: including Automated Privacy Compliance, which uses the privacy management platform developed by software company OneTrust;
- IHL Excellence: a legal ops optimisation service: Hexagon®;
- Real Estate Evolved: a portfolio management tool: Lease Infinity; and
- Community +: a service which allows legal advice to be procured on a direct, seconded basis.

Once the solutions had been developed, but before they'd been launched, the strategist went on an internal roadshow to explain the benefits of the solutions to the partners (who were mainly agnostics and the odd sceptic). This included letting the partners know how to leverage the new products, in connection with the business development team, in a way that took up as little time as possible.

In March 2021, the suite of services was launched. As one of the authors, Tony Randle, said at the time, "they will help [clients] with their business objectives and free up their time – what they have told us is their most precious commodity". Subsequently the firm developed further solutions, including a financial services compliance solution (at the time of writing, the only consultancy model in the legal market for this type of work). In 2022, the initiative won the "Best Strategic Reimagination" at the Managing Partners Forum (MPF) Awards.

5.2 Case study 2: Procuring a document checking system to increase internal efficiency

The case study looks at the importance of getting heavies on board to push proposals forward and get the wheels turning on a tech project. Like the case study above, this case study also uses some of the other archetypes set out earlier in this chapter.

Finetuning contracts sounds simple enough. For years, Word itself has included functionality which is second nature to most lawyers: the much-used 'spelling and grammar' function; keyboard shortcuts, such as 'Ctrl + F'; and the more advanced 'find and replace' function, which, if truth be told, doesn't always find, but often is a bit too keen to replace (changing 'PM' to 'project manager', for example, could suddenly mean that a meeting time is changed to '12.30 project manager').

Tech is great, until it isn't! There's also a lot of off-the-shelf functionality that isn't used or is underused in Word. The firm decided to look at the many other products which are becoming available as Word plug-ins to take document checking to the next level for lawyers. One partner in particular (a strategist) saw the opportunity to increase internal efficiency by procuring a Word plug-in to automatically check documents, such as cross-references, definitions, dates and so on. This task was routinely being undertaken by trainees or junior lawyers. Having made initial enquiries, the strategist estimated that an automated system could save at least 30 to 60 minutes a day (amounting to about 17 days a year) as the reviews would be completed more quickly and consistently, as well as more accurately.

Initially the strategist engaged a techie partner who supported the concept. Together with experienced business-support personnel from the projects and innovation team, they began identifying solutions available on the market. And found one in particular that, on initial scrutiny, seemed appropriate in both functionality and cost. However, to confirm that this system would do the job needed to involve several more people in the firm to trial the system in a live environment to confirm that:
- the functionality was indeed good enough to do what was required of the system;
- the time saved by using the system would deliver the return on investment that the strategist estimated; and
- the system was sufficiently intuitive to use that lawyers would actually use it.

To undertake that detailed testing would require a cross-discipline cohort of professional support lawyers to commit a considerable amount of their valuable time to the project. And that would equally require getting very senior partners onboard to agree that level of resource support at a time when other projects were competing for resource.

Therefore:

- the strategist arranged for the firm's Divisional Heads (heavies) to see a demo of the system at work. Although all the heavies had seen the written business case in advance of the demo, they hadn't realised just how impressive and powerful the software was, or what it would achieve for the firm, until they saw it in action.
- After the demo, the heavies ensured that priority was given to testing the system fully, concluding the procurement and implementing its launch to the firm.

Many law firms have advanced lawyers within them who see themselves as tech or innovation champions. What this case study shows, however, is that there's nothing quite like showing the advantages of innovation to the heavies in a firm, who can really help to move things along at pace if they like what they see.

6. Practical tips on advanced lawyers

We set out below some practical tips on advanced lawyers. These have been split into:

- collective tips (tips for senior partners and management); and
- individual tips (tips for individual partners).

6.1 Tips for senior partners/management

- Play each partner to their own strengths. Not every partner can innovate and not everyone wants to. But for those who do, encourage and facilitate their efforts.
- Set the relevant partners' clear objectives in relation to technology and innovation and give them the headspace to achieve them. And be sure that meeting objectives is rewarded. Without those things, a culture of innovation will never embed at partner level.
- Task the client partners with being inquisitive about clients' current unmet needs and anticipated future needs. And reassure the client partners that they're not responsible for finding solutions to those needs, but identifying the needs in the first place is certainly their job.
- Ask your partners to consider how the services they give their clients might be offered in ways that are more affordable to the client. (As the authors mention in Chapter 6, lawyers want to provide advice, but clients often just want affordable solutions to their needs.) Inevitably, the partners' responses are likely to be conservative, so be prepared to challenge them. (And if they need any motivation to give this due

consideration, point out to them that if they can't think of solutions then chances are that there is another firm out there who will.)

- It might be a daunting prospect for the leadership team in your firm to give your partner cohort the message that change is coming. Many of the partners will naturally regard themselves as the legal equivalents of rocket scientists and will find it hard to countenance that their imperious place in the order of things might be in peril. However, the reality is that peril only exists for them if they fail to recognise that change is coming. As Jim Collins says: "Yes, leadership is about vision. But leadership is equally about creating a climate where the truth is heard and the brutal facts confronted."[18]
- There are those who shout loudly and tend to get heard; and those who don't shout loud enough or at all (and who we need to make a special effort to listen to. They may be the silent majority).
- Consider asking fellow partners to consider into which archetype they would put themselves and then ask them if that is where they really want to be:
  - the heavies;
  - 3 Bs (brilliant but busy);
  - techies;
  - strategists;
  - agnostics;
  - sceptics.
- But tread carefully. Some of the archetypes are usually the most keen to out themselves and celebrate what they do. The agnostics and sceptics, less so. Asking such partners outright might be tricky or counterproductive.
- Apply a balanced score card approach to partner appraisals that takes into account innovation initiatives adequately. Otherwise even those partners who have the most to offer to push the firm forward in its evolution will instead continue to chase billing targets at the expense of the potential benefit to the broader firm.

6.2 Tips for individual partners
- Ask yourself with which archetype you most associate. Are you comfortable with your conclusion? Or would you rather be a different archetype and, if so, how can you change your behaviours to achieve that?
- Chances are that you are currently good at your job, enjoy your job and are valued for doing your job. Ask yourself whether any of those three things might be compromised if your firm falls behind the times.
- Be positive and empathise with your firm's management in their efforts to modernise your firm. It is not an easy task and one made much harder with a dissentient partner cohort.

- Challenge your leadership group if they are not demonstrating that they have a vision and strategy, and related aims, for modernising your firm.
- Realise the opportunity that change offers you. For the right partner with the right attitude and skills, you have the chance to carve your niche, while the legal sector's thinking on innovation is still relatively nascent.

Notes

1   Dr Larry Richard, "Herding Cats: The Lawyers Personality Revealed" (Managing Partner Forum), www.jdsupra.com/post/fileServer.aspx?fName=6ff978fa-f9f1-441e-b65f-e14ae5cd8174.pdf.
2   L Empson, "Leadership, Power, and Politics in Law Firms" in R Normand-Hochman and H Gardner (eds), *Leadership for Lawyers* (Globe Law and Business, 2015), pp89–102, https://openaccess.city.ac.uk/id/eprint/15430/1/Leadership%20power%20and%20politics%20in%20law%20firms%20Empson.pdf.
3   *Ibid.*
4   Melissa Healy, "Psychologists ask: What makes some smart people so skeptical of science?" (*Los Angeles Times*, 21 January 2017), www.latimes.com/science/sciencenow/la-sci-sn-science-skepticism-psychology-20170120-story.html.
5   In recent years, research suggests that 'survival of the friendliest' might have given homo sapiens just what it needed to get to where we are today. As science journalist Kate Ravilious notes: "It may be some of our seemingly deepest vulnerabilities – being dependent on others, feeling compassion and experiencing empathy – that could have given us the edge." (Kate Ravilious, "Survival of the friendliest? Why Homo sapiens outlived other humans" (*New Scientist*, 24 November 2021), www.newscientist.com/article/mg25233625-000-survival-of-the-friendliest-why-homo-sapiens-outlived-other-humans/.)
6   Charles Darwin, *The Origin of the Species and the Voyage of The Beagle* (Vintage, 2009) p913.
7   Keiko Nakao and Judith Treas, "The 1989 Socioeconomic Index of Occupations: Construction from the 1989 Occupational Prestige Scores", GSS Methodological Report No 74, May 1992, https://gss.norc.org/Documents/reports/methodological-reports/MR074.pdf.
8   Tom W Smith and Jaesok Son, "Measuring Occupational Prestige on the 2012 General Social Survey", GSS Methodological Report No 122, October 2014, https://gss.norc.org/Documents/reports/methodological-reports/MR122%20Occupational%20Prestige.pdf.
9   Having done a search on Google using the search term 'Millennial' and 'avocado'. The search was undertaken on 31 August 2022.
10 Nina Edy, "Thought millennials went crazy for avocados? Meet Generation Z" (City AM, 15 September 2017), www.cityam.com/thought-millennials-went-crazy-avocados-meet-generation-z-2/.
11 DP Costanza, JM Badger, RL Fraser *et al*, "Generational Differences in Work-Related Attitudes: A Meta-analysis" (2012) 27 *J Bus Psychol* 375–394, https://doi.org/10.1007/s10869-012-9259-4.
12 Eden King, Lisa Finkelstein, Courtney Thomas and Abby Corrington, "Generational Differences At Work Are Small. Thinking They're Big Affects Our Behavior" (*Harvard Business Review*, 1 August 2019), https://hbr.org/2019/08/generational-differences-at-work-are-small-thinking-theyre-big-affects-our-behavior.
13 Differences, as Professor Bobby Duffy notes, are 'period effects' (things like the pandemic or the 2008 financial crisis) which affect members of society differently; 'lifecycle effects': as we age, we change (in the authors' cases: get grumpier). We start a job, leave home and so on; and 'cohort effects': this is being born at a certain time, in a certain place. This makes someone, say, a Baby Boomer or a Millennial. Having been educated and socialised in different ways, these cohorts can also have different ways of looking at and interacting with the world.
14 See n 12 above.
15 David Kingman, *All Consuming Pressure* (Intergenerational Foundation, 2019), www.if.org.uk/wp-content/uploads/2019/10/All-Consuming_pressure_draft_Final.pdf .
16 Shiv Malik, "Adults in developing nations more optimistic than those in rich countries" (*The Guardian*, 14 April 2014), www.theguardian.com/politics/2014/apr/14/developing-nations-more-optimistic-richer-countries-survey.
17 Sean Keach, "I-GONE World's best Apple expert reveals EXACT year iPhone 'will become obsolete'" (*The Sun*, 26 November 2021), www.thesun.co.uk/tech/16857962/apple-iphone-obsolete-ar-vr-headset-release/.
18 "Confront the Brutal Facts" (Jim Collins), www.jimcollins.com/concepts/confront-the-brutal-facts.html.

Part 5:
The future

Change isn't new. We lawyers have already seen, and thrived off, a massive technology-driven transformation in our profession over the last few decades.

It wasn't so long ago that there were no mobile phones, no emails, and word processing was something new that was only done by the magicians in the document production unit (remember DP?). Some readers may even remember office telex machines which, in their own time, represented the state-of-the-art in electronic business communication.

In those days it was harder to do our job. Every change to a document had to be put in a queue in the DP department. Before Deltaview was introduced, there was no document comparison software, so two articled clerks would sit together, one reading aloud from one document and the second marking the changes on the other version of the document with coloured pens and a ruler. The work was tedious, took longer and was inevitably less accurate than now.

Therefore, when document comparison software was first introduced in the early 2000s, every articled clerk in the land shouted 'hooray' in unison. The software freed them from a truly horrible part of their daily job; it seemed miraculous. We might even have described it as disruptive (a term which, at that time, was only used to describe an unruly toddler at a child's birthday party, but not to describe technology). But fast forward 30 years and software now exists which can review and make *legal* drafting amendments to a contract in a matter of seconds.

Perhaps each is equally miraculous in its own way, in the context of when it came along. But there's a fundamental difference. The task of comparing documents manually could have been done by anyone who could read, had an eye for detail and a lot of patience. It didn't really require someone with legal training to do it. Contrast that with AI contract review software, which does what *only* a legally trained and experienced lawyer (or experienced contract professional) can do. The difference is, the authors suggest, that the former was clever, but the latter is truly disruptive.

With every technological advance the lawyer's job has become more efficient and less laborious. It has led to faster and more accurate outcomes for clients.

And so we can be absolutely certain that the changes that we can all expect to come our way over the next decade or two will be at least equally (and probably even more) miraculous, life-changing, exciting, challenging and enabling in equal measure. This part looks at this change in more detail and what you can do to prepare for it.

In the 1987 film, *Wall Street*, the singularly unlikeable Gordon Gekko made a speech that captured the zeitgeist of that era. It's often simplified to: "Greed is good. Greed is right. Greed works." As you enter this part of the book, the authors would like to suggest a modern-day twist on Gekko's speech:

"Change is good. Change is right. Change works."

Chapter 12:
Horizon-gazing

At sea-level, stood on a beach, we can't see further than about three miles.

At the top of Everest, on the other hand, our line of sight soars to over 200 miles – the distance, as the crow flies, of London to Cornwall.

But even if we were to draw an imaginary circle of this radius around Everest's summit, and had the skills, stamina and strength to drag ourselves up this behemoth of a mountain, we'd still not see everything within that invisible circle.

If we take the standard route up, for example, we can't see the base camp where we started from. Neighbouring features, like Lhotse – itself the fourth highest peak in the world – obscure the view too. It's what mountains do.

After a lifetime of training and years of sacrifice, we might scratch and claw our way to the top. But then see nothing. The clouds roll in and remove the world's highest panorama from view, like an overzealous museum curator moving a precious artefact out of the elements for safekeeping. Even our exhausted climbing partners, from time to time, block what we can see as they edge towards you on the way up.

Put simply, you'd see what the landscape and circumstances allow us to see.

However, the common perception of horizon-gazing is that all lines of sight are unencumbered, as though, by sheer luck, we're on the only conical-shaped mountain in a landscape that's otherwise flatter than a Dutch polder.

You can almost see it all and thus work out what's coming, and what to do next. In the main, everything's neat and, if we know the rules, predictable.

If only it were that easy.

The problem with horizon-gazing in real life is that, without fail, it involves humans in some way: messy, passionate, irrational and unpredictable humans. And being unpredictable, humans can, of course, be measured, dispassionate and rational too. We do it all with a predictable unpredictability. (Species status: 'it's complicated'.)

Therefore, in this chapter, what the authors see in our field of vision is a subjective affair. Think more the ups and downs, blind spots and shadows forming in the mist of the mountains, rather than the certainty and monotony of the flatlands. The authors have selected the features that have piqued our interest or caught our imaginations and, in some cases, we've highlighted the things we've not had the time to look at earlier in the book. It's a very human affair.

The authors know, of course, we've missed things. But we're okay with that. After all, even if the mountain was infinitely high we'd only ever be able to see half the world; the hemisphere on the other side would remain forever out of view. The purpose of this chapter is to whet our appetites for some of the changes to come. We'll try to give as high a mountain as possible and nudge the reader to do their own reading and research into the areas that most interest them. It's time for us to grab a bit of Kendal Mint Cake, work through the inevitable sugar rush, and plan our own expeditions to the metaphorical summits of our own choosing.

Climber George Mallory, when asked "why climb Everest?", allegedly retorted "because it's there".[1]

The same answer could equally be given for planning for the future. We just need to start. As we look ahead of us, 'change3' means that we need to redouble our efforts to see and manage what's coming. We need to embed a future-focused mindset in our firms.

After all, if we ignore the future, we forsake the agency we have in shaping the future we want. We risk becoming irrelevant if we cannot evolve to give our clients the service they need and deserve.

In this chapter, we examine:
- horizon-scanning in the business of law; and
- horizon-scanning in the practice of law.

The chapter then goes on to look at some case studies and set out practical tips so that the reader can look to the future with confidence.

1. Horizon-scanning in the business of law

We start with the business of law.

Most of us read the legal and other press from time to time, but things get missed. In a time of information overload: a must-have piece of legaltech or new way of working could prove to be a gamechanger for a firm, but they're lost in a fog of information. A more methodical and formal approach means we lessen the risk of overlooking things that could really make a difference.

When we look to the future, we need to ask:
- What do firms need to take notice of and what can they ignore?
- What about future-gazing for our clients? (There may be legaltech and innovation which could be a gamechanger for them too.)

1.1 Formal horizon-scanning
In firms, formal horizon-scanning is often done by partners who have been tasked to do it. They are sometimes helped by project management teams, professional support lawyers and the IT team.

They may use materials from a variety of sources:
- The Law Society has published a suite of materials, which it links to on its *Future Worlds 2050* project website;[2]
- the *Playbook for Strategic Foresight and Innovation* contains guidance on "futuretelling";[3] and
- in the public sector, *The Futures Toolkit* from the Government Office for Science sets out four tools for gathering intelligence about the future and processing what's unearthed.[4]

1.2 Informal horizon-scanning
Horizon-scanning also relies on something that can all too often be dismissed by many people: our gut feelings. As *The Futures Toolkit* notes:[5]

Horizon Scanning is relatively straightforward but does rely on intuition and insight – which can feel counterintuitive to those who are more practiced in evidence based strategic thinking. The hardest part for many [horizon-scanners] is knowing whether something they have read is interesting or different enough to include in the scan. Scanners should always err on the side of being irrelevant.

The brain has been described as "a large predictive machine".[6] Intuitive thoughts may seem to appear out of thin air in a scattergun fashion, but trusting our instincts can still have value: they may well be trying to shine a light on something important. And if we back it up with formal analysis we may be onto something.

1.3 Seeing through the hype

A colleague bursts into the room. They catch your eye and rush over. Pleasantries done, they start talking about an amazing bit of tech that "revolutionises" how lawyers work. Little of it makes sense, although it does sound impressive. You nod in all the right places, but your head is spinning. In a time of 'change3', how do we know what to get excited about and what to quietly ignore (for now)? Some organisations have started to chart the ebbs and flows of hype, which clings to so much tech.

In particular, research and consulting firm Gartner creates well-known guides – "Hype Cycles" – on technology, which are updated relatively regularly and split into five key stages. Its aim is to cut through the hype that clings to new innovations. What's more, its analysis (such as its September 2021 *Hype Cycle for Legal and Compliance Technologies*)[7] can be a useful, if somewhat jargon-heavy, tool to work out where today's 'Big New Thing' sits on the cycle.[8]

The five Hype Cycle stages[9] are:
- Innovation Trigger (formerly the Technology Trigger): after a 'eureka!' moment, word gets out that a snazzy bit of tech is the smarter, faster and better solution to a problem that's been bugging the legal profession for years.
- Peak of Inflated Expectations: The buzz builds. Numerous breathless articles admonish lawyers for paying little or no heed to this new 'Big New Thing'. Often a frenzied bubble of investment follows. The world will never be the same!
- Trough of Disillusionment: it turns out the tech has numerous teething difficulties. Expectations weren't managed. What were we thinking? The brave new world is dead.
- Slope of Enlightenment: long live the brave new world! The brave souls who stuck with the new tech have bedded it in and, well, it's

not too bad after all. In fact, it's pretty impressive. They've worked out what works and what doesn't and are reaping the benefits.
- Plateau of Productivity: everyone else piles in. The tech becomes the 'new normal'.

When we're investigating an item of tech, we may or may not agree with where Gartner places it. At worst, Gartner may use a term which is so wide it's difficult to see why they've placed it where it is on the cycle. Some key technologies may also find themselves scattered throughout these cycles and are difficult to pin down.

AI is a particularly well-known miscreant in this area. The tech has been through good spells and bad spells over the years. These are sometimes referred to as 'AI summers' and 'AI winters' – so splitting up this tech and placing it on Gartner's model isn't an obvious task. And the true promise of AI always seems to be for tomorrow, not today (although, as we see in the case study in Chapter 5, AI-powered tech, such as that found in contract review tools, is having an impact).

The authors' view is that the Hype Cycles and accompanying insight can be of some use to firms looking to understand trends and patterns in the marketplace generally. But, as with all methodologies, they should be taken with a pinch of salt.

1.4 Understanding the market in England and Wales
Numerous reports have been published to understand the state of where we are in England and Wales:
- In 2019, the Law Society published its report *Lawtech Adoption Research*.[10] Its 'market maturity' model, like Gartner's, has five key stages of tech adoption:
  - Innovators;
  - Early Adopters;
  - Early Majority;
  - Late Majority; and
  - Laggards.
- In 2022, the LSB published a report: *Social acceptability of technology in legal services*.[11] The LSB report (commissioned jointly with the SRA) also included stages, but it had one less stage of tech adoption than the Law Society above.

None of the timelines mirror each other in full. Unlike Gartner, for example, the Law Society and the LSB are less concerned about the innovation end of the model and are much more interested about the adoption end; that is: when any given item of tech starts to hit a critical mass in the sector (this

Forecasting the future isn't easy, but this hasn't stopped some from trying.

often happens after what it calls the "chasm": the stage between the Early Adopters and Early Majority). This is roughly how the models compare:

Figure 1. Authors' comparison of market maturity models

Gartner	Innovation trigger	Peak of inflated expecta-tions	Trough of disillu-sionment	Slope of enlightenment		Plateau of productivity		
Law Society	Innovators			Early adopters	**Chasm**	Early majority	Late majority	Laggards
LSB	Early adopters					Early majority	Late majority	Resistors

Understanding where we are at any given time with any given bit of technology is important. It helps us ask questions such as "do we buy this tech now? Or should we wait a bit?" But as the above shows, it is equally important to be aware of the differences in the available models to optimise the timing of any adoption.

The Law Society report also makes an important point:

> *It is very hard to forecast the timescale in which 'maturity' is likely to happen. Experience tells us that, for most sectors, technologists tend to overestimate the speed of maturity.*[12]

Forecasting the future isn't easy, but this hasn't stopped some from trying. For example, the Law Society, in the conclusion to its 2019 report, nailed its colours to the mast for the five-year period from 2019 to 2024. It thinks that, for example:

- the highest impact will be with AI (and machine learning) in BigLaw firms and in-house. Adoption of AI will be "good" in Biglaw firms, but a bit less so in-house. AI (and ML) will have just a "medium" impact in 'PeopleLaw' firms (such as high-street firms);
- cloud-based on-demand services will also have a high impact in BigLaw firms and in-house, but adoption levels will be lower than with AI (and ML);
- blockchain won't have a big impact and there'll be "no or rare adoption" (although see our views later on blockchain); and
- robotic process automation (RPA) and natural language processing (NLP) will sit in the middle with a "medium" impact across the board, but various levels of adoption.

And there's plenty of technology that doesn't figure in this report, such as smart contracts.

The key with horizon-gazing is to accept its inherent uncertainty and find the sweet spot between underpreparing and overthinking. We can spend too long thinking about every future variable. Do too little of it and we might head off in the wrong direction. Do too much of it and we might end up doing nothing at all. In particular, the extent of future regulation of law firms is unknown. The LSB notes: "Legal services regulators must tend the flame of technological innovation. They must minimise the risks that it creates, while helping it to do as much good as possible."[13] The detail of how this will be done is still to be played out.

But in the practice of law there's a lot which is happening now. In what follows, we look at how regulation itself is likely to change. The rules of making the rules are being rethought to deal with a world of 'change3'.

2. Horizon-scanning in the practice of law generally

The practice of law: the bread and butter of what lawyers do. What will regulation look like? How will it work in the future? These are questions that all lawyers need to ask themselves. How we do things now isn't necessarily how we will do things in the future.

This chapter starts by looking at trends in future regulation to understand how new technology and innovation might be regulated or, indeed, not regulated. We then explore some specific areas which we need to be aware of.

2.1 Understanding the growing impact of 'code is law'

First, we need to step back and remind ourselves that rules which regulate our lives, and our online lives in particular, are not just confined to statutory law, case law and any soft law, such as guidance and codes of practice. What's more, other codes, such as computer code, increasingly tell us what we can and can't do.[14] If we ignore any of these rules then, to be frank, we won't be able to see the bigger picture.

Tech companies, in particular, influence many aspects of our lives through the code (and rules within it) that *they* write and the terms and conditions by which we agree to be bound. Consider how Apple and Google in effect decided how the NHS COVID contact tracing app would work in practice. An update to the app was blocked by these companies. In effect, the government played second fiddle to Big Tech.

We underestimate the power of this code at our peril. Lawyers will need to be aware of how these rules will increasingly rule our lives.

2.2 Regulating good ol' law (the traditional type)

But let's not get too ahead of ourselves. There will *still* be plenty of traditional new law for us to get our teeth into, although, there's no doubt this law is struggling to keep up with 'change3' and the exponential exploding into life of technology and innovation.

But our institutions, politics and laws aren't following the same trajectory. Theirs is a more sedate world. Modernising our institutions and creating new laws is like trying to make an oil tanker change course. It takes time, if it happens at all.

The result? There's a growing gap. Tech expert Azeem Azhar calls it an "exponential gap"; others refer to it as a "pacing problem".[15]

Figure 2. Comparison between the pace of technological change and pace of political change

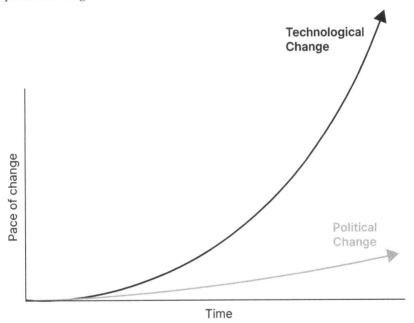

When advising in the future, we're going to come across this gap much more: the law hasn't caught up with the reality on the ground. This is likely to get even worse in the years to come, unless we forge a different, more agile path. We need to be honest with ourselves: our systems aren't up to the task.

(a) More regulation

Big Tech recognises the growing gap and says it would like to see more regulation. Microsoft's Brad Smith, for example, says: "Tech companies have become too important to be left to a *laissez-faire* policy approach today. They need to be subject to the rule of law and more active regulation."[16] Facebook's CEO, Mark Zuckerberg, has called for tighter regulation on online harms.

In its integrated review, *Global Britain in a competitive age*, published in March 2021, the government also referred to the need for "ethical and legal frameworks that foster public trust and early adoption".[17]

(b) Better regulation

Regulation needs to be done better too. In July 2021, DCMS set out its *Plan for Digital Regulation*. In it the Department for Digital, Media, Culture & Sport (DCMS) set out its "new, ground-breaking approach" to digital regulation. The government said it will take a "proportionate and agile" approach, which will get rid of "unnecessary burdens" and thus offer "clarity and confidence to businesses and consumers".[18]

There's certainly lots of ambition in these statements. And who'd disagree with any of them? They're statements, perhaps, of the obvious. In practice, only time will tell whether these sorts of joined-up thinking initiatives, including the creation of the Digital Regulation Cooperation Forum (DRCF), will bear any fruit. In the meantime, there are plenty of other challenges that we face too, as we consider the types of regulation on which we'll be advising our clients.

- There's the tendency to add to regulation, and not subtract from it.
- There's the tendency to think that Big Tech represents all tech firms and regulate accordingly. The internet, of course, isn't just Silicon Valley and its overseas equivalents.
- There's 'cakism' (having your cake and eating it). This is where authorities proclaim that they want a 'win-win' solution, even where one isn't on the table. They want to, for example, deregulate, but also safeguard consumers at the same time. They're trying to square circles that can't always be squared.
- Finally, there's the pressure to do something even where something doesn't need to be done. There's nothing the press loves more, from time to time, than whipping itself up into a frenzy of indignation – and often ignorance – about a new tech craze. 'Ban it!', they scream. All the while, technology like AI, which is everywhere, but somewhat invisible, has been mostly ignored to date.

LawtechUK says that policymakers need to ensure that "the law itself is fit for purpose" and helps in the "adoption of technologies and modern ways of working".[19] But governments, of all colours, struggle to regulate tech well and in a timely manner. Regulation is tough to get right; and usually lags behind innovation. It's full of time-consuming compromises. Are we lawyers ready for this messy world? We'll need to be.

(c) More self-regulation and standards
There are alternatives to hard law and soft law. The government also wants to encourage, where appropriate:
- self-regulation; and
- non-regulatory measures like technical standards.

We are likely to see more of these approaches in the future.

Unfortunately, we lawyers tend to pooh-pooh technical standards, even though they're rules, albeit of a different kind to what we're used to. We seem to prefer parliamentary laws and judgments from courts. They have a certain cachet that standards don't seem to have (perhaps it's because, from the first day of law school, we've been taught, in detail, how these top-down rules are made). Standards, on the other hand, are often collaborations put together out of the limelight of legislative or court procedure, such as the technical, commercial and industrial standards developed by the ISO.

The authors' view is that we'll need to be canny at recognising where the 'regulatory gap' exists; be more comfortable dealing with less traditional ways of rulemaking; and also be fine with advising where there are no rules at all.

We also think that there's scope for the certification of certain types of technology (eg, an ISO-style standard for legaltech), but perhaps more realistically some form of assurance scheme might be a more pragmatic place to start. For example, that client confidential information is secured appropriately, that functionality and accuracy levels make the technology fit for its intended use case and so on. Not only could this safeguard the consumers of legal advice delivered through technology (and thereby foster their trust) but it would also make it much easier for law firms to adopt technology confident that it works, rather than having to test it to destruction in trials before buying, as we currently do.

In the next section:
- we look at some of the areas where we're likely to see significant change (these are in alphabetical order); and
- we also look at how firms can scan the horizon for such changes.

There's no doubt that there are many areas where more up-to-date or new rules would be welcome. For example, the Social Market Foundation, in an October 2021 report (sponsored by Mishcon de Reya), called for a legal modernisation commission to "modernise English law so that it is 'fit' for the 21st century economy".[20] This would include creating rules for:

- new tech such as AI, additive manufacturing (including 3D printing), biotechnology and blockchain;
- new business concerns, such as CSR and ESG; and
- the changes in the way businesses are run, such as the growth in digital trade.

AI, in particular, is an area where comprehensive rules are at present conspicuous by their absence. How long can this hold?

3. Horizon-gazing specific areas for FutureLaw

As with horizon scanning in the business of law, a similar approach works for the practice of law. When we look to the future, we need to ask:

- What legal developments do firms need to take notice of for their own businesses?
- What legal developments do our clients need to know about and be ready for?

Many businesses adopt more formal horizon-scanning techniques. For example, global food and drink multinational Nestlé has to track legal developments in the almost 200 countries and territories in which it operates. To this end, it has created an online tool, Legal and Compliance Radar, for various functions in its business to "visualise and track legislative and regulatory trends".[21] The multinational started with data privacy and has moved onto other areas with a tech flavour and also sustainability. Nestlé is also seeing to what extent it can use technology, such as algorithms, to fine-tune the tool and to ensure interoperability with other platforms.

With 'change3' and the increasing amount of hard law, soft law and other rules, horizon-scanning in the practice of law is something that we all need to get better at.

The authors don't set out an exhaustive list below. There are so many areas which we could have covered. So we've had to be pretty brutal in what we've left out for fear of the book ballooning into an unwieldy encyclopaedia of developing laws. There are plenty of books which look at developments in specific areas of law in a more detailed way from data governance in AI and legaltech to guides to cryptoassets for private clients.

What about other new areas of law, such as autonomous vehicles and the related liability issues? Or drones, where we've already started to see an increase in regulation in recent years? Or even cutting-edge science, such as neurotechnology: one report in August 2022 suggested that in the future lawyers may be able to bill clients by "units of attention"?[22] Alas, they're not for this book on this occasion.

Even where we deal with a topic, there's a cut-off point. For example, we look at the metaverse, but not whether new laws of meta-workplace safety will be needed to protect staff and stop abuse or bullying; or what IP ownership rights will be in this space.

Nevertheless, here are some of the main areas which the authors think lawyers need to keep a keen eye on in the years to come.

3.1 Algorithms

An algorithm is a set of automated instructions which tells a computer what to do to complete a task. Algorithms can be:

- simple: making a cup of tea, for example, is an algorithm: there are steps that need to be followed to get from an empty to a full mug ready to drink; or
- complicated: increasingly complicated algorithms, including those which are powered by AI, will be the 'engines' that make the tech we use smarter.

To be optimally efficient (and to deliver consistently high-quality output), the legal profession needs to improve significantly the processes by which we practise law. For example, methodologies like contract playbooks, which often contain flowcharts and checklists, are a type of algorithm. And getting these algorithms right from the start will be vital. The trick is to develop robust playbooks from the outset so that any computer automation of them is based on the right processes and outputs (see Chapter 5). As with most things, algorithms are only as good as their creators.

We should also expect to see more regulation of algorithms in the future, so we'll need to keep an eye on developments. There's no doubt that the power of algorithms, and the biases that can inadvertently be baked into them, are underestimated. They can affect, for example, the most basic of things we do in life, such as where we live (through the algorithms used when we apply for a mortgage); where we work (through the algorithms used to peruse CVs); and what qualifications we gain (standardisation algorithms, which were used to award GCSE and A-level grades in 2020 caused a public outcry when many grades were downgraded). The law will increasingly want to peer under the covers to see what is going on.

We're also likely to see more guidance:

- Already, the ICO produces guidance on the use of algorithms in the context of personal data.
- In November 2021, the Central Digital and Data Office (CDDO), which is part of the Cabinet Office, published one of the world's first national algorithmic transparency standards for the government and public sector. The hope is that it will help to deliver greater transparency in the public sector. In particular, the algorithmic transparency template asks policymakers to provide two types of information:
  - 'Tier 1' information: this is how and when the algorithmic tool is being used:
    - What problem is being solved using the algorithm?
    - What's the justification or rationale for using the algorithm?
    - How can people find out more about the algorithm or ask a question?
  - 'Tier 2' information: this is where much of the detail is set out.

Will this influence the templates for any future regulation of algorithms? Alas, only time will tell. We shouldn't be surprised if it does. Algorithms may also end up being regulated under laws to do with our next subject: AI.

3.2 AI

[The] consideration of AI is another example of how everything changes, and nothing changes. The technologies and opportunities are new, but the fundamental principles – of maintaining trust, of asking if data is being used fairly and transparently – remains constant.
Elizabeth Denham[23]

Everything changes; and yet nothing changes. At a fundamental level, the future of AI will see us tracing a path between these two contradictory statements. So much has changed in terms of the AI that is now commercially available to apply in the practice of law. But, so far, not much has changed, as far as the law relating to AI is concerned. And it's not just a legal path that we need to tread. There are other paths on AI that lawyers need to navigate too: moral and ethical, to name just two. At times, all of these paths will converge; at times, they'll diverge. These paths will flit and dance around the regulatory landscape. The hope is that, in the main, they do so together; the worry is that they do not. This is an area of deep complexity.

Given the speed of change, there's certainly never been a greater urgency for lawyers, of all disciplines, to think about AI in a more profound way, even if the amount of specific laws on AI at the moment aren't going to worry the editors of *Halsbury's Laws of England* anytime soon. There are innumerable moral, ethical and philosophical quandaries to think through. What approach should we take in using this technology? How much of our lives, and free will, do we want to expose to AI? To what extent can we use AI to regulate AI itself?

In September 2021, the *Harvard Business Review* was in no doubt that "AI regulation is coming"[24] globally. The frustration for many lawyers is that the law has barely begun its AI journey. At present, the complaints are coming through thick and fast. The Office for AI says, for example, that it's unclear and unpredictable. To complicate matters further, the remits of some regulators overlap and, worst of all, there are gaps in the law where there's no regulation at all:

- To fill any regulatory gaps, it's unlikely that we'll see a 'General AI Regulation' in the United Kingdom. The government believes there's "a big limitation in what can be covered in cross-cutting legislation on AI".[25] Instead, the Office for AI says that the government's approach will be "proportionate", "risk-based" and "light-touch".[26] In particular, regulation will be "context-specific". It also proposes "to delegate responsibility for designing and implementing proportionate regulatory responses to regulators", ensuring coherence through bodies such as the Digital Regulation Cooperation Forum (DRCF). If regulators take different approaches AI laws are likely to become complex quickly. And given the role that AI will play in our society is "light-touch" regulation enough?
- Guidance, which often fills legal gaps, is still in its infancy. The Law Society *Lawtech and Ethics Principles*,[27] published in 2021 are a useful start for law firms. The ICO also has guidance on the use of AI in the context of processing personal data. But guidance is still neither deep nor wide enough generally.

Already the practical and beneficial effects that AI is having on the profession are turning out to be remarkable (as, for example, we show in Chapter 2). The time to look at AI isn't 10 years in the future. Or in five years. It's now. The opportunities are there to be seized.

Be in no doubt, AI will upend many areas of law and a lot of new laws will be needed to deal with it. As we show in Chapter 2, AI will be used by lawyers to help them do what they do in a smarter, faster and better way. Lawyers will also advise their clients on AI rules and guidance, and possibly the ethics too. The Centre for Data Ethics and Innovation in its 2021 "roadmap to an effective AI assurance ecosystem" noted that businesses using AI "will increasingly rely on ... independent assurance providers to assess and manage AI risks, and to demonstrate and monitor regulatory compliance" and that it's "an area in which the UK is well positioned to

We also need to keep an eye on developments so we can future-proof our use of AI to the extent that we can. After all, retrofitting compliance is a thankless task, and often isn't even possible.

excel, drawing on strengths in legal and professional services".[28] In December 2022, an independent 'industry temperature check' report noted that "AI assurance can provide organisations with 'a competitive edge', through building customer trust and managing reputational risk".[29] Are we ready to take advantage of this competitive edge?

We also need to keep an eye on developments so we can future-proof our use of AI to the extent that we can. After all, retrofitting compliance is a thankless task, and often isn't even possible. Keeping an eye on international developments too can help many businesses achieve best practice before their competitors.[30]

If we succeed in using AI to its best advantage, the results in the business of law, in particular, could mean:
- freeing up lawyers' time to place a greater emphasis on EQ (see Chapter 9); and
- a better work/life balance: the long-hours culture could be a thing of the past if we can crack Parkinson's Law (where work expands to fill the time given to it) and implement other potential changes like a four-day work week. Productivity, client satisfaction and profitability can all increase, while seeing less burn out, more enjoyment, better output, and greater job satisfaction. What's not to like!

3.3 Blockchain (including smart contracts and cryptoassets)
Sorry to be a wet blanket. Writing a description for this thing [ie, Bitcoin] for general audiences is bloody hard. There's nothing to relate it to.
Satoshi Nakamoto[31]

Who is Satoshi Nakamoto, who gave the above quote? As it happens, we don't know. The name is possibly a pseudonym for the elusive individual (or individuals) who developed Bitcoin, which is still the most well-known (and most successful) use of blockchain. The Bitcoin software was released in 2008, and the founder of this cryptocurrency has been the subject of frenzied speculation as to their identity over the years. Having been shown by Nakamoto how blockchain technology can be used to give Bitcoin its decentralised and immutable features, people have speculated for years what the technology will be used for. It's an area which is stuffed full of jargon and initialisms, which can make it hard even for the most techie of lawyers to get their heads around.

But we need to understand what's going on in this sphere sooner rather than later. As we mention in Chapter 2, in January 2022, the Master of the Rolls, Sir Geoffrey Vos, said that "every lawyer will require familiarity with the blockchain, smart legal contracts and cryptoassets".[32] As always, we don't need to understand *everything* about the underlying tech, but we do need to understand what it can do for our clients and in our businesses. Indeed, the authors believe that blockchain will become hugely useful in, for example, verification of title. In 2017, HM Land Registry launched its Digital Street initiative and explored whether it could use blockchain to deliver transformational change in property ownership.[33]

So what is blockchain? At its simplest, blockchain is a type of distributed ledger technology (DLT). DLT technologies typically store, synchronise and manage digital records across vast networks of computers. In the case of blockchain, data is stored in the ledger in blocks, with each new block that is added to the ledger being linked (cryptographically) to the last block (hence 'blockchain').

Recording information in this way in a blockchain means that it shouldn't be possible to change the data in any existing block as this would break the 'link' to the next block (and all subsequent blocks in the chain) – a principle known as 'immutability' – and this would be identified by the computers managing and verifying additions to the blockchain. This prevents changes, fraudulent or otherwise, to the existing data on the blockchain. Once data is on the blockchain, it stays there.

The main use of this technology is currently in cryptocurrencies like Bitcoin and Ethereum. In the DLT world, there is a saying that "all blockchains are DLT, but not all DLT are blockchains". Blockchain is considered to be a form of DLT but not the only form. For example, a DLT doesn't necessarily need to have a data structure in blocks or have those blocks linked in a 'chain'.

In the legal sphere, DLT technologies can also be used in smart legal contracts. However, for many reasons, some remain agnostic about this technology, including:

- The benefits of blockchain haven't always been explained well. We need to go back to basics and craft narratives. Lawyers are busy people. Often the materials on this subject bamboozle us with jargon. So we lose interest. For example, the comprehensive *Blockchain Legal and Regulatory Guidance*, a leading legal resource on blockchain (see below), includes prose such as "when NFTs first became technically possible in 2017, when Ethereum added a new standard, ERC-721, to its platform, one of the first uses was a game called CryptoKitties, which allowed users to trade and sell virtual kittens".[34] As great as this resource is, for a lot of people, language like this makes little sense (as lovely as virtual kittens sound).
- What's more, despite a lot of the breathless copy by 'cryptopians',

blockchain isn't the solution to everything. But no one seems to be able to agree what its impact will be. Contrast the Law Society's report on legaltech adoption to 2024, which reckons that blockchain's impact will be low, with "no or rare adoption",[35] with Sir Geoffrey Vos' statement above, saying "get ready for big changes". Some say that conventional technologies could solve many of the problems that blockchain proports to solve if businesses "put their minds to it".[36] So who's right and who's wrong?

Well, time has certainly moved on since the Law Society's report. It seems likely that, in the next few years, blockchain's time will arrive to some extent.

There's certainly been a lot of work in this area, in particular:
- in November 2019, the UK Jurisdiction Taskforce published its *Legal statement on cryptoassets and smart contracts;*[37]
- in April 2021, the UK Jurisdiction Taskforce published its *Digital Dispute Resolution Rules;*[38]
- in January 2022, the TLA and the Law Society published the second edition of *Blockchain Legal & Regulatory Guidance.*[39] This guidance has ballooned from 141 pages in its first edition to 236 pages in this edition. Updates to this guidance will be published regularly; and
- in March 2022, the Law Commission published its report on electronic trade documents.[40] In July 2022, it also published new proposals to reform the law relating to digital assets.[41]

Ultimately, the benefits of DLTs such as blockchain go to the heart of our relationships in business and in life: trust. Professionals such as lawyers are 'trust intermediaries' who facilitate transactions – think of escrow and solicitor's undertakings, for example. In the digital future, trust is likely to reside increasingly in technology like blockchain. No single entity is in charge of a blockchain, as it's decentralised and isn't stored in one place and additions to the blockchain need to be verified (through a set consensus mechanism) by those computers managing and verifying the blockchain, so the theory is therefore that it can't be manipulated easily for fraudulent or other purposes by a bad actor.

However, the key question that we need to ask when looking to use any type of blockchain is can we trust it in practice? As cryptographer and computer security expert, Bruce Schneier, notes in *WIRED*: "You need to trust the cryptography, the protocols, the software, the computers and the network. And you need to trust them absolutely, because they're often single points of failure."[42] Blockchain is only as strong as the weakest link in the above factors. An open and decentralised blockchain is also difficult to square

In the years to come key stakeholders, including lawyers, will need to become far more familiar with this technology, to grapple with these challenges and come up with answers.

with data protection such as the GDPR in respect of personal data stored on the blockchain on a number of levels including the right to erasure (now the UK GDPR).

In the years to come key stakeholders, including lawyers, will need to become far more familiar with this technology, to grapple with these challenges and come up with answers.

(a) Smart contracts and smart 'legal' contracts

Elon Musk is reported as having said: "I'm too dumb to understand smart contracts."[43] A bit too self-deprecating perhaps? The authors think so as, compared with many other technologies, the concepts are easier to grasp (and Elon Musk is no intellectual slouch).

Smart contracts are not new. The idea was introduced some 20 years ago, but we were only able to use smart contracts with the introduction of Ethereum (a decentralised blockchain – first launched in 2015 – that uses Ether as its native cryptocurrency). Nowadays there are many blockchains that have smart contract functionality.

A smart contract is simply a program that typically runs on a blockchain. It's machine-readable computer code (in whole or in part) that has a degree of automation coded into it, which is linked to the occurrence of a specific event or meeting of a condition. A smart contract may or *may not* be legally binding, depending on whether it meets the rules for the formation of a legally binding contract.

A smart legal contract is a type of smart contract that *is* a legally binding contract. Traditional principles of contract law also still apply. Smart legal contracts may be stored on a blockchain (although not all are). Typically, the contract includes equations such as: 'if x does y, then payment goes to z'. Smart legal contracts have potential application in a vast number of use cases, from, for example, the automated production of management accounts under investment agreements to the automatic payment of dividends to investors. And combined with the Internet of Things, the scope is even broader. Imagine a car leasing agreement, which typically limits the annual mileage and obliges regular servicing. The car already has inbuilt monitors of mileage and servicing, so the car could confirm contractual compliance or breach and send that data to the smart contract which could then automatically deduct payment from the driver for non-compliance. (This stuff makes Robocop look positively Dickensian.)

Smart legal contracts appear in one of three forms.
- Natural-language contract with the performance of it using computer

code. Performance, in whole or part, is done automatically. This form is unlikely to raise (many) novel legal issues.

- Hybrid contract where some obligations are defined in computer code and the rest in natural language. How far code is used varies widely.
- Code-only contract (ie, where no natural language version exists). This form presents the most potential challenges on contract formation and interpretation. These are likely to be rare given that it would be difficult to distil a complex commercial contract into computer code.

Smart legal contracts are increasingly being considered by businesses. In November 2021 the Law Commission noted that additional legislation isn't needed for smart legal contracts to work in England and Wales:

Current legal principles can apply to smart legal contracts in much the same way as they do to traditional contracts, albeit with an incremental and principled development of the common law in specific contexts. Although some types of smart legal contract may give rise to novel legal issues and factual scenarios, existing legal principles can accommodate them.[44]

However, the Law Commission does state further work is required on the law on deeds and private international law "to support the use of smart contract technology in appropriate circumstances".[45]

But smart legal contracts do raise new considerations:

- What are the rules of legal interpretation for computer code? For example, how is the concept of the 'reasonable person' to be interpreted? It can't mean a reasonable computer as no such thing exists. Therefore, perhaps it means a 'reasonable coder'?
- Standardisation is also needed. To date there hasn't been a universally accepted way of digitising commercial and legal documentation. The UK Legal Schema aims to fix this by creating a "generalised universal structured data format for the creation of digital contract".[46]
- Self-executing smart legal contracts could bring down a company or financial institution before a human being is able to intervene. What safeguards are built in? What happens if there are coding errors?
- Will lawyers who work with smart legal contracts need to become coders? (Or at least have the skills to vet or validate the code of a smart legal contract?)

Using smart legal contracts is a learning curve for many lawyers, but it looks likely that many more lawyers are going to have to step onto this curve in the years to come.

(b) Cryptoassets

Cryptoassets are a type of digital asset. They include crypto-tokens such as:

- cryptocurrency 'coins' (like Bitcoin) that have their own blockchain;
- cryptocurrency 'tokens' that don't have their own blockchain, but instead run on top of an existing blockchain (using smart contracts); and
- non-fungible tokens (NFTs).

These cryptoassets are already having a big impact. And the press is having a field day reporting on them.

Cryptoassets can be traded, used as a store of value, or used to represent another asset:

- NFTs, in particular, are linked to data which represents digital artwork. And, like real art, they can be worth a lot of money. A series of NFTs sold for $91.8 million in December 2021.[47]
- Central bank digital currencies (CBDC) are increasingly being looked at and adopted (The Bahamas introduced the 'Sand Dollar' as a currency in 2020). At the time of writing, the Bank of England is considering how it might work, although it hasn't yet made the decision to introduce one.
- In June 2021, El Salvador adopted Bitcoin as legal tender in the country – the first country in the world to do so. Although, at the time of writing, it's too early to say whether this development is a success or not, particularly given the volatility (or "growing pains")[48] of the cryptocurrency, many businesses elsewhere in the world are starting to accept cryptocurrencies.

In July 2022 the Law Commission proposed that a distinct category of personal property be developed, "which is better able to accommodate the unique features of digital assets"[49] (provisionally called 'data objects'). (NFTs, for example, do not sit well in the traditional categories of choses in action or choses in possession.) This would include reforming the law on crypto-tokens such as cryptocurrencies and NFTs. These reforms are also intended to help make England and Wales the jurisdiction of choice and a global hub for digital assets (in particular, for crypto-tokens and crypto-token systems).

Law firms in the United Kingdom are starting to take notice. In February 2022, gunnercooke said that it would accept payment in certain cryptocurrencies.

The firm represents cryptocurrency developers, platforms and exchanges, so accepting the currency was a natural progression. The question is, however, when will other firms follow gunnercooke's lead? Perhaps, until the ecological issues around cryptocurrency are addressed,[50] ESG considerations will hold back broader adoption.

With blockchain and digital assets (and, of course, other technologies in this book too), lawyers can play a key role in making the systems work and also making them as safe and trusted as possible. Day in and day out, we deal with the real-world complexities of businesses and the complex taxes and laws which are levied on, and govern, these businesses. We can help our clients understand the risks and potential liabilities. The question is whether we put our hands up now to highlight and help to fix any nascent problems.

And if understanding all of this is proving a bit too much, it's worth reminding ourselves to not get too het up with details of the technology. The authors find that, when this happens, use cases are often more important than a deep understanding of the underlying technology.

3.4 Brexit
We move from one complex subject to another: Brexit.

"I think British politics and public life are going to go through an even more turbulent decade" journalist Andrew Marr tweeted in November 2021.[51] We suspect Marr is right. The Dissolution of the Monasteries after Henry VIII's break with Rome – another big row in the tradition of big rows with Europe – started a flurry of litigation and land deals.[52] We've been here before. And it's become clear that no split of this size is done at pace or without a degree of pain.

What can we expect next? David Charter, Europe Correspondent for *The Times*, predicted the referendum result in 2012 within half a percentage point. His forecast for the years ahead? In a sense, much of the same: "The familiar pattern of frequent arguments, muddles and joint initiatives that has always marked Britain's relationship with the continent continued unabated."[53] On the other side of the Channel, the Prime Minister of Luxembourg, Xavier Bettel, summed up the UK approach in 2016 as "before, they were in and they had many opt-outs; now they want to be out with many opt-ins".[54] Has much changed since then?

It might only be about 21 miles from South Foreland in Kent to Cap Gris Nez near Calais, but it can sometimes feel like the English Channel is getting wider. In November 2021, Dr Eoin Drea noted that on the EU side "it remains remarkable that for such a seismic event, Brexit continues to be most noticeable by its absence in the formulation of future European Union strategy".[55] But at the time of writing, like jilted partners, the two mostly have their backs to each other, hackles raised, with stern 'I'm-not-interested-any-more' expressions on their faces. After almost five decades of formal partnership, it's as though both sides are bored with one other.

Lawyers, however, can't afford to be bored. We can't, for example, ignore the reality of the European Union's legacy in our laws (finding the law can be challenging at the best of times. Brexit hasn't made things any easier). Nor can we ignore the realities of the trade agreement with the bloc.

At the time of writing, it's still difficult to determine the extent to which the United Kingdom will diverge or shadow the European Union:

- Will we go back to the common law tradition? Barnabas Reynolds, a partner at Shearman & Sterling LLP and Global Head of the Financial Services Industry Group proposes that much EU-derived law should be removed. It goes against the United Kingdom's common law tradition and is "restrictive and protectionist".[56] A less codified, common law approach to regulation is also proposed by the government;[57] or
- Will we shadow the European Union? The GDPR showed the 'Brussels effect' where EU law on data protection became, in effect, the gold standard for global business. Microsoft extended the GDPR to all of its consumer customers worldwide in 2018.

Following David Charter's prediction, it'll probably be a mix of the above – a very British fudge, we could call it – depending on the sector and industry in question. TechUK in February 2022 suggested that, in terms of "regulating the digital economy", the United Kingdom is heading down a third path "between the more *laissez-faire* approach of the USA and a comparatively proscriptive approach from the EU".[58] As lawyers, particularly those who have multinational clients, we need to be alive to these dynamics so that we can point out potential issues and opportunities in the United Kingdom and the European Union and, with the help of colleagues or contacts in the bloc, advise our clients accordingly. It looks as though, for many of us, not being aware of EU laws (as they develop) isn't a luxury that we can afford.

3.5 Climate crisis and environmental issues

The world is all we have. Not the title of the latest Bond film, but a stark and simple reminder that we live on a planet with finite resources. It's also one which is heating up (the authors wrote this section during the third, record-breaking heatwave of 2022). The World Economic Forum (WEF) in its *Global Risks Report 2022* asked businesses to "identify the most severe risks on a global scale over the next 10 years".[59] Five out of the top 10 severe risks were environmental with "climate action failure", "extreme weather" and "biodiversity loss" coming in as the first, second and third most worrying risks. The UK Climate Change Risk Assessment in 2022 reported "strong evidence that even under low warming scenarios the UK will be subject to a range of significant and costly impacts unless significant further action is taken now".[60]

In the years to come, a lot of the technology and trends set out in this book will be used in the fight against climate change, including AI. Additive manufacturing (ie, 3D printing) can reduce transit costs. But lawyers have an important role to play too, both in the practice and in the business of law.

In the business of law:
- in our firms:
  - we haven't snapped back to the climate-unfriendly pre-lockdown patterns of leaving the house every day for work, as we explore in Chapter 3. Hybrid working is here to stay (although how it works in practice is still settling down);
  - we no longer default to meeting in person. We think about it: 'do we really need to spend a whole day travelling the length of the country for a 30-minute meeting?';
  - in procurement many law firms aim to buy better and buy less;
  - many firms are also committed to eliminating their contribution to carbon emissions entirely;
- for our clients: progressive firms are watching developments, such as the government's ambition to make the United Kingdom the best place in the world for green and sustainable investment and helping our clients develop their businesses into these new areas.

In the practice of law, many of us are playing our part:
- the International Bar Association is urging lawyers "to consider: taking a climate conscious approach to problems encountered in daily legal practice";[61]
- the Law Society has adopted a similar resolution. It calls on lawyers to adapt to new norms in the sector and to "realise the full potential of the law, solicitors and law firms as a progressive force in tackling the climate crisis".[62] This includes developing career paths for lawyers "who wish to transition into distinct disciplines related to climate change or enhance their practice area by focusing on ways in

which that practice can advance net-zero targets, such as clean energy, green real estate, ESG, sustainable finance law and similar climate related aspects". The Law Society is due to publish guidance on climate change matters in early 2023.

The Chancery Lane Project, a *pro bono* initiative which, in its words, is "fighting the climate crisis with contracts"[63] is at the forefront of change in private practice in particular. As chair, Matthew Gingell, says: "Every day, in offices across the world, lawyers are using our tools to make a difference and up the ante in the Race to Zero."[64]

To this end, the Chancery Lane Project has published:
*   climate clauses, containing standard climate-related clauses to incorporate into precedents and commercial agreements;
*   toolkits, containing timelines and transition maps; and
*   a glossary, containing standard climate-related definitions to draft climate-aligned contracts.

Some of their clauses have been incorporated into LexisNexis and Thomson Reuters precedents.

English and Welsh lawyers are in a privileged position to bring about change (many of the clauses have been translated to be relevant in US juris-dictions). And while there are those who aren't too keen on using some of the clauses (they can be detailed), it's likely that most lawyers will increas-ingly see them in practice.

Former president of Ireland and erstwhile UN special envoy for climate change, Mary Robinson, said that "lawyers should wake up"[65] and do some-thing about the climate crisis. As the above shows, they are doing so.

And as smart contracts develop and technology relating to property design, management, monitoring and use (proptech) features more and more in buildings, there will certainly be plenty for lawyers to do.

3.6 Globalisation
Globalisation has had a rough time of it in recent years. New Brexit trading rules, China's lengthy zero-COVID strategy[66] and the war in Ukraine, in par-ticular, have highlighted how vulnerable just-in-time supply chains are. In a report in March 2021, the US National Intelligence Council (NIC) called it a "more contested world".[67] The result is that a lot of organisations are moving to a just-in-case model to build more resilience into their supply chains and businesses.

While aspects of globalisation are contested, and the way we deal with them is changing, many aspects of it are here to stay. Technology, in particular, has unleashed powerful forces which can't be undone. The genie's out of the bottle.

In a time of 'change3' and what some call the 'polycrisis', businesses need to be able to weather the storms that are arriving on our shores with increasing regularity. The BCG Henderson Institute, Boston Consulting Group's think tank, calls it "becoming an all-weather company".[68] Law firms aren't immune to this need, as COVID and other unexpected events have shown. The exodus of law firms from Russia in 2022 is another stark reminder of how quickly times can change and how firms need to react to them.

If businesses get this right, they should find that they can bounce back better when the biblical rain stops and the clearing up after the storm is done. BCG Henderson Institute research indicates that more resilient businesses don't fall as far when a shock hits and that they tend to recover more quickly. The extent of the recovery is greater too.

None of this means that we turn our backs on the world ('deglobalisation'). While aspects of globalisation are contested, and the way we deal with them is changing, many aspects of it are here to stay. Technology, in particular, has unleashed powerful forces which can't be undone. The genie's out of the bottle.

What's more, many of the solutions to the problems we face may come from almost anywhere on the planet. The *FT Omdia Digital Economies Index 2022–26* shows that the fastest growing digital economies in that period are likely to be in countries like India, Vietnam and Israel. If we close our minds to developments overseas, we may also be closing down opportunities.

3.7 Metaverse

This is a bit of a last-minute entry to this book. It might be an exciting new development; or, for lawyers and law firms, it might fizzle out into relative obscurity – for now at least. One partner to whom we spoke told us: "welcome to Hype Central". It's clear, however, that Facebook rebranding itself in October 2021 as Meta means the metaverse is difficult to ignore. As the *New Scientist* noted in January 2022, the company's "metamorphosis certainly amped up the metaverse hype".[69]

What is it? Put simply, the metaverse is a 3D virtual-reality world accessed through headsets. According to Mark Zuckerberg, CEO of the social media giant Meta, this next iteration of the internet will "be even more immersive – an embodied internet where you're in the experience, not just looking at it".[70] He adds that we'll "be able to teleport instantly as a hologram to be at the office without a commute". More opportunities will open up to us, Zuckerberg thinks, if we spend much less time commuting. And this'll help to shrink our carbon footprints too.

At the time of writing, MetaQuest 2 (the virtual reality headset developed by Meta's Reality Labs) offers its users a beta version of Horizon Workrooms, a "VR workspace for teams to connect, collaborate and create".[71] But the metaverse isn't something that Facebook has a monopoly on. Other businesses are increasingly keen. Microsoft Mesh ("here can be anywhere")[72] offers mixed reality applications to users through avatars with "Holoportation" where users can project themselves as their "most lifelike, photorealistic self".[73] In law firms, lawyers may start to use these technologies internally (perhaps for training purposes) or to, say, connect with certain clients overseas (and with clients within relative proximity, but who want to embrace the metaverse in their daily work pattern).

Outside the legal sector, businesses are already starting to embrace this technology. Manchester City FC and Sony, for example, are building a metaverse version of the Etihad stadium so that fans can watch live games from anywhere in the world. Lawyers will increasingly be required to advise on legal issues in the metaverse from IP queries ("do our IP licences extend to the metaverse?") to issues on ownership and 'meta-property' (the first eviction order for meta-squatters can't be far off).

Law firms are slowly testing the waters of this new world. German law firm Gleiss Lutz and US law firm ArentFox Schiff, for example, have opened offices in Decentraland, a virtual world which is overseen by the non-profit Decentraland Foundation. As Anthony Lupo, firm chair of ArentFox Schiff, said in February 2020: "We don't know what the metaverse will be in five years, but we're not waiting five years to find out. We're going to help iterate that future."[74]

For now the authors categorise this as 'one to watch' for most firms. Internet speeds may need to catch up with the requirements of this technology. In the meantime, what's your avatar going to be?

3.8 Non-virtual places

The authors don't think it's time to write off towns and cities just yet. Our (non-virtual) urban areas remain the logical places to get together thanks to their networks of railways, airports and motorways. Physical places still have great significance in business and society, including in lawyering. People want to congregate to share ideas and just to be together for that elusive buzz; something which is notoriously tricky to replicate online.

This isn't to say, of course, that people won't communicate with one another virtually. The climate crisis certainly means that law firms will need to be mindful of lowering their carbon emissions, but meetings in real life (IRL – isn't it amazing that we need a term for 'in real life' now?) will still happen. People will visit offices to get together to connect, collaborate, create and celebrate (the 'four Cs').

Many meetings will increasingly be hybrid too, for example:
- The authors' firm set up a state-of-the-art innovation suite, *The Studio*, when it moved into its new London office in 2021 (see Chapter 3). This suite is a place where:
  - some attendees may be physically present, some may attend virtually; and
  - clients and others can get together too (it's not just for lawyers);
- Brodies moved to Capital Square in Edinburgh in 2022 and used it as an opportunity to rethink the most effective way of working for their lawyers. The firm has, for example:
  - built a virtual courtroom where litigation, arbitration, mediation and other forms of dispute resolution can take place without everyone needing to be present; and
  - designed its offices to the WELL Building Standard, which aims to put people's health and wellness at the centre of design. The result is that people want to come into the office. As managing partner Nick Scott said at the time, this technology, and the flexibility it engenders, means that opportunity is opened up "to connect with a greater range of talented people". He added (and the authors agree) that "whatever the future looks like, it won't bear much resemblance to my 1990s' expectation that almost everything should be achieved at a single desk".[75]

There's no doubt hybrid working will be a game-changer for our towns and cities. But with a bit of imagination and flair we can create spaces so that, when we do head into the office, we enjoy being there with our colleagues and clients.

The authors' selection of topics above will, no doubt, omit some that readers would have included. Possibly because of different personal interests and priorities; possibly because a reader may have a different view from a different mountaintop.

Even if you can't see everything within the field of view that is available to you, that doesn't mean you can't start to prepare. On the contrary, you can and you must. Some of your view might be obscured, but you can usually work out roughly what lies ahead and how best to deal with it. As the old maxim goes: by failing to prepare you are preparing to fail.

And any preparations don't need to be perfect. As we've said often in this book, we need to be mindful not to let perfection be the enemy of good. When we're looking at something as uncertain and unknowable as the future – from the Rumsfeldian 'known knowns' to his (often mocked but completely logical) 'unknown unknowns' – and planning how we'll react to it, good is often good enough (and in any event is all we have).[76]

But doing something, no matter how small, soon adds up.

In a world of 'change3', we need to be pragmatic: we won't typically have the time to dot the i's and cross the t's, as much as it may upset the secret perfectionist in most of us lawyers (we're reminded of a colleague who decided to redo a whole set of board minutes as they stated *inter alia* instead of *inter alios*. Is this sort of thing worth delaying a deal over?).

What's more, we often have to make do with what we've got.

In 1921, when the Mount Everest Reconnaissance Expedition did a recce of the area to find a feasible route to the summit, the team was photographed sporting knickerbockers, putees (a type of leg binding) and Norfolk jackets (a garment which looks more suited to going for a walk in the park rather than going up a mountain). Playwright George Bernard Shaw, when shown a portrait of the team, quipped "Connemara picnic surprised by a snow-storm".[77]

It's no picnic preparing to climb a mountain like Everest and the ragtag clothing of the Everest team looked ill-suited to the task. However, despite first appearances, the Expedition's kit did the job. In the end, it didn't matter what they looked like. It worked.

Many lawyers fall into a similar trap of overthinking things, worrying that there must be a correct way of horizon-gazing; that their way of approaching the challenges and opportunities ahead of them doesn't quite feel right; and that they may end up using all the 'wrong kit'. As a result, they think they won't get to their desired destination. As we mention earlier, we can't be perfectionists. Doing even a bit of horizon-gazing is better than doing none at all.

4. Case studies

4.1 Case study 1: The Regulatory Horizons Council

In 2019, the government set up the Regulatory Horizons Council (RHC). The independent expert committee's goal is to "[scan] the horizon for technological innovation and trends" and "[make] recommendations to government on broad priorities for regulatory reform".[78]

In December 2020, the RHC set out its potential priority areas.[79] There were four priority areas in the first tranche, for which reports were published between June 2021 and November 2021, namely:

- genetic technologies;
- fusion energy;
- unmanned aircraft (ie, drones); and
- medical devices.

In the second tranche, the RHC is looking at the "crosscutting issue of regulation and innovation, hydrogen in maritime, neurotechnologies and artificial intelligence as a medical device".[80]

Other possible future areas for the RHC to look at include:

- mobility as a service (platforms and user interfaces in transport);
- hydrogen fuel cells in transport;
- battery technology in transport; and
- using wireless technologies in food, water and agriculture (including 5G);
- 3D printing in manufacturing (eg, aerospace, automotive and bio-printing); and
- robotics and autonomous systems.

There's a lot, of course, that isn't on that list. The RHC's raw data indicated a mind-boggling 542 emerging innovations of interest.[81] In a world of 'change3', it's inevitable that bodies like the RHC need to prioritise what it looks at. The RHC itself has admitted that as a new organisation it's still fine-tuning its methodology to work out how it does this.

The RHC is only able to make recommendations. It sits at the starting blocks of any proposed regulatory solutions. But if the government finds the committee's work to be of use, lawyers who advise on regulation in the areas the RHC examines:

- would do well to consider what it proposes as it's likely to give initial indications as to where regulation could be heading. As the report on drones indicated, recommendations can also, for example, extend to ensuring that the UK engage with international standards bodies. Regulation doesn't always mean, say, passing primary or secondary legislation to deal with challenges posed by new technologies;

- that said, a few years of work from the RHC will be needed to see to what extent its views are followed. So far, the Secretary of State for Business, Energy and Industrial Strategy has responded to the initial four RHC reports above with responses that are somewhat formulaic.

The Government Office for Science also publishes *Trend Decks* which set out trends in key areas such as the climate crisis, demographics, technology and, of particular interest to lawyers, governance and law.[82]

In March 2022, the RHC undertook evaluation interviews and a retrospective on the first tranche of reports it published. Interviewees said that they liked the independence of the RHC. There was also "consistent mention of [the reports'] utility and insightfulness, and in some instances, their ability to highlight to experienced policy officials some of the issues or concerns with the relevant field".[83] However, interviewees also said it was usually too early to say whether the RHC had had any impact and that the information in the reports wasn't always new. Some interviewees also suggested using "'technical advisors' to support the deep dives and provided expert advice on a more regular basis". This could be a good opportunity for the clients of some law firms to participate in the work that the RHC does.

The view of the RHC on regulation generally can also be found in its reports: *The Future of Technological Innovations and the role of Regulation* and *Closing the Gap: getting from principles to practice for innovation friendly regulation*.[84]

4.2 Case study 2: The future influence of English law

The laws of England and Wales have travelled far and wide. Sir Roger Gifford, Lord Mayor of London from 2012 to 2013, said that the jurisdiction has "produced an international contract law that is essentially English law and is viewed the world over as a gold standard":[85]

- according to TheCityUK, in 2020 net exports of UK legal services amounted to about £5.4 billion and, in 2021, the UK ranked second for legal services fee revenue globally;[86]
- according to the Ministry of Justice, English law is the most popular choice of law globally for commercial contracts. The economic value of English law, both in the United Kingdom and overseas, underpins trillions of pounds of business in numerous industries and sectors;

- the United Kingdom's soft power is "underpinned by our model of democratic governance, legal systems and Common Law heritage";[87]
- London is a leading global legal centre, including in dispute resolution and arbitration.

The United Kingdom has more influence than it realises for a nation of its size, even though events like the parliamentary logjams and Brexit battles of 2016 to 2019, in particular, hit its confidence a bit:

- the NIC said in March 2021 that "the United Kingdom is likely to continue to punch above its weight internationally given its strong ... financial sector and its global focus", adding that the United Kingdom is in a position to exercise influence during the next two decades and it, together with other major countries and blocs, is "likely to be consequential in shaping geopolitical and economic outcomes as well as evolving norms and rules";[88]
- the UK government notes the need to "[promote] UK legal services, ensuring that the principles and values on which our domestic system is built remain the global standard".[89]

And yet despite all of this, the power of the English legal system is often underappreciated. Do we take for granted how much English law is used? Are we doing enough to turn this asset to our advantage? The authors, and others, think that the answers to these questions are a simple "yes" and "no".

The widespread use of English law, according to one report by the Social Market Foundation, "has seen it become – it has been suggested – something akin to an 'international public utility'".[90] But it's a utility that shows signs of decline: gaps in the law and a civil justice system under pressure, among other things, are chipping away at this resource. Ultimately, this report worries that "a failure to invest in English law ... gives rise to major risks for the UK economy".[91]

The report makes four recommendations:

- There should be a long-term and "more coherent" approach to the system of civil justice and civil English law. The government should be singing the praises of the system more.
- There should be reform of how the system of civil justice works and how it is structured. Modernisation of the courts is vital. How much longer can we put up with leaky roofs, dodgy electrics and faulty heating in our court buildings?
- English law needs to be modernised in two key ways: where it has fallen behind (insurance law is given as an example); and where

there are gaps in it (such as AI). To gauge the scale of the challenge, the government should set up a "time-limited, adequately resourced expert legal modernisation Commission". An alternative, the authors suggest, would be to give this role to the Law Commission of England and Wales.

- English law is also at risk because of its improper use in other jurisdictions. The government should undertake a review of where English law is used abroad and see what action it can take to protect it.

This matters because there is competition. A study in 2019 by the Singapore Academy of Law found that English law is used less in Asian markets. Closer to home, Brexit means that Ireland is now the largest English-speaking common-law jurisdiction in the EU. In 2019, it launched the *Ireland for Law* initiative. Events have been held in London, Paris and New York to showcase what Irish law can offer. IT problems and a shortage of judges may hamper this initiative for now, but these can be fixed. Other jurisdictions are hungry for a slice of the action.

And it's always easier to destroy a reputation than it is to build one up. Take the Libor scandal, which tarnished the City's reputation and created a lot of uncertainty in the markets as institutions and businesses transitioned to successor rates. The cost is estimated to have run into the billions of dollars.

We're reminded of the great Hemingway line from *The Sun Also Rises*: "How did you go bankrupt?" "Two ways ... gradually and then suddenly".[92] If we're not careful, the advantage we enjoy of practising English and Welsh law could be lost – quicker than we think. It's time to do more to acknowledge this extraordinary commercial advantage and what we can do to not let it slip away.

5. Practical tips on horizon-gazing

We set out below some practical tips on horizon-gazing.

These tips are split as follows:
- understanding where you are now;
- working with external contacts; and
- working with internal stakeholders.

5.1 Understanding where you are now
- Before you look up, look down. Where are you? It's difficult and more time-consuming to chart a course to an end destination if you don't know where you are now.
- Equally, even if you think you know where you are, double-check. Market research and consulting firm Ipsos runs *Perils of Perception* studies from time to time to explore the gap between what people perceive to be the reality and reality itself. These types of studies show that things are not often what they seem. People often overestimate how bad things are while underestimating how good things are.
- Mindset is important. Approach the exercise as one that seeks new opportunity rather than defensively preserving your current position.

5.2 Working with external contacts
- Speak to your clients: if you want to know where your world is headed you need to know where theirs is headed too.
- Enlist industry and sector gurus to help with your future gazing. This is important enough to invest in some outside help.

5.3 Working with internal stakeholders
- Ask your partners to do the exercise of considering where the puck is moving in their practice areas. How many of them have been charged with doing that in the past? Can they all do it? If they can't, then are they really plugged into their practice areas deeply enough?
- Create a place where everyone in your firm can submit feedback from clients etc on the future. Make it easy to capture this vital data.
- Ensure that someone senior in your firm has overall responsibility for having a 'helicopter view' of all the future-gazing feedback that is feeding through. Without such a view, wider trends that may have an impact across the firm might be missed.
- Ensure that the conclusions of future gazing are fed into your firm's vision, strategy and related aims. It's all very well collating the views, but quite another to ensure something is done as a consequence.
- Put future-gazing on the board agenda as a standing item (at least

quarterly). Ensure someone is responsible for presenting on market news/trends against that agenda item. If one thing is certain, it is that change is going to happen. Therefore, recognise that and give it the priority at board level that it deserves.

- Don't be afraid to accept the conclusions that start to dawn on you as you work through the exercise of future-gazing. Uncomfortable as they may seem while they are shadowy figures in the distant mist, they will be a hell of a lot scarier when they are in plain sight standing just feet away from you with their lawyer-disintegrator-ray guns in hand!

Notes

1   Huw Lewis-Jones, *Mountain Heroes Portraits of Adventure* (Conway, 2011), p243.
2   "Our world in 2050: what lies ahead for you and your business?" (Law Society, 27 March 2022), www.lawsociety.org.uk/topics/research/future-worlds-2050-project.
3   "How can we start building our innovation aptitude?" (Innovation Leadership Group), www.innovation.io/playbook.
4   Government Office for Science, *The Futures Toolkit* (November 2017), https://assets.publishing.service.gov.uk/government/uploads/system/uploads/attachment_data/fil e/674209/futures-toolkit-edition-1.pdf.
5   *Ibid.*
6   Valerie van Mulukom, "Is it rational to trust your gut feelings? A neuroscientist explains" (*The Conversation*, 16 May 2018), https://theconversation.com/is-it-rational-to-trust-your-gut-feelings-a-neuroscientist-explains-95086.
7   "Hype Cycle for Legal and Compliance Technologies, 2021" (Gartner, 19 July 2021), www.gartner.com/en/documents/4003713.
8   One particular criticism is that they are not cycles.
9   "Gartner Hype Cycle" (Gartner), www.gartner.co.uk/en/methodologies/gartner-hype-cycle.
10 Law Society, *Lawtech Adoption Research* (February 2019), https://prdsitecore93.azureedge.net/-/media/files/topics/research/law-society-lawtech-adoption-report-2019.pdf.
11 *Social acceptability of technology in legal services* (Legal Services Board and Solicitors Regulation Authority, March 2022), https://legalservicesboard.org.uk/wp-content/uploads/2022/05/Acceptability-of-technology-in-legal-services-research-report-FINAL-M arch-2022.pdf.
12 Law Society, *Lawtech Adoption Research* (February 2019), https://prdsitecore93.azureedge.net/-/media/files/topics/research/law-society-lawtech-adoption-report-2019.pdf.
13 Noel Semple, "Tending the Flame: Technological Innovation and the Legal Services Act Regime" (A paper prepared for the Legal Services Board, 6 August 2019), www.legalservicesboard.org.uk/wp-content/uploads/2019/09/Semple-Final-version-for-publication.pdf.
14 In 1999, lawyer and creator of the Creative Commons licence standards, Lawrence Lessig, wrote about 'code is law', or it certainly behaves like it. By and large, the day-to-day 'lawmakers' for much of the tech we use are the creators of it, and not our local MPs. If a piece of software behaves and says you can't do something, then you can't, unless you can find a permissible workaround. This is 'code is law' in action.
15 Gary E Marchant, Braden R Allenby and Joseph R Herkert (eds), *The Growing Gap Between Emerging Technologies and Legal-Ethical Oversight* (Springer Dordrecht, 2011). The subtitle of the book is "The Pacing Problem".
16 Brad Smith and Carol Ann Browne, *Tools and Weapons* (Penguin, 2021), p33.
17 Cabinet Office, *Global Britain in a Competitive Age: the Integrated Review of Security, Defence, Development and Foreign Policy* (16 March 2021), www.gov.uk/government/publications/global-britain-in-a-competitive-age-the-integrated-review-of-security-defence-development-and-foreign -policy.
18 Department for Digital, Culture, Media and Sport, *Digital Regulation: Driving growth and unlocking innovation* (6 July 2021), www.gov.uk/government/publications/digital-regulation-driving-growth-and-unlocking-innovation.
19 LawtechUK, *Shaping the Future of Law – The LawtechUK Report 2021* (July 2021), https://technation.io/wp-content/uploads/2021/07/LawtechUK-Report-2021-Final.pdf.
20 Richard Hyde, *Law and the open economy* (Social Market Foundation, November 2021), www.smf.co.uk/wp-content/uploads/2021/11/FINAL-Mishcon-1.pdf.
21 Leanne Geale, "Developing a legal and compliance radar" (*Practical Law In-House Blog*, 13 July 2022), http://in-houseblog.practicallaw.com/developing-a-legal-and-compliance-radar/.

22 Michael Cross, "Prepare now for 'internet of brains' – Law Society" (*Law Society Gazette*, 9 August 2022), www.lawgazette.co.uk/law/prepare-now-for-internet-of-brains-law-society/5113367.article.

23 Elizabeth Denham, "The certainty of change: regulation in a time of political and social challenges" (ICO, 26 November 2021), https://ico.org.uk/about-the-ico/media-centre/news-and-blogs/2021/11/the-certainty-of-change-regulation-in-a-time-of-political-and-social-challenges/.

24 François Candelon, Rodolphe Charme di Carlo, Midas De Bondt and Theodoros Evgeniou, "AI Regulation is Coming" (*Harvard Business Review*, September–October 2021), https://hbr.org/2021/09/ai-regulation-is-coming.

25 Office for Artificial Intelligence, Department for Digital, Culture, Media and Sport, and Department for Business, Energy and Industrial Strategy, *National AI Strategy* (22 September 2021), https://assets.publishing.service.gov.uk/government/uploads/system/uploads/attachment_data/fil e/1020402/National_AI_Strategy_-_PDF_version.pdf.

26 Department for Business, Energy and Industrial Strategy, Department for Digital, Culture, Media and Sport, Office for Artificial Intelligence, *Establishing a pro-innovation approach to regulating AI* (18 July 2022), www.gov.uk/government/publications/establishing-a-pro-innovation-approach-to-regulating-ai/establishing-a-pro-innovation-approach-to-regulating-ai-policy-statement. See also Centre for Data Ethics and Innovation, "The roadmap to an effective AI assurance ecosystem" (8 December 2021), www.gov.uk/government/publications/the-roadmap-to-an-effective-ai-assurance-ecosystem.

27 "Lawtech and ethics principles report" (Law Society, 28 July 2021), www.lawsociety.org.uk/topics/research/lawtech-and-ethics-principles-report-2021.

28 Centre for Data Ethics and Innovation, "The roadmap to an effective AI assurance ecosystem" (8 December 2021), www.gov.uk/government/publications/the-roadmap-to-an-effective-ai-assurance-ecosystem.

29 Centre for Data Ethics and Innovation, "Industry Temperature Check: Barriers and Enablers to AI Assurance" (7 December 2022), www.gov.uk/government/publications/industry-temperature-check-barriers-and-enablers-to-ai-assurance.

30 See, for example, the work done by AI Verify in Singapore (see: "Singapore launches world's first AI testing framework and toolkit to promote transparency; Invites companies to pilot and contribute to international standards development" (Infocomm Media Development Authority, 25 May 2022), www.imda.gov.sg/Content-and-News/Press-Releases-and-Speeches/Press-Releases/2022/Singapore-launches-worlds-first-AI-testing-framework-and-toolkit-to-promote-tran sparency-Invites-companies-to-pilot-and-contribute-to-international-standards-development).

31 "Re: Slashdot Submission for 1.0" (Satoshi Nakamoto Institute, 5 July 2010), https://satoshi.nakamotoinstitute.org/posts/bitcointalk/167/.

32 Michael Cross, "Every lawyer will require familiarity with crypto, says MR" (*Law Society Gazette*, 11 January 2022), www.lawgazette.co.uk/news/every-lawyer-will-require-familiarity-with-crypto-says-mr/5111085.article.

33 "Digital Street: HM Land Registry tests blockchain for property conveyancing" (*Internet of Business*), https://internetofbusiness.com/digital-street-hm-land-registry-exploring-blockchain-for-conveyancing/.

34 Law Society, *Blockchain: Legal & Regulatory Guidance Second Edition* (2022), https://prdsitecore93.azureedge.net/-/media/files/topics/research/blockchain-legal-and-regulatory-guidance-second-edition-2022.pdf?rev=d15fe95a00ca4d179b7d6df97950fd5a&hash=141 33E112A070BBEAE2A1D342B6DC61A.

35 Law Society, *Lawtech Adoption Research* (February 2019), https://prdsitecore93.azureedge.net/-/media/files/topics/research/law-society-lawtech-adoption-report-2019.pdf.

36 Andrew Hampshire, *Creating Value Through Technology* (*Bloomsbury Business*, 2020), p4.

37 "Cryptoassets & Smart Contracts – Legal Statement" (LawtechUK, 1 May 2021), https://lawtechuk.io/explore/cryptoasset-and-smart-contract-statement.

38 "UKJT Digital Dispute Resolution Rules & Guidance" (LawtechUK, 1 May 2021), https://lawtechuk.io/explore/ukjt-digital-disputes-rules.

39 "Blockchain: legal and regulatory guidance (second edition)" (Law Society, 11 January 2022), www.lawsociety.org.uk/topics/research/blockchain-legal-and-regulatory-guidance-second-edition. For the first edition see: "Blockchain: legal and regulatory guidance report" (Law Society, 7 September 2020), www.lawsociety.org.uk/topics/research/blockchain-legal-and-regulatory-guidance-report.

40 "Electronic trade documents" (Law Commission), www.lawcom.gov.uk/project/electronic-trade-documents/.

41 "Digital assets" (Law Commission), www.lawcom.gov.uk/project/digital-assets/.

42 Bruce Schneier, "There's No Good Reason to Trust Blockchain Technology" (*WIRED*, 6 February 2019), www.wired.com/story/theres-no-good-reason-to-trust-blockchain-technology/.

43 Billy Bambrough, "Elon Musk Reveals Bitcoin Creator Satoshi Nakamoto Theory, Admits He Doesn't 'Get' Ethereum And Issues Dogecoin Mars Prediction Amid Crypto Price Crash" (Forbes, 28 December 2021), www.forbes.com/sites/billybambrough/2021/12/28/elon-musk-reveals-bitcoin-creator-satoshi-nakamoto-theory-admits-he-doesnt-get-ethereum-and-issues-dogecoin-mars-pre diction-amid-crypto-price-crash/?sh=2d0c2a225d0e.

44 "Smart Contracts" (Law Commission), www.lawcom.gov.uk/project/smart-contracts/.

45 *Ibid.*

46 Legal Schema, *A Structured Data Format for Digital Contracts in the UK* (*LawTechUK*, June 2021), https://technation.io/wp-content/uploads/2021/06/LegalSchemaFinal.pdf.

47 Fang Block, "PAK's NFT Artwork 'The Merge' Sells for $91.8 Million" (*Barron's*, 7 December 2021) www.barrons.com/articles/paks-nft-artwork-the-merge-sells-for-91-8-million-01638918205.

48 Omid Malekan, "What Skeptics Get Wrong About Crypto's Volatility" (*Harvard Business Review*, 6 July 2022), https://hbr.org/2022/07/what-skeptics-get-wrong-about-cryptos-volatility.

49 "Law reforms proposed for digital assets, including NFTs and other crypto-tokens" (Law Commission, 28 July 2022), www.lawcom.gov.uk/law-commission-proposes-reforms-for-digital-assets-including-crypto-tokens-and-nfts/.

50 Cryptocurrencies require vast amounts of power to verify them. The Cambridge Bitcoin Electricity Consumption Index (at the University of Cambridge) estimates in real time the annualised energy consumption of Bitcoin. At the time of writing, it's the equivalent of about one-third of the United Kingdom's entire electricity consumption. Ethereum is moving from a 'proof-of-work' basis to a 'proof-of-stake' basis, which it is hoped will alleviate the problem. The Ethereum Foundation says it will use 99.95% less energy in this way. Time will tell.

51 Andrew Marr (@AndrewMarr9), "I think British politics and public life are going to go through an even more turbulent decade, and as I've said, I am keen to get my own voice back", Twitter, 19 November 2021, https://twitter.com/andrewmarr9/status/1461676535157563406?s=11.

52 Joyce Youings, *Sixteenth-Century England* (Penguin, 1991), pp175–176.

53 David Charter, *Au Revoir, Europe* (Biteback Publishing, 2012), p306.

54 Harry Cooper, "Luxembourg PM: EU countries should shut borders to teach lesson" (*Politico*, 11 October 2016), www.politico.eu/article/luxembourg-pm-xavier-bettel-eu-countries-should-shut-schengen-borders-to-teach-lesson/.

55 Dr Eoin Drea, "Europe has learned nothing from Brexit" (*Politico*, 24 November 2021), www.politico.eu/article/europe-brexit-lessons-single-market-economy/.

56 Barnabas Reynolds, *Restoring UK Law: Freeing the UK's Global Financial Market* (Politeia, 2021), www.politeia.co.uk/wp-content/Politeia%20Documents/2021/FEB%20-%20Barney%20Reynolds/Restoring%20UK%20Law_%20Freeing%20the%20UK%27s%20Global%20Financial%20Market%281011956366.65.docx%29%20MASTER.pdf?_t=1612457531&mc_cid=c5cac04c93&mc_eid=UNIQID.

57 Department for Business, Energy and Industrial Strategy, *Reforming the Framework for Better Regulation* (July 2021), https://assets.publishing.service.gov.uk/government/uploads/system/uploads/attachment_data/file/1005119/reforming-the-framework-for-better-regulation.pdf.

58 "Regulating the Digital Economy after Brexit, what is the UK's approach?" (TechUK, 3 February 2022), www.techuk.org/resource/regulating-the-digital-economy-after-brexit-what-is-the-uk-government-s-approach.html.

59 "Global Risks Report 2022" (World Economic Forum, 11 January 2022), www.weforum.org/reports/global-risks-report-2022/.

60 HM Government, *UK Climate Change Risk Assessment 2022* (17 January 2022), https://assets.publishing.service.gov.uk/government/uploads/system/uploads/attachment_data/file/1047003/climate-change-risk-assessment-2022.pdf.

61 "IBA President: The legal profession must be prepared to play a leading role in climate crisis" (International Bar Association, 7 May 2020), www.ibanet.org/article/d1e68796-a00f-460e-9b24-0ab1d8d07b5c.

62 "Creating a climate-conscious approach to legal practice" (Law Society, 28 October 2021), www.lawsociety.org.uk/topics/climate-change/creating-a-climate-conscious-approach-to-legal-practice.

63 "The lawyers fighting the climate crisis with contracts" (The Chancery Lane Project, 3 September 2021), https://docs.google.com/document/d/1gRuJBBPl9EX4AhoHg8rrp3S7O3B9n_BUXJEXvlqK_GA/edit.

64 Nick Hilborne, "Green contract project targets in-house lawyers" (*Legal Futures*, 20 September 2021), www.legalfutures.co.uk/latest-news/green-contract-project-targets-in-house-lawyers.

65 Paul Rogerson, "Cop 26: Lawyers must wake up to climate 'madness', says former Ireland president" (*Law Society Gazette*, 29 October 2021), www.lawgazette.co.uk/news/cop-26-lawyers-must-wake-up-to-climate-madness-says-former-ireland-president/5110339.article.

66 At the time of writing, this is starting to loosen up: Stephen McDonell, "China Covid: Xi's face-saving exit from his signature policy" (BBC News, 5 December 2022), www.bbc.co.uk/news/world-asia-china-63857194.

67 National Intelligence Council, *Global Trends 2040* (March 2021), www.dni.gov/files/ODNI/documents/assessments/GlobalTrends_2040.pdf.

68 Martin Reeves, Saumeet Nanda, Kevin Whitaker and Edzard Wesselink, "Becoming an All-Weather Company" (BCG Henderson Institute, 9 September 2020), www.bcg.com/publications/2020/how-to-become-an-all-weather-resilient-company.

69 Chris Stokel-Walker, "The metaverse: What is it, will it work, and does anyone want it?" (*New Scientist*, 5 January 2022), www.newscientist.com/article/mg25333680-800-the-metaverse-what-is-it-will-it-work-and-does-anyone-want-it/.

70 Mark Zuckerberg, "Founder's Letter, 2021" (Meta, 28 October 2021), https://about.fb.com/news/2021/10/founders-letter/.

71 Horizon Workrooms (MetaQuest),
    www.oculus.com/experiences/quest/2514011888645651/?locale=en_GB›.
72 Microsoft Mesh (Microsoft), www.microsoft.com/en-us/mesh.
73 *Ibid.*
74 Kathryn Rubino, "First Biglaw Firm To Buy Serious Property In The Metaverse" (Above the Law, 15
    February 2022), https://abovethelaw.com/2022/02/first-biglaw-firm-to-buy-serious-property-in-
    the-metaverse/.
75 "The world of work is evolving; so are our offices" (Brodies, 28 March 2022),
    https://brodies.com/insights/working-at-brodies/the-world-of-work-is-evolving-so-are-our-
    offices/.
76 In February 2002, Donald Rumsfeld (then-US Secretary of State for Defense) said: "there are known
    knowns; there are things we know we know. We also know there are known unknowns; that is to
    say we know there are some things we do not know. But there are also unknown unknowns – the
    ones we don't know we don't know". (See News Transcript: DoD News Briefing – Secretary
    Rumsfeld and Gen Myers (US Department of Defense, 12 February 2002),
    https://archive.ph/20180320091111/http://archive.defense.gov/Transcripts/Transcript.aspx?Transcr
    iptID=2636#selection-401.0-401.53.
77 Wade Davis, *Into the Silence* (The Bodley Head, 2011), p212.
78 "Regulatory Horizons Council (RHC)" (GOV.UK), www.gov.uk/government/groups/regulatory-
    horizons-council-rhc.
79 Regulatory Horizons Council, *Briefing Note: Potential Priority Areas for the Council* (23 December
    2020),
    https://assets.publishing.service.gov.uk/government/uploads/system/uploads/attachment_data/fil
    e/949318/potential-priority-areas-for-the-council.pdf.
80 "Regulatory Horizons Council (RHC)" (GOV.UK), www.gov.uk/government/groups/regulatory-
    horizons-council-rhc.
81 Regulatory Horizons Council, *Retrospective August 2019–August 2020* (August 2020),
    https://assets.publishing.service.gov.uk/government/uploads/system/uploads/attachment_data/fil
    e/943738/RHC_team_retrospective.pdf.
82 "Trend Deck Spring 2021" (Government Office for Science, 28 June 2021),
    www.gov.uk/government/collections/trend-deck-spring-2021.
83 Department for Business, Energy and Industrial Strategy, "Tranche 1: Findings from the
    Regulatory Horizons Council evaluation interviews and retrospective" (11 March 2022),
    www.gov.uk/government/publications/evaluation-of-the-regulatory-horizons-council-findings-
    from-tranche-1/tranche-1-findings-from-the-regulatory-horizons-council-evaluation-interviews-a
    nd-retrospective-accessible-webpage.
84 Department for Business, Energy & Industrial Strategy, "Future of technological innovations and
    the role of regulation" (27 August 2021), www.gov.uk/government/publications/future-of-
    technological-innovations-and-the-role-of-regulation and Department for Business, Energy &
    Industrial Strategy, "Closing the gap: Getting from principles to practices for innovation friendly
    regulation" (15 June 2022), www.gov.uk/government/publications/closing-the-gap-getting-from-
    principles-to-practice-for-innovation-friendly-regulation/closing-the-gap-getting-from-principles-
    to-practices-for-innovation-friendly-regulation.
85 Select Committee on Soft Power and the UK's Influence, *Persuasion and Power in the Modern
    World* (HL 2013-14, para 175).
86 "Legal excellence, internationally renowned: UK legal services 2022" (TheCityUK, 7 December
    2022): www.thecityuk.com/our-work/legal-excellence-internationally-renowned-uk-legal-services-
    2022/.
87 Cabinet Office, "Global Britain in a Competitive Age: the Integrated Review of Security, Defence,
    Development and Foreign Policy" (16 March 2021), www.gov.uk/government/publications/global-
    britain-in-a-competitive-age-the-integrated-review-of-security-defence-development-and-foreign
    -policy.
88 National Intelligence Council, *Global Trends 2040* (March 2021),
    www.dni.gov/files/ODNI/documents/assessments/GlobalTrends_2040.pdf.
89 Cabinet Office, "Global Britain in a Competitive Age: the Integrated Review of Security, Defence,
    Development and Foreign Policy" (16 March 2021), www.gov.uk/government/publications/global-
    britain-in-a-competitive-age-the-integrated-review-of-security-defence-development-and-foreign
    -policy.
90 Richard Hyde, *Law and the open economy* (Social Market Foundation, November 2021),
    www.smf.co.uk/wp-content/uploads/2021/11/FINAL-Mishcon-1.pdf.
91 *Ibid.*
92 Ernest Hemingway, *The Sun Also Rises* (Scribner, 1954), p136.

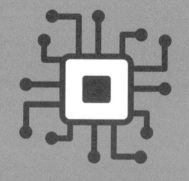

Conclusion

Tech won't replace the legal profession, but lawyers who use tech will replace those who don't. Lawyers who act like robots will be replaced by robots. Lawyers who combine tech and EQ will thrive above all.
The authors

In the previous chapters we've looked in detail at the events, developments and trends that are transforming, and will continue to transform, our everyday working lives. There's been a lot to take in.

So perhaps here we should simplify things a bit by setting out some fundamental tenets to encapsulate the major themes of this book.

In the 1940s, writer and futurologist Isaac Asimov laid down his well-known 'Three Laws of Robotics'. He wrote them when he was just 21 years old. Almost 40 years later, he said his laws were obvious and that people, at a subliminal level, knew them. It was just that the laws "never happened to be put into brief sentences until I managed to do the job".[1]

It would seem no one has yet tried to do a similar job for the legal profession.

So these are what the authors think are the three laws of legal practice in the digital age:

- first law: tech won't replace the legal profession, but lawyers who use tech will replace those who don't;
- second law: lawyers who act like robots will be replaced by robots;
- third law: lawyers who combine tech and EQ will thrive above all.

Let's briefly look at these in turn:

First law

We don't subscribe to the dystopian predictions that tech will become so advanced that human lawyers will become few and far between any time soon – there's too much that humans do that machines can't do and won't do for quite some time. For example, we're a long way from machines being able to negotiate; to assess relative bargaining positions; to form a view on when to concede a point; and when to bang the table and be willing to walk away.

But we lawyers do have to take action to ensure that we build the future that we want to see and not one that is imposed upon us. And that means we need to be investing in tech right *now*. Sceptics argue that seeking out faster and cheaper ways only goes to cannibalise the work we already do and that we want to hang onto: that when lawyers develop and use tech, it's like turkeys voting for Christmas. But here's the thing: Christmas is going to happen anyway, whether or not the turkeys send in their postal votes. If we don't forge ahead to create this brave new world for ourselves then others (probably tech-led businesses) will do it anyway. But if the tech overlords see that the lawyers have realised the opportunity that tech offers and are doing something about it, then they will be far more wary of entering a market that we lawyers are actually far better placed to continue to dominate. The key? Don't be a turkey.

In Chapter 2, we looked at a 2020 survey which found that 76% of legal professionals were aware of the rise of legaltech, but only 28% were ready.[2] Now's the time to get tech-savvy. If not now, when?

Second law

If all that a lawyer does is apply legal knowledge to a given set of circumstances, without adding any value over and above that, then it's 100% inevitable that sooner or later a robot will come along that will completely replace that lawyer because the robot will be faster, more accurate and less expensive. (And judging by the many lawyers of that type who have chosen that approach, and whom the authors have met over the years, the robot will probably be more likeable as well.)

So don't be that sterile, lifeless, grey lawyer in the corner of the room. Competing against data-hungry, hyper-efficient computers for the things they do best is a non-starter. If we currently only do work that could easily be replaced by a few complicated algorithms, it's time for a rethink. How to thrive? The third law shows you how.

Third law
Combine tech and emotional intelligence. In Chapter 9, we saw how EQ is our secret weapon. EQ-powered lawyers and AI-powered tech will transform how we practise law.

And it's this third law that excites the authors more than anything else about the potential future of our profession. We'll see increased efficiency through tech, but we'll also see increased client service and satisfaction through humans concentrating more of their efforts on the EQ side of legal practice, such as:
- getting to fully know our clients and their businesses and their markets;
- showing clients that we care about them and not just about the next piece of work they're going to give us;
- developing our compassion and ability to make our clients feel supported – making them feel assured that we've got their backs.

In other words, with the power of technology we can now devote more time to developing all those EQ skills – the so-called soft skills which in fact are some of the hardest skills to master in life.

It's interesting to consider that, over the last four decades, technology has advanced in power exponentially, and yet in all that time we have not really advanced the human side of lawyering much at all!

And in case anyone is sceptical about the value of the human side of lawyering in a tech-driven world, think about it this way: tech is going to be a great leveller when it comes to technical legal ability. The purely technical knowledge of thousands of lawyers might well be available to every firm in a single bit of software. When that happens, the only distinguishing factor between law firms will be the experience that we give our clients – not just what we do for them, but how we make them feel.

1. Heading into the future

How do we cope with the relentless change we've explored in the previous chapters? More excitingly, how do we embrace change to shape that golden age of lawyering?

We three authors believe that there are three fundamental approaches which underpin everything we explore in this book and which will help to evolve us to the next level. These bigger picture attitudes will guide us to the solutions that we need. They'll transform the practical tips set out in the previous chapters into something that works for us all.

Ultimately, they are the need to be:
- prudently optimistic;
- active; and
- people-focused.

Let's look at each of these in turn:

1.1 Be prudently optimistic
We want to be optimistic, but too often our innate prudence holds us back.

Prudence is at the heart of what we lawyers do; our blood runs thick with it. When we think of prudence, we typically picture self-discipline; we think of being mindful of what we say and how we say it; of planning ahead to avoid bad things happening (rather than to make good things happen); of being circumspect, careful and shrewd. For the ancient Greeks, it was the most important of all virtues.

While generally not considered to be a vice as such, a notable side effect of being prudent is a tendency, at times, to be negative. Researchers in the Netherlands have found that a more negative emotional state such as pessimism, correlates with greater prudence. We think that a lot of lawyers can relate to this.

In a 2001 article "Why Lawyers Are Unhappy",[3] US researchers noted that in other realms of life pessimists are "losers on many fronts", but they add – and here's the clincher – there's one "glaring exception": "pessimists do better at law". Other academics have suggested that many lawyers may self-select studying law because of their gloomy nature.

The way others see us is also instructive. Specialists on the psychology of lawyer behaviour in the US say that in addition to the words "pessimistic" and "negative", the most common words that people who work with lawyers use, when describing them, are "sceptical", "critical" and "cynical".[4]

But don't write off optimism just yet. As with many things in life, it turns out that things are a bit more nuanced than this. What's more, we should take care not to conflate prudence and pessimism.

Being prudent as a lawyer does not mean settling down into the world we know now, winding up the drawbridge and sheltering from the slings and arrows of an unknown future. In the end, this approach won't work, as there's always a point when we have to come out again. A siege mentality can only get us so far.

The authors hope this book has shown you that there is "a larger prudence in living boldly"[5] because, often, more possibilities open up that way; possibilities that lead to necessary change.

Taking adventurous, farsighted decisions sometimes means taking more risk, but these decisions can still be prudent ones. Dare we say it, we can allow ourselves some optimism. After all, to be prudent is to look to the future. Survival is the ultimate optimistic act.

As lawyers, think of all the Herculean efforts we've made to qualify, survive and (the authors hope) thrive in our chosen profession.

Is that not a future worth being optimistic about and fighting for?

Our clients, the rule of law, the reputation of our profession, justice: are they not worth fighting for too?

The authors believe they are.

As has been made clear in the previous chapters, technology, in particular, is going to turbocharge how we practise law. It'll free us up to do the things that humans do best. This means that we'll be able to:
- truly work hand-in-glove with our clients. We'll spend more time to get to know our clients better and understand, in a more profound way, what they need; we'll have their backs like never before;
- develop our teams, avoid burning them out and watch them flourish; ultimately, we'll see them become much better lawyers; and
- use our years of experience to make judgement calls that no amount of clever data capture by itself can replicate. This is the stuff we can't write down: reading a room, gauging the mood, unjamming impasses; finding humane solutions to very human problems.

Of course, optimism isn't always easy, nor should it be naïve.

There's no doubt that, as lawyers, we're experts at the worst-case scenario. But this default downcast approach risks being all-consuming, crowding out any attempt to be excited about the future of our profession. There's growing evidence that it's making many of us ill. We are worrying perhaps a bit too much.

It would be easy to say that unprecedented changes in the legal profession mean that we lawyers have little to no agency in what happens next; that all bets are off, and we'll just have to shrug our shoulders and submit to the fatalistic approach of 'whatever will be will be' and accept that the robots will take over eventually.

This book is an antidote to that: it's a realistic, prudent and optimistic best-case scenario handbook.

And, fundamentally, we've good reasons to be optimistic in the face of the pressures for change that we identify. Who on this planet has more experience of the practice of law and the provision of legal services than we lawyers?

Who else have, for centuries, been the go-to trusted advisers when someone needs to be guided through the legal minefield?

Who else applies such high standards of ethics to the practice of law?

And, most important of all, who else knows better what clients want when accessing legal services?

Yes, there will be change in every one of these aspects: dramatic change. Yet who's best to steer a new course than those who have been charting the waters for the longest?

1.2 Be active

In recent years the United Kingdom has faced a number of unprecedented challenges; from Brexit to COVID to astronomical household energy bills.

As a result, we've seen far too much of the word 'unprecedented' itself. It's fair to say its use has exploded in print and online. And it is certainly not a positive development.

The use of the term shows "an abdication of responsibility",[6] because if there isn't a precedent, then there can't be an expectation that we know what to do next. It absents us from the responsibility that we owe to our profession, our clients and our staff.

Even worse, without any precedents – something that we precedent-loving lawyers can feel nervous about – the argument goes that we can almost say and do what we like in terms of what happens next, skewing expectations about what is feasible in the years to come.

Following this logic, it would be easy to say that unprecedented changes in the legal profession mean that we lawyers have little to no agency in what happens next; that all bets are off, and we'll just have to shrug our shoulders and submit to the fatalistic approach of 'whatever will be will be' and accept that the robots will take over eventually. It's time, perhaps, simply to surrender to our fate, in the style of glib news anchor Kent Brockman in *The Simpsons*: "I, for one, welcome our new robot overlords."

As is often the case, things aren't quite as simple as that.

In the case of COVID, for example, the government was aware for years that a global pandemic could arise. *The National Risk Register*, in its 2017 matrix of risk, placed pandemic flu and emerging infectious diseases as being highly likely to occur.[7] Recorded history is peppered with numerous diseases far more deadly than COVID, which precludes COVID or its effects from being accurately described as unprecedented. (More accurately, what is unprecedented is the reaction of many national governments to the pandemic and the incredible scientific work to develop vaccines.)

As for Brexit, although in *Canary Wharf (BP4) T1 Ltd v European Medicines Agency*[8] it was held that Brexit wasn't "relevantly foreseeable" in 2011, there's an argument that it was on the political agenda from early 2013 when the then-Prime Minister, David Cameron, announced he wanted to hold a "straight in-out referendum".

These predictions weren't perfect – how could they be? – but they show that unprecedented events, or aspects of them, aren't always quite as unprecedented as they might first seem.

There is a wealth of material out there on the future of the legal profession and the law. Regulators, lawyers, academics, technologists and other stakeholders are all studying the road ahead of us, spotting patterns and trends, and looking to give us the tools and knowledge we need to take considered action.

As lawyers, each of us needs to step up, understand what are the agents for change facing the practice of law and delivery of legal services and, most importantly, to actively choose the future we want for ourselves and the profession generally and do everything we can to make it happen.

But, in the best tradition of lawyers, we mustn't forget to question new technology too. In these times of 'change3', it's vital that we think laterally, ask 'stupid' questions and use our imaginations. As always, we need to be wary of solutions in search of problems.

Right now, there's no better time to back up our optimism with action.

The key? We need to build the future we want to see, as opposed to seeing an unwanted future being built for us by others.

So far in this 'be active' section, we've looked inwards to the inner world of the law.

However, we also need to look at the outer world; to know and understand what's going on outside our profession in the wider world and make our voices heard.

More than anything, as a profession we have one big obligation: to embrace science and technology. And understand it to the extent that at least we know what it can do.

Stephen Hawking once asked: what does the future hold, particularly for the young? He responded: "I can say with confidence that their future will depend more on science and technology than any previous generation's has done."[9] We *all* need to know more about these subjects as otherwise we risk creating a world where only a super-elite are literate in advanced science and technology. Hawking called this world a "dangerous and limited one".[10] What's more, if lawyers don't 'get' tech, tech often doesn't 'get' the law. Lawyers often assume, for example, that developers know the law. More often than not, they don't.

We lawyers have an active role to play in shaping the societies we live in by protecting the rule of law, but also by keeping a watchful eye on technology and working with others to learn about tech and teach them the legal things they need to know.

We can only do this if we get out of our legal bubble from time to time so that we can:
- ensure that the pressure for change and the fundamental need to recognise the dramatic effects it will have on our firms are acknowledged at the very highest level within our organisations;
- get every senior lawyer and head of supporting functions within our firms to read this book. Until they have, most will simply not have an informed appreciation of what is going on around them;
- create an environment in which innovation thrives within our firms. This may involve giving space and support to those who have proved most innovative in the past, or formally creating an innovation team (or both). Remember: it doesn't need to be the most senior people who are the most innovative. Also remember: this isn't something simply to delegate to the existing IT team within the firm. To use the advantage that we lawyers have when compared with the tech giants, we need to have our lawyers front and centre in this effort;
- speak to our clients about innovation. How are they using technology? What frustrations do they currently have relating to the legal services

they receive or the way in which they conduct their own in-house legal team? From clients, we can both learn and generate ideas for innovation;

- become familiar with technology providers. This should, of course, include those already in the business of offering legal technology solutions. But it should also include a wider range of technicians and developers who may be open to assisting us in implementing our ideas for legal technology by applying their currently non-legal software to legal use cases;

- consider others with whom we can potentially partner to test and develop our ideas. Together we can kick the tyres to see whether an exciting new project is a goer. They may also offer more effective routes to market for the commercialisation of our ideas; and

- look overseas for inspiration: in France, lawyers have set up an association of lawyers who create legaltech (AvoTech). Local bar associations have also set up incubators like the IBP (l'Incubateur du Barreau de Paris).

At an individual level, here are some tips for how each of us can get more involved:

- commit to get to know others with an interest in tech: have a coffee with a developer friend or a virtual catchup with an academic;

- read *WIRED* or the *New Scientist* (or both); watch *Click*;

- attend webinars or, even better, give a webinar and teach people what they really need to know. The good news? Doing webinars has never been easier;

- attend talks and give talks;

- attend a conference;

- write articles for LinkedIn;

- speak to journalists (they are always eager to hear about new developments in the ways we work and how that can benefit society);

- contact a politician (that's what they're there for);

- go into a bookshop (remember them? They're where you buy books in real life) and browse for an hour, pick up a few books, read them and – here's the bonus – put them on your Teams-curated bookshelf; look learned;

- don't just use Big Tech, understand it;

- speak up when you spot something that isn't quite right. The EU-UK 'Brexit' trade deal of December 2020, for example, mentioned "modern e-mail software packages" like "Netscape Communicator 4.x.", even though this hasn't been used for well over two decades. (Oh dear!) If you see a howler, flag it up;

- get involved in networks like TechUK, and the AI for Services Network;

- set up initiatives; and
- most importantly: never stop learning.

In other words, we need get out there and surround ourselves with people who can put the wind in our sails. It could be in the virtual world or perhaps in the real world. Or a bit of both. It doesn't matter. And, of course, we should look to have fun when doing so.

This may sound like a wish list of nice-to-dos. In the busy working life of a lawyer, who has time to do any of this? (The billable hour can sometimes hold us back from doing non-billable activities.) But, of course, we don't have to do all of the above. (We wouldn't try to bring all 10 bags of shopping into the house in one go on our weekly trips to the supermarket.) But it is only through building up networks of trusted relationships that progress can be made and we can do the things highlighted in the previous chapters. And by doing this, other colleagues may be encouraged to do the same.

1.3 Be people focused

In 1998, theoretical physicist Michio Kaku, in his *fin-de-siècle* book *Visions*, speculated what life would look like in 2020.

To his credit, he was spot on (or close enough) with many of his predictions, GPS in cars, smart speakers and video calls: "At ten o'clock two staff members 'meet' with you via the wall screen."[11] But he didn't get it all right. Futurologists never do.

He was a little too optimistic about how much tech would be available, say, down the local Tesco or Waitrose: "We're low on computers. Pick up a dozen more at the market while you're at it."[12] These 'computers' would be inch-sized, clip-on 'tabs' that would allow you to magically open a door or turn your lights on and off.

(Almost, Michio, almost. Just give it a few more years ...)

The good news is that he predicted lawyers would "flourish", as they "are almost impossible to replace with computers".[13] For now, the statistics back this up. Since the date of Kaku's book the number of solicitors has continued to climb. In brief, futurologists think technology will, in most respects, complement what lawyers do, not replace them. (And we authors agree; hence the first part of our first law of legal practice: technology will not replace the legal profession.)

It's clear, however, that we can't afford to ignore technology (hence the second part of the second law of legal practice: lawyers who use technology

Too often the depiction of legaltech feels either cold or dystopian, or both, as though humans have no place being with it. If AI is being discussed in an article, we'll be treated to the almost obligatory, clichéd pictures of a humanoid, skin plastered in integrated circuits and a head like one of the androids in I, Robot.

will replace lawyers who don't). But lawyers often struggle to engage with tech. As a result, we think legaltech needs to show its human side more. It needs to be resolutely more people-focused. Or, more precisely, it needs to be portrayed as a powerful ally and not as a threatening competitor.

Too often the depiction of legaltech feels either cold or dystopian, or both, as though humans have no place being with it. If AI is being discussed in an article, we'll be treated to the almost obligatory, clichéd pictures of a humanoid, skin plastered in integrated circuits and a head like one of the androids in *I, Robot*. Perhaps, if we're lucky, it'll be holding its hand aloft, fingers curled inward slightly as if half-holding some sort of invisible ball. Finish off with a smile as inscrutable as that in the Mona Lisa and there's our default, blank-faced robot. Somehow, it manages to be enigmatic and creepy at the same time.

Frankly, some of the images look as daft as pictures of the future from the 60s or 70s, where everyone is walking around in silver jumpsuits.

None of this is helpful.

There's evidence that many people's attitudes towards robots and similar technology are based on science fiction rather than science reality or 'Hollywood Robot Syndrome'. For less tech-savvy lawyers, research suggests that this engenders negative attitudes towards this sort of tech. It doesn't have to be this way.

The authors wonder whether fear of a tech-enabled future is also feeding into a negative narrative in some parts of the profession. We often speak to partners whose children are about to embark on a law degree or training contract. The conversation usually ends up along the lines of, "oh, but I do worry about what the future holds for them. It won't be like when we started in the law".

Well, instead of worrying for them, let's inform them, reassure them, nurture them and give them the opportunities they deserve.

More than ever, we need the best minds to be motivated to become involved in the provision of legal services, rather than choosing other professions or sectors in which there is more appetite for change. We need to remind them that the profession remains a people business.

Indeed, rather than accepting a brain drain out of the legal profession, to the extent that it withers for lack of new blood, now more than ever law firms should be encouraging both those who aspire to be lawyers and those with tech skills who aspire to be successful in the business of law – there is a great future for both in a law firm in the digital age.

Before the authors sign off, let's travel a few years into the future and imagine how this might all pan out. It's popular currently to ask someone what letter of advice they'd write to their younger self. Well, here's our twist on this – a letter from the future from our collective older selves.

A message from 2030:

Hi. I hope you're well!

I'm writing to you from our new collaborative work suite in the Artichoke, a new skyscraper not far from the Gherkin. (Remember that? You can barely see it now.) It opened during the record-breaking heatwave of 2029 and is one of the Capital's first green skyscrapers. Our offices now absorb more carbon that they emit!

Anyhow, 2030 eh? For you, it's still most of the decade away. You're still getting your head around COVID and its aftermath. What an awful and sad time that was. Did we learn much from it? Well, it's a mixed bag. Scientists still struggle to get funding to deal with future pandemics. And our memories are short too: the start of COVID sometimes feels as far away in time as the fall of the Berlin Wall. I think, to be fair, everyone just wanted to forget the worst of it and get on with their lives.

The Roaring Twenties they tried to call the decade, but it didn't quite stick. The economy had its usual ups and downs. As for the end of handshakes and hugs? They came back. People are people, after all. Hybrid working stuck too: people loved the flexibility and, frankly, being treated like adults.

So what does the practice of law look like today at the cusp of the Thirties?

I remember one report in the early 2020s which said lawyers who remain in the profession (they were called the 'human survivors', if I recall) will need to take performance-enhancing medication to compete with our tech overlords. Well, that hasn't happened. But, a lot has.

We use a load more data than a decade ago. And we use AI much more too. Like all good technologies, it's so ubiquitous, it's as good as invisible. Even the metaverse is starting to take off (it took a while).

So what are my thoughts about what you should do and think about now?

- *Is the firm united around a common vision and mission? I recall the (apocryphal?) story of the cleaner at NASA during the Apollo missions: the one where the president, John F Kennedy, asks them why they're working so late. They answer: "I'm helping put a man on the moon." Quite. In a world full of technology and innovation, every single colleague, and what they do, matters more than ever. What would a randomly picked member of staff say about us?*

- *Get the right people and treat them well. The 'Great Resignation' after the worst of the pandemic – when people quit their jobs after deciding that life was too short and the law (or private practice) wasn't for them – was a wakeup call for many firms. Some just threw money at the problem, but the wise worked out the root cause to keep their people motivated and happy.*

- *Do your colleagues or partners motivate and inspire you? If they don't, why not? Is everyone out for themselves. If so, get out! Life's too short.*

- *Talking of which, don't forget to have a life. I read an article 20 years ago in which a palliative care nurse revealed their dying patients' regrets. The common stand-out one? No one looks back at their life and says 'I wish I spent more time at the office'. Always take time to see your loved ones and friends. Do something you love outside of work too.*

- *Don't burn out chasing the impossible: 'Parkinson's Law' still exists in 2030 ("work expands so as to fill the time available for its completion").[14] You are allowed downtime: it's when I have my best ideas. The neanderthal 'all-nighter' at work is thankfully all but extinct as tech has taken away so much of the drudge work. (How did you ever think it was OK to deprive yourselves and your associates of sleep and expose your clients to the increased risk that you would make a mistake while exhausted?)*

- *Embrace change. It won't be a constant though: it's more like how tectonic plates grind against each other. For a while, little happens and then – bang! – pent-up energy rips through the present and nothing seems the same after that.*

- *Don't be an absolute perfectionist. You don't have the time. (Even AI still isn't 100% accurate! But, my goodness, we are achieving an awful lot with 'just' 99%!)*

- *Don't fear failing. Fail fast, learn from it, iterate and move on. As lawyers, we're getting much better at putting our hands up when something goes wrong and learning from it.*

- *Be bold: moving forward involves taking risks. Don't avoid risk, rather embrace it and manage it, particularly earlier in your career where you probably have less to lose!*

- *Seize the opportunities in front of you. Remember when we discussed the 'Great Unmet Legal Need'? Well, the legal profession finally got its* act together and this has added £6 billion to the annual value of legal services supplied by our profession. We still have more to do. Some of the tech is so deceptively simple and consumers just love how the human element that law firms offer makes for such a great experience. (So much for the end of lawyers!) I can't work out why this market was so ill-served for so long.

- Get used to welcoming non-graduates in senior positions. Solicitor apprenticeships took a while to get going, but one member of our board qualified through this route. This is happening at other firms too. And long may it continue.
- Get the right data – you'll be using much, much more of it. Data mining has transformed our insights. Our instinctive gut feelings still have their uses, but data has transformed so many of our decisions for the better.
- Treat personal data with respect too. (It makes it much easier to comply with the Data Protection and Artificial Intelligence Act 2029, too.)
- Go the extra mile for your clients and customers. Last week some new clients from Poland visited. Without asking, our receptionist went out and bought some Polish sweets (Śliwka Nałęczowska) and put them in the meeting room to make them feel at home. The clients were really touched by this lovely gesture. The little things still go a long way.
- Be prepared to see some areas of practice upended. Conveyancing has been revolutionised. Some firms have entered into joint ventures with logistics experts. The lawyers 'do the legals' and the logistics companies arrange for fully coordinated removal lorries to do their thing. There's no more twiddling thumbs in the van outside a new house for hours waiting for completion to happen. Law firms are really starting to partner with other experts.
- Tell stories to win hearts and minds. We still don't tell enough stories. Language is our tool. And make things easier and more engaging to understand. Our clients are no longer willing to pander to our penchant for legalese and writing that is like wading through treacle.
- If you have the choice of being right or being kind, try to be kind. This is such an underestimated thing to do. Don't smugly correct people or be a show off with how much you know. If you need to correct someone, do it in a kind way. And if you're right and someone is wrong but you don't need to correct them, then just don't!
- Embrace diversity and inclusion and never treat it as a tick-box exercise. Do it because it is the right thing to do.
- Change your mindsets. You can do tech. And where you can't, at the very least learn about the power of what it can do.
- Enjoy dealing with more satisfied clients. Technology and innovation have meant that clients can track their matters 24/7 and lawyers have more time to dedicate to looking after them.

- *Keep a keen eye on all the changes that are afoot. Learn to recognise those which matter and those that don't. Experience helps!*

One final thought: focus on building good personal relationships with people in and out of the firm. It's never too early to start doing this. Or, in other words, don't spend a minute more looking at a clause than you have to (AI now takes away a lot of the strain anyway). Find the balance between knowing your stuff and getting to know the people you come into contact with every day much better.

To conclude this message from 2030: have fun, be confident and good luck! You've got lots to look forward to in the years ahead …

Some things in this book we'll have predicted with uncanny accuracy. For these, we hereby take full credit. As for any predictions that turn out to be slightly awry, we'll add ourselves to the long, illustrious list of those who've done the same.

But whatever the future holds, we can, and must, allow ourselves to be hopeful: to see change as an enabler and not as a threat. We don't promise a future where technology and innovation solve every problem, but we do promise a future in which technology and innovation will play a funda-mental and empowering role in what we do.

Finally, we said at the start that this is a book of hope. And the authors are hugely optimistic about the future of the profession. Some theorists predict that all professions (not just lawyers) are on their way out, like dying stars. Well, even if that theory proves ultimately to be correct – whether lawyers will still exist in a thousand years is impossible to say – before a star even-tually dies it goes through a long stage when it expands dramatically in size and becomes a red giant. We believe that the legal profession is about to become a red giant; we are about to enter a golden age of lawyering, where tech will enable us to do more than ever before, and to do it more quickly, more accurately and at lower cost. And this will free up lawyers to prioritise developing and applying their human skills and emotional intelligence to give our clients not only better outcomes but also to have an amazing expe-rience from lawyers like never before.

And in case this all sounds just a little bit crazy to you, remember this: even if it's crazy, do you like the sound of it? Because if you do, there is absolutely nothing stopping you from being part of making it happen. One of the greatest business minds and futurists on the planet famously praised the ones who are crazy enough to think they can change the world, because they are the ones who do.

Good luck!

Thank you for reading.

Glossary

Bear in mind that in this area pinning down the terms below can be tricky as experts often disagree as to the exact scope of some of them.

Other glossaries are available. For example, the Law Society publishes a useful guide to race and ethnicity terminology and language.[15] It also includes some tips on choosing the most appropriate and respectful language to use.

Term	Description	So what?
Algorithm	Algorithm is explained in Chapter 11.	
Artificial general intelligence (AGI) or 'general' AI	AGI is a type of 'strong AI': where computers are as clever as a human. When, or if, it happens, Professor Stuart Russell, in his 2021 Reith Lecture at the BBC says it will be the "biggest event in human history".[16] In February 2022, some suggested that we're getting closer to this point: academics Tamay Besiroglu and Ilya Sutskever, co-founder and Chief Scientist at OpenAI, said "it may be that today's large neural networks are slightly conscious".[17] Others, like Professor Murray Shanahan, pooh-poohed the idea. Shanahan said: computers are slightly conscious "in the same sense that it may be that a large field of wheat is slightly pasta".[18] The debate rolls on.	If you see the term AGI don't confuse it with AI. For the moment, AGI sells sci-fi books and films; it doesn't yet exist, so it won't help firms for some time to come (predictions range from about 2040 to past 2100). But AI is getting stronger all the time, and at an ever-increasing rate. The result? We can anticipate that AI will perform an increasing proportion of the intellectual aspects of lawyers' work over time. (See the diagram after this glossary.)
Artificial intelligence (AI)	AI is explained in Chapter 2.	

continued on next page

Term	Description	So what?
Artificial narrow intelligence (ANI) or 'narrow AI'	ANI is a type of 'weak AI': where computers aren't as clever as a human.	This is where AI is now. Don't read much into the jargon of 'narrow' and 'weak' – there isn't much distinction in practical terms. (See the diagram after this glossary.) Also, don't underestimate just how much this so-called 'weak' AI can do for lawyers right now, let alone as it develops over the next decade.
Artificial super intelligence (ASI) or 'super AI'	ASI is a type of 'strong AI': where computers are more clever than a human.	Like AGI, ASI is the stuff of sci-fi books and films. Like artificial general intelligence, it doesn't yet exist so it won't help firms. (See the diagram after this glossary.)
Big data	The easiest way to understand big data is to think of the letter 'v'. Some talk of the four, five or six v's of big data – or even more. For our purposes and to keep things simple, three v's suffice: they are the volume of data (hence 'big data'), variety of data; and velocity of data (the speed of flow of data). Big data is also characterised by the logistical difficulties in managing it.	Big data is still quite new to lawyers. But through, for example, AI-powered data mining of big data – such as the data which firms hold, but don't yet use – remarkable insights will be gained.
Blockchain	Blockchain is explained in Chapter 12.	

continued on next page

Term	Description	So what?
Chatbot	A computer program that mimics human conversation, using algorithms or AI (NLP). Users typically interact with chatbots by typing questions into an interface on a website. They can be prompted to do so by a simple 'how can I help you today?' pop-up message.	Client-facing chatbots are increasingly used on websites to answer common questions 24/7, 365 days a year. Chatbots can streamline how new queries are dealt with, directing them to the most relevant team. At the moment, the Law Society says that firms "are only flirting with the idea"[19] of legal information being made available via chatbots. This is likely to change.[20]
Data democratis- ation	Data democratisation is making data available to the average person who doesn't have specialised technical knowledge, without the involvement of data experts or other gatekeepers such as the IT department.	More sharing of data means having the data available when it is needed and not stuck in data silos. It means more potential insights by those who are best placed to make the most use of the data. It also means that more data is available for training AI and the insights that that brings. Product data management (PDM) software can help to remove data siloes and manage data more effectively.
Data exhaust	Data exhaust are the trails or by-products of data processing, which are often ignored or discarded as they don't seem immediately useful. This 'unconventional' data includes data such as websites visited and clicked-on-links.	More use of data, including data exhaust, means more potential insights. It means not letting data go to waste and thus using it more productively. Most firms' websites, for example, collect geolocation data from visitors, but this information is often unused. Webpages on topical subjects could be analysed to see the areas where queries are coming from. National? International? If so, where? With this insight, firms can, for example, tailor websites and focus their marketing campaigns.

continued on next page

Term	Description	So what?
Data hub	Data hubs are more structured than a data lake and typically contain high quality data. Data hubs centralise key data.	Data hubs are not commonly used in firms.
Data lake	Data lakes include databases from numerous sources. The data can be structured and unstructured. Unlike data warehouses, data lakes can be a dumping ground for medium- or low-quality data the use of which hasn't yet been ascertained: the 'this-might-be-handy-one-day' type of data.	Because data lakes typically contain much more data than data warehouses, they give data scientists and data analysts the data fuel they need to train technologies such as AI (and machine learning and deep learning in particular). They're also used to store data for analytics and reporting purposes.
Data mining	Data mining is finding patterns and trends, and thus insight, in existing databases. The term is a bit of a misnomer. It isn't mining data itself, rather it is mining patterns and trends in the data. Lawyers therefore typically need to collate and present two types of data for insights: the data in the database itself, as well as patterns-and-trends data from data mining. An example of the first kind of data would be data points in 10 contracts which show that limitation of liability is capped at 100% of the contract value in five contracts and 120% in the other five. The data-mined data would show a pattern or trend of a limitation of liability cap at 110% of the contract value.	Data mining (and customer profiling) paid dividends for Tesco through its loyalty card scheme. Sir Terry Leahy, chief executive between 1997 and 2011, said that it was the most significant factor in Tesco's success.[21]

continued on next page

Term	Description	So what?
Data silo	Data which is stored and not available to the entire business, but just parts of it. They are also known as 'information silos'.	Data silos are an obstacle to using data (see data democratisation).
Data warehouse	Data warehouses are more structured than a data lake, containing numerous databases of high-quality data.	Data warehouses are typically more time-consuming and costly to build and maintain than alternatives (see data lakes). They are typically used to store data for analytics and reporting purposes.
Deep learning (DL)	DL is a subset of machine learning (ML), which itself is a subset of AI. DL uses algorithms which are inspired by how the human brain works. DL models are also called 'deep neural networks'. With ML, for example, the computer can be taught to recognise a bog-standard limitation of liability clause. DL takes it one step further and can teach itself the concept of what a limitation of liability clause is and therefore recognise less obvious versions of such a clause. It 'gets' what the clause is trying to do. When teaching ML, the AI has to be told whether something is right or wrong; whereas DL gets on with things like a keen student – with the teacher just 'popping by from time to time' to make sure they're on the right track.	While ML enables the AI to operate with less human intervention, DL takes it a step further by using human brain modelling (neural networks) and lots of data to result in less ongoing human intervention. DL is also capable of analysing unstructured data in a way that ML cannot easily do. At the moment, think of DL as a stretch goal of AI within the legal sphere, although legaltech start-ups, like US-based Legal Robot, are using DL to do things like understand legal language. (See the diagram after this glossary.)

continued on next page

Term	Description	So what?
Distributed ledger technology (DLT)	Distributed ledger technology (DLT) is explained in Chapter 12.	
Innovation	The use of this term has been on an upward trajectory since about 1960.[22] The word is almost a cliché. But it still works as, frankly, there's not a compelling alternative. As for a definition? The UK Innovation Strategy refers to it simply as "the creation and application of new knowledge to improve the world".[23]	Don't overuse the word: just because something is new doesn't necessarily mean that it's innovative. People can start to balk and become cynical if there's yet another 'next big thing' in the business (think 'innovation fatigue').
Lawtech	The word is a portmanteau of 'law' and 'technology'. Often used interchangeably with 'legaltech', many argue there's a material difference between the two terms: "legaltech is for lawyers, and lawtech is for clients" notes the Lawtomated website.[24] As tempting as it is, it's often not quite as simple as that. According to LawtechUK, a government-backed initiative within Tech Nation – "lawtech is technology that supports or enables the delivery of legal and court services".[25] But this could include, say, Microsoft Word. Is this the intention?	Whatever we decide to call it is probably not worth losing any sleep over. However, be aware that others may define the term and related terms such as 'legaltech'. For example, the Law Society Lawtech and Ethics Principles published in July 2021[26] gives 'lawtech' a similar definition to LawtechUK, ie, "technology which supports or enables the provision of legal services and dispute resolution systems". Like the Tech Nation definition to the left, is this too wide? We need to consider too how any definitions impact on the application of any guidance.

continued on next page

Term	Description	So what?
Legaltech	Like 'lawtech', the word is a portmanteau of 'legal' and 'technology'. (It's sometimes also spelt 'LegalTech'.) In this book the authors favour this term over 'lawtech' as the general trend seems to be in favour of the former and it is regarded by some as a wider term.[27]	As with 'lawtech', whatever we decide to call it, is not worth losing any sleep over.
Low-code	Computer code is the instructions for a computer to do something. Lines of such code tell the computer what to do: they're the building blocks of apps and software (etc). Code is often written in a language such as C++, Java, JavaScript, Python and SQL (pronounced 'sequel') for software; or, say, HTML and CSS for websites. No-code development platforms (NCDPs) allow people who don't know how to code to develop apps and software (etc).	Low-code applications are where a basic understanding of code is needed. They allow those with such a basic understanding to create software solutions. But be wary of suppliers who claim that a product is low-code (or even no-code) as, from the authors' experience, they're sometimes anything but the intuitive solution we might expect them to be.
Machine learning (ML)	ML is a subset of AI: ML uses algorithms to get computers to do things, without them being explicitly programmed. It focuses on using large amounts of data to imitate how humans learn so accuracy is gradually improved. With ML, we need to 'train the brain': it's similar to a child with a massive IQ and potential, but we need to teach them and help them realise their potential. Like a child, we need to tell the computer when it's right or wrong but, unlike a child, it'll never make the same mistake again. ML can be supervised, unsupervised or reinforced.	If your ML is unsupervised, we don't have to teach it. However, the limitation of ML, as compared to DL, means that it might just be a stepping stone to a more autonomous AI solution. As for ML which is supervised, this can be time- and resource-intensive: it took the authors' firm two years to supervise its AI-powered product to go from 50% to 94% accuracy. (See the diagram after this glossary.) (Developments in the technology of ML are reducing the training time required.)

continued on next page

Term	Description	So what?
Metaverse	Metaverse is explained in Chapter 12.	
Natural language processing (NLP)	NLP is a branch of AI. It's where computer science, linguistics and AI join so humans and computers can interact with each other. E-mail filters and smart assistants such as Siri, Alexa and Cortana are examples of technology that uses NLP. In the legal world, NLP is used by LexisNexis' and Thomson Reuters' search engines, and to power speech-to-text dictation solutions. It's also used in Cia (see the case study in Chapter 5).	NLP means strings of words can be recognised by AI. NLP helps to understand context better. For example, on 'limit of liability', NLP would pick up, for example, 'liability limit', 'cap on liability', 'liability cap' or 'limit on liability' (where it has been trained to do so). The more it is trained the more it will recognise and, therefore, the more accurate it will be.
No-code	See 'low-code'.	No-code applications are where no understanding of code is needed. They allow those with no expertise in coding to create software solutions. See 'low-code' above for what you may need to be slightly wary of when thinking of using such a product. Don't assume that no-code equals no effort.
Quantum computing (QC)	QC is when computers use quantum mechanics to function. QC can help to solve problems that even current supercomputers struggle to handle. It's still a nascent technology and scaling the technology up is a significant challenge. The government acquired its first quantum computer in June 2022. In November 2021, Boris Johnson, the then-Prime Minister, said he wanted the United Kingdom to	Quantum computing will be faster than normal computers and help to accelerate, for example, the development of AI to get closer to being AGI and ASI. This is one to watch for the long term. Will it be, for example, China or the United States who cracks this? Whoever succeeds may therefore have the 'keys to the future'.

continued on next page

Term	Description	So what?
Quantum computing (QC) *continued*	secure "the single biggest share" of the global quantum computing market by 2040 (that's quite an ambition).[28]	According to investor and hedge fund manager Ray Dalio, QC with AI could see the "greatest shift in wealth and power that the world has ever seen".[29]
Regtech	At the moment, regtech is used much more in the highly-regulated FS sector. The FCA says regtech "focuses on technologies that may facilitate the delivery of regulatory requirements more efficiently and effectively than existing capabilities".[30] This is a useful definition that we can use too when looking at regtech with a legal flavour – or 'legal regtech'. Put simply, it's tech that allows firms to comply with regulation – and often guidance under it – in a smarter, faster and better way.	'Regtech' is a portmanteau of 'regulation' and 'technology'. It is often seen as a type of fintech, although this isn't particularly helpful as it could constrain the development of regtech in other sectors outside of the FS sector, such as the legal sector.
Robotic process automation (RPA)	RPA is form of business process automation. It's where technology, through software, does the repetitive tasks that people normally do. Scott Littlehales of managed IT services provider, Littlefish, prefers to call RPA "intelligent automation".[31] (The authors agree: the use of the term 'robotic' may not be that helpful as it conjures up images of physical robots scooting around doing the tasks that they've been given.)	An example of RPA in a firm is a system (or bots) automatically collecting key information on clients from, say, Companies House or the Land Registry (as opposed to this being done manually). Using RPA can speed up processes and bring down costs.
Smart contract	Smart contract is explained in Chapter 12.	
Smart legal contract	Smart legal contract is explained in Chapter 12.	

continued on next page

Term	Description	So what?
Software as a service (SaaS)	SaaS is where instead of downloading software onto a computer or server, it's accessed via an app or via an internet browser instead.	SaaS applications need an internet connection to work. They offer many advantages, such as the seller being able to update and correct bugs in the software easily. It also makes adoption of the software easier because a firm's IT department doesn't need to install it on the firm's systems (other than perhaps installing a link to a website through which the software is accessed).
Science, technology, engineering and mathematics (STEM)	STEM is an acronym for the fields of science, technology, engineering and mathematics. The less-used 'STEAM' acronym includes the field of arts: an attempt to bridge the humanities/ science gap.	Sometimes dubbed 'the curriculum of the future', STEM subjects will play a larger role in firms who will increasingly employ lawyers with STEM backgrounds or other STEM experts, such as data scientists.
Strong AI	See artificial general intelligence (AGI) and artificial super intelligence (ASI).	
Technology	How we love to eulogise this word! And we become frustrated if things don't turn out quite as expected. As *New York Times* columnist Bret Stephens says, technology promises its users an effortless experience even where, by its "intrinsic nature", it can't be easy.[32] He gives the example of Google where doing a search is easy, but knowing what to	When we think of technology, we always need to think of people. We can't have one without the other. Technology is about people and tech; not people or tech. Even the most 'people-free' technology usually needs input from people to get it going and to keep it running. And ultimately, technology is used to serve people and not the other way around.

continued on next page

Term	Description	So what?
Technology *continued*	actually look for isn't; or dating apps like Tinder, where liking someone by swiping right is a doddle, but finding that special someone is a country mile from that.[33] Of course, this is a simplification, there are always exceptions to these rules, but a lot of technology in this book does ask a bit more of us than we realise. We love the promises it seduces us with, but we, the human side of the equation, often still have work to do too.	
Weak AI	See artificial intelligence (AI).	

Figure 1. The nature of artificial intelligence

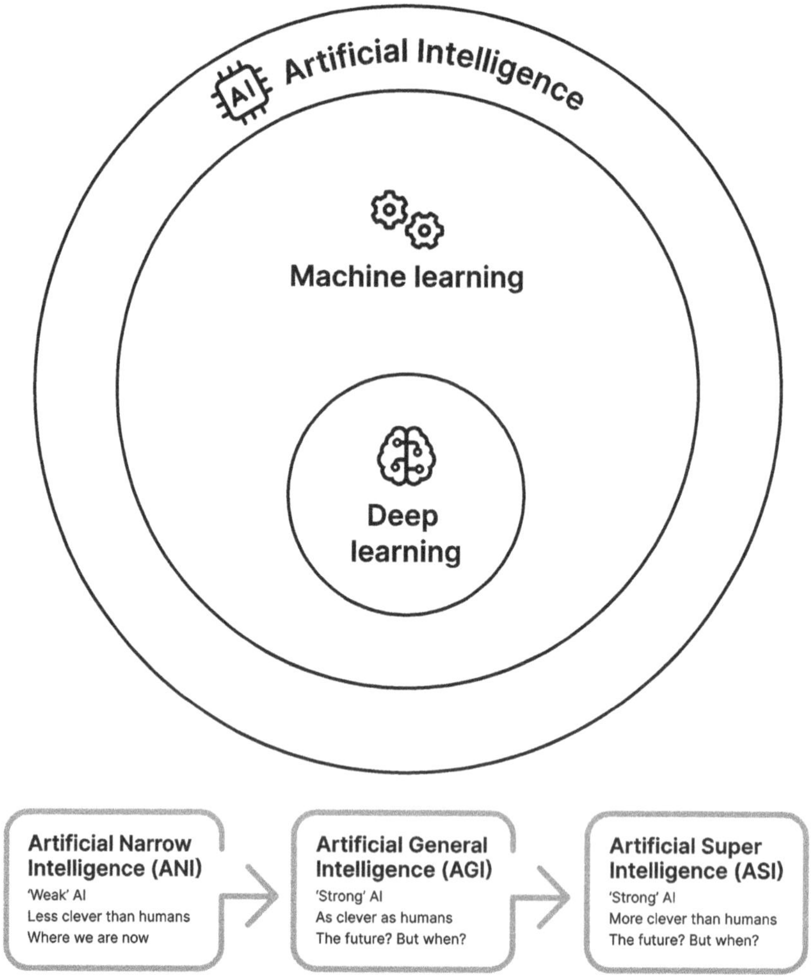

Notes

1   Isaac Asimov, "The Three Laws" (*Compute!*, November 1981, Issue 18), p18.
2   "The COVID crisis catalyses legal tech adoption among law firms" (Wolters Kluwer, 16 November 2020), www.wolterskluwer.com/en-gb/expert-insights/the-covid-crisis-catalyses-legal-tech-adoption-among-law-firms.
3   Dr Martin EP Seligman, "Why Are Lawyers So Unhappy?" (Lawyers With Depression, 20 September 2016, 16 November 2007), www.lawyerswithdepression.com/articles/why-are-lawyers-so-unhappy/.
4   Dr Larry Richard, "Resilience and Lawyer Negativity" (*What Makes Lawyers Tick?* 19 September 2012), www.lawyerbrainblog.com/2012/09/resilience-and-lawyer-negativity/.
5   AC Grayling, *The Meaning of Things* (Weidenfeld & Nicolson, 2001), p41.
6   John Authers, "Don't Blame Me for Unprecedented Use of This Word" (*Bloomberg UK*, 7 May 2020), www.bloomberg.com/opinion/articles/2020-05-07/coronavirus-unprecedented-overuse-fuels-false-market-hopes#xj4y7vzkg.
7   Cabinet Office, *National Risk Register of Civil Emergencies – 2017 Edition* (September 2017), www.gov.uk/government/publications/national-risk-register-of-civil-emergencies-2017-edition.
8   *Canary Wharf (BP4) T1 Ltd v European Medicines Agency* [2019] EWHC 335 (Ch).

9   Stephen Hawking, *Brief Answers to the Big Questions* (John Murray, 2018), p203.
10   *Ibid*, p208.
11   Michio Kaku, *Visions* (Oxford University Press, 1998), p67.
12   *Ibid*, p66.
13   *Ibid*, pp123, 124.
14   C Northcote Parkinson, "Parkinson's Law" (*The Economist*, 19 November 1955), www.economist.com/news/1955/11/19/parkinsons-law.
15   "A guide to race and ethnicity terminology and language" (Law Society, 10 February 2022), www.lawsociety.org.uk/en/topics/ethnic-minority-lawyers/a-guide-to-race-and-ethnicity-terminology-and-language.
16   The Reith Lectures (BBC Radio 4), www.bbc.co.uk/programmes/m001216j.
17   Anthony Cuthbertson, "Artificial intelligence may already be 'slightly conscious', AI scientists warn" (*Independent*, 18 February 2022), www.independent.co.uk/tech/artificial-intelligence-conciousness-ai-deepmind-b2017393.html.
18   *Ibid*.
19   "Chat show: How chatbots can grow your business" (Law Society, 11 January 2019), www.lawsociety.org.uk/en/campaigns/lawtech/features/chat-show.
20   "Norton Rose Rolls Out 'Parker' the Legal Chat Bot for GDPR" (*Artificial Lawyer*, 16 May 2018), www.artificiallawyer.com/2018/05/16/norton-rose-rolls-out-parker-the-legal-chat-bot-for-gdpr/.
21   Denise Winterman, "Tesco: How one supermarket came to dominate" (BBC News, 9 September 2013), www.bbc.co.uk/news/magazine-23988795.
22   Having done a search on Google Books Ngram Viewer using the search term 'innovation', https://books.google.com/ngrams .
23   Department for Business, Energy and Industrial Strategy, *UK Innovation Strategy* (July 2021), https://assets.publishing.service.gov.uk/government/uploads/system/uploads/attachment_data/fil e/1009577/uk-innovation-strategy.pdf.
24   "Legaltech vs lawtech. What is the difference between legaltech and lawtech? Is there one and does it matter?" (*Lawtomated*, 19 January 2021), https://lawtomated.com/legaltech-vs-lawtech-what-is-the-difference-between-legaltech-and-lawtech-is-there-one-and-does-it-matter/. On legaltech see: "How Do You Define 'Legal Tech'?" (Artificial Lawyer, 20 October 2021), www.artificiallawyer.com/2021/10/20/how-do-you-define-legal-tech/.
25   LawtechUK, *Shaping the Future of Law – The LawtechUK Report 2021* (July 2021), https://technation.io/wp-content/uploads/2021/07/LawtechUK-Report-2021-Final.pdf.
26   "Lawtech and ethics principles report" (Law Society, 28 July 2021), www.lawsociety.org.uk/topics/research/lawtech-and-ethics-principles-report-2021.
27   Esther Salmerón-Manzano, "Legaltech and Lawtech: Global Perspectives, Challenges, and Opportunities" (2021) 10(2) *Laws* 24, https://doi.org/10.3390/laws10020024.
28   Rowena Mason, "West must choose between Russian gas and supporting Ukraine, PM warns" (*The Guardian*, 15 November 2021), www.theguardian.com/politics/2021/nov/15/west-must-choose-between-russian-gas-and-supporting-ukraine-pm-warns.
29   Ray Dalio, *Principles for Dealing with the Changing World Order* (Simon & Schuster, 2021), p475.
30   "Call for input on supporting the development and adopters of RegTech", Feedback Statement FS16/4 (Financial Conduct Authority, July 2016), www.fca.org.uk/sites/default/files/publications/feedback/fs-16-04.pdf.
31   Scott Littlehales, "Legal technology sponsored briefing: RPA in legal – be cynical of the hype and do not get left behind" (*Legal Business*, 29 October 2018), www.legalbusiness.co.uk/co-publishing/legal-technology-sponsored-briefing-rpa-in-legal-be-cynical-of-the-hype-and-do-not-get-left-behind/.
32   Bret Stephens, "How Plato Foresaw Facebook's Folly" (*The New York Times*, 16 November 2018), www.nytimes.com/2018/11/16/opinion/facebook-zuckerberg-investigation-election.html.
33   *Ibid*.

About the authors

Paul Caddy
Head of Insight, Shoosmiths
paul.caddy@shoosmiths.co.uk

Paul Caddy is Head of Insight at Shoosmiths, having previously practised as a commercial and data protection lawyer, with a particular focus on new technologies. Qualifying in 2000 at Veale Wasbrough Vizards, he has worked in private practice (Osborne Clarke and Laytons), in business and with leading legal publishers, such as LexisNexis (LexisPSL) and Thomson Reuters. Paul joined Shoosmiths in 2019.

Paul studied law, French and Spanish at UWE, Bristol and helped to develop Laytons' international presence through membership of the International Bar Association. He is a prolific writer and, through thought leadership, is determined to help drive change in the legal sector, not only through the use of legaltech, but by focusing on the human side of legal practice too.

David Jackson

CEO, Shoosmiths

david.jackson@shoosmiths.co.uk

David Jackson is the chief executive of Shoosmiths LLP and a specialist commercial, outsourcing and technology lawyer. Before taking on his current leadership role, David spent over 20 years in both private practice and in-house, supporting major corporates and multinationals on complex, high-value commercial agreements.

In particular, he led Shoosmiths' leading Commercial Practice for over 10 years and helped to position the firm as a pioneer in the legaltech space, bringing to market several groundbreaking products including legal operations platform matters+ and AI-powered contract review tool Cia, as well as Shoosmiths' award-winning connected services business, Shoosmiths8.

Since 2022, David has led Shoosmiths as CEO and is responsible for delivering the firm's strategy and driving operational excellence in the business to help serve its clients. In 2023, David was listed in *The Lawyer* Hot 100.

Tony Randle

Head of Client Strategy, Shoosmiths

tony.randle@shoosmiths.co.uk

Having practised law (corporate, project finance and commercial) over 35 years, Tony Randle has more experience than most of the ever-changing landscape of lawyering. During the last decade, he has focused on developing different ways of approaching legal service delivery, including new processes and legaltech solutions. As well as leading Shoosmiths' connected services business, Shoosmiths8, he is also responsible for client strategy, ensuring that Shoosmiths is constantly evolving to meet client needs in the best ways.

Through conference appearances, articles and podcasts Tony is a prolific thought leader on legal innovation. He was listed in *The Lawyer* Hot 100 in 2022 and sits on various bodies seeking to promote the use and development of technology in the practice of law.

Index

About Globe Law and Business

Globe Law and Business was established in 2005. From the very beginning, we set out to create law books that are sufficiently high level to be of real use to the experienced professional, yet still accessible and easy to navigate. Most of our authors are drawn from Magic Circle and other top commercial firms, both in the United Kingdom and internationally.

Our titles are carefully produced, with the utmost attention paid to editorial, design and production processes. We hope this results in high-quality publications that are easy to read and a pleasure to own. Our titles are also available as ebooks, which are compatible with most desktop, laptop and tablet devices. In 2018 we expanded our portfolio to include journals and Special Reports, available both digitally and in hard copy format, and produced to the same high standards as our books.

In 2021, we were very pleased to announce the start of a new chapter for Globe Law and Business following the acquisition of law books under the imprint Ark Publishing. Our law firm management list is now significantly expanded with many well known and loved Ark Publishing titles.

We are also pleased to announce the launch of our online content platform, Globe Law Online. This allows for easy search and networked access across firms. Key collections include the Law Firm Management Collection, Private Client and Energy and the Energy Transition. Email me at sian@globelawandbusiness.com for further details or to arrange a free trial for you or your firm.

Sian O'Neill
Managing director
Globe Law and Business
www.globelawandbusiness.com

Related title

Globe Law
and Business

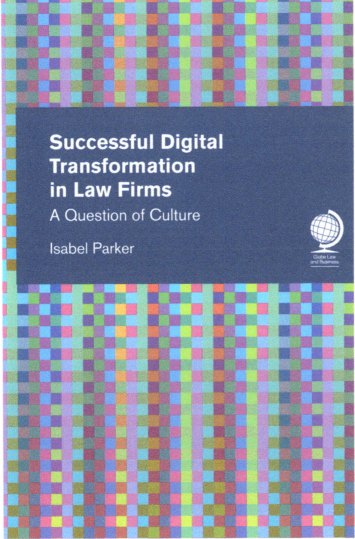

Successful Digital Transformation in Law Firms

A Question of Culture

Isabel Parker

Globe Law
and Business

" "

Thoroughly enjoying Isabel Parker's book on successfully implementing digital transformation. Although it's predominantly for law firms, the principles apply to in-house as well. Highly recommend!

Eletra Japonas
CEO and Founder, tlb; Co-founder, oneNDA

Related title

Globe Law
and Business

The Handbook for Legal Innovation

NICOLA SHAVER

In addition to strategy suggestions, *The Handbook for Legal Innovation* delves deeply into methodologies for change. Shaver provides an overview of effective methods drawn from other industries that can be leveraged within legal to support and supercharge innovation efforts, equipping lawyers and legal innovation leaders with tools that will help them drive real change within their organisations.

Go to **www.globelawandbusiness.com/THLI**
for full details including free sample chapters